South-Western

OFFICE

2000

TECHNOLOGY
AND
PROCEDURES

PATSY FULTON-CALKINS, PH.D., CPS
ADJUNCT PROFESSOR
EDUCATIONAL CONSULTANT

JOIN US ON THE INTERNET
WWW: http://www.thomson.com
EMAIL: findit@kiosk.thomson.com   A service of I(T)P®

South-Western Educational Publishing
an International Thomson Publishing company I(T)P®

Cincinnati • Albany, NY • Belmont, CA • Bonn • Boston • Detroit • Johannesburg • London • Madrid
Melbourne • Mexico City • New York • Paris • Singapore • Tokyo • Toronto • Washington

D1517543

Team Leader: Karen Schmohe
Project Manager: Inell Bolls
Production Coordinator: Jane Congdon
Editor: Carol Spencer
Marketing Managers: Tim Gleim, Al Roane
Art and Design Coordinator: Michelle Kunkler
Cover Design: Ann Small
Internal Design: Wilson Design
Photo Editor: Alix Parson

ISBN: 0-538-66981-0

  5 6 7 8 9 BC 02 01 00 99

Printed in the United States of America

Library of Congress Cataloging-in-Publication Data
Fulton-Calkins, Patsy, 1934-
        Office 2000: technology and procedures / Patsy Fulton-Calkins.
        p.   cm.
        Rev. ed. of: Office procedures and technology for colleges. 10th
ed. c1994.
        Includes index.
        ISBN 0-538-66981-0 (softcover)
        1. Office practice.   2. Office practice—Automation.
3. Universities and colleges—Business management.   I. Fulton
-Calkins, Patsy, 1934-   Office procedures and technology for
colleges.   II. Title.
HF5547.5.F84 1998   97-22052
651—dc21   CIP

PREFACE

You are entering the business world at an exciting and challenging time. Exciting because of the numerous changes taking place daily in the offices of businesses and challenging due to the constant learning in which you will need to be engaged. Career opportunities in the twenty-first century will continue to be available for office professionals. These opportunities promise work duties that will be broader in scope and more demanding in nature as the Information Age provides increased technological means of performing work. In a world in which the virtual office is a reality (performing work in any place at any time), you will probably work more independently than ever before. However, coupled with this independence is constant communication through various methods including the Internet, interactive video, and voice messaging. To be successful, you must continue to develop excellent oral and written communication skills, teamwork skills, and creativity and critical thinking skills, in addition to having commanding technological skills.

Office 2000: Technology and Procedures is written for you, the individual who is interested in making the office professional field and its related areas a career. Presently, you may be a full-time student or already working in the business world and taking this course to help you upgrade your skills. Whatever your present status, by committing yourself to careful study of the material presented in this text-workbook you will increase your knowledge and employability opportunities.

TEXT-WORKBOOK ORGANIZATION

Office 2000: Technology and Procedures is organized into six parts, with a total of fifteen chapters.

PART 1: THE HIGH TECH WORKPLACE
Chapter 1: Understanding the Office Environment
Chapter 2: Planning Your Career
Chapter 3: Utilizing Computer Hardware and Office Equipment
Chapter 4: Using Software

PART 2: SUCCESS BEHAVIORS
Chapter 5: Developing Effective Communication Skills
Chapter 6: Responding Ethically in the Work Environment

PART 3: OFFICE COMMUNICATIONS
Chapter 7: Telecommunications and the Telephone
Chapter 8: Letters, Memos, and Reports
Chapter 9: Office Callers and Presentations

PART 4: MEETINGS, CONFERENCES, AND TRAVEL
Chapter 10: Planning Meetings and Conferences
Chapter 11: Making Travel Arrangements

PART 5: MAIL AND RECORDS MANAGEMENT
Chapter 12: Handling the Office Mail
Chapter 13: Managing Documents

PART 6: CAREER ADVANCEMENT
Chapter 14: Managing Stress and Time
Chapter 15: Leading Others

LEARNING AIDS

This text-workbook has been designed to reinforce your learning in a variety of ways. So that you may know what is expected of you, learning objectives are given at the beginning of each chapter. Then at the end of the chapter, you are asked to state whether you accomplished the objectives and, if so, how. Learning aids to assist you in the accomplishment of these objectives include:

- Self Checks in each chapter

- Technology, Human Relations, and Communication Tips throughout each chapter

- Chapter summaries

- Chapter glossaries which list terms you need to know

- Discussion items that provide for class and/or small group discussion about the concepts presented

- Case studies for analyzing office situations

- English Usage Challenge Drills for reviewing and reinforcing grammar rules
- Office tasks tied directly to the objectives of the individual chapter
- Numerous opportunities to work with your classmates on projects so that you may develop team building skills
- Numerous opportunities to present orally in class to assist you with developing good presentation skills

SUPPLEMENTARY ITEMS

In addition to the material presented in the text-workbook, these additional items are available for your learning.

- A Student Data Template Disk which includes office tasks, information, and forms
- Additional office tasks to give you added learning opportunities
- Chapter tests, part tests, and a final exam to reinforce your learning

YOUR SUCCESS

As an author who cares about your learning and success on the job, I urge you to concentrate on expanding your knowledge and development of the following very important job skills for the twenty-first century throughout this course.

- Critical thinking
- Creativity
- Openness to change
- Oral and written communication skills
- Teamwork skills
- Ethical behaviors

In every chapter in this text-workbook, you have a chance to develop and expand these skills by being aware of their importance and consciously attempting to improve in these areas as you read the text-workbook, complete the various learning activities provided, and work in teams with your classmates. Learn, grow, and have fun in the process.

FEATURES NEW TO THIS EDITION

- Emphasis on twenty-first century skills
- New chapter—Chapter 15: Leading Others

- New topic on oral presentation skills
- Four new profiles of office professionals, with the office professional depicting diversity in race, ethnicity, gender, and age. One office professional is from outside the United States—Australia.
- A multinational company orientation with the student completing office tasks for Jacqueline Marquette, vice president of community relations, Koronet International (a multinational firm).
- Tips on technology, human relations, and communication
- Student Self Checks
- English Usage Challenge Drills
- Assessment of chapter objectives
- Case studies from professionals
- Office tasks with an emphasis on teamwork and technology
- Chapter tests
- Four-color text
- Expanded Instructor's Manual
- Student Data Template Disk with additional case studies

THE AUTHOR

Dr. Patsy J. Fulton-Calkins' experience in the field is extensive. Her past experience in the office includes working as a secretary for large corporations for six years. She holds the CPS certification. Her teaching experience includes over thirteen years at the university, community college, and high school levels. Subjects she has taught include business and community college education courses at the university level; office procedures, business communications, CPS review courses, communications courses at business sites, keyboarding, shorthand, and bookkeeping at the community college level; and vocational office education, business law, and general business at the high school level.

In addition to her teaching experience, she has worked as an administrator for twelve years in the following positions:

- Chancellor of Oakland Community College, the chief executive officer, Oakland County, Michigan
- President of Brookhaven College, Dallas, Texas

- Vice President of Instruction at El Centro College and Cedar Valley College, Dallas, Texas

- Division Chairperson of Business and Social Science, Cedar Valley College, Dallas, Texas

Her present position includes consulting with major universities and community colleges across the nation and adjunct teaching at the university level.

Her educational credentials include a BBA, an MBEd., and a PhD. Honors include Outstanding Alumnus, University of North Texas; Transformation Leader in Community Colleges; Who's Who in America, Who's Who in American Education, Outstanding Woman in Management; Paul Harris Fellow of Rotary International; Beta Gamma Sigma, National Honorary Business Fraternity; and Piper Professor.

ACKNOWLEDGMENTS

Thanks to the following reviewers for their helpful comments as this text-workbook was being developed:

Reviewer	School Affiliation
Misty W. Ballentine	Greenville Technical College, Greenville, SC
Dr. Marilyn R. Chalupa	Ball State University, Muncie, IN
Dr. Carolyn Ashe Jones	University of Houston-Downtown, Houston, TX
Carol Silvis	Newport Business Institute, Lower Burrell, PA
Mary U. Valenti	Harford Community College, Forest Hill, MD
Nancy Varnadoe	Eastern Idaho Technical College, Idaho Falls, ID
Gloria Weatherspoon	South Ohio College, Cincinnati, OH
Patsy Zink	Oklahoma State University, Okmulgee, OK

My thanks also to my husband, Richard W. Calkins, president of Grand Rapids Community College, for his thoughtful comments on my work and his understanding during the long hours of production.

CONTENTS

PART 1

The High Tech Workplace

Bernice Fujiwara, CPS
Administrative Secretary
First Hawaiian Bank
Honolulu, Hawaii

A Success Profile

I attribute my success to a combination of several things: a supportive family (including my husband of nineteen years, my two boys who are 9 and 12 years of age, my parents, and my sisters), hard work, Professional Secretaries International, and being at the right place at the right time.

My educational background includes a secretarial diploma from Cannon's School of Business. I was inducted into Cannon's Business College Alumni Hall of Fame in April 1993. However, my education has not stopped. I have completed a number of courses from the American Institute of Banking: principles in banking, economics, law and banking, residential mortgage lending, and analyzing financial statements. In addition, I have attended numerous workshops and courses on various computer programs, gaining a proficiency in IBM® WordPerfect®, Microsoft® Excel®, Lotus®, and Macintosh® Word processing. In 1986 I attained the Certified Professional Secretary rating by passing a two-day, six-part examination covering (1) behavioral science in business, (2) business law, (3) economics and management, (4) accounting, (5) office administration and communication, and (6) office technology.

I have been with First Hawaiian Bank for twenty-two years. My career began as a steno-receptionist; I am currently the administrative secretary to an executive vice president. My present responsibilities include: assisting in customer service, being a liaison between division and regional managers, composing and editing letters and memos, coordinating bankwide branch manager's meetings, taking minutes in various meetings, preparing and following up on management reports, preparing itineraries for executive travel, and assisting the executive in nonprofit organization activities. In addition, I supervise one secretary.

The most enjoyable part of my job is coordinating our semiannual branch manager's meeting. My responsibilities for this meeting include making hotel reservations, preparing the meeting agenda, attending the meeting, and assisting with dinner arrangements. The bank has fifty-seven branches in Hawaii and two in Guam; I enjoy meeting and talking with our branch managers.

I receive tremendous satisfaction from my work when I am able to do a task faster by using technology or by organizing the task another way. I am always looking for ways to do a job faster and easier. I feel that office professionals sometimes get into a rut by doing the same things the same way day in and day out. When I improve a procedure, even though it may be a simple one, I think to myself—why didn't I think of this sooner? When I am able to save time doing the mundane tasks, I have more time to organize and plan for other projects.

The most stressful part of my job is needing to do ten things at once because my executive is extremely busy and needs my support. I have learned that it takes good communication between an administrative assistant and the executive to get the job done. The administrative assistant needs to know the purpose or reason for the project to organize appropriately and meet the necessary deadlines. Many times the executive does not know the process or details necessary to get the job done. The administrative assistant needs to use good judgment in deciding what needs to get done first. Another stressful part of my job includes unhappy customers who scream at me over the telephone. I have learned that I need to listen and ask the right questions. I have to know my company well—the organization, the people, and the products so that I may refer them to the correct area.

My hobbies include working on handcrafts such as needlepoint, ceramics, and Japanese washi-paper dolls. I enjoy making almost anything by sewing, gluing, and so forth. I also enjoy my aerobic classes, walking, going to the beach to swim while my boys go boogie-boarding (like surfing), and playing basketball with my boys.

I have been a member of the Hawaii Chapter of Professional Secretaries International since 1980. Our club is engaged in numerous activities such as offering scholarships to students in the secretarial field (which means that we do fundraising), assisting with community service projects, and providing continuing education for our members. I am proud of the special recognition I have received through PSI, including:
• 1992–93 International Secretary of the Year for PSI
• 1992–93 Southwest District Secretary of the Year for PSI
• 1992–93 Hawaii Division Secretary for PSI

BERNICE FUJIWARA'S CASE

Here is a case I prepared from my varied experiences as an administrative assistant. I hope you learn from this case. Decide how you would have handled the case by answering the questions at the completion of the situation. Then, turn to the end of Part I (page 107) to see how I solved the case.

THE SITUATION

Your executive holds weekly or monthly meetings with the staff. These meetings usually average one hour; you take minutes at these meetings. You have a heavy workload and feel that the time used in attending the meetings could be used more productively in activities such as arranging customers' calls, making travel arrangements, planning meetings, and a myriad of other activities for which you are responsible. Once the meetings are over, it takes another hour to prepare the minutes. On the day of the meetings, you find you are behind in opening mail, answering correspondence, and completing projects. Your executive has noticed it too. In fact, your executive has commented about your being behind on your work.

Would you speak to your executive? If so, how would you approach the subject? What would you suggest?

CHAPTER 1

UNDERSTANDING THE OFFICE ENVIRONMENT

LEARNING OBJECTIVES

1. **Describe the ever-changing office.**
2. **Identify the role and responsibilities of the office professional.**
3. **Determine skills and qualities necessary for the office professional.**
4. **Create a professional growth plan for this semester.**

You will be entering the office of the twenty-first century, which will be characterized by change in these major areas:

- *a workforce that is more diverse than ever before, with many different cultures working together;*
- *a business economy that continues to expand in its global operations;*
- *a workplace with **state-of-the-art technology** (the latest available);*
- *a workplace that is **virtual** (work can be performed anywhere and at anytime using technology).*

To survive and thrive in this workplace, you will need to acquire the knowledge, skills, and qualities that will allow you to become a valued part of the organization. This chapter will help you begin that development, and throughout this course you will continue that development.

Take a moment now to reread the learning objectives at the beginning of this chapter. It is important for you to begin each chapter with an understanding of exactly what you are expected to achieve. The learning objectives will help you focus your study and use your time efficiently. At the end of each chapter, you will be asked the following questions:

- *Did you achieve the objectives?*
- *If so, explain how.*
- *If not, explain why.*

THE EVER-CHANGING OFFICE

Why is the office environment ever-changing? A major part of the answer to this question is that you and I live in the **Information Age.** As is suggested by the term "Information Age," we are living in a time of tremendous explosion of knowledge. Technology is an integral part of this Information Age.

Consider for a moment the tremendous changes that have taken place in the office over a few short years. In the past, the typewriter was the standard piece of equipment for document preparation. The microcomputer did not exist; the mainframe computer performed all computer applications. Many applications were done manually. The telephone was the standard piece of telecommunications equipment. The conference call was one of the most sophisticated techniques available when communicating with several people. Presently, office professionals use computers, voice mail, electronic mail (e-mail), fax machines, and printers and copiers. **Software office suites** are available for the office professional's use which allow the addition of graphics, **clip art,** and spreadsheets to correspondence. Office professionals may work from their home or another location outside the office in a virtual environment or virtual office. The changes are

The technological workplace. *Courtesy of International Business Machines, Inc.*

numerous and will continue as new technology is constantly introduced.

A DIVERSE LABOR FORCE

From the period of 1994 to 2005, employment is projected to increase by 17.7 million or 14 percent.[1] This workforce will be increasingly diverse, with minorities and immigrants constituting a larger share of the workforce than they do today. African Americans, Hispanics, and Asians will continue to become an increasingly larger percentage of our workforce.

Projections given in the 1996–97 *Occupational Outlook Handbook* are:

By 2005:

- Hispanics will be 11 percent of the workforce.

- African Americans will be 12 percent of the workforce.

- Asians and all other minorities will be 5 percent of the workforce.

- African Americans, Hispanics, and Asians will be approximately 35 percent of all labor force entrants.

- Women will continue to be a growing part of the workforce. Constituting 48 percent of the workforce.

- The number of workers 55 and above is projected to grow approximately twice as fast as the total labor force between the 1990s and 2005.[2]

These projections will have a very real impact on the office.

Multiculturalism

Multiculturalism by definition means relating to or including several cultures. **Culture** is defined as the ideas, customs, values, skills, and arts of a spe-

---

[1]U.S. Department of Labor, Bureau of Labor Statistics, *Occupational Outlook Handbook* (Washington, D.C.: U.S. Government Printing Office, 1996–97), 1.

[2]U.S. Department of Labor, Bureau of Labor Statistics, *Occupational Outlook Handbook* (Washington, D.C.: U.S. Government Printing Office, 1996–97), 5–6.

cific group of people. Certainly America has been racially and culturally diverse since its very beginning. According to Takaki, by 2056 most Americans will trace their descent to Africa, Asia, Spain, the Pacific Islands, Arabia, or other countries—almost anywhere but white Europe.[3]

As you work in this diverse office, you need to be aware and sensitive to the varying cultural differences and backgrounds. You must understand that individuals, because of their different backgrounds, may view situations differently than you do. Your openness to new ideas and different perspectives will be essential. It will not always be easy to remain open to differences, but it is well worth the effort that it will demand from you. Only through awareness, understanding, and acceptance of different cultures can we expect to work in a harmonious, productive office world.

The office of 2000 is more diverse than ever before.
Courtesy of International Business Machines, Inc.

Gender Differences

Not only do women continue to enter the workforce in greater numbers but they are also assuming positions of greater authority and responsibility. In the past, it was assumed that the office support role

---

[3]Takaki, Ronald, *A Different Mirror: A History of Multicultural America* (Canada: Little, Brown & Company, 1993), 2.

COMMUNICATION TIP

America is composed of a mosaic of different cultures, races, and ethnicities. Our openness to each other will help us build a more harmonious world.

was filled by women. Even though women continue to dominate this field, the field is now open to men. It was also assumed in the past that all supervisory positions would be held by men. Again, this assumption is no longer valid. More and more women are assuming management positions. In addition, the office professional role itself is changing drastically. As an office professional, whether you are male or female, you may find yourself supervising others. Your supervisory role will probably not occur at the beginning of your career but after you have acquired some experience. In fact, in this course, you will be studying supervisory techniques (Chapter 15) to help prepare you for this role.

What do these gender differences mean in the office? As office workers, we cannot assume that women and men react differently to situations because of their gender. *People,* with different backgrounds and different cultures, react differently to situations, but it is not because they are male or female. As we grow up, the socialization process in our culture tends to treat men and women differently. For example, women may be encouraged to express their feelings more. Thus, sometimes women are **stereotyped** (a perception or image held of people or things which may be favorable or unfavorable) as being more emotional. We cannot assume, however, that women are more emotional than men. Our culture has merely allowed women to express their feelings more. Your role in the office is to be aware of the stereotyping that can occur for women as well as men and to not let your attitudes or decisions be based on these stereotypes. *Your focus must be on understanding and accepting differences.*

Senior Workers

You learned earlier that the number of people 55 and older in the workforce will continue to increase into the twenty-first century. Thus, you will probably work with people who are from 18 to well over 60. Certainly, each generation of our population grows up with differing national and local influences in their lives. For example, the generation of young Americans who served in the Vietnam conflict experienced very different situations than those born after that time. Young people who are in their teens today have grown up in an age of technology. Many have learned to use computers at an early age and several enjoy playing video games, for example. Age differences certainly may mean that we view the world

from varying perspectives; but, again, just as we cannot categorize people because of differences in race, ethnicity, or gender, we also cannot categorize them because of their differences in age. Our task is to understand and accept each person as an individual.

A GLOBAL ECONOMY

The American economy is a global one. Businesses in the United States are not confined to state or national boundaries. **Multinational** is a term which refers to a business that operates both within the United States and in countries outside the United States. With technology, the world has become the marketplace. For example, General Motors® and Ford® Motor Company, two of the largest corporations in America, have plants all over the world. Just as American businesses are establishing plants and offices abroad, so are other countries establishing plants and offices in America. Truly, businesses today are global in their production and marketing of goods and services.

Our economy is a global one. *Photo by Mimi Ostendorf/Photonics Graphics.*

DOWNSIZED AND FLATTENED ORGANIZATIONS

In marketing a product or service, greater efficiency means greater profitability for the company and its owners. To achieve greater efficiency and to provide flexibility for the future, the organizations of the '90s have engaged in downsizing. Numerous companies have made media headlines due to laying off thousands of workers. This downsizing is expected to continue. To reduce costs and improve efficiency, productivity, and quality, organizations have also flattened the organizational structure. This flattening is expected to continue into the twenty-first century.

Temporary Employees

To get the work done in a downsized environment, businesses are employing more part-time and temporary employees. For example, if a business identifies a problem in a certain area of the company, the business may bring in a consultant for a defined period to determine the problem and make recommendations for improvement. Businesses also frequently use the assistance of temporary agencies. These temporary agencies supply the business with various types of temporary help, including accounting assistants, administrative assistants, and human resources assistants.

Statistics show that twice the number of temporary workers are employed by businesses today than there were four short years ago.[4] A growing number of these temporary workers are highly educated professionals who enjoy the opportunity of working for a variety of companies. In addition to office professionals working in temporary positions, technical writers, engineers, and graphic artists are a few of the myriad of professionals who enjoy working as temporary employees. The following are some of the advantages of working as a temporary employee:

- flexibility
- challenge of working in new situations
- relatively high pay
- fewer hours on the job, with more time for family

Organizational Structures

For years we talked about the organization as a hierarchy. A **hierarchy** is organized according to rank or authority with the chief executive officer (CEO) at the top of the organization. The organization chart resembles a pyramid. Notice Figure 1-1 which shows an organizational chart. Such a structure assumes that knowledge and information flows from the top down. In the past, this theory of knowledge flowing from the top had some relevance. For example, the CEO may have begun a small bicycle manufacturing company. Through the years, that CEO built the company into a medium-sized organization, knew each step of the process of manufacturing and marketing a bicycle, and could perform any job within the company.

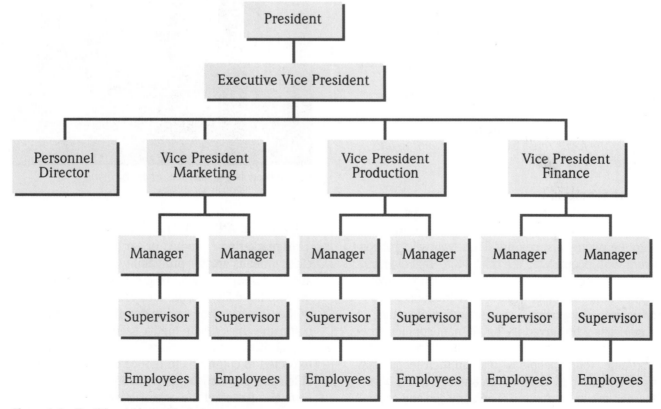

Figure 1-1   Traditional hierarchical structure.

---

[4]"You, Inc.," *U.S. News & World Report* (October, 1996), 71.

Part 1: The High Tech Workplace

Today, with the knowledge explosion, such is no longer true in most cases. For example, the CEO of a large telecommunications company cannot know all aspects of the company. Employees within the company have specialized skills and knowledge which the CEO does not have. The changes in the knowledge base dictate a flatter organization with specialized teams working throughout the organization. No one person has the ability to do all the work of the organization.

The flattened organizational structure shown in Figure 1-2 has fewer levels than the hierarchy as shown in Figure 1-1. Notice that the levels of management have been reduced greatly, and notice that teams exist with project managers as team leaders. This team concept has come about as a result of the focus on quality which is discussed in the next section.

Quality Focus

Dr. W. Edwards Deming, an American statistician, developed the quality concept. This concept emphasizes the importance of continually improving a product or service to stay competitive with other businesses. Improvement of a product or service means that constant evaluation must occur. For example, as a car is being manufactured, each phase of the manufacturing process must include product evaluation to ensure a quality product. Teams of individuals within the organization must understand the goals and quality focus of the organization and how to contribute to that focus in their particular segment of the delivery of the product or service.

Deming emphasized that the leadership of an organization must help people do a better job. He stressed that improvement must be made in management effectiveness as well as individual worker effectiveness. The concept today is known as total quality management (**TQM**) or continuous quality improvement (**CQI**) and is widely accepted by American business. It has spawned the team approach to product and service development, with the development of standards of quality within and across businesses. Figure 1-3 shows the concepts graphically and lists Deming's management principles.

The implementation of TQM concepts can change the work of the office professional. For example, the office professional may

- be involved in a planning team that affects the direction of the business;

- have an opportunity to identify customer service problems and make suggestions through the team for improvement;

- be part of a team who is responsible for producing a service or product.

THE WORKPLACE—WHERE AND WHEN?

The workplace of the twenty-first century may be at an established place or building. It also may be at home or at any number of other locations. The workweek may be from eight- or nine-to-five or it may be extremely flexible hours.

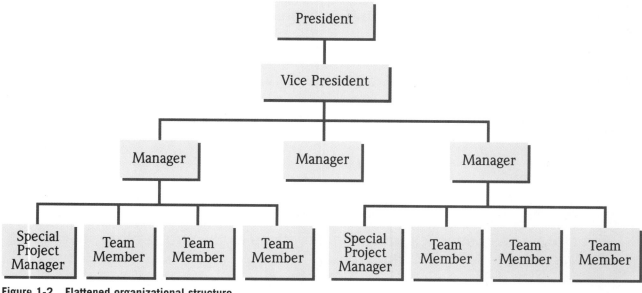

Figure 1-2   Flattened organizational structure.

Deming's Management Principles

1. Create constancy of purpose toward improvement of product and service, with the aim to become competitive and to stay in business and to provide jobs.

2. Adopt a new philosophy. We are in a new economic age. Western management must awaken to the challenge, must learn their responsibilities and take on leadership for change.

3. Cease dependence on inspection to achieve quality. Eliminate a need for inspection on a mass basis by building quality into the product in the first place.

4. End the practice of awarding business on the basis of price tag. Instead minimize the total cost. Move toward a single supplier for any one item, on a long term relationship of loyalty and trust.

5. Improve constantly and forever the system of production and service, to improve quality and productivity, and thus constantly decrease costs.

6. Institute training on the job.

7. Institute leadership. The aim of leadership should be to help people and machines and gadgets to do a better job. Leadership of management is in need of overhaul, as well as leadership of production workers.

8. Drive out fear so that everyone may work effectively for the company.

9. Break down barriers between departments. People in research, design, sales, and production must work as a team, to foresee problems of production and use that may be encountered with the product or service.

10. Eliminate slogans, exhortations, and targets for the workforce, asking for zero defects and new levels of productivity.

11. Eliminate work standards on the factory floor. Substitute leadership. Eliminate management by objective. Eliminate management by numbers, numerical goals, substitute leadership.

12. Remove barriers that rob the hourly worker of his pride of workmanship. The responsibility of the supervisor must be changed from sheer numbers to quality. Remove barriers that rob people in management and engineering of their right to pride of workmanship. This means, among other things, abolishment of the annual or merit rating and of management by objective, management by numbers.

13. Institute a vigorous program of education and self-improvement.

14. Put everyone in the company to work to accomplish the transformation. The transformation is everyone's job.

W. Edwards Deming, OUT OF THE CRISIS (Massachusetts: Massachusetts Institute of Technology, 1993).

Figure 1-3

TECHNOLOGY TIP

To help you keep informed on such innovations as the virtual office, read *PC Magazine* and *Home Computing*.

Virtual Office

As you learned earlier in this chapter, the virtual office is one in which work can be performed anywhere and at anytime using technology. Today, many workers have traded the traditional office for the virtual office. The telecommuting-to-work lifestyle is here to stay. More than 7 million people now telecommute at least one day a week, and telecommuting is growing at a solid 20 percent per year.[5] It is projected that millions more workers will be doing so in the future.

The concept started several years ago as **telecommuting,** working from home or another established location via computer hookup. Today, work can be performed using cellular phones, fax machines, modems, voice mail, e-mail, laptop and handheld computers, and so on. Local telecommuting centers are available which provide for all types of conferences. Job interviews may even be held through telecommuting centers with the interviewer, for example, being in China and the interviewee being in Michigan.

IBM® is one company that has established the "mobile workforce," which is a virtual office concept. Mobile workers have the ability and resources to perform their jobs anywhere. Employees determine where and when they will work. One employee describes a typical day as being armed for mobility with an IBM ThinkPad® laptop computer, cellular phone, printer, and a two-line business speaker phone that transfers unanswered phone calls to the company's branch office voice mail system. The employee may work at home all day, work at home in the morning, meet clients in the city in the evening, or work at the office for a portion of the day. The employee avoids rush-hour traffic, saving both the employee and IBM hours of wasted time. A few other advantages to the program for IBM are

- decreased real estate and other occupancy-related expenses;

- increased individual productivity by reducing commute time;

- improved employee morale with workday flexibility.[6]

American Express® is another company that has put many of their employees in virtual offices. Their sales staff are outfitted with laptop computers, cellular phones, and pagers. To help the employees feel a part of an organization, the company mandated regular Monday morning conference calls between sales staffs and managers, monthly social events, and a buddy system in which each sales associate teamed with another to share ideas. With workers spending less time in offices and more time selling, sales calls at American Express have jumped 40 percent.[7]

The virtual office allows you to work any place and any time.
Courtesy of International Business Machines, Inc.

Changing Workweek

In addition to the flexible workweek provided by the virtual office, the workweek may be a compressed workweek, a flextime one, or even one in which the job is shared with another individual.

With a **compressed workweek,** employees work the usual number of hours (thirty-five to forty); however, the hours are compressed into four days. For example, a thirty-five-hour week consists of three days of nine hours each and a fourth day of eight hours.

Another departure from the eight- or nine-to-five workday is the **flextime** approach (the staggering of working hours to enable an employee to work the full quota of time but at periods defined by the company and the individual). Flextime helps to reduce traffic congestion at the traditional peak hours and allows employees needed flexibility in their schedules.

---

[5]"Your Home Office: A Multiplicity of Choices," *Managing Office Technology* (January, 1996), 25.

[6]Thomas, John B., "Virtually At Work," *World Traveler* (March, 1996), 53–57.

[7]"You, Inc.," *U.S. News & World Report* (October, 1996), 79.

Still another departure from the traditional workday is the **job-sharing** plan. Under this arrangement, two part-time employees perform a job that otherwise would be held by one full-time employee. Such a plan may be suitable for a mother or father with small children or workers who want to ease into retirement.

THE OFFICE PROFESSIONAL'S ROLE AND RESPONSIBILITIES

With the availability of technology and the emphasis on greater efficiency and productivity through flattened organizational structures and teams, the office professionals of today and tomorrow will find that their role is continually shifting. With this shifting role generally comes greater responsibility.

THE SHIFTING ROLE

For years the office professional's title was confined to secretary, receptionist, and such specialized titles as legal and medical secretaries. Today, although these titles are still in use, the emerging titles reflect the shifting role. A few of these titles are administrative assistant, executive assistant, payroll assistant, and human resources assistant. The shifting role is reflected in the duties of the office professional, those duties include:

- researching and preparing reports complete with graphics and spreadsheets;
- assisting with the planning and direction of the company through working on organizational teams;
- leading TQM teams focusing on increased quality of products and services;
- supervising support staff.

The office professional serves on quality teams.
Hewlett Packard.

In addition to the administrative assistant and executive assistant titles, there are numerous other office professional roles which include such titles as office assistant, office manager or supervisor, records manager, records and information assistant, accounting and payroll assistant, to name a few. Job roles and responsibilities differ among these various positions; however, certain knowledges and skills are essential in all office professional roles. These knowledges, skills, and qualities will be discussed in the next section and emphasized throughout this course. The term **office professional** will be used consistently throughout the text to denote the office support person.

JOB RESPONSIBILITIES

As mentioned in the previous section, the job responsibilities of the office professional have increased in complexity and accountability as compared to several years ago. With technology, many executives now answer their own voice mail and e-mail, key certain correspondence directly on the computer, and do much of their own scheduling through electronic schedules provided with computer software. This change frees the office professional to become more involved in creating correspondence and in becoming a valued member of a number of office teams.

Job responsibilities of the office professional will vary depending on educational level, work experience, and even the initiative of the employee. Figure 1-4 lists some of the basic responsibilities that are fairly generic to all office professional positions.

TWENTY-FIRST CENTURY SKILLS AND QUALITIES

If the office professional is to succeed in a world of technology and rapid change, certain skills and qualities are needed. It is important that you begin now to develop these skills and qualities.

ORAL AND WRITTEN COMMUNICATION SKILLS

Office professionals spend a majority of their time communicating with others. Such communication may be in the form of written letters, memorandums, reports, e-mail, faxes, telephone calls, voice mail messages, or face-to-face communications. Regardless of the form it takes, you must be extremely proficient in the communications area.

Communication skill implies that you have a mastery of the English language. The office professional must be able to apply the rules of grammar, punctua-

Basic Job Responsibilities of the Office Professional

- Composing and keying various types of documents, including letters, memorandums, and reports
- Researching report information within the defined parameters set by the employer
- Participating in quality teams, with the more experienced office professional serving as team leader
- Solving day-to-day problems within the role of the office professional
- Communicating both orally and in writing with individuals both within and ouside the office
- Scheduling appointments
- Setting up meetings and conferences
- Organizing time and work
- Maintaining correspondence and records in both electronic and manual files
- Making travel arrangements for the executive
- Using telecommunications technology including the telephone, voice mail, and fax
- Interviewing and making recommendations on the employment of office support personnel
- Supervising office support personnel
- Taking and transcribing minutes from various types of meetings
- Making recommendations on equipment purchase
- Purchasing office supplies
- Handling incoming and outgoing mail
- Processing paperwork that involves mathematical calculations (expense reports, budgets, invoices, purchase orders, petty cash, and so forth)

Figure 1-4

tion, and capitalization. Many times the employer expects the office professional to be the English expert, relying on the professional to correct any grammatical errors that the employer may make.

Spell checkers, available on word processing programs, are extremely helpful aids for the office professional. Once a document has been completed, you should always use the spell checker to identify any misspelled words. However, the spell checker does have limitations. For example, if you key "off" when you actually mean "of" the spell checker will not identify the error because the word is not spelled incorrectly. This means that you must be an extremely good proofreader even with the tools that are provided on your computer software. Take the time to proofread each document you produce thoroughly and carefully.

Note-taking skills are essential in the office. At times you will be asked to take notes at a meeting or to take directions from your employer. These notes may be taken manually or by using a laptop computer. Most jobs today do not require symbol shorthand skill; however, you may find symbol shorthand or alphabetic shorthand an appropriate skill to add to your skills. It certainly can only enhance your employability. Regardless of the method you use to take notes, you must have the ability to record and transcribe notes accurately or to follow the oral directions given in the note-taking process.

HUMAN RELATIONS SKILLS

As an office professional you will come in contact with a number of people. Within the company you will work with co-workers, your supervisor, and other executives. Contacts outside the company will include customers and other visitors to your office, all with different backgrounds and experiences. If you are to be effective, you will need to understand, accept, and work well with them. Human relations skills are like most of our other skills. We must constantly develop and improve these skills if we are to grow in our abilities. Take the following short Human Relations Self Check. Check the suggested responses at the end of this chapter. Where do you need to improve? Commit now to working on the improvement of these areas during this course.

Human Relations Self Check

Respond to the following comments by marking "yes" or "no" after the statement.

1. I understand that differences exist in culture, race, and ethnicity. *Y*

2. I respect others' differences in culture, race, and ethnicity. *Y*

3. I expect all individuals to react to situations just as I do. *N*

4. I listen carefully when others are talking. *Y*

5. I ignore body language when others are talking. *N*

6. I am conscious of the words I use in my written communications. *Y*

7. I avoid dealing with conflict. *Y*

8. I evaluate individuals when they are talking to me. *Y & N*

9. I trust people who are older than I am. *N*

10. Men are better supervisors than women. *N*

CRITICAL THINKING SKILLS

Critical thinking can be defined as a unique kind of purposeful thinking in which the thinker systematically chooses conscious and deliberate inquiry. Critical comes from the Greek word **"krinein,"** which means to separate, to choose. When we think critically about a subject, we try to see it from all sides before coming to a conclusion. Critical thinking requires us to see things from perspectives other than our own and to consider the possible consequences of the positions we take. If you are to succeed in the complex world of the twenty-first century, you must be able to think

critically about the day-to-day decisions you make in an office. Figure 1-5 lists some questions you should consider when thinking critically.

Critical Thinking Questions

- What is the purpose of my thinking?
- What problem or question am I trying to answer?
- What facts do I need to address this problem or question?
- How do I interpret the facts or information I receive?
- What conclusions can I make from the information I received?
- Are my conclusions defensible?
- Have I dealt with the complexity of the situation?
- Have I avoided thinking in simple stereotypes?
- What will be the consequences if I put my conclusions into practice?

Figure 1-5

ORGANIZATIONAL SKILLS

A skill frequently listed in job advertisements is the ability to organize work. As an office professional, you must be able to establish priorities, determining what needs to be done first. You must organize your work station and files, whether they are paper or electronic. You must organize your time so that your work flows smoothly and tasks are finished as needed. Chapter 14 on Managing Stress and Time will help you understand more about organizing your work and time.

TECHNOLOGY SKILLS

Success today demands that you be technologically competent. You must be

- proficient on a computer;
- knowledgeable about the most current software packages, including word processing, spreadsheet, databases, and presentation software;

- competent in using telecommunications equipment;
- competent in using printers and copiers;
- willing to continually learn new office technology.

SUCCESS QUALITIES

In addition to technology skills, certain qualities are essential for the success of the office professional. These qualities include openness to change, creativity, flexibility, dependability, confidentiality, integrity, and initiative.

Openness to Change

Because change will continue to play such an important role in the office world, you must not only learn to cope with it but you must embrace it. Embracing change means accepting and preparing for change and being creative and flexible. Try to predict the changes you will face and prepare yourself for them. For example, you know that technology will continue to play an important role in the office; therefore, keep current on the latest technological changes that might impact your workplace.

Be creative and flexible when dealing with change. **Creativity** can be defined as the ability to combine existing ideas or things in new ways. When a change occurs, it is usually possible to connect that change to some already existing idea or way of doing something. **Flexibility** demands that you be able to see and choose from multiple options to determine the most appropriate one in a given situation. Review the steps listed in Figure 1-6 to help you understand how to deal with change.

Dependability

Dependability means many things. It means being at work on time if you are working at an established location. If you are working in a virtual environment, it means being productive in the performance of the objectives you must achieve in your job. It means the willingness to put in additional time when required on important assignments. It means doing what you say you will do and when you say you will do it.

Confidentiality

As an office professional, you will have access to information that is extremely confidential. You will be preparing documents that contain confidential information; you will also be told information that is confidential or you may overhear confidential conversations between executives. You must always maintain the **confidentiality** of the information received or the confidences shared. To let any confidential information leak outside your office may cause irreparable damage to your employer, others within your organization, customers, and your organization.

Integrity

Integrity is defined as the adherence to a code of behavior. In the office environment, the code of behavior means in part that you are honest. It means that you do not take equipment or supplies which belong to the company for your own personal use. It means you spend your time on the job performing the duties of the job—not making and receiving numerous personal phone calls. It means that you uphold high standards of ethical behavior. You do not engage in activities in which your morals or values may be questioned.

Initiative

Initiative is defined as the ability to begin and to follow through on a plan or a task. Initiative means the ability to take the tasks given you and complete them in an appropriate manner. It means having the ability to set appropriate work goals for yourself. The most highly valued office professional has the ability to analyze a task, establish priorities, and see the work through to completion. The professional who takes the initiative to make suggestions to the employer about needed changes or revisions is truly worth his or her weight in gold.

Dealing with Change

Follow these steps in dealing effectively with change.

- Understand why it is necessary to change. Determine what circumstances have occurred that have necessitated change.
- Determine what objectives will be achieved by the changes that are proposed.
- Establish guidelines for achieving these objectives.
- Determine the benefits or rewards that will occur as a result of the change.
- Once the change has occurred, evaluate the effectiveness of the change and your effectiveness in working through the change.

Figure 1-6

A PROFESSIONAL IMAGE

The office professional with a positive professional image constantly presents to the public the essential skills and success qualities discussed in the previous sections. In addition, the office professional presents a positive personal appearance, dresses in appropriate business attire, and is always well groomed. The office professional pays attention to hair style, personal hygiene, appropriate jewelry and accessories, physical condition, good posture, and proper eating habits. Depending on the office, appropriate business attire may include a suit and tie for men and a suit or dress for women. Other offices may be more relaxed with shirts without a tie for men and skirts or slacks and blouses or sweaters for women. A number of offices today have a day once a month or even once a week in which casual dress is appropriate, even if the remainder of the days are considered standard business attire. Some companies are now allowing employees to dress in business casual on a daily basis.

The professional image is an inclusive one. A positive personal appearance without the necessary skills and qualities is meaningless. The office professional who expects to succeed must be successful in combining the necessary skills and qualities with an appropriate personal appearance. Together, these three areas ensure a positive professional image.

PROFESSIONAL GROWTH

In our constantly changing office world, it is essential for you to continue your professional growth. This professional growth can be through:

- attending classes in a college or university;

- attending seminars and workshops provided by your company or outside firms;

- reading business periodicals;

- participating in professional organizations.

PERIODICALS

Numerous periodicals are available with articles to assist you in enhancing your knowledge and skills. Several of these periodicals and their addresses are listed in Figure 1-7. It is important that you begin now to become familiar with these periodicals by reading selected articles.

Professional Periodicals

From Nine to Five
Dartnell Corporation
4660 Ravenswood Avenue
Chicago, IL 60640

Managing Office Technology
Penton Publishing, Inc.
PO Box 95795
Cleveland, OH 44101

The Office Professional
212 Commerce Boulevard
Round Rock, TX 76664

The Secretary
Professional Secretaries International
10502 NW Ambassador Drive
Kansas City, MO 64195-0404

Working Woman
PO Box 3276
Harlan, IA 59593-2456

Business Week
McGraw-Hill, Inc.
1221 Avenue of the Americas
New York, NY 10020

Fortune
Time and Life Building
Rochester Center
New York, NY 10020-1393

The Wall Street Journal (a newspaper)
Dow Jones Company, Inc.
200 Liberty Street
New York, NY 10281

Figure 1-7

PROFESSIONAL ORGANIZATIONS

Listed here are several professional organizations that provide growth opportunities for the office professional.

- Professional Secretaries International (PSI)—This organization is the largest organization of secretaries, with chapters throughout the United States and several countries abroad. PSI administers a certification program that is widely respected and applies to all office fields. Upon successful passage of the examination, plus the

The Certified Professional Secretary

WHAT: Certification is granted to individuals who pass a written examination and have certain verified minimum secretarial experience. The certificate and CPS designation signify a professional goal and pride in one's profession.

HOW: To take the examination, an application must be submitted to the Institute for Certification. Certain minimum requirements must be satisfied before taking the examination; a fee is payable in advance.

The examination is given twice a year at over 250 locations in the United States, Puerto Rico, Jamaica, Malaysia, the Virgin Islands, and Canada. It is administered on one day in the months of May and November.

The CPS examination is made up of three parts:

I. Finance and Business Law

II. Office Systems and Administration

III. Management

Recertification is mandatory every five years, with requirements for recertification given at the time of certification. Upon recertification, an applicant is awarded a dated certificate that is valid for five years.

An educational review program at a local community college or university is advised prior to taking the examination.

WHY: CPS holders may receive special consideration for promotion and salary increases. Many holders of the certificate have used it as a stepping stone into supervisory and/or management positions. Many colleges grant college credits to individuals with CPS certificates. The CPS designation leads to opportunities for leadership positions within professional organizations oriented toward office and secretarial work.

Figure 1-8

required work experience, you are awarded the certified professional secretary (CPS) designation. The letters CPS after an office professional's name are indicative of the achievement of the highest professional standard within the field. Figure 1-8 gives more details about this certification. PSI publishes *The Secretary.*

- National Association of Legal Secretaries (NALS)—This organization sponsors a professional legal secretary (PLS) examination and certification programs. The two-day examination consists of these seven parts:

  - written communication skills

  - human relations and ethics

  - legal secretarial procedures

  - legal secretarial accounting

  - legal terminology, techniques, and procedures

  - exercise of judgment

  - legal secretarial skills

  The NALS publishes the NALS *Docket* (recently named @ *LAW*).

- The American Association of Medical Assistants (AAMA)—This organization is for office staff, nurses, technicians, and assistants employed by physicians or accredited hospitals. The organization sponsors a certification program which culminates in the certified medical assistant (CMA) designation. The examination tests general, medical, administrative, and clinical knowledge. It also publishes *The Professional Medical Assistant.*

- The American Association for Medical Transcription (AAMT)—This organization is for office staff,

17

assistants, and technicians employed by physicians or hospitals. It sponsors a certification program called certified medical transcriptionist (CMT) and publishes a magazine called the *Journal of the American Association for Medical Transcription.*

• The National Association of Educational Office Personnel (NAEOP)—The NAEOP sponsors a program that issues certificates based on education, experience, and professional activity. It also publishes *National Educational Secretary, Beam,* and *Crossroads.*

• Association of Records Managers and Administrators (ARMA)—This association sponsors the certified records manager (CRM) designation.

• Executive Women International (EWI)—This organization is composed of executive secretaries and administrative assistants and provides opportunities for professional growth and service.

COMPANY SCENE

Throughout this course, you will be working for Koronet International, 3500 Division, Grand Rapids, MI 49503-3295. The company was founded in 1920 in Grand Rapids, Michigan, with only 20 employees. Since that time, it has grown to over 6,000 employees, with four locations in the United States—Michigan, Texas, North Carolina, and California. The company is also international, having locations in Japan, Korea, and Mexico, as shown in Figure 1-9. It is one of the largest manufacturers of office furniture in the world. Its sales are in excess of $18 billion per year. Its stock is listed on the New York Stock Exchange and presently lists for $38 per share of common stock. Koronet International has been paying dividends to its investors for the last three years of over $3 per share. The Japan location opened in 1980, with the Korea location following in 1988, and the Mexico location opening in 1995. All locations are meeting projections at the present time.

Your job title is executive assistant. You report directly to Jacqueline Marquette, vice president of community relations. Koronet takes its social responsibility role seriously. The company has always taken an active role in the educational, environmental, and social concerns of the community, both in its national and international locations. It is considered a good corporate citizen by the communities in which it is located. Koronet is proud of this role and strives to continually enhance this image. Its profitability picture has been secure for years. Downsizing occurred in its home office in Michigan

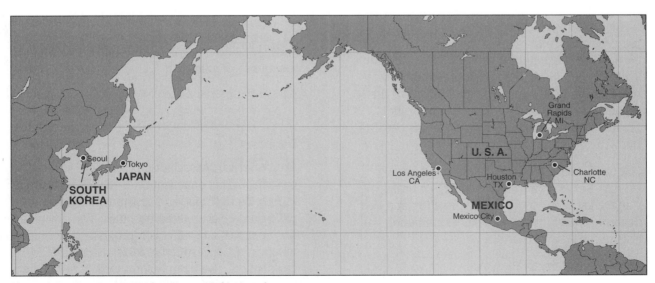

Figure 1-9 Koronet International's worldwide locations.

two years ago. This downsizing resulted in the early buyout of 100 employees which was 5 percent of the total staff of 2,000 employees in the home office. It resulted in a slight morale problem within the home office; however, steps have been taken to make the employees feel more a part of the decision-making process through TQM.

Your duties are extremely varied. They include assisting Jacqueline Marquette with setting up meetings with government and educational leaders within the local community to determine issues of common concern. At one point, you traveled to Japan with your employer and two other support staff to help set up a community conference in Japan. This is the only time that you have traveled outside the company; however, you do communi-cate frequently with Japan, Korea, and Mexico through fax and video teleconferencing. Other duties include:

- researching and preparing all types of correspondence
- participating in TQM teams
- organizing your employer's schedule
- scheduling meetings
- making travel arrangements
- handling the mail
- filing correspondence
- supervising one part-time clerk

CHAPTER SUMMARY

This summary will help you remember the important points covered in this chapter.

- The office of the twenty-first century will be (1) more diverse than ever before, (2) global in operations, (3) technologically up-to-date, (4) virtual.

- It is projected that the entering workforce entrants in 2005 will be 35 percent African Americans, Hispanics, and Asians.

- Women will continue to be a growing part of the workforce; they will occupy diverse positions in the workforce, including all levels of management.

- The workforce will be older, with the number of workers 55 and above growing approximately twice as fast as the total labor force between the 1990s and 2005.

- As you work in the diverse office, you will need to be aware of and sensitive to the varying cultural differences and backgrounds.

- We cannot assume that women and men react differently to situations because of their gender.

- Age differences may mean that we view the world from different perspectives.

- Businesses in the United States are not confined to state or national boundaries; they may be multinational.

- To reduce costs and improve efficiency, productivity, and quality, organizations have downsized and flattened their organizational structures.

- The quality concept developed by W. Edwards Deming is now used by numerous American businesses in an effort to improve quality and productivity.

- Today, a number of workers have traded the traditional office for the virtual office—one in which work may be done at any time and in any place.

- Workweeks today may be flexible, with hours varying from the traditional eight- or nine-to-five. The compressed workweek, flextime, and job-sharing are examples of flexible workweeks.

- The office professional's role is shifting due to technology, with duties that include researching and preparing reports complete with graphics, clip art, and spreadsheets; assisting with the planning and direction of the company through teams; and supervising support staff.

- The office professional needs these skills:

  oral and written communication skills

  human relations skills

  critical thinking skills

  organizational skills

  technology skills

- The office professional must develop these success qualities:

  openness to change

  dependability

  confidentiality

  integrity

  initiative

- The total professional image (including knowledges, skills, and qualities mentioned previously), in addition to personal appearance, are essential for success.

- Professional growth can occur through attending classes or seminars and workshops, reading business periodicals, and participating in professional organizations.

CHAPTER GLOSSARY

The following terms were introduced in this chapter. To help you review, definitions are given here.

- **State-of-the-art technology** (p. 5)–The latest technology available.

- **Virtual workplace** (p. 5)–Where work can be performed virtually anywhere and at anytime using technology.

- **Information Age** (p. 5)–An age when there has been a great explosion of knowledge due mainly to the technological revolution.

- **Software office suites** (p. 5)–Software packages that include word processing, spreadsheets, graphics, and scheduling.

- **Clip art** (p. 5)–Art that is pre-drawn and available on software for transfer to documents for illustration purposes.

- **Multiculturalism** (p. 6)–Relating to or including several cultures.

- **Culture** (p. 6)–Ideas, customs, values, skills, and arts of a specific group of people.

- **Stereotype** (p. 7)–A perception or image held of people or things which may be favorable or unfavorable.

- **Multinational** (p. 7)–Refers to business operations that are both within a country and outside the country.

- **Hierarchy** (p. 8)–Organization that is structured by rank or authority of each position.

- **TQM or CQI** (p. 9)–Total quality management or continuous quality improvement which emphasizes continued improvement of both goods and services through team approaches within a business.

- **Telecommuting** (p. 11)–Working from home or another established location via computer hookup.

- **Compressed workweek** (p. 11)–Regular workweek hours compressed into four days.

- **Flextime** (p. 11)–Staggering of working hours to enable employees to work the full quota of time but at periods defined by the company and the individual.

- **Job-sharing** (p. 12)–Two part-time employees performing a job that otherwise would be held by one full-time employee.

- **Office professional** (p. 12)–A term used to denote an office support position. In this text, it is used throughout as a means of clarifying the position.

- **Critical thinking** (p. 14)–A unique kind of purposeful thinking in which the thinker systematically chooses conscious and deliberate inquiry.

- **Krinein** (p. 14)–Greek word meaning to separate or choose.

- **Creativity** (p. 15)–The ability to combine existing ideas or things in new ways.

- **Flexibility** (p. 15)–Ability to see and choose from multiple options to determine the most appropriate one in a given solution.

- **Dependability** (p. 15)–An individual's capacity to be reliable, supportive, trustworthy, and productive.

- **Confidentiality** (p. 15)–The ability to keep secrets; not revealing information, such as legal information, which is needed only by certain people within the organization and could be harmful to individuals and the company if revealed to others.

- **Integrity** (p. 15)–Adherence to a code of behavior.

- **Initiative** (p. 15)–The ability to begin and to follow through on a plan or a task.

DISCUSSION ITEMS

These discussion items provide an opportunity for you to test your understanding of the chapter through discussion with your classmates and your instructor.

1. What is meant by the virtual workplace? What implications does this term have for you in working in the twenty-first century office?

2. Explain how the office of the future will be more diverse. What does the diversity suggest for you as a future office employee?

3. What impact does the global economy have on today's office?

4. Explain the difference between the traditional hierarchy and the flattened organization structure.

5. What significant contributions have been made by W. Edwards Deming to the business world?

6. Identify five skills that are necessary in today's office.

CASE STUDY

Koronet International has introduced TQM in an effort to improve quality and productivity. You were asked to be part of a team that looks at the improvement of internal communication. You were pleased to be asked to be a part of the team and you took the assignment seriously. Before the first meeting, you had identified several communication problems that seem to be ongoing in the organization. You brought these communication problems up at the meeting; that is, failure to respond to e-mail promptly and failure to answer telephone calls. Two of the individuals who work in the adjacent office to yours became very upset with you. They assumed that your statements referred to situations you had encountered with them. They exploded in the meeting, making these comments:

"I can't answer every e-mail you send me within the hour. Get off my back. The next time you have a complaint about me, talk with me personally."

"I'm sorry if you have to pick up my phone occasionally, but I don't have anyone to assist me in the office like you do."

You tried to let these individuals know that you were not talking about individual cases. You were attempting to identify problems that needed to be addressed in order that the customer might be better served. However, because the meeting did not get off to a good start, you feel responsible. You want to be a contributor to the process. What should you do? Think through the following items, and prepare responses.

- What is the problem?

- Do the upset employees have cause to be concerned about your behavior?

- Should you talk to these employees before the next meeting? If so, what should you say?

- How can you present problems or issues at the next meeting without causing the volatility of the last meeting?

CHAPTER 2

PLANNING YOUR CAREER

LEARNING OBJECTIVES

1. **Identify and use effective decision-making techniques.**
2. **Determine sources of job information.**
3. **Prepare a resume and letter of application.**
4. **Develop job interview skills.**
5. **Complete an employment application.**
6. **Discover how to succeed and advance your professional career.**

How do I go about planning my career and finding the job I want? If this question is not an important one to you at present, it will become increasingly important as you finish your education and look for a job. If you are to be effective in planning, you must understand how to make good decisions. Effective decision-making, steps in applying for a job, the job interview, and the follow-up of the interview are presented in this chapter.

Looking for a job is the next step. © *Jeff Greenberg.*

PLAN YOUR CAREER

You probably have decided that you want a career as an office professional. However, you may not have given any thought to the type of company that will best match your goals. Would you like to work for a service industry, a health related industry, a government agency, a banking institution, a legal firm, or a manufacturing industry, to name a few. Would you like to move up in the company? Do you want to find a job where you now live or are you willing to move? Do you want to work for a large firm or a small company? All these questions are important considerations. Clear goals will help direct your job search into productive channels.

CAREER GOALS

In order to set appropriate goals, you need to analyze yourself. Take an inventory of your strengths and weaknesses. It is perfectly okay to admit to certain weaknesses; all of us have them. Only from understanding what they are can you grow.

Ask yourself the following questions:

- What are my strengths?
- What are my weaknesses?
- What have I achieved?
- Where have I failed?
- What do I enjoy doing?
- Where do I want to be in five years? In ten years?
- Do I enjoy working with people?
- Do I enjoy working independently and alone?

Keep in mind that your goals will change over time and that you will not always reach all of your goals. However, if you never set goals, you will certainly never reach them.

Take a few moments now to respond to the items in the following Self Check.

Self Check

- List three of your strengths.
- List three of your weaknesses.
- List two of your accomplishments.
- Are there areas in which you have failed? If so, what are they? List one or two.
- What do you enjoy doing?
- Where do you want to be in five years? In ten years?

EFFECTIVE DECISION-MAKING

Setting goals and reaching them also involve making effective decisions. A **decision** is the outcome or end product of a problem, concern, or issue that needs to be addressed and solved. The process by which a decision is reached includes five steps. The steps are depicted in Figure 2-1.

Decision-Making Steps

- Evaluate the decision
- Test the alternatives and make the decision
- Generate alternatives or possible solutions
- Establish the criteria
- Define the problem or purpose

Figure 2-1

Define the Problem or the Purpose

This first step may sound simple, but it is usually the most difficult. In attempting to define the problem or purpose, it is helpful to ask yourself a series of questions. Here are some questions that may be helpful.

- What decision am I trying to make or what problem am I trying to solve?
- Why is it a problem?
- Why is the decision necessary?
- Who is involved?
- What will be the outcome of this decision?

Assume that you are trying to decide what job offer to take. You have two offers. One is with a large company in the city in which you live. The other job offer is with a small but growing company in another state. Your answers to the questions might be:

- I am trying to make a decision about which job I choose. I want a job that is challenging and has growth potential. I do not object to living in another state; however, I do not know much about North Carolina (the state where the company is located).
- It is a problem because I want to be happy in my job; if I do not make a right decision, I will not be happy.
- The decision is necessary because (a) I am finishing my education; (b) I need money to help support myself; (c) I want employment where I can have a challenging job.
- There is no one else involved at the present time. I am not married and I have no family members living with me.
- The outcome of the decision will be that I am employed in a position that provides me challenges and opportunities, with an appropriate starting salary.

When you finish answering the questions, it is a good idea to frame the problem into a statement. You might frame this statement:

My purpose is to find an office professional position that is challenging with a company that provides growth opportunities. This company should be located in a city that has affordable housing, offers numerous cultural events, and has pleasant weather conditions so that I can bike and hike at least eight months of the year.

Establish the Criteria

The next step in the decision-making process is to determine the criteria you need to make a sound decision. In setting your criteria, ask these two questions:

- What do I want to achieve?
- What do I want to avoid?

Your answers to these questions might be:

- I want to grow on the job; I want to be promoted to positions of greater responsibility and higher pay.

- I want to live in a city that has pleasant climate and a multitude of cultural activities.

- I want to live in a city where good housing is available at a reasonable cost.

- I want to avoid a company that provides no promotional opportunities.

- I want to avoid living in a city that does not offer the activities that I enjoy.

Generate Alternatives or Possible Solutions

The next step in the decision-making process is to begin generating alternatives or possible solutions. For example, you might list the job duties of each position, promotional opportunities available, and the starting salaries available. You might call the chamber of commerce in the city of North Carolina to get information. In addition, you may want to spend a few days in the city checking out the cultural activities, the climate, and the housing situation.

Test the Alternatives and Make the Decision

The effective decision-maker tests each alternative and makes the decision by

- eliminating alternatives that are unrealistic or incompatible with the person's needs;

- giving thought to the alternatives that seem appropriate in the situation;

- selecting the alternative that appears the most realistic, creative, or appealing for the criteria established.

Evaluate the Decision

The last step in the decision-making process is evaluation. Evaluation serves two purposes:

- It helps you decide if you have made the right decision.

- It helps you improve your decision-making skills for the future.

In evaluating your decision, here are some questions you can ask yourself.

- What was right about the decision? What was wrong?

- How did the decision-making process work? How can it be improved in the future?

- What was learned from the decision? What changes should be made for the future?

Assume that you chose the job with the large company in your city. You have been with the company for a year now, and there have been no promotional opportunities. In evaluating your initial decision, you discover that you did not look carefully at what career paths were available in the company. You have learned that in the future you will be more careful in asking the right questions of the interviewer and in analyzing the situation.

This decision-making model is an appropriate one for making decisions in any area. As you go through this course, you may want to refer to the decision-making model again to help you make good decisions.

DETERMINE SOURCES OF JOB INFORMATION

One of the first things to do as you look for a job is to get all the information you can about available job opportunities. Information is available through the following sources:

- personal networks

- placement offices

- newspaper advertisements

- employment agencies

- the Internet and the World Wide Web

- professional organizations

- company walk-ins

- temporary agencies

PERSONAL NETWORKS

Networking is defined in this context as the process of identifying and establishing a group of acquaintances, friends, and even relatives who can assist you in the job search process. Most employees are aware of job openings within their company. Many companies list positions on e-mail, job hotlines, and bulletin boards.

27

Networking can be a source of job information. *Courtesy of International Business Machines, Inc.*

PLACEMENT OFFICES

Many colleges maintain a placement office. Visit this office. Your school may not have enough employment calls from employers to provide positions for all students, but usually you will find that the counselors at your school are well informed about job opportunities in the community. They know the employers who need entry-level workers, and they can match a job to your qualifications and abilities.

NEWSPAPER ADVERTISEMENTS

Employers and employment agencies list positions available in local newspapers. These advertisements give an excellent review of the types of positions and qualifications required, and usually provide information about the salaries offered. Figure 2-2 shows several advertisements.

EMPLOYMENT AGENCIES

There are two types of employment agencies: private and state operated. **State-operated employ-** ment agencies are supported by tax dollars. As a taxpaying citizen, you can take advantage of the services provided by your state agency free of charge.

Private employment agencies charge a fee for their services. Either you or the employing firm must pay for these services. Find out if you are expected to pay the fee. It is usually stated as a percentage of your beginning salary. Generally, you must sign a contract with private employment agencies. Information regarding how the fee is determined should be included in the contract. Read any contract carefully before signing it. When private employment agencies advertise jobs that are fee paid, the employer pays the fee when the applicant is hired.

Employment agencies screen applicants for the employer. When you go to an agency, you should be prepared to complete an application and take several tests. Examples of the tests are

- keyboarding speed and accuracy

- grammar, punctuation, and proofreading skills

- mathematical aptitude

- skill in operating computers

THE INTERNET AND WORLD WIDE WEB

The **Internet** is a group of computers which are connected all over the world, allowing people to communicate with each other. In fact, the Internet is the world's largest group of connected computers. A variety of information is available through the Internet. This information is gathered in a huge assortment of computer files; the information may be accessed through any number of sources. For example, you may get on the Internet and then

---

ADMINISTRATIVE ASSISTANT QUALITY MANAGEMENT

We are seeking a detail-oriented individual to assist in the daily talks of quality improvement. Responsibilities include preparing reports, developing forms and summarizing peer review data. Excellent interpersonal and organizational skills, and analytical ability, as well as expertise on computer required (Word-Perfect for Windows, Quatro Pro, Paradox); knowledge of medical terminology preferred. Please send resume or apply in person to Human Resources, Pine Wood Medical Center, 300 36th Street, Grand Rapids, MI 49502

ADMINISTRATIVE ASSISTANT

NEBC has an immediate need for an Administrative Assistant to join our team.

Responsibilities include performing secretarial and administrative duties in support of the Executive Director. Must have working knowledge of standard office procedures, proper phone etiquette, and the ability to communicate verbally and in writing. Must work well under pressure with various levels of staff. Proficiency in Microsoft Word, Excel, and Power Point is essential.

We offer excellent salary and comprehensive benefits. Send your resume, along with daytime phone number to NEBC, PO Box 593, New York, NY 10119-5436

NEBC

Figure 2-2   Newspaper advertisements.

access data about companies worldwide through the **World Wide Web (WWW).** The Internet provides your connection to computers internationally; the World Wide Web provides the computer files with the data you need on the international businesses. The WWW contains numerous files with information on a multitude of topics.

Assume that you want information concerning job openings. You access the Internet and the computer files of the World Wide Web. Many major companies including high tech companies such as 3M®, AT&T®, Novell®, Rockwell®, and Unisys® post company profiles and job openings on WWW. The database is searchable by company name, location, job description, and title. Through this computer network, you can get immediate access to thousands of job opportunities.

PROFESSIONAL ORGANIZATIONS

If you are a member of a professional organization, check to see if they maintain a listing of jobs in the area. You should also ask individual members if they are aware of any openings.

COMPANY WALK-INS

If you are interested in obtaining a position with a certain company or in a particular type of business, the **direct canvass** or **cold canvass** (going directly to the business without having an appointment or without knowing if there is a job available) is sometimes a more successful procedure. If you have a gift for selling yourself, you might find this type of approach beneficial. Before you engage in the direct canvass approach, however, it is a good idea to find out as much as you can about the company.

TEMPORARY AGENCIES

A **temporary agency** (one that offers temporary work) is not a source of job information in the usual sense; however, a temporary agency can help you know more about where you want to work. If you are not clear concerning the type or size of company where you wish to work, you might try working for a temporary agency for a period of time. They can place you in a number of different companies. Without any long-term commitment, you can gain an understanding of where you want to work as a full-time employee.

Temporary agencies also provide an alternative to a full-time job. For example, individuals with young children may decide to work for a temporary agency. As a "temp" they can accept jobs on a part-time basis which allows for more time with their children.

Direct canvass of individual companies is one method of obtaining job information.

You learned in Chapter 1 that many companies are downsizing today. With this downsizing, they often hire temporary workers. It usually is a cost-saving measure for the company. It also allows greater flexibility because the company has less of its staffing dollars tied up in full-time personnel. Some companies may also use temporary agencies as a way to get first-hand knowledge of employees. For example, the businesses may hire an individual from a temporary agency, be extremely pleased with the employee's work, and offer the employee a full-time job.

LEARN ABOUT THE COMPANY

Once you have identified a company or companies where you are interested in applying, spend some time learning about the company. How do you do this? There are several ways.

- Ask friends, relatives, or acquaintances what they know about the organization.

- Check library publications such as *Standard and Poor's* and *Moody's*.

- Obtain an annual report of the company; most companies will send you one upon request.
- Consult your local chamber of commerce.
- Ask your placement office at the college for information.

To find out about local companies, visit the chamber of commerce. © *Jeff Greenberg.*

When evaluating a company, here are some items to consider.

- What is the company's product or service?
- Is the company multinational? Does the company have branches in other states?
- What has been the profit picture of the company for the last several years?
- Is the company financially secure?
- Is the company growing?
- Does the company have a good reputation in the community?
- Are there good relationships between the employer and employees?
- Is the company an equal opportunity employer?
- Are there opportunities for advancement?

WRITE A LETTER OF APPLICATION

Once you are satisfied that you are interested in the company, your next step is to obtain an interview. The **letter of application** is the key to obtaining that interview. It is basically a sales letter because it attempts to sell your abilities. Prepare your letter thoughtfully. The appearance, format, arrangement, and content of the letter are extremely important in making a good impression and in obtaining your objective—an interview.

LETTER GOALS

The three basic goals of a letter of application are to arouse interest, describe your abilities, and request an interview.

Arouse Interest

In the opening, provide the employer with a brief statement of your qualifications. Let the person know you are interested in the company and what you can do for the company. Consider the following examples of effective beginnings.

Example 1. *The position you have advertised sounds challenging. My Associate of Arts Degree in Business Information Systems and my part-time experience as an office assistant while attending college have given me the skills necessary to fill the job.*

Example 2. *Your employment announcement calls for an office assistant who is interested in learning the latest technology and has good office skills. My training at Grand Haven College for the last two years has provided me with these skills.*

In both cases you let the prospective employer know that you are interested in the position and that you believe you have the skills needed for the job.

Describe Your Abilities

The next paragraph of the letter should describe in more detail the abilities you have. It should also call attention to your enclosed resume, vitae, or data sheet (explained in the next section).

In May of this year I will graduate from Grand Haven College. During my two years at Grand Haven, I have taken courses in office procedures, accounting, management, business communications, computers, and organizational behavior. I have good computer skills and an excellent working knowledge of Microsoft Word and WordPerfect, in addition to spreadsheet, database, and presentation software.

Request an Interview

Because the purpose of the letter is to get an interview, you should ask directly for the interview. For example:

Please give me an opportunity to discuss my qualifications with you. My telephone number is 555-2041.

A letter of application is shown in Figure 2-3.

```
                    2341 Broadmoor NE
                    Grand Rapids, MI 48501-1655
                    October 23,--


          Mr. Anthony Rush
          Human Resources Manager
          Koronet International
          3500 Division
          Grand Rapids, MI 49503-3295

          Dear Mr. Rush:

          Your employment announcement for an executive assistant
          specifies an individual with interpersonal, organizational, and
          analytical skills, plus expertise in Word for Windows.  My two
          years of training in office systems at Grand Haven College and
          my one year of work experience have given me the skills and
          knowledge which you desire.  I am very interested in this
          position and in working for Koronet International.  I am very
          willing to work hard in demonstrating my capabilities.

          During the last two years, I have completed an Associate Degree
          in Office Systems. My courses included business communications,
          organizational behavior, management, accounting, office
          procedures, and computer science.  I can keyboard at 80 wpm and
          am proficient in operating telecommunication equipment and
          copiers.  Prior to beginning college, I worked for one year at
          Martin Paper Company where I was a receptionist and did some
          keyboarding and filing.  The enclosed resume gives further
          details concerning my qualifications and experience.

          May I have the opportunity to discuss my qualifications with
          you?  You may reach me at 555-7750 between 2:00 and 5:00 p.m.

          Sincerely,

          Martha G. Hornecek

          Martha G. Hornecek

          Enclosure
```

Figure 2-3   Letter of application.

Additional hints on writing a letter of application are given in Figure 2-4. Careful reading of these hints will help you in writing application letters.

PREPARE A RESUME

The **resume, vitae,** or **data sheet** is a concise statement of your background, education, skills, and experience. Because the term resume is probably the most frequently used, it will be used in this text. Figure 2-5 shows the format and style of a typical resume in chronological format (listing education and experience in date order with the most recent education and experience listed first). Just as the letter of application is a sales letter, so the resume is a piece of sales literature. It represents a very important product—you.

To a certain degree, a resume reflects what is important in the changing business world. For example, prior to the antidiscrimination legislation of the 1960s and 1970s, almost all resumes had a section labeled "personal data." This section included such information as age, marital status, number of children, height, weight, and hobbies. Our laws now state that it is illegal to discriminate on the basis of national origin, ethnic group, gender, creed, age, or race. Most authorities, therefore, recommend that personal items be left off the resume. What the prospective employer needs to know is whether you have the qualifications for the job.

However, although employers are limited by law on what they can ask you to provide, you can submit any data you wish on a resume. If you feel that some of your personal characteristics will assist you in getting the job, list them.

RESUME SECTIONS

The sections of a resume may vary, depending on your situation and how you want to present your qualifications. There is no one perfect model; however, certain parts are common to most resumes. The parts are given here.

Career Objective

This section lets the reader know about your present career goals. For example:

Career Objective: *A position as an office professional in a challenging business with opportunities to use my technology and human relations skills.*

Notice that this objective did not specify a particular type of company. If you are certain that you are interested in a specialized field, you may note that objective. You also might list your long-term goal. In that case, your objective might be:

Career Objective: *A position as an office professional in a law firm, with a long-range goal of being a law office manager.*

Letter Writing Hints

- Key the letter in proper form using an acceptable letter style.

- Print your letter on high-quality bond paper. Most office supply stores will have paper that they recommend for use in writing letters of application and resumes.

- Use correct spelling, punctuation, capitalization, and grammar. Always use the spell checker if available.

- Keep the letter short. Put the details in the resume.

- Address the letter to a specific person. Never address an application letter "To Whom It May Concern." If you do not have a name, take the time to find out by calling the company or checking with the placement office, agency, or the person who told you about the job.

- Send an original letter for each application. Do not send photocopies.

- Do not copy a letter of application from a book. Make your letter representative of your personality.

- Use three paragraphs.

- Use reader's name within the letter.

- Mail in a large envelope so your letter and resume will "stand out" from other No. 10 envelopes on the employer's desk.

Figure 2-4

Capabilities

This section gives you a chance to identify your skill strengths. You can list the computer software in which you are proficient, your keyboarding speed, and the various technological equipment that you can operate.

Education

In this section, list the schools you have attended and the degrees obtained (if applicable). If you graduated many years ago, it is usually not necessary to list your high school. If you are a recent high school graduate, you should list it. You might also want to list the courses or programs that you have taken that would be helpful in getting the position.

Work Experience

List the companies where you have worked, the dates of employment, and your duties. You may want to reverse the order of education and experience on your resume. For example, if you have had excellent experience that directly relates to the job for which you are applying, you may wish to list the experience first. Remember, the resume is a sales piece. You want to call attention to your best-selling features first.

The usual order for listing both education and experience is in reverse chronological order. In other words, you list your most recent work and educational experience first, followed by the next most recent, and so forth. Notice the resume in Figure 2-5 which shows this type of order. It is referred to as a **chronological resume.** However, you may wish to focus on the skills and abilities that are more applicable to the present job you are seeking. If so, you may cluster your education, experiences, and activities into categories that support your career goals. This type of approach is usually more appropriate for the individual who has considerable experience. This resume is shown in Figure 2-6 and is referred to as a **functional resume.**

Extracurricular Activities, Memberships, and Honors

If you have participated in special activities, maintained memberships in professional organizations, or achieved honors, you may wish to list these. Such activities illustrate that you have many interests and leadership qualities. Employers are usually impressed with such characteristics. This involvement and recognition can provide an added advantage for you.

MARTHA G. HORNECEK
2341 Broadmoor NE
Grand Rapids, MI 48501-1655
616 555-7750

Career Objective
A position as an executive assistant with the opportunity to use technological skills and human relations skills.

Capabilities
Keyboarding at 80 wpm; proficiency in Microsoft Word, WordPerfect, Lotus, and Microsoft Office; competency in operating telecommunications equipment and printers and copiers.

Education
Grand Haven College, Grand Rapids, Michigan, September 1997 to May 1999, Associate Degree in Office Systems.

Courses studied: Business communications, organizational behavior, management, office procedures, accounting, English, psychology, math, and computer science.

Grisham High School, Granville, Michigan, September 1993 to May 1996.

Work Experience
Student assistant in the business department of Grand Haven College, September 1998 to June 1999. Responsibilities included producing tests, copying materials, and records management.

Receptionist, Martin Paper Company, June 1996 to August 1997. Responsibilities included greeting visitors, setting appointments, keyboarding correspondence, and answering the telephone.

Honors
Phi Theta Kappa, President
Dean's List
Most Outstanding Student in Business Department

References
Dr. Morris Adams, Grand Haven College, 4789 Keist NE, Grand Rapids, MI 49546
(616)555-8354

Ms. Mary Lee Patterson, Grand Haven College, 4789 Keist NE, Grand Rapids, MI 49546
(616)555-8323

Mr. Lee Quang, Martin Paper Company, 2500 28th Street SE, Cascade, MI 49646
(616)555-9040

Figure 2-5 Chronological resume.

MELINDA PEREZ
8354 Westbend Drive
Dallas, TX 75214-2365

CAREER OBJECTIVE
A position as an executive assistant, with a long-range goal of an office manager.

QUALIFICATIONS
Five years of office experience, assuming more responsibility in each position. Keyboarding skills of 100 wpm, with proficiency in telecommunications. Associate Degree in Office Systems, plus 20 hours junior level work.

EDUCATION
Associate Degree in Office Systems, Brookdale College, Dallas, Texas. Twenty hours of work toward a BBA at the University of the Northwest, Denton, Texas.

WORK EXPERIENCE
Executive Secretary to Vice President, Human Resources, TOX International, Plano, Texas. Supervised two clerical personnel, keyboarded correspondence, arranged meetings, prepared monthly reports. Accounting Assistant to Business Services Division of Apple Industries, Dallas, Texas. Entered data on computer for numerous business reports and personnel forms; prepared bills for vendors.

PROFESSIONAL MEMBERSHIPS
Executive Women International
Professional Secretaries International

REFERENCES
Furnished upon request.

Figure 2-6 Functional resume.

References

You may list references on the resume or you may choose to list the section with the statement, "References will be furnished upon request." Notice in Figure 2-5 references are listed and in Figure 2-6 they are not. Either method is appropriate.

Even if you do not have references listed on your resume, you will need to have at least three references when you begin your job search. Three references are considered a minimum number, with five usually considered a maximum. The most effective references are previous employers, followed by references from your instructors. Personal references are considered to be less effective. Do not use the names of close relatives or your minister (unless it is for a church-related job).

Choose your references carefully. Attempt to select those individuals who know your qualifications well and will take the time to respond to a reference request. Before you list a person as a reference, it is essential that you obtain permission from the person.

RESUME FORMAT

The resume has no one set format—use one that is clear and concise. Just as the application letter must be free from spelling and grammatical errors, so must the resume. It should be prepared on a good grade of 8½-by-11-inch bond paper. For a student, a one-page resume is usually adequate. If you have extensive work experience, your resume may need to be two or even three pages long. Remember the rule is to present the necessary information as concisely as possible. No prospective employer wants to read through five or six pages of poorly presented, wordy material.

FILL OUT THE EMPLOYMENT APPLICATION

You will be asked to fill out an **employment application.** You may do this before or after being interviewed. Figure 2-7 shows an employment application form similar to those found in many businesses today. In some businesses, all applicants fill out a form. Other firms ask only those who are seriously being considered for a position to fill out a form. Some businesses request that applicants print or type the information requested on the form. Others require the applicant to handwrite the form. If you are asked to handwrite the form, use your best handwriting and a pen. Fill in all blanks. If you have no response, write "none" or "not applicable."

Read each question carefully before answering. Avoid asking unnecessary questions of the individual who has given you the form. Spell correctly. Carry a pocket dictionary in case you need to look up the spelling of a word. Be prepared. Have all the information with you that you need: dates you attended schools, dates of employment, and complete addresses of previous employers and references. You will also need your social security number.

Be careful to not spoil the form because you do not want to ask for another one. A standard question included on the application is the reason for leaving your last position. State your reason in its most positive light. For example, if you were fired from your job, you might say, "Skills did not match what was needed by the organization." Be certain to answer all questions truthfully. Some firms may discharge you, even after months of satisfactory work, if they discover that you were untruthful on the application.

PREPARE FOR THE INTERVIEW

The interview will not be an ordeal if you adequately prepare for it. Knowledge of what to do and what to say will help eliminate a great deal of nervousness. In the interview, the employer will judge your appearance, personality, human relations skills, self-confidence, and other traits. The interviewer will question you about your experience and abilities as identified in your letter of application and resume. The interview is an opportunity for the prospective employer to get to know you and for you to get know the employer. Although it may be a new experience for you, approach it with confidence.

HUMAN RELATIONS TIP

Good human relations skills will help you get the job you want. Throughout this course, practice those skills.

If you have not had much experience in interviewing, it is a good idea to accept interviews for positions you do not think you are interested in to give you much needed practice. You may just find that you were wrong; the job may turn about to be something that you are interested in.

PORTFOLIO INFORMATION

You may wish to prepare a **portfolio** of your work to take with you in the interview. A portfolio is a compilation of samples of your work. The work should be arranged attractively in a binder. Some possible items for inclusion are

- letters that you have written to demonstrate your writing style;

- spreadsheets that you have prepared;

- reports including graphics;

- presentation software slides.

LOCATION OF INTERVIEW

Be sure you know the exact time and location of the interview. Do not rely on your memory. Write down the time, address, and person's name you are to see and take it with you. When traveling to the interview location, allow time for unexpected delays. You do not want to be late for the interview. Excuses for being late will not erase the poor impression you would have already made by your lateness.

NUMBER OF INTERVIEWS

It is possible that you will have more than one interview for a particular position. For example, you may be interviewed first by a human resources professional. Next, you may see the person to whom you would report and possibly have an interview with your prospective team members within the company.

TEAM INTERVIEWS

Some companies like to have team interviews. For example, the group of people who will work with you may interview you as a group. Usually, the teams do not consist of more than five or six people. Although this type of interview sounds intimidating, it need not be so. Pay careful attention to the individuals' names as they are introduced. Remember to focus on each individual as the person asks a question. Listen carefully and answer it succinctly. When you ask a question, ask it of the group unless one person has said something that you wish to follow up. Make eye contact with all individuals if the question or statement is meant for the entire group.

VIRTUAL INTERVIEW

You learned in Chapter 1 about the virtual office—one where work may be performed from anywhere at anytime using technology. Businesses are now in certain situations using the **virtual interview** (a prospective employee may be interviewed anywhere at anytime using technology).

Assume that you are applying for a job in Canada. You live in Grand Rapids, Michigan. Rather than flying to Canada for the interview and either you or the company assuming the travel expense, you are interviewed in Grand Rapids. The company makes arrangements for you to go to a facility that has teleconferencing capabilities. The room in Grand Rapids is linked electronically to a room in Canada. The interviewer from Canada can see you and you can see the interviewer. The interview is conducted without you leaving Michigan and without the interviewer leaving Canada.

If you are going to take part in a virtual interview, you need to be extremely well prepared. Most of us get a little nervous when we know that a camera is involved; however, your goal is to relax and treat the situation just as you would if the person interviewing you were in the same room with you. Because the situation is unique, here are some points to help you have a successful virtual interview.

- Greet the interviewer warmly and with a smile just as you would in person. Repeat the interviewer's name; for example, say: "I'm happy to meet you, Mr. VanDoss."

- Sit in the chair provided. Sit back in the chair—not on the edge of your seat. Sitting on the edge of the chair can connote nervousness.

- Try to forget the camera is there. Do not concentrate on it. Concentrate on the interviewer and the questions.

- Dress in colors that look good on you—black or gray does not generally come across well on camera. Be certain that you are not wearing jewelry that jingles or clangs. This noise on camera is even more noticeable than in person.

- Pay attention to the body language and small nuances of the interviewer. Do not spend an inordinate amount of time answering any one question. Be warm and informative, but also be concise.

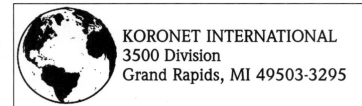

KORONET INTERNATIONAL
3500 Division
Grand Rapids, MI 49503-3295

Name _____ Social Security Number _____
       LAST   FIRST   MIDDLE

Present Address _____ Tel. No. _____
          NO.   STREET   CITY   STATE   ZIP

U.S. Citizen? _____

Have you ever been convicted of a crime? _____ If yes, describe in full _____

Have you ever been employed by Koronet? _____ If so, when? _____

Have you ever had or do you now have a worker's compensation claim pending for an injury while working for any employer? _____

If yes, give date and nature of accident _____

List relatives working for Koronet

_____
            NAME   RELATIONSHIP

List acquaintances now employed by Koronet

_____

_____

_____

Person to be notified in case of emergency: _____
                                                 NAME

Home Address _____ Tel. No. _____

Business Address _____ Tel. No _____

SCHOOL	NAME AND ADDRESS OF SCHOOL	COURSE OF STUDY	DATES ATTENDED	DIPLOMA, DEGREE OR CERTIFICATE
High School				
College				
Other (Specify)				

Figure 2-7 Employment application.

Employment Record

Present or Last Employment

Name of Firm	Type of Business	Supervisor	Job Title	Salary
Previous Employment Name of Firm	Type of Business	Supervisor	Job Title	Salary
Previous Employment Name of Firm	Type of Business	Supervisor	Job Title	Salary

List Other Employers:

_____

_____

U.S. Military Experience: Branch of Service _____ Date Entered _____

Do you have a valid Driver's License? _____ Type _____ Was it ever suspended? _____

Have you ever been bonded? _____

REFERENCES (not former employers or relatives)

NAME AND OCCUPATION	ADDRESS	PHONE NUMBER

Applicant's Signature _____

Figure 2-7   *(Continued)*

- Enunciate carefully. Poor enunciation is more pronounced on camera than in person.

- Once the interview is over, thank the person and leave the teleconferencing room.

- Notice the hints given below for traditional interviews. Many of these hints will also apply in a virtual interview process.

HELPFUL HINTS

Observe the following suggestions to help you make a good impression during the interview.

- Dress appropriately. The safest look during the interview is a conservative one, even if you are applying for a creative position. For both men and women, a suit is appropriate attire. Wear a color that looks good on you. Both men and women should keep the amount of jewelry to a minimum.

- If you wear a coat, hang it in the reception area. Do not take it into the office where you are being interviewed. You do not want to be burdened with numerous belongings.

- Good grooming is critical. Women may wish to have their hair done professionally the day before the interview; men need to be certain their hair is cut appropriately.

- Get a good night's rest before the interview so that you will be alert.

- Carry a briefcase. If you are female, try to do without a handbag. There will be one less item for you to juggle. Have an extra copy of your resume in your briefcase in case the interviewer has misplaced the one you mailed. Have a pad and pen in your briefcase if you need to take notes. Also, have your list of references ready if you need to fill out an employment application.

- Greet the receptionist with a friendly smile, stating your name and the purpose of your visit.

- Give a firm handshake when meeting the interviewer.

- Wait to sit down until invited to do so.

- Maintain appropriate eye contact.

- Try not to act nervous—avoid nervous gestures such as playing with your hair or jewelry.

- Display good humor and a ready smile.

- Show genuine interest in what the interviewer says and be alert to all questions.

- Do not talk too much. Answer the questions carefully.

- Be enthusiastic; demonstrate pride in your skills and abilities.

- Be positive. Do not criticize past employers, instructors, schools, or former colleagues.

- Try to understand your prospective employer's needs and show how you can fill them.

- Be prepared to tell the interviewer something about yourself—a commonly asked question at the start of the interview.

- Express yourself clearly and with a well-modulated voice.

- Be prepared to ask questions; give some thought to the questions you will ask before the interview. The interviewer will usually give you a chance at the end of the interview to ask questions. Some often asked questions are given in Figure 2-8 on page 39. Listen carefully to the answers you are given to the questions.

- Be prepared to take tests. You may expect to take tests consisting of basic skills such as keyboarding, spelling, math, proofreading, vocabulary, and reasoning ability. The law demands that any test given relate to the job for which you are applying.

- At the close of the interview, attempt to determine what will be the next step. Will there be another interview? When can you expect to hear the results of the interview?

HUMAN RELATIONS TIP

Do not forget to greet the receptionist or office professional when you enter the office with a smile and your name, and thank the person as you leave the office. Such gestures indicate interest and concern for others.

Commonly Asked Interview Questions

Questions at the Beginning of the Interview
- How did you learn about this position?
- Are you familiar with our company?
- Why are you interested in our company?
- Why do you think you are qualified for the position?

Questions Regarding Your Interest in the Job
- Are you presently employed? If so, is your present employer aware of your interest in changing jobs?
- Why do you want to change jobs?
- Why did you enter this field?
- What is the ideal job for you?
- If you could have any position, what would it be? Why?
- What would you like to be doing three years from now? Five years from now?

Questions Regarding Education
- What formal education have you had?
- Why did you choose your major area of study?
- What was your academic average or class standing when you were in school?
- What honors did you earn?
- In what extracurricular activities were you involved?
- Which courses did you like best? The least? Why?

Questions Regarding Experience
- Have you ever been fired or asked to resign from a position?
- Why did you leave your previous job?
- Have you had any problems with previous supervisors?
- Which duties performed in the past have you liked the best? The least? Why?
- What are your greatest strengths?
- What do you not do well?
- Why should I hire you?
- What salary do you expect to receive?

Note on Salary: You should have an idea of an appropriate salary before going to the interview. You may check the job advertisements of your local paper for area salaries. Your placement office is another good source for local salary information.

You can ask the interviewer the starting rate for the company. If you are willing to take that rate, you merely respond that the rate is appropriate. If you feel that the starting salary is below the average rate for that particular type of work, you may reply that you had hoped to start at a slightly higher salary, but that you are primarily interested in an opportunity to show what you can do and take advantage of the chances for promotion (if this is true). If not, you can say you are not interested in the salary offered. However, be certain before you respond that you are not interested. Your chances of getting additional salary may not be good, and you may well lose a possible job offer.

Figure 2-8

- Reiterate your interest in the job at the end of the interview (that is, if you are still interested).

- Smile pleasantly and thank the interviewer for the time.

- Smile and thank the receptionist as you leave.

Commonly Asked Questions

Take a few moments to read the commonly asked questions in Figure 2-8. Using the Self Check below, formulate answers to five of these questions. If you have concerns about the appropriateness of your answers, check with your instructor.

Self Check

Answer the following questions:

- Are you familiar with our company?
- What is the ideal job for you?
- What honors did you earn in school?
- What are your weaknesses?
- Why should I hire you?

Questions That You Might Ask

When the interviewer asks for any questions you might have, here are some appropriate ones.

- Would you please describe the specific duties of the job?

- Would you like for me to explain anything on my resume in more detail?

- Could you tell me about the people with whom I will be working if I were accepted for the position?

- Can you tell me about the advancement prospects?

- When will you make a decision about hiring?

- Are fringe benefits associated with the position?

INTERVIEW NO-NO's

So far, suggestions have been made about what to do during the interview. Here are some suggestions for what you should not do.

- Avoid nervous gestures and movements such as fidgeting, tugging at your clothes, and stroking your chin.

- Do not put personal belongings or your hands on the interviewer's desk.

- Do not argue. You are not participating in the interview to prove a point.

- Do not interrupt. Let the interviewer complete all questions or statements before you speak.

- Do not ask too many questions. Ask important questions only. If you ask questions regarding when you can expect your first raise, when you will be promoted, when you can expect a vacation, or the length of coffee breaks, the interviewer may decide that you are not interested in working.

- Do not tell jokes. Leave that up to the interviewer.

- Do not comment on the furnishings in the interviewer's office.

- Do not brag. If the company hires you, you may have to live up to your boasts.

- Do not criticize. If you are hired, you will have ample time and opportunity to make constructive suggestions for improvement.

- Do not smoke. Most companies today have no-smoking policies, and smoke is offensive to a number of people.

- Do not chew gum.

HUMAN RELATIONS TIP

Know when to leave the interview. Take your signal from the interviewer. Do not take up time with needless chatter once the interview is over.

```
2341 Broadmoor NE
Grand Rapids, MI 48501-1655
October 30, —


Mr. Anthony Rush
Human Resources Manager
Koronet International
3500 Division
Grand Rapids, MI 49503-3295

Dear Mr. Rush:

Thank you very much for the courteous interview you gave me
this morning.

Because of my education and experiences, I am confident that I
can be an addition to your team at Koronet. My skills in
keyboarding, communications, and human relations will help me
perform at a high level. Please give me the opportunity to
prove that I can be a valuable employee.

You may reach me at home by calling 555-7750. I hope to hear
from you soon.

Sincerely,

Martha G. Hornecek

Martha G. Hornecek
```

Figure 2-9   Follow-up letter.

INTERVIEW FOLLOW-UP

Promptly after the interview, write a **follow-up letter** thanking the employer for the interview and reviewing points of special interest. A sample of a letter you might write is given in Figure 2-9. Notice that the letter begins by thanking the interviewer.

A second follow-up letter may be advisable a week or two after the first one. You should not annoy the employer unnecessarily. However, if no action is taken in regard to the application within a reasonable time, a very short letter is not out of place. The second letter should merely remind the employer of your having filed a letter of application and should express willingness to return for another interview if necessary.

Of course, it is possible that after the interview you may decide that you are not interested in the position. In such a case, you should promptly send a courteous letter in which you express your appreciation for having been considered and explain why you do not wish the position. Although you are not interested in the present position, you may at a later point be interested in a position with the company. If so, the courteous way in which you declined the first position will help you in being considered a second time. The rule in such a situation is to keep all doors open if possible.

SUCCEED ON THE JOB

Once you have successfully gone through the interviewing process and have actually been hired, your task is to put together the skills and knowledge that you have and perform the job well. Listen to what co-workers and supervisors tell you. Observe and learn what is expected and what is accepted in the office. Make sure you have a clear understanding of your job duties and how you will be evaluated. Most companies have job descriptions which detail the responsibilities of particular jobs. If you are not given one, ask for it. If one does not exist, ask your supervisor to go over the duties with you.

PERFORMANCE APPRAISALS

Usually, formal evaluations are done on job performance. These evaluations are called **performance appraisals.** For the beginning employee, this evaluation may occur during the first three to six months, and then annually or semi-annually thereafter. You may be asked when you are first employed to establish short-range goals that you will be accomplishing. If so, you will then be evaluated on the accomplishment of those goals; your employer may use a form that is the same for all employees in your classification within the company. Figure 2-10 shows a performance appraisal

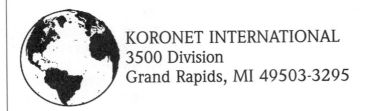

KORONET INTERNATIONAL
3500 Division
Grand Rapids, MI 49503-3295

Employee Name _____

Job Title _____

Supervisor _____

Assessment

4 Performance demonstrates consistent and important contributions which surpass defined expectations of the position.

3 Performance demonstrates attainment of the defined expectations of the position.

2 Performance has not reached a satisfactory level. Improved performance on this factor is needed to achieve defined expectations of this position.

1 Performance demonstrates deficiencies which seriously interfere with the attainment of the defined expectations of the position.

Organizational Skills	Assessment			
Prioritizes tasks.	4	3	2	1
Plans steps to accomplish tasks.	4	3	2	1
Meets deadlines.	4	3	2	1
Attends to detail.	4	3	2	1

Attendance	Assessment			
Adheres to scheduled work hours.	4	3	2	1
Uses leave appropriately.	4	3	2	1
Uses break period appropriately.	4	3	2	1
Adjusts work schedule at supervisor's request.	4	3	2	1

Quality	Assessment			
Performs work accurately.	4	3	2	1
Demonstrates neatness.	4	3	2	1
Demonstrates thoroughness and attention to detail.	4	3	2	1

Job Knowledge	Assessment			
Uses required job skills.	4	3	2	1
Demonstrates knowledge of organizational functions needed to perform the job.	4	3	2	1
Demonstrates knowledge of procedures needed to perform the job.	4	3	2	1

Figure 2-10 Performance appraisal.

Cooperation

	Assessment			
Appreciates and respects responsibilities of others.	4	3	2	1
Provides assistance and guidance to others.	4	3	2	1
Accepts guidance from supervisor.	4	3	2	1
Works toward workgroup and company goals.	4	3	2	1

Communication

	Assessment			
Conveys ideas effectively.	4	3	2	1
Responds to ideas conveyed by others.	4	3	2	1
Demonstrates appropriate professional courtesy.	4	3	2	1
Demonstrates sensitivity to a diverse staff.	4	3	2	1

Problem-Solving Skills

	Assessment			
Demonstrates the ability to identify the problem.	4	3	2	1
Demonstrates the ability to select the best solution.	4	3	2	1
Follows through on chosen solution.	4	3	2	1
Takes action to prevent future problems.	4	3	2	1

Supervision Required

	Assessment			
Supervision required.	4	3	2	1
Does not require supervision to accomplish routine jobs.	4	3	2	1
Gives constructive feedback to supervisor.	4	3	2	1
Responds to supervision in a positive manner.	4	3	2	1

Initiative

	Assessment			
Seeks additional job knowledge.				
Seeks new ideas and methods to improve results.	4	3	2	1
Develops new ideas and methods to improve results.	4	3	2	1
Exhibits self-motivation to achieve workgroup goals.	4	3	2	1
	4	3	2	1

Supervisor's Comments

_____

_____

_____

_____

Employee's Comments

_____

_____

_____

_____

Employee's Signature _____ Date _____

Supervisor's Signature _____ Date _____

Figure 2-10   *(Continued)*

43

form. Whichever method is used, here are some possible areas for evaluation.

- Ability to perform the job assignments
- Maintenance of good working relationships with your employer and other employees
- Adherence to company policies regarding attendance, punctuality, sick leave, and so forth
- Contribution to overall company goals

Remember, during your evaluation, your job performance is being evaluated. Be open to criticism and how you may perform better. Do not take the statements of the evaluator personally. A good evaluator tries to help you improve—not to hurt you. Notice Figure 2-11 which gives some tips to help you during the evaluation process.

JOB ADVANCEMENT

Advancing on the job may mean doing the job you presently have more and more effectively and efficiently. Your first job, in all likelihood, will be at entry level. Take time to learn your job well, to work well with others, and to learn new ways of doing your job better. Keep current on all new equipment, software, and procedures related to your job. Increase your verbal, nonverbal, and written communication skills. Remember that you gain valuable work experience on whatever job you are assigned. Concentrate on doing each task of your job to the best of your ability.

Advancing on the job may also mean taking advantage of any promotional opportunities that come your way. Remember that promotion more frequently comes to the individual who has performed well at specific levels in the company. Be ready for a promotion should the opportunity present itself. Learn as much about other jobs in the company as you can. Know how your present position fits with the overall organizational structure of

Evaluation Tips

- Listen to what the evaluator is saying.
- Discuss the issues openly and honestly. Maintain a calm and professional demeanor.
- Give the evaluator significant information relating to your performance that the evaluator may not have.
- Maintain eye contact with the evaluator.
- Accept an adverse evaluation as a criticism of your performance, not of you as an individual.
- Resolve to correct your mistakes. Tell the evaluator that you will do so.
- Discuss with your evaluator how you might improve your performance.
- If the evaluator is not clear about the directions you should take for the future, ask for an explanation. You may want to do performance objectives for the next period of work.
- Accept praise with a smile and a thank you. Let the evaluator know that you will continue to work hard for the company.

Figure 2-11

the company. Stay informed on openings in the company.

Keep a file of previous evaluations (assuming they are good ones) and any letters of praise from your boss or co-workers. The file may also contain special projects you have completed which show the range of your abilities. For example, if you researched and wrote a report that included spreadsheets and graphics, it would be a good idea to keep a copy to demonstrate your abilities.

HUMAN RELATIONS TIP

Do not join the gripers in the organization. Remember that most gripers spend their time talking rather than doing. Be an action-oriented worker; do your job well and look for opportunities to grow and learn.

LEAVE A JOB

You may decide to leave a job. Whatever your reasons for leaving, whether you are unhappy with the position and decide to leave on your own or whether you are being forced to leave due to a layoff in the company or being fired, you must be professional in how you handle your departure.

EXIT INTERVIEW

Most companies do an **exit interview** with the employee. A sample exit interview form is shown in Figure 2-12. This exit interview is usually done by an impartial party, not your immediate supervisor. A staff member in the personnel office is usually the one to do the exit interview.

This exit interview is not a time to get even, to make derogatory remarks about your supervisor, or to unduly criticize the company. Keep in mind the old adage about not burning your bridges. If you are leaving on your own, you may wish to return some day. Regardless of the reason for leaving, you will probably need a reference from the company. Be honest but not vindictive in the exit interview. For example, if you are leaving for a job with greater opportunities for growth, say, "I have decided to accept a position with greater responsibilities." You do not need to give all the details for your move.

LAYOFF OR TERMINATION

You may have to face the situation of being laid off or fired. Assume first that you are being laid off. The situation may be a downsizing of the company. Other jobs may be eliminated in addition to your own. Keep in mind that you did not cause the situation. Even though the situation is difficult, your skills, abilities, and experience on the present job will help you to find another position. Keep a positive outlook and begin to determine what you want to do next.

Now assume that you have been fired. Your feelings of fear, rejection, and even insecurity are normal. It is time to take a hard look at what skills you have. Listen to what your employer tells you about your performance. What can you learn for the future? What steps do you need to take to see that you do not find yourself in the same situation again? Where do you need to improve? Talk with your family, your friends, and your closest advisers.

EXIT INTERVIEW/TERMINATION FORM

TO BE COMPLETED BY SUPERVISOR

Name _____   Social Security No. _____
　　　　Last　　　　　　　First　　　　　M.

Job Title _____   Eligible for Rehire _____ Yes _____ No

Date of Hire _____   Termination Date _____   Comments _____

TO BE COMPLETED BY EMPLOYEE LEAVING

	Satisfactory	Unsatisfactory	No Opinion	Comments
1. Work load/ responsibilites				
2. Working conditions				
3. Satisfaction received from work				
4. Attention to employee ideas				
5. Supervision				
6. Employer benefits				
7. Advancement opportunities				
8. Other				

Reason for Termination _____

Post Employment Plans _____

Additional Comments _____

Supervisor's Signature _____ Date ____

Employee's Signature _____ Date ____

Figure 2-12　Exit interview form.

CHAPTER SUMMARY

This summary will help you remember the important points covered in this chapter.

- Effective decision-making involves these steps:

  a. Defining the problem or the purpose

  b. Establishing the criteria

  c. Generating alternatives or possible solutions

  d. Testing the alternatives and making the decision

  e. Evaluating the decision

- Sources of job information include:

  a. Personal networks

  b. Placement offices

  c. Newspaper advertisements

  d. Employment agencies

  e. The Internet and World Wide Web

  f. Professional organizations

  g. Company walk-ins

  h. Temporary agencies

- When you decide on a company where you will apply for a position, it is important for you to learn about the company. You may do so by checking the library for publications, obtaining an annual report, consulting your local chamber of commerce, asking your placement office, or asking friends and relatives who may work for the company.

- The goals of a letter of application are to arouse interest, describe your abilities, and request an interview.

- The resume, vitae, or data sheet is a concise statement of your background, education, skills, and experience. Resume sections include career objective, capabilities, education, work experience, extracurricular activities, memberships, honors, and references.

- Each blank on an employment application form should be filled out. Be certain to read the form carefully before filling in each blank. Be truthful; reflect your background and experience accurately.

- The interview is extremely important. The interview may be in person or through a virtual environment. You must carefully prepare for it and present yourself to the very best of your ability. Review the sections Helpful Hints, Commonly Asked Questions, Questions That You Might Ask, and Interview No-No's to help you remember how to present yourself well.

- Once the interview is over, a follow-up letter should be written thanking the employer for the interview and reviewing points of special interest.

- Once you obtain a job, it is important to succeed on that job. You must put your skills and knowledge together and perform well. You must listen to what co-workers and supervisors tell you. You must also observe and learn what is expected and what is accepted in the office. Find out your job duties and how you will be evaluated.

- Formal performance appraisals are usually done within three to six months after you begin work. After that time, appraisals are done on an annual or semiannual basis. Areas for evaluation include:

  a. ability to perform the job assignments;

  b. maintenance of good working relationships with your employer and other employees;

  c. adherence to company policies regarding attendance, punctuality, sick leave, and so forth;

  d. contribution to overall company goals.

- To advance on the job, it is important that you do each task of your job extremely well. It is important that you keep current on all new equipment, software, and procedures related to your job. You need to increase your verbal, nonverbal, and written communication skills. Learn as much about other jobs in the company as you can. Know how your present position fits with the overall organizational structure of the company. Stay informed on openings in the company.

- If you decide to leave a job (on your own or due to a layoff or termination), handle the leaving professionally. Do not burn your bridges. Do not make negative comments about your supervisor, the job, or the company.

- If you are laid off or terminated, remember that feelings of fear, rejection, and even insecurity are normal. Take a period of time to analyze your skills. Listen to what your employer tells you about your performance. Discover what you can learn from the situation that you may use effectively in the future. Before looking for another job, give yourself enough time to release your anger, evaluate your strengths and weaknesses, and consider your career goals. In both situations it is normal to be upset and even angry. It is certainly not a good idea, however, to lash out at your employer or colleagues at work. Talk through your anger with your family and friends.

CHAPTER GLOSSARY

The following terms were introduced in this chapter. To help you review, definitions are given here.

- **Decision** (p. 26)–The outcome or end product of a problem, concern, or issue that needs to be addressed and solved.

- **Networking** (p. 27)–Process of identifying and establishing a group of acquaintances, friends, and even relatives who can assist you in the job search process. (Networking can be defined in different ways; this definition pertains to its use in this chapter.)

- **State-operated employment agencies** (p. 28)–Those employment agencies that are supported by tax dollars and provided to customers free of charge.

- **Private employment agencies** (p. 28)–Privately owned employment agencies that charge a fee of the employer or the client when providing services.

- **Internet** (p. 28)–The world's largest group of connected computers, allowing people from all over the world to communicate.

- **World Wide Web (WWW)** (p. 29)–One of several features of the Internet; it contains a huge assortment of computer files with all types of information.

- **Direct canvass or cold canvass** (p. 29)–Visiting companies without an appointment to seek job information.

- **Temporary agency** (p. 29)–One that offers temporary work to prospective employees; temporary agencies pay the employee directly and charge the company for their services.

- **Letter of application** (p. 30)–A letter applying for a job with the goals of the letter being to arouse the prospective employer's interest, describe the abilities of the person writing the letter, and request an interview.

- **Resume, vitae, or data sheet** (p. 31)–Concise statement of background, education, skills, and experience which is sent with the letter of application when seeking a job.

- **Chronological resume** (p. 32)–A list of a person's credentials, listing education and experience in reverse date order. For example, the most recent job experience is presented first, followed in reverse date order by the remaining job experience.

- **Functional resume** (p. 32)–Resume that presents education, experience, and activities in clusters which support the credentials of the job applicant for the position being sought.

- **Employment application** (p. 34)–Form used by companies for prospective employees to fill out concerning their education, background, and experience.

- **Portfolio** (p. 35)–A compilation of samples of an individual's work.

- **Virtual interview** (p. 35)–A prospective employee may be interviewed anywhere at anytime using technology.

- **Follow-up letter** (p. 41)–A letter thanking the prospective employer for an interview and reviewing points of special interest.

- **Performance appraisals** (p. 41)–Evaluation of an employee completed by the employer.

- **Exit interview** (p. 45)–Interview completed by the employer when an employee leaves the company.

DISCUSSION ITEMS

These discussion items provide an opportunity for you to test your understanding of the chapter through discussion with your classmates and your instructor.

1. Identify and explain the steps in the decision-making process.

2. Explain what should be included in a resume.

3. List ten helpful hints for making a good impression during the interview.

4. Identify ten things that you should not do during an interview.

5. What is the purpose of a follow-up letter?

6. What is the purpose of performance appraisals? What possible areas might be included in a performance evaluation?

CASE STUDY

Arturo Herrera has just finished a two-year business course in college. He has done well in school. He is proficient in WordPerfect, Microsoft® Word, Lotus, and Microsoft® Office. His math and English skills are good, and he works well with people. He has applied at five different companies for an office job, but he has been turned down for all jobs. Arturo knows he has the skills necessary to handle the jobs; he does not understand why he has not been hired. Here is what happened on his last job interview.

Arturo was ten minutes late for the interview. He left home in time to get to the interview promptly, but he had trouble finding a parking place. When he went in, he told the receptionist that he was sorry that he was late but that he could not find a parking place. Arturo was anxious over being ten minutes late, so he decided to have a cigarette to calm down while waiting for the inter-view. He did not see the no-smoking sign until after he had already lit the cigarette. He did put out his cigarette immediately.

The first question that the interviewer asked him was, "Could you tell me a little about yourself?" Arturo thought he did a thorough job with the question. He spent ten minutes telling the interviewer about his life, starting from grade school. When the interviewer asked him if he had worked before, he said that he had only had summer jobs. He told the interviewer that he had been on four interviews previously and he felt that the interviewers were unfair when they did not offer him the job.

What mistakes did Arturo make? How can he correct these mistakes in the future?

How should he prepare for the next job interview?

OFFICE TASKS

OFFICE TASK 2-1 (Objective 1)

Identify one important decision you have to make in the next year. State the problem or purpose in a statement form. Using each of the decision-making steps, describe how you will go about making this decision. In other words, establish the criteria, generate alternatives or possible solutions, test the alternatives, and make the decision. State how you will evaluate that decision.

If you have trouble identifying a decision that you will make, use the one given here.

You have been offered a part-time office position beginning within the month. You will be required to work 25 hours per week. You cannot continue to take care of your family (you have two small children), take 15 hours of course work, and do the part-time job. You do need the money; however, you can exist without it although it will be difficult. If you take less course work, you cannot graduate this year.

Identify the problem; and using each of the decision-making steps, describe how you will go about making the decision.

OFFICE TASK 2-2 (Objectives 2 and 3)

If you have access to the Internet, check to see what office positions are listed (an address on the WWW which you can use is **http://www.careermosaic.com/cm**).

If you do not have access to the Internet, go to the classified ads in your local paper. Pick one that you wish to apply for and then prepare a resume and letter of application. If your software package has a resume template included, you may want to use that form in preparing your resume. You will not actually be mailing this letter of application and resume; however, you will be using a real-life situation in that the job opening is a real one.

OFFICE TASK 2-3 (Objective 4)

Work with your classmates as teams of four on this project. Using the position that you applied for in Office Task 2-2, now assume that you are going on an interview. Role play that interview with your classmates, with one of you acting as the employer, one being the interviewee, and the other two members observing. When you have finished, the two members observing are to critique your performance. Please review pages 34 through 41 in your text before beginning this task. Go through the following steps again, with the next member being the interviewee, one the employer, and the other members being the observers until each member of the team has played each role.

OFFICE TASK 2-4 (Objective 5)

Complete the employment application given on the Student Data Template Disk, file OT2-4. Print out a copy of the form and then handwrite your answers.

OFFICE TASK 2-5 (Objective 6)

As a team of three or four, interview an employed office professional. The interview may take place over the Internet rather than in person. Ask the individual the following questions:

- To what do you contribute your success in this position?

- Does your company do a performance appraisal? If so, how often? (If possible, obtain a copy of the performance appraisal form.)

- What advancement opportunities are available in your company?

- Are internal candidates considered for promotional opportunities?

Report your findings orally to the class.

ENGLISH USAGE CHALLENGE DRILL

Correct the following sentences. Cite the grammar rule that is applicable to each sentence. Before you begin, refresh your memory of grammar rules by reviewing pronouns in the *Multimedia Reference for Writers* (if available to you), by reading the rules in the reference guide to this text, or by using another printed reference guide.

1. The eclipse of the sun was an astonishing sight for both him and I.

2. The instructor spoke with her and I about the project that is due next week.

3. The winner of the speech contest was me.

4. I wondered whom would go to the polls in the presidential election.

5. Rebecca admires who?

ASSESSMENT OF CHAPTER OBJECTIVES

Now that you have completed the chapter and the office tasks, take a few moments to review the following learning objectives which you were given at the beginning of this chapter. Did you accomplish these objectives? If so, explain how in the space provided. If you were unable to accomplish these objectives, give your reason for not doing so. Your instructor may want to review your answers.

I accomplished these objectives:

1. Identify and use effective decision-making techniques. Yes _____ No _____

   Explain how you accomplished this objective.

   _____

   _____

   _____

2. Determine sources of job information.
   Yes _____ No _____

   Explain how you accomplished this objective.

   _____

   _____

   _____

3. Prepare a resume and letter of application.
   Yes _____ No _____

   Explain how you accomplished this objective.

   _____

   _____

   _____

4. Develop job interview skills. Yes _____ No _____

   Explain how you accomplished this objective.

   _____

   _____

   _____

5. Complete an employment application.
   Yes _____ No _____

   Explain how you accomplished this objective.

   _____

   _____

   _____

6. Discover how to succeed and advance your professional career. Yes _____ No _____

   Explain how you accomplished this objective.

   _____

   _____

   _____

Provide reasons for failing to accomplish any of the objectives.

_____

_____

_____

_____

UTILIZING COMPUTER HARDWARE AND OFFICE EQUIPMENT

LEARNING OBJECTIVES

1. Classify computer systems.
2. Identify computer hardware components and explain their functions.
3. Define the function of computer networks.
4. Identify the types of copiers available.
5. Explain the basic features of copiers.
6. Demonstrate a knowledge of how to maintain and select copiers.
7. Explain the fax process and selection criteria.
8. Use computers, copiers, and fax machines.

Have you ever wondered how we lived in a world without today's technology which provides us with computers and telecommunications equipment, among other things? For most of us, such a world is hard to imagine. Technology is an ever-present part of our daily existence. We encounter computers in grocery stores as the products we buy are run through scanners to record prices. As we shop in department stores, our purchases are registered and our bill totaled by computers. In education, computers help us to learn how to read, write, perform mathematical computations, and even learn foreign languages. Our children learn to play computer educational games at extremely early ages. As we get in our cars, we encounter numerous computer control systems. Our telephones are answered by machines which we have programmed. We tape our favorite television programs for showing at a time convenient to us. Medical doctors diagnose some diseases through laser technology. The impact of technology on our lives is almost endless.

The office world is no exception. Technology is an integral part of that world, and the future promises even greater dominance of technology. Today, computers have become synonymous with the complete processing of information—from the time of its creation to the output of that information to the appropriate audiences. Copiers and fax machines are used multiple times each day by office professionals. Your success as an office professional is dependent on your ability to use computer technology to process words and data quickly and efficiently and copier and fax technology to produce and send the numerous documents you prepare daily. In this chapter, you will gain an understanding of the hardware components of computers, how computers and copiers are classified, and how you may utilize computer, copier, and fax technology effectively in your work.

COMPUTER HISTORY

Although you have probably grown up with computers, an overview of the history may be helpful to you. Blaise Pascal, the French mathematician, physicist, and religious philosopher, is widely credited with building the first digital calculating machine in 1642. It performed only the addition of numbers. In 1671 Gottfried Wilhelm von Leibniz invented a computer that could add and multiply. These machines remained mere curiosities until more than a century later when Charles Xavier Thomas in 1820 developed the first commercially successful mechanical calculator that could add, subtract, multiply, and divide. In 1890 Herman Hollerith and James Powers developed devices that could automatically read information that had been punched into cards. This keypunch, sorting, and tabulating equipment allowed the 1890 U.S. census to be completed in two years as opposed to the seven years that it had taken to complete the 1880 census using manual methods. By the late 1930s, punched-card machine techniques had become so well established and reliable that Howard Hathaway Aiken, in collaboration with engineers at IBM, began construction of a large, automatic digital computer. This computer was called the Mark I and could perform all four arithmetic operations in addition to handling logarithms and trigonometric functions.

With the outbreak of World War II came a desperate need for computer capability, especially for the military. New weapons systems were produced for which trajectory tables and other essential data were lacking. In 1942 John Eckert, John Mauchly, and their associates at the Moore School of Electrical Engineering built a high-speed electronic computer. This machine became known as ENIAC (Electrical Numerical Integrator and Calculator). Eckert and Mauchly later developed the UNIVAC-1, the first electronic computer offered as a commercial product. The UNIVAC became famous when it correctly predicted Dwight Eisenhower's victory in the 1952 presidential election. General Electric, in 1954, was the first private American company to purchase one of these computers.

Since that time we have seen an explosion of computer power in a revolution that is part of the Information Age. Truly, it is a revolution. The computer and the numerous other technological devices that it has spawned have revolutionized the way we work and play.

COMPUTER CLASSIFICATIONS

Generally, computers are classified into the following three main categories:

• Mainframes and supercomputers

• Minicomputers and superminis

• Microcomputers and supermicros

MAINFRAMES

Mainframes are the largest computer systems. A mainframe is capable of processing large amounts of information at very fast speeds. Mainframes can support a number of auxiliary devices such as terminals, printers, disk drives, and other input and output equipment. The mainframe is usually the main computer used in a large organization. It is used in companywide applications such as payroll, accounting, inventory, and purchasing. Large companies generally have computer managers, programmers, and technicians whose jobs are to operate, program, and maintain the mainframe. Mainframes, with the peripheral equipment such as printers and disk drives, are usually housed in separate rooms with appropriate air-conditioning for heat control and false floors to accommodate the multitude of cables required to connect terminals and peripherals.

SUPERCOMPUTERS

The mightiest and most expensive mainframes are called **supercomputers.** They are used in organizations that must process huge amounts of information. For example, the federal government uses supercomputers for tasks that require mammoth data manipulation such as national census data processing, worldwide weather forecasting, and weapons research.

Supercomputers are now bigger and faster than ever before. For example, a supercomputer can operate at 1.06 **teraflops** (one teraflop equals one trillion operations per second). The fastest previous speed on a supercomputer was 368 **gigaflops** (one gigaflop equals one billion operations per second). The speed and capacity of these supercomputers will allow researches to develop new drugs, predict weather, improve automotive and airline safety, and map DNA to prevent genetic diseases.

MINICOMPUTERS AND SUPERMINIS

A typical **minicomputer** is more compact in size, has a slower processing speed, and has a more limited storage capacity than a mainframe computer. Minicomputer systems are generally less expensive than a mainframe. The capability of the minicomputer system usually limits its use to smaller businesses. A large company may have a mainframe computer at its central location and minicomputers at various branch sites. In such situations, the mainframe and minicomputers are usually **interfaced** (interconnected) so that they can communicate with each other. The term **"supermini"** was coined to describe minicomputers at the top of the size and price scale. Superminis require only about one-fifth the physical space of a mainframe and do not require a specially prepared room.

Mainframes and minicomputers are used extensively in large and medium-sized companies. *Photos courtesy of International Business Machines, Inc.*

MICROCOMPUTERS AND SUPERMICROS

The **microcomputer** is the smallest of the computer systems. Microcomputers were made possible by the advances in technology in the 1970s which permitted the manufacture of electronic circuits on small silicon chips. A single miniature chip (called a **microprocessor**) contains the circuitry and components for arithmetic, logic, and control operations. Microcomputers are also widely known as **personal computers** or **PCs**. In the office, most office professionals, managers, and executives have PCs on their desks. Today, PCs are very powerful. In fact, they have more capabilities and storage capacity than the early mainframes. The addition of **hard drives** (internal storage capacity) allows the PC to store huge amounts of data. The power of the PC is continuing to increase with such technological inventions as the **Pentium® processor chip** (a type

of microprocessor) which provides for increased speed and performance capability of the PC. Large and mid-size companies will also have a mainframe or minicomputer in addition to the PC on the desk of many employees.

The **supermicros** are the upper-end microcomputers. Supermicros have been called "desktop mainframes" due to their power. They have a high-speed microprocessor and significantly increased memory and hard disk storage capacity. Super-micros are **multiuser** (able to serve several users at the same time) and **multitasking** (able to run more than one application package per user).

A need for microcomputers that can be carried to different work sites and locations has produced the **portable microcomputer.** These portables are of two basic types—laptop and notebook. Another type of portable, with limited capabilities, is the palmtop.

Laptop Computers

The **laptop computer** gets its name from the fact that it can rest comfortably on the lap during use. Laptop computers may be battery powered or AC powered and come with built-in display screens. Compactness, portability, and affordability are the laptop's main assets.

Notebook Computers

Closely related to the laptops are **notebooks.** They are smaller than laptops and generally fold to fit inside a briefcase. Notebooks are now available with Pentium processor chips which allow for the speed and performance capabilities of many desktop computers. **Hard drives** (internal storage capacity), **floppy drives** (external storage), and **CD-ROM drives** (provide for the running of CD-ROM software) are available on notebooks. Ports are also available for connecting a video camera and hooking up to a television.

Palmtops (small enough to fit in a pocket or purse) are used to jot down notes, check schedules, or look up phone numbers quickly when away from the office. A palmtop is not practical for word processing because the keyboard is so tiny that keying is a two-finger operation.

The convenience of using laptops and notebooks has contributed to their widespread use. Executives who travel frequently may use the laptop or notebook on the plane or in the hotel. Documents can be faxed back to the office for immediate distribution. Office professionals may also find the portable convenient to record minutes or notes of a meeting. Once the meeting has concluded, the office professional can produce a record of the meeting quickly and easily with minor editing.

Notebook computers may be used in airports as well as on airplanes. *Courtesy of International Business Machines, Inc.*

Due to the relative inexpensiveness of PCs, they are also purchased extensively for home use. For example, PCs are used to balance personal checkbooks, to pay bills, to assist in investment strategies, to do homework assignments, to review news articles on the Internet, to talk with people all over the world, and even to play games. With the price of PCs decreasing, the home market is expected to continue to grow.

The computer classifications you have just learned are useful in understanding the categories of computers. As an office professional, you will be using a PC almost exclusively. Throughout the

remainder of this text, the term "computer" will be used to refer to the microcomputer or PC.

COMPUTER HARDWARE

Computer hardware with which you need to become familiar includes the following:

- Input devices
- Central processing unit
- External storage devices
- Output devices

INPUT DEVICES

As information is created, it is necessary to enter the information into the computer. Devices used to communicate with the central processing unit of the computer (the part of the computer that processes data) are called **input** and **output devices** or **I/O devices.** The basic input device for the computer is the computer keyboard; however, a number of other devices are available including scanners, touch screen monitors, mouse and trackballs, pens and tablets, and voice input. You will learn about output devices later in this chapter.

Computer Keyboards

The standard computer keyboard includes an **alphanumeric keypad,** a **cursor control keypad,** a **function keypad,** and a **numeric keypad.** The alphanumeric keypad allows you to enter documents on the computer. The cursor control keypad allows you to position the cursor to begin keyboarding. The function keypad controls the various electronic functions of the computer, and the numeric keypad allows you to enter numbers quickly.

A keyboard is an input device.

Scanners

Scanners, also referred to as **optical character readers (OCRs)** allow you to scan typed, printed, or handwritten information from paper and transfer the information to a computer. They can electronically process pages of reports, articles, memos, receipts, and various other documents. Scanners are used as an economical means of inputting material into the computer as they eliminate the need to rekey or rewrite information. Scanners fall into four categories:

- Handheld
- Sheetfed
- Flatbed
- Production level

Handheld Scanners. With handheld devices, the operator manually draws the scanning head over a document on a flat surface. These scanners are used widely for reading product codes, for inventory purposes, at such businesses as grocery stores and department stores; recording packages received and delivered by delivery businesses; and reading file folder labels for document tracking.

Sheetfed and Flatbed Scanners. Sheetfed scanners are compact devices wide enough to feed through an 8½-inch-wide sheet of paper. Flatbed scanners are larger, have more features, and are usually higher in price than the handheld or sheetfed scanners. Flatbeds are capable of processing color graphics and photos. These scanners are used in offices to scan information previously keyboarded when the volume is not extremely high.

Production-Level Scanners. If there are numerous scanning needs, the office uses a production-level scanner. Examples of firms that may use production-level scanners are law firms, insurance companies, financial institutions, and institutions with multiple branches or locations. These scanners are used when volumes are too high for flatbed technology to handle sufficiently.

Magnetic Ink Character Readers and Bar Code Scanners. Two special types of scanners include **magnetic ink character readers (MICRs)** and **bar code scanners.** MICRs are used by banks and credit unions to read the magnetic ink numbers preprinted on checks and deposit slips. Bar code scanners are used widely in grocery stores to record the bar codes printed on various products. This information is fed into the computer which then computes the grocery bill of the individual.

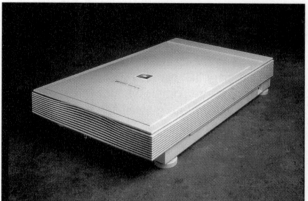

Sheetfed and flatbed scanners. *Hewlett Packard.*

Touch Screen Monitors

Touch screen monitors display choices and instructions on the screen. The user then touches the desired choice. Here are some ways in which touch screens are used.

- to enter orders, record sales, and print receipts by stores and restaurants
- to provide the public with directions at such places as shopping centers, office buildings, and museums
- to let shoppers create and print customized greeting cards

- to let preschoolers run educational programs unassisted—takes less eye–hand coordination than a mouse does

- to let people with impaired motor skills run simple applications

Mouse and Trackball

A **mouse** is a small hand-controlled device that allows the user to move the cursor and choose menu commands without using the keyboard. The mouse has become a standard part of the PC as most software packages now employ a **graphical user interface (GUI)** rather than being driven by keystrokes. A GUI uses drop-down menus and various icons for executing commands and choosing program options. For example, if you want to change the print size of the document on which you are working, you may use the mouse to click on the icon at the top of the screen which then gives you a drop-down menu where you may select the size of print you wish. The mouse is used for a variety of functions including printing copy, opening files, formatting, and so forth.

An option to the mouse is the **trackball roller.** Here a stationary ball is rolled with the tips of the fingers to move the pointer on your screen. Trackball rollers can be custom installed on some keyboards or they can be clipped to the side of a portable computer. A mouse and trackball are shown in the following photos.

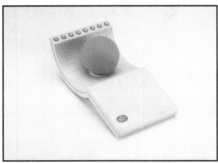

Mouse and trackball. *Photos courtesy of International Business Machines, Inc.*

Pens and Tablets

Images can be created on a screen with the use of **light pens.** As you move the pen against the screen, movements appear as light on the screen.

TECHNOLOGY TIP

When using a mouse, make sure it fits your hand. They come in right- and left-handed models. Be sure to place it next to the keyboard, at the same height, to avoid always reaching for it.

TECHNOLOGY TIP

Try using a trackball instead of a mouse; it does not require as much arm or wrist movement.

You can produce lines and drawings through the use of light pens. The pens are called light pens because of their sensitivity to light on the screen, not because they produce light.

Closely related to a light pen is a **touch tablet.** The same type of technology is used with a touch tablet as with a light pen. The basic difference between the two is the surface on which a person draws or writes. With a light pen, the monitor is used, and with a touch tablet, an accompanying pad is used in place of the monitor screen.

Touch tablet. *Hewlett Packard.*

Voice

Voice recognition systems allow the user to input data to the computer with spoken words. Today, fields using voice input include medicine, finance, and transportation. For example, medical doctors can report the analyses of pathology slides by voice and a biologist can tell a microscope to scan up or down. Voice input has still not been developed to its full potential. In the future, it is anticipated that voice input will be a major source of direct input to the computer, eliminating the need for keyboarding.

CENTRAL PROCESSING UNIT

Once data has been entered into the computer through the input media mentioned in the previous section, processing takes place in the **central processing unit (CPU)** of the computer. This unit is the brain of the computer. It accepts the data from the input devices, processes the data according to the program used, and delivers the results through some type of output device. Figure 3-1 depicts this

process. The **program** that the computer uses is a series of instructions directing the computer to perform a sequence of operations. In Chapter 4, you will learn more about programs that give operating instructions to the computer.

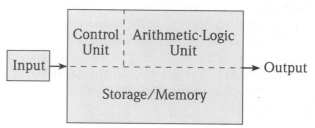

Figure 3-1   CPU process.

The CPU of a mainframe is housed in a fairly large unit. However, the CPU of a microcomputer is smaller than a thumbtack. The CPU consists of

- a memory component;
- an arithmetic-logic component;
- a control unit.

Memory

Data are transferred from the input device, such as the keyboard, to the memory unit of the computer. Data remain in this unit until the computer processes the data. The memory unit also holds the results of processed data until the data are transferred to an output device such as floppy disks.

The memory capacities of computers are not the same. Before explaining memory capacities, you need to understand some basic computer terminology such as **bits** and **bytes.** A bit (binary digit) is the smallest unit of computer information. Eight bits make one byte, which is the amount of information that makes up a single character (a letter, number, or symbol). Memory and storage are measured in bytes or multiples of bytes.

Thousand-byte units are called **kilobytes (KB);** million-byte units are called **megabytes (MB);** billion-byte units are called **gigabytes (GB);** and trillion-byte units are called **terabytes.** The size of the memory capacity varies by computer. As applications and **software** (a set of instructions that tells the computer what to do, such as word processing software) are developed that require more memory or storage capacity, greater capacity has been made available on the computer. It is expected that in the future the memory or storage capacity will continue to increase.

The two most common categories of memory are **random access memory (RAM)** and **read-only memory (ROM)**. Both RAM and ROM memory are present on all computers. ROM allows you to turn your computer on and off. The contents of ROM cannot be modified; it can only be read—not changed. RAM allows you to change data. When you work with a word processing document, you are using RAM.

Arithmetic-Logic Unit

This unit adds, subtracts, multiplies, and divides numeric data. It also compares both alphabetic and numeric data.

Control Unit

As its name implies, the control unit regulates the different functions of the computer system. All instructions to the computer are interpreted here. For example, the unit directs the input-output devices, giving them instructions as to when to input data and when to output data. It also interprets instructions for all arithmetic-logic operations. It tells the arithmetic-logic unit when to add, subtract, multiply, and divide. It coordinates the transfer of data to and from the main computer storage.

Because this chapter deals with technical information, take a few moments now to answer the questions on the Self Check. Once you have completed the Self Check, refer to the answers at the conclusion of this chapter. If you did not do very well, you might want to reread the first part of this chapter before proceeding to the last part of the chapter.

EXTERNAL STORAGE DEVICES

The ability to store information is an important part of any information processing system. You have already learned that the internal storage capability of computers has a finite limit. Therefore, auxiliary storage devices are commonly used. The types of storage devices used most commonly are

- disks
- optical or laser disks
- hard disks
- magnetic tape

Disks

Disks are indispensable storage mediums for the computer. The first size available was a 5.25-inch disk; however, that disk is rarely used today. The size that is used almost exclusively is the 3.5-inch disk. Both disks are referred to as **floppy**. The 3.5-inch is housed in a nonremovable, fairly rigid plastic case. The amount of data that can be stored on a disk is expressed in terms of **density**. The density of disks is referred to as **double sided** and **high density**. For example, a double-sided and high-density 3.5-inch disk may store 1.44MB (megabytes). To give you a yardstick as to what this means, a typical printed page, using single spacing, contains 2,500 to 3,000 characters. Thus 1MB holds 400 pages of single-spaced text. Proper care must be taken when using and storing disks; this care is discussed in Chapter 4.

Self Check

- List the three main categories of computers.
- What is a Pentium processor?
- List six input devices.
- What are the components of the CPU?
- How are memory capacities on the computer expressed?

External storage devices. *Photo by Alix Parson.*

Optical or Laser Disks

There are three types of **optical disks** or **laser disks**—CD-ROM, WORM, and erasable. The **CD-ROM (compact disk read-only memory)** is a durable, nonmagnetic storage medium. The CD-ROM is used to supply software packages such as word processing, spreadsheets, graphics, and databases to the computer because it can only be read, it cannot be edited. Most computers now have CD-ROM capability which allows the user to access libraries of information, including graphics and video.

CD-ROMs can be used to store information in a variety of forms, such as video and graphics. *Photo by Guennady Maslov/Photonics '95.*

Write once, read many (WORM) gets its name from the fact that it is written only once and read any number of times. A WORM disk is nonerasable and is used in applications that require the data to be written once as a permanent record. For example, banks and accounting firms use WORM as a means of maintaining a permanent, unalterable audit trail.

The **erasable disk** can be reused by writing over the data that is there. Thus, it is suitable for applications that call for temporary document storage. For example, in the office you may have disks that have data that is obsolete and can be destroyed such as memorandums or letters. You can use the disk again by deleting the data or writing over the data.

Hard Disks

Hard disks (also called **magnetic disks**) are secondary storage for mainframe and minicomputers. However, the hard disk that is of more importance to you is the hard disk drive that operates as an internal storage device for the computer. As an office professional, you will often store information on the hard disk drive. Even if you intend to transfer information to a floppy disk at a later point, the usual process is to store it on the hard disk drive first. In fact, most software programs now automatically store the information you are keying to the hard drive and let you determine how often you want it saved. With icon programs, it is a simple process of clicking on the appropriate icon and then telling the computer how often you wish to save the data. The hard disk drive allows quicker access to stored information than the floppy disk. Once you have stored information on the hard drive, it is a good idea to store it also on a floppy disk as a backup, particularly if the information is extremely important. For example, you probably would not back up a routine memo that has been sent and you will not need again, but you would back up a financial report. If you are constantly working with data that must be backed up, backup software is available, with some of this backup software being free from the software company.

Magnetic Tape

Magnetic tape has been used as a storage medium for mainframe computers for years, and it is still used today. Tape can also be a storage medium for minicomputers and microcomputers. The basic usage of tape consists of transferring information to tape for archival or replacement purposes. For example, software programs may be transferred to tape to provide a backup if something happens to the program stored on the hard drive. Payroll information may be transferred to tape for a backup in case of loss of data through a computer malfunction. Information stored on the tape can be restored to the hard disk later if needed. Tape drives for microcomputers may be internal drives which are installed in an empty bay in the front of your computer or external drives which are self-contained units that plug into a connector on the back of your computer.

OUTPUT DEVICES

The main two output devices are monitors and printers. If you want **soft copy** (copy shown on the monitor only—a printed copy is not necessary), the video display monitor or **cathode ray tube (CRT)** is appropriate. If you want **hard copy** (printed on paper), the printer is appropriate. A good example of soft copy is in the sending of e-mail messages. Most of the time the receiver of the e-mail merely reads the message on the monitor and saves it in the computer or destroys it immediately. No printed copy is needed.

Monitors

Monitors come in four standard sizes: 9 inch, 12 inch, 13 inch, and 14 inch, with 13 inch and 14 inch being the most popular sizes for desktop monitors. Portable computers generally use a 9-inch screen. Large-screen monitors measure at least 19 inches diagonally and are able to display a two-page spread for a desktop publishing program. Monitors 25 to 35 inches in size are referred to as **presentation monitors.**

Monitors are available in black-and-white, **monochrome** (one color), or color. The three most popular one-color alternatives are green, blue, or amber. These hues have been found to be the easiest on the eyes over long stretches. Color monitors use three primary colors—red, green, and blue. Using these three colors and mixing them in various combinations or proportions, you can obtain every other color of the spectrum in all possible tints, tones, and gradations from very dark to very light.

Printers

The most commonly used output device is the printer. Printers may be classified as either impact or nonimpact. Printers differ from one another in the speed and quality of their output and in the ability to produce color. The printer used most frequently in offices today is the laser printer—a nonimpact printer.

Impact Printers. The first printer to dominate the market years ago was the **impact printer.** It utilizes a device that prints characters on paper by physically impacting or hitting the paper. The dot matrix printer is the impact printer used today. The dot matrix printer does not provide as high quality a product as does the laser printer. It is mainly used where high quality is not essential and where printed documents are going to remain in-house.

Nonimpact Printers. Two types of **nonimpact printers** in use are the ink-jet printer and the laser printer. With the ink-jet printer, characters are formed on the page by tiny streams of ink spraying through a nozzle onto the paper. Ink-jet printers can produce color. They are less expensive than the laser printer but not capable of producing at the quality or speed of the laser printer.

The laser printer uses a beam of light to form images on light-sensitive paper. Laser printers print at extremely fast speeds and produce a high-quality

product. They can print color. Laser printers are the printer of choice of most offices due to the speed and quality of the copy produced. The following photo shows a laser printer.

Laser printer. *Hewlett Packard.*

Network Printers and Print Sharing

Some offices network or link several computers to one printer. Network printers run at faster speeds than do desktop printers, have a higher quality, will run large sizes of paper, and can run less expensively. If an office is working with computer-aided design, computer-aided engineering, or other specialized functions that require larger sizes of paper (such as 11″ × 17″), a **network printer** (a printer attached to a local area network) can provide the speed and quality needed. Color printers are also being networked to help justify the costs of purchasing and running these printers. Digital printers are being used in the networks to take advantage of their capabilities such as sorting, stapling, bundling, and hole punching. To help you understand more about local area networks, read the next section on Computer Networks.

Another option to a printer on every desk is **printer sharing.** Printer sharing allows both networked and non-networked users to access the same printers. Because printers are not attached to a network, no printer downtime occurs if there are network problems. Printer sharing can be cost effective and provide for a higher quality printer in certain office situations.

COMPUTER NETWORKS

Computers and other peripheral equipment such as printers, as you have just learned, can be linked through networks. These networks may be

- **Local Area Networks (LANs)** which link various types of technological equipment within a building or several buildings within the same geographic area such as an office park or college campus;

- **Metropolitan Area Networks (MANs)** which link technological equipment over a distance equal to the size of a city and its surrounds (approximately 31 miles);

- **Wide Area Networks (WANs)** which link technological equipment in an area of hundreds of thousands of miles. Notice Figure 3-2 which depicts graphically a WAN network.

Almost all desktop computers are networked via LANs, MANs, or WANs. These connections allow computers to talk to each other over distances. For example, a LAN allows for **electronic mail (e-mail)** to be sent between computers within an office. Networking through MANs or WANs allows electronic mail to be sent to computers at distant locations.

The growth of technology and the need for sharing information worldwide have spawned worldwide networks. The Internet, a worldwide network, and the World Wide Web, one of the features of the Internet, are being used extensively by businesses and individuals.

INTERNET

You learned in Chapter 2 that the Internet is the world's largest group of connected computers, allowing people from all over the world to communicate. Let us now take that definition and expand

Figure 3-2 Wide Area Network (WAN).

on it. The Internet is an open, worldwide network in which supercomputers are connected; these supercomputers act as servers to connect smaller computers. To get on the Internet, you need to make contact with the larger computers through a modem which connects your computer to telephone lines; cable access will probably be possible in the future. If you are using the Internet at school or on the job, the company or school is paying a fee for the use of the Internet. To use the Internet from your home computer, you may access a commercial database such as America Online[SM], CompuServe®, Prodigy®, and Microsoft Internet Explorer®. These companies charge a monthly fee for services. As new companies are coming into this market, the fee per month is decreasing.

Presently, the Internet is growing extremely fast, with data byte size doubling every three months. It takes Alta Vista® (an Internet search engine) six days to scan the net one time. As of April 1996, there were 22 million pages of information available on the Internet. One page may be as small as an individual's resume or as large as an automobile manufacturer's model documentation. Currently, about 1 million pages of information are being added each month.[1]

It is projected that in the immediate future consumers who do not own personal computers will be able to access the Internet through their television sets. A number of companies are in the process of making low-cost products that will turn television sets into Internet-access devices and make surfing the World Wide Web as simple as changing television channels. In fact, as you read this book, you may already be able to access the Internet through television.

Here are some examples of services available on the Internet.

- Electronic mail (e-mail)—you can exchange e-mail with people all over the world. Figure 3-3 illustrates this concept. Electronic mailing lists enable you to join group discussions over the Net. **Mail servers** (programs that respond to e-mail messages) let you retrieve information.

- Information retrieval—There are files of information ranging from U.S. Supreme Court decisions, library card catalogs, texts of books, digitized pictures, and software which are available through the Internet. As a specific example, if you are interested in the latest happenings in Europe, you can obtain access to online European news services.

- Bulletin boards—A system called **Usernet** is an online bulletin board with messages on thousands of different topics ranging from computer information to politics to cycling.

To give you some idea of the magnitude of users on the Internet, in the late 90s there were over 30 million people around the globe using the Net more or less regularly.[2] This number is continuing to increase.

INTRANET

The **Intranet** is a network that allows businesses to provide access for their employees to the Internet, but, as a usual rule, does not allow persons from the outside to have access to the information within the company. To help you understand the relationship between the Intranet and the Internet, think of the Internet as a worldwide network of computers and the Intranet as a business network of computers with a wall in between. People from the Intranet can break through the wall to access information from the Internet. However, individuals from the Internet cannot break through the wall to access the information on the Intranet unless the business decides to make certain information available to select interested parties on the outside.

WORLD WIDE WEB

You learned in Chapter 2 that the World Wide Web is one of several features of the Internet. The WWW is a huge collection of computer files—several million with the number growing daily—scattered across the Internet. These files contain all types of information, including sounds, videos, and still graphics. A company might develop, for example, a **Web page** that advertises its services.

---

[1]Eagan, J., "Taming the Internet," *U.S. News & World Report* (April, 1996), 60–64.

[2]Eagan, J., "Taming the Internet," *U.S. News & World Report* (April, 1996), 60–64.

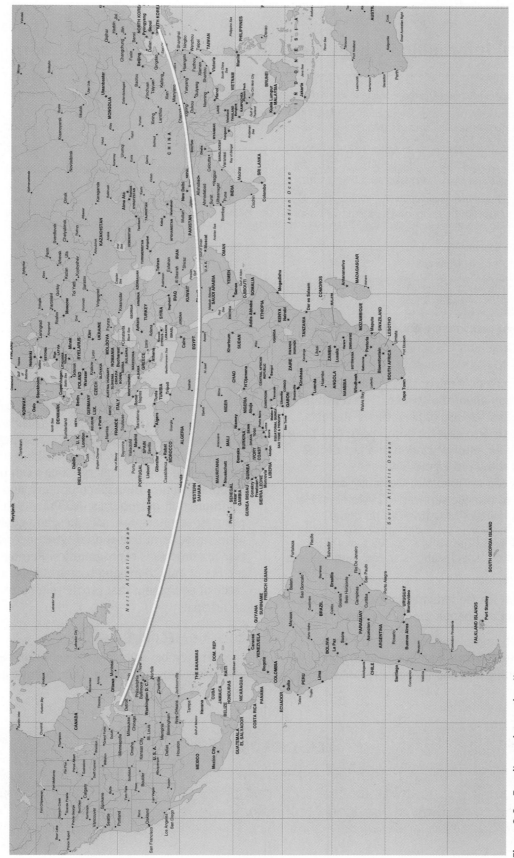

Figure 3-3 E-mail sent internationally.

Chapter 3: Utilizing Computer Hardware and Office Equipment

General Information About the University of Michigan-Dearborn

The University of Michigan-Dearborn is one of the three campuses of the University of Michigan operating under the policies of the Board of Regents.

The campus, located on 196 acres of the former estate of automotive pioneer Henry Ford, was founded in 1959 as a senior-level institution offering junior, senior, and graduate-level courses and degrees. In 1971, UM-D became a comprehensive university campus offering four year degree programs in liberal arts and sciences and graduate programs at the master's degree level.

More than 8,000 highly selective students, representing a wide range of academic interests and diverse backgrounds, are currently enrolled at the University of Michigan-Dearborn.

As part of the University of Michigan, UM-D enjoys the association with a large multi-university and the advantages of moderate size. Through expanded evening course offerings, professional development programs and cooperative education programs, UM-D continues to respond to the educational needs of commuting students from the Detroit metropolitan community.

Related Information:

☐ History of the University
☐ Administrative Organizations
☐ Applying to the University of Michigan-Dearborn
☐ Check out our campus map

Figure 3-4   Home page from the World Wide Web.

A college or university might develop a Web page with information about the college, with a picture of the college, for the use of perspective students. The Web page is also called a **home page** (the main Web presence for an organization or a person). A home page is shown in Figure 3-4.

Businesses can use the Web to market sales and products and to provide services to customers. Here are some examples of how this can be done.

- Save printing and updating costs by placing product information, specifications sheets, and so forth on the Web.

- Use the Web to give individuals and other companies information about a product or service.

- Use the Web to provide answers to frequently asked questions about a product and to obtain troubleshooting lists and lists of service locations.

OFFICE COPIERS

As an office professional, you will be using copiers daily. You must be knowledgeable about copier categories, features, quality, maintenance, selection, and efficiency of use. Making copies is not confined to only copiers. Copies can be made on fax machines, through computers, and through **multifunction peripherals (MFPs)** which include printers, scanners, fax machines, and copiers. An all-inclusive term that is used when referring to the copying process is **reprographics.** Reprographics refers not only to making copies but also to any piece of equipment that produces multiple copies of an original.

COPIER CATEGORIES

There are basically four categories of copiers available—personal copiers, low-volume copiers,

TECHNOLOGY TIP

Keeping current on technologies that impact your office means reading technology publications such as *Modern Office Technology* and *PC World.* Commit to reading at least one technology publication each month.

mid-volume copiers, and high-volume copiers. These divisions are based on the monthly copy volumes each copier can handle and the speed at which the copier operates. In addition to these categories, intelligent copier-printers and multifunction peripherals also can make copies.

Personal Copiers

Personal copiers are used in small offices and in homes, with the majority of the use being in the home. Typically, these machines are low-cost units that run 3 to 12 copies per minute. They are not typically recommended for companies or people who run more than 50 copies per month. These copiers are lightweight, portable, and can be placed on top of a desk.

Low-Volume Copiers

Low-volume copiers are machines that produce from 10 to 45 copies per minute and up to 50,000 copies per month. Some of the features on the low-volume copiers include handling two sizes of paper, automatic paper selection, reduction and enlargement of copies, and duplexing. These copiers are used in small offices as the only copier and in large offices as satellite machines in decentralized locations (throughout the office at numerous locations rather than in one location).

Mid-Volume Copiers

Mid-volume copiers generate between 45 and 80 copies per minute, producing as many as 150,000 copies per month. These machines have more features than low-volume copiers. Some of the standard features include document editing, programmable memory, highlight color, and reduction and enlargement. Mid-volume copiers are floor console models and are found in semi-central locations (at two or three locations throughout the office) within an office.

High-Volume Copiers

High-volume copiers are used in a centralized copy center (one location within the company) where they can serve an entire organization. These copiers are capable of producing up to 150 copies per minute, with monthly volumes as high as 500,000 copies. They are the most expensive of the copiers and produce the greatest numbers of copies per minute (from 60 to 120 copies per minute). Some of the features that mark high-

volume copying include insertion of tabs and covers and finishing options such as stapling.

Intelligent Copier-Printers

An intelligent copier-printer is a high-end copier that is capable of receiving input from other machines. For example, information can be keyed into a microcomputer and sent by electronic signals to the intelligent copier. To be considered intelligent, the copier must have a significant amount of memory which allows it to accept input from one or more machines and provide hard copy output. Some of the functions of an intelligent copier-printer are

- printing as many as 135 pages per minute;

- communicating with other intelligent copier-printers;

- merging data from other intelligent machines;

- reproducing line art, photographs, and text.

Intelligent copier-printer. *Courtesy of The Document Company Xerox.*

Color Copiers

Full-color copiers are available today that print high-quality copies in a matter of seconds. These copiers will also produce prints in black and white. If a company is creating color brochures or various other graphics which demand color and producing these documents in large quantities each month, a color copier can be more cost effective than having the work done by a printing company.

Multifunction Peripherals

A multifunction peripheral is a machine that combines two, three, or four functions. Generally these functions are printing, faxing, copying, and scanning. Some advantages of the machines are

- time saved in walking to and from various office machines;

- space saved when one machine replaces three;

- productivity increased when users can execute functions directly from the PC;

- cost savings as maintenance and supplies come from a single source.

Disadvantages of multifunction peripherals include

- malfunctioning due to several different operations on one machine;

- the relative newness of the market;

- quality concerns.

Even with these disadvantages, it is anticipated that more of these machines will be used in the future.

COPIER FEATURES

Although the features on copiers are varied and numerous, the following are some productivity-enhancing features that can be important to offices.

- Automatic document feeder—Feeds a stack of up to 50 one-sided or two-sided originals.

- Automatic magnification selection—Detects different size originals and adjusts automatically to copy them all onto a single paper size.

- Automatic paper selection—Automatically selects a copy that is the same size as the original.

- Computer forms feeder—Feeds unseparated computer paper continuously.

- Dual page copying—Copies facing pages of a book or report onto a single sheet.

- Image editing—Eliminates cutting and pasting by deleting sections of an original.

- Interrupt memory—Allows a user to interrupt a long copy run for a quick copy without disrupting the original copier setting.

- Job memory—Maintains in memory frequently copied jobs and recalls the settings instantly.

- Reduction and enlargement—Reduces or enlarges originals from 200 to 500 percent.

- Weekly timer—Turns the copier on and off each day.

- Edge eraser—Erases black borders that sometimes appear when copying facing pages of books.

- Duplexer—Makes two-sided copies from one-sided or two-sided originals.

COPIER QUALITY

Have you ever received a document copy that you could not read? was not straight on the page? had pages that were missing? Did you answer "yes"? Most of us have experienced at least one of these problems. Numerous errors are made in the copying process. Perhaps the machine malfunctions in some way or the machine needs toner. The collating may not be done properly, so pages are left out. Refer to Figure 3-5 for items that you should consider to ensure quality results when copying documents.

Quality Checklist

1. Keep paper clips and staples away from the copier to prevent any copier malfunction.

2. Check the copier screen to see that it is clean.

3. Know exactly how many copies you need to make.

4. Ask these questions about the copies:

   - Is the copy free of spots?

   - Is the copy easy to read? Is the ink dark and clear?

   - Is the copy straight on the page?

   - If the original was in pencil, can the copy be read?

   - If color has been used, did the color reproduce well?

   - Have all pages of the document been copied?

   - Have the pages been collated correctly?

5. Did you leave the copy room straight and orderly?

Figure 3-5

COPIER MAINTENANCE

When the office copier is inoperable, productivity suffers and frustrations increase. Many times the breakdown could have been avoided if proper maintenance had occurred. Refer to the suggestions given in Figure 3-6 to learn how to minimize copier breakdowns.

Maintenance Checklist

1. Designate a key operator. One person (situated close to the copier) should be responsible for simple repairs, replenishing supplies, and calling a repair person when necessary.

2. Choose an appropriate location. A copier needs proper ventilation and adequate temperature control. The user needs sufficient space to place paper and other supplies.

3. Note problems that occur. Inform the key operator so that the repair person may be told. If one or two problems are occurring consistently, the repair person needs to know the situation.

4. Pay attention to the control panel. When the control panel instructs you to add toner, do so. If toner is not added when needed, the quality of the copies will suffer as well as the internal mechanics of the machine.

5. Use proper paper. Paper that has been folded or that has rough edges may cause paper jams. Check the paper before you load it in the copier. It is wise to fan the stack of paper before loading it in the tray so that sheets will feed through singularly. Because paper is affected by humidity, keep the paper in its package until you are ready to use it.

6. Be careful. Do not attempt to make repairs or retrieve a jammed sheet unless you know the proper procedures. If you are making minor repairs, take off any dangling or large jewelry that might get caught in the machine. Also, be certain that the copier is not too hot before attempting minor repairs.

Figure 3-6

ABUSES

Although for many years we have had the technology to reduce the amount of paper in the office, the reverse has been true. The amount of paper has increased, and the ease of copying materials has contributed to that increase. Industry sources indicate that American businesses produce as many as 400 billion copies annually and up to 35 percent of those images may be unnecessary.[3] That is over 100 billion wasted sheets every year. For example, an employee may make ten copies of a document when he or she knows that only eight are actually needed. The additional copies are made "just in case" they are needed, and most of the time the employee winds up throwing the extra copies away. Unfortunately, there is also widespread use of office copiers for personal use.

Control Systems

To curb copying control abuses, one solution that offices have gone to is the installation of a copy control device. Each system operates somewhat differently but the same basic features exist in all systems. For example, if a keypad system is used, the user enters an account number into a keypad and access is granted to the copier. With a card system, the card is good for a set number of copies. When the card is inserted into the machine, copying costs can be automatically charged back to the appropriate department or division. Each department or division of the company can then check copy costs against a specific account. If abuses are occurring, appropriate action can be taken.

Public entities such as libraries and schools control copying costs by using coin-operated copiers. The user of the copier pays for the copies directly by inserting money into the copier or by purchasing a debit card which has a specific value. As copies are made, the cost is deducted from the card.

Ethical Considerations

Each employee in a company should be extremely ethical in the use of copying machines. Ethics in such a situation means:

- You do not copy documents for your own personal use.

---

[3]"Controlling Copier Usage," *Managing Office Technology* (September, 1995).

- You are consistently prudent in making the appropriate number of copies.

- You do not copy restricted materials (explained in the copyright section that follows).

COPYRIGHT LAW

A portion of the Federal Copyright Law is shown in Figure 3-7. Because you may be responsible for a great deal of copying, you need to be informed about the law. Here are some of its highlights.

- Money, postage stamps, U.S. bonds, Federal Reserve notes, or other securities of the United States may not be reproduced.

- Birth certificates, passports, draft cards, naturalization and immigration papers may not be reproduced.

- Driver's licenses, automobile registrations, and certificates of title may not be reproduced.

- Documents that contain the personal information of an individual are protected by the Right of Privacy Act. They may not be reproduced without the individual's permission.

- Material that retains a copyright may not be reproduced without the owner's permission. The fair use provisions allow some exception to this provision.

The fair use clause means that individuals do have the right to reproduce copyrighted materials without permission under certain fair and reasonable circumstances. In determining whether the use of a work in any particular situation is fair, refer to Figure 3-7 which gives four provisions to be considered. Whether the copying to be done falls within the fair use provision must be decided on an individual basis.

Further technological advances have impacted the copyright process even more. Almost all software is copyrighted. Statements are included on software that spell out the copyright restrictions.

The Federal Copyright Law P.L. 94-553

106. The fair use of a copyrighted work including such use by reproduction in copies of phone records or by any other means specified by that section, for purposes such as criticism, comment, news reporting, teaching (including multiple copies for classroom use), scholarship, or research is not an infringement of copyright. In determining whether the use made of a work in any particular case is a fair use, the factors to be considered shall include:

- The purpose and character of the use, including whether such use is of a commercial nature or is for nonprofit educational purposes,

- The nature of the copyrighted work,

- The amount and substantiality of the portion used in relation to the copyrighted work as a whole, and

- The effect of the use upon the potential market for or value of the copyrighted work.

Figure 3-7

For example, under the copyright laws neither the documentation nor the software may be copied, photocopied, reproduced, translated, or reduced to any electronic medium or machine readable form without prior written consent from the company.

In 1994, the National Information Infrastructure Working Group on Intellectual Property Rights, a committee of the Clinton administration's policy group on information technology, asked the U.S. Patent and Trademark Office to address the shortcomings of the 1976 Copyright Act. The task was to determine if copyright holders and "fair users" of

HUMAN RELATIONS TIP

Integrity means that you never copy personal items at work.

Copier Selection Questions

Ask these questions before selecting a copier.

- How many copies will be made per month?

- What features are needed? Is reduction and enlargement essential? editing? duplexing? collating?

- Will color copying be needed? If so, can color be reproduced with a high degree of accuracy?

- What is the purchase price of the machine?

- What is the cost per copy?

- What is the cost of supplies?

- Is the vendor an authorized representative for the brand?

- Does the vendor have an established reputation?

- Does the vendor carry parts for the brand?

- Does the vendor provide quick, reliable service?

- What is the cost of service? Is a service contract available? If so, how much does it cost?

- Ask for a demonstration of the copier; then ask these questions:

  - Are the copies clean and crisp?

  - Is there a clear definition between black and white areas?

  - Are the grays in photos clear?

  - Is the machine easy to operate?

  - Is the interior easily accessible for removing jammed paper and replacing toner?

Figure 3-8

copyrighted material could agree to a new set of guidelines that address technological trends in education. The result was the establishment of the Conference on Fair Use (CONFU). This group is addressing the guidelines in four areas: multimedia, distance learning, visual archives, and digital libraries. It is not expected that the guidelines will do away with the 1976 Copyright Act. It is expected, however, that the guidelines will address technological trends such as distance learning and digital libraries and will provide more clarity of copyright rules.

COPIER SELECTION

Because a copier is used so extensively, it is important that consideration be given to the type of copier that will best serve the needs of the business. To help you understand some of the questions to be asked when considering the purchase of a copier, review Figure 3-8.

HUMAN RELATIONS TIP

Integrity means that you do not violate the copyright law when copying materials.

THE FAX PROCESS

A **facsimile (fax) machine** is a type of copier that electronically sends an original document from one location to another via communication networks. With a fax you may communicate with other persons within the same building, in the same city, across the nation, or across the world. The fax machine has become a standard piece of office equipment.

FAX FEATURES

A number of features are available on fax machines. Several of these features are presented here.

- **Fax broadcasting** is the ability to personalize and transmit to multiple locations simultaneously. You fax a single document and then a computer individualizes and faxes it to hundreds or thousands of recipients in minutes. Broadcasting is often accomplished at a fraction of the cost of direct mail or overnight services. Transmissions can be scheduled twenty-four hours a day. However, most are sent after business hours when telecommunication rates are lower and fax machines are not busy. The message sits in the recipients' machines, ready to be read first thing the next morning.

- **Fax-on-demand** is the service of storing information for instant retrieval via telephone and fax. It allows you to automate your organization's repetitive actions. For example, customers may call asking for product literature, specification sheets, or price lists. Callers follow a voice-prompted menu to choose documents, and then enter their choices and fax numbers on their telephone keypads. The documents are then sent to the designated fax machine.

- **Color fax** makes it possible to scan any high resolution color image and transmit it anywhere in the world in a few minutes via standard telephone lines. Images can be edited and output to a full-color printer, color display monitor, or other output device.

- A **portable fax** (a telephone handset and a small fax machine) will fit in a briefcase. If the executive is traveling and does not have a portable fax machine, machines are available in hotels across the country. Many office supply and copying stores also offer fax machine services.

- Businesses have had problems with junk mail clogging fax machines. With a special device attached to your fax, you can eliminate the receipt of junk faxes. The device requires that the sender know your security code and your fax number. If the sender does not know the security code, the machine blocks the message. Another way of controlling junk fax is to purchase a fax machine that only allows communication with user-selected numbers stored in the machine's memory.

- As you learned earlier, multifunction machines allow the combination of two, three, or four functions. A fax may be a multifunction machine, combining printing, faxing, copying, and scanning or two or three of these functions into one machine.

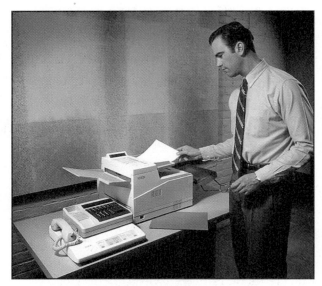

Fax machines provide for almost instant communication anywhere in the world. *Courtesy of The Document Company Xerox.*

FAX SELECTION

In selecting a fax, here are some questions you should ask before making the purchase.

- How will I be using the fax? What are my applications? Will I be sending more documents or receiving more documents?

- How much memory will I need? What features do I need?

- What type of image quality is needed? Is faxing photographs or graphics a priority?

- Do I need document security? **Confidential mailboxes** (mailboxes to which no other person has access) are available if document security is an issue. Security devices are also available that enable the user to send **scrambled signals** (signals in code).

- What is the vendor's reputation? How long has the company been in business? Is the service quick and efficient? If the company's home office is not in your city, is there a service center where you are located?

THE FUTURE—TECHNOLOGY DOMINATED

New discoveries in technology are constant. Advances will continue in the area of **artificial intelligence** (the exploration of using computers for tasks requiring human characteristics of intelligence, imagination, and intuition). Stated simply, the differences between intelligent computing and conventional computing can be summarized in this manner. In conventional computing, the human gives a problem to the computer and tells it how to solve the problem. In intelligent computing, the human gives the problem to the computer but does not tell it how to solve the problem. Artificial intelligence can be separated into several systems, namely

- expert systems

- natural language

- computer vision

- robotics

Expert systems allow the computer to be expert on a particular subject. Some expert systems are presently used in the fields of medicine, science, engineering, geology, and computer systems. **Natural language** refers to being able to communicate with the computer in our native language. **Speech-recognition systems** are natural language systems that understand and accept the human voice. **Vision systems** refer to the ability of a computer to identify features of real objects or images of objects as in a photograph and use this information to solve a problem. **Robots** are another area of artificial intelligence. The ultimate intelligent robot might be one that utilizes expert systems, speech recognition, and vision technologies. Advances will continue to be made in these areas which will affect the office environment.

Consider this example of the possible capabilities of the future "intelligent" word processor. An office professional sits down at the word processor on Monday morning and communicates *verbally* with the computer. (The computer understands the employee's language.) The employee gives the computer only the essential information necessary for a report the employer is waiting on in Japan. The computer composes the report, using correct format and grammar. After a few seconds of work, the computer asks the office professional to review the report, if necessary. The employee decides to review it auditorily. The computer than reads the report. The employee determines some details are missing and verbally adds those details to the report. Once the report is finished, it is sent by e-mail to the employer in Japan.

On a personal level, advances will be made that may impact your life. Bill Gates in his book, *The Road Ahead,* discusses possibilities that will be available to us. Technology will be available to allow our house to provide the environment we wish. For example, through wearing an electronic pin, you may give the house information to meet your needs. When your house is dark, the pin will cause a moving zone of light to accompany you through the house. Music will move with you (if you choose). This music will be music of your selection. Other individuals in the house will have the option of listening to their own music. The house can give you information about upcoming vacations. For example, if you are planning to visit Hong Kong, you might ask the screen in your home to show you pictures of the city. Images will materialize on the walls of the room and vanish after you leave.[4]

It is expected that computers will be able to map the human genome for genetic-based personal identification and diagnostics. Researchers will look for ways to treat diseases before they occur. For example, if a person carries the gene that gives a 90 percent probability of contracting Lou Gehrig's disease, treatment could start in an attempt to stop the advent of the disease. Through technology, it may also be possible to manipulate the genetic code to make the aging process a more pleasant experience.[5]

---

[4]Gates, Bill, *The Road Ahead* (Pennsylvania: Quebecor Printing/Fairfield, Inc., 1995).

[5]Roe, Mary Ann, "Technology Research and Application," *Community College Journal* (August/September, 1996), 15–19.

Chips may be implanted in our bodies. The chip may serve as combination credit cards, passport, driver's license, personal diary, and so forth. No longer would we need to worry about losing our credit cards while traveling. Ultra-tiny computers might also provide enough intelligence for microscopic machines that could be injected into our bodies. These computers could perform such tasks as repairing muscle and brain cells.[6] A dream world? No, the world in which you and I may possibly live.

Clearly, technology will continue to invade our entire life—both our life at the office and our life at home.

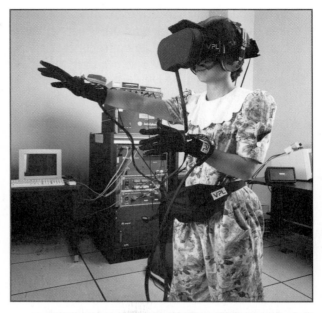

Virtual reality will provide increased opportunities for the future. *Top photo courtesy of NASA. Bottom photo courtesy of Ford Motor Co.*

[6]Cornish, Edward, "The Cyber Future: 92 Ways Our Lives Will Change by the Year 2025," *The Futurist* (January/February, 1996).

CHAPTER SUMMARY

This summary will help you remember the important points covered in this chapter.

- Computers are classified into three main categories: mainframes and supercomputers, minicomputers and superminis, and microcomputers and supermicros.

- Computer input devices include computer keyboards, scanners, touch screen monitors, mouse and trackball, pens and tablets, and voice recognition.

- The central processing unit is the brain of the computer. The parts of the CPU are the memory, arithmetic-logic unit, and the control unit.

- The two most common categories of memory are random access memory and read-only memory.

- External storage devices include: disks, optical or laser disks, hard disks, and magnetic tape.

- Computer output devices include monitors for a soft copy and printers for a hard copy.

- Computers and peripheral equipment are linked through networks that can be local area networks, metropolitan area networks, or wide area networks.

- The Intranet is a network within a business that allows Internet access by the employees of the business but, as a general rule, does not allow external access to the business's data by individuals outside the company.

- The Internet is a special network linking the world's largest group of computers. Through the Internet, people from all over the world can communicate. The World Wide Web is one of several features of the Internet; it contains a huge collection of computer files containing all types of information, including sounds, videos, and still graphics.

- Office copiers can be divided into four categories—personal copiers, low-volume copiers, mid-volume copiers, and high-volume copiers. These divisions are based on the monthly copy volumes that each copier can handle and the speed at which the copier operates.

- The intelligent copier-printer is a high-end copier that is capable of receiving input from other machines.

- Multifunction peripheral machines combine two, three, or four functions, such as printing, faxing, copying, and scanning.

- Copier features are numerous with automatic document feed, automatic magnification selection, dual page copying, image editing, and job memory being a few.

- Copy quality is important. Some of the items that should be considered to maintain quality are copy easy to read, ink dark and clear, copy straight on page, color reproduced well, pages collated correctly, copier screen clean, staples and paper clips kept away from the copier.

- Making unnecessary copies is an abuse that is widespread. In fact, it has been estimated that up to 35 percent of copies made are unnecessary.

- Keypad and card systems are two methods that businesses use to contain copy costs.

- When making copies, you should be certain that the copyright law is not being violated.

- In selecting copiers, some important considerations are number of copies that will be made per month, features needed, colors necessary, vendor reputation, quality of service, purchase price of machine, cost of supplies.

- Fax features include fax broadcasting, fax-on-demand, and color fax. Portable fax machines and multifunction fax machines are available in addition to the regular fax machine.

- In selecting a fax, some considerations are use of fax, memory needed, features needed, image quality necessary, document security, vendor's reputation, service from vendor.

- Technology continues to increase. For the future we can expect advances in artificial intelligence. These advances will be in expert systems, natural language, computer vision, and robotics, to name a few. Technology will continue to impact our entire life—both professionally and personally.

CHAPTER GLOSSARY

The following terms were introduced in this chapter. To help you review, definitions are given here.

- **Mainframe** (p. 52)–The largest computer system.

- **Supercomputer** (p. 52)–The mightiest and most expensive mainframe.

- **Teraflop** (p. 52)–A trillion operations per second.

- **Gigaflop** (p. 52)–A billion operations per second.

- **Minicomputer** (p. 52)–A mid-size computer; smaller, slower in processing speed, and more limited in storage capacity than the mainframe computer.

- **Interfaced** (p. 52)–Computers that are interconnected.

- **Supermini** (p. 52)–A minicomputer at the top of the size and price scale for minis.

- **Microcomputer** (p. 53)–The smallest of the computer systems.

- **Microprocessor** (p. 53)–A single miniature chip containing the circuitry and components of a microcomputer.

- **Personal computers (PCs)** (p. 53)–A term used widely for microcomputers.

- **Hard drives** (p. 53)–Internal storage capacity for a computer.

- **Pentium processor chip** (p. 53)–A type of microprocessor which provides increased speed and performance capability for the PC.

- **Supermicros** (p. 53)–Upper-end microcomputers.

- **Multiuser** (p. 53)–Computers that are able to serve several users at the same time.

- **Multitasking** (p. 53)–Computers that are able to run more than one application package per user.

- **Portable microcomputer** (p. 53)–Computer that can be carried from place to place.

- **Laptop computer** (p. 53)–A type of portable computer small enough to rest on the user's lap.

- **Notebook computer** (p. 53)–A type of portable computer; it is smaller than a laptop.

- **Hard drive** (p. 53)–Internal storage on a PC.

- **Floppy drive** (p. 53)–External storage for a PC.

- **CD-ROM drives** (p. 53)–Provides for the running of CD-ROM software on PCs.

- **Palmtops** (p. 53)–Portable computers small enough to fit in a pocket or purse.

- **Input and output devices** (p. 54)–Devices used to communicate with the central processing unit of the computer; also called I/O devices.

- **Alphanumeric keypad** (p. 54)–PC keypad with alphabetic and numeric characters.

- **Cursor control keypad** (p. 54)–Keypad that allows the operator to move the cursor up, down, and to both sides.

- **Function keypad** (p. 54)–Keypad that controls the various functions of the software package such as search, spell check, and so forth; these functions will differ considering the software package being used.

- **Numeric keypad** (p. 54)–A separate keypad consisting of numbers only; designed to speed the entry of numbers.

- **Scanners** (p. 55)–Machine that allows you to scan typed, printed, or handwritten information from paper and transfer the information to a computer. Scanners are also referred to as optical character readers (OCRs).

- **Magnetic ink character readers (MICRs)** (p. 55)–A type of scanner.

- **Bar code scanners** (p. 55)–Scanners used in grocery stores and other businesses to record the bar codes printed on various products.

- **Mouse** (p. 56)–A small hand-controlled device that allows the user to move the cursor and choose menu commands without using the keyboard.

- **Graphical user interface (GUI)** (p. 56)–A device that uses drop-down menus and various icons for executing commands and choosing program options.

- **Trackball roller** (p. 56)–A stationary ball rolled with the tips of the fingers to move the pointer on the screen.

- **Light pens** (p. 56)–Produces lines and drawings on a computer screen.

- **Touch tablet** (p. 57)–Similar to a light pen except a pad is used rather than a computer screen.

- **Voice recognition** (p. 57)–A system that allows the user to input data to the computer with spoken words.

- **Central processing unit (CPU)** (p. 57)–The brain of the computer which accepts data from the input devices, processes the data, and delivers the results through some type of output device.

- **Program** (p. 57)–A series of instructions directing the computer to perform a sequence of operations.

- **Bit** (p. 57)–A binary digit.

- **Byte** (p. 57)–One byte is equal to eight bits, which is the amount of information that makes up a single character.

- **Kilobytes (KB)** (p. 57)–Memory capacity of a computer expressed in thousand-byte units.

- **Megabytes (MB)** (p. 57)–Memory capacity of a computer expressed in million-byte units.

- **Gigabytes (GB)** (p. 57)–Memory capacity of a computer expressed in billion-byte units.

- **Terabytes** (p. 57)–Memory capacity of a computer expressed in trillion-byte units.

- **Software** (p. 57)–A set of instructions that tells the computer what to do.

- **Random access memory (RAM)** (p. 58)–Memory in a computer that allows you to change data. You are working with RAM in a word processing program.

- **Read-only memory (ROM)** (p. 58)–Memory in a computer that allows you to read but not change any data.

- **Floppy** (p. 58)–A disk that may be 5.25 or 3.5 inches used as external storage for the microcomputer.

- **Density** (p. 58)–Amount of data that can be stored on a disk.

- **Double sided and high density** (p. 58)–Refers to the amount of disk density.

- **Optical disks or laser disks** (p. 59)–A type of disk that provides external storage for a computer.

- **Compact disk read-only memory (CD-ROM)** (p. 59)–A type of disk that supplies software packages to the computer.

- **Write once, read many (WORM)** (p. 59)–A disk that is nonerasable and is used for applications that require the data to be written once as a permanent record.

- **Erasable disk** (p. 59)–A disk that can be reused by writing over the data.

- **Hard disks (also called magnetic disks)** (p. 59)–Secondary storage for mainframe and minicomputers.

- **Soft copy** (p. 59)–Copy that is not in print but is shown on a monitor.

- **Cathode ray tube (CRT)** (p. 59)–Video display monitor.

- **Hard copy** (p. 59)–Printed copy.

- **Presentation monitors** (p. 60)–Monitors 25 to 35 inches in size.

- **Monochrome** (p. 60)–Refers to monitors that are one color.

- **Impact printer** (p. 60)–Printer that prints characters on paper by physically impacting or hitting the paper.

- **Nonimpact printer** (p. 60)–Printer that does not hit the paper; this type includes the ink-jet printer and the laser printer.

- **Network printer** (p. 60)–A printer attached to a local area network.

- **Printer sharing** (p. 61)–Printer that can be shared by both networked and non-networked users.

- **Local area networks (LANs)** (p. 61)–Networks that link various types of technological equipment within the same geographic area such as an office.

- **Metropolitan area networks (MANs)** (p. 61)–Networks that link technological equipment over a distance equal to the size of a city and its surrounds.

- **Wide area networks (WANs)** (p.61)–Networks that link technological equipment in an area of hundreds of thousands of miles.

- **Electronic mail (e-mail)** (p. 61)–Mail sent between computers within networked locations.

- **Mail servers** (p. 62)–Programs that respond to e-mail messages.

- **Usernet** (p. 62)–Online bulletin board with messages on thousands of different topics.

- **Intranet** (p. 62)–A network within a business that allows Internet access by the employees of the business but, as a general rule, does not allow external access to the business's data by individuals outside the company.

- **Web page** (p. 62)–A page on the World Wide Web network.

- **Home page** (p. 64)–The main Web presence for an organization or a person.

- **Multifunction peripherals (MFPs)** (p. 64)–Peripherals that have several functions such as printing, scanning, faxing, and copying.

- **Reprographics** (p. 64)–Refers to the process of making copies and to any piece of equipment that produces multiple copies of an original.

- **Personal copiers** (p. 65)–Copiers that run from 3 to 12 copies per minute and not more than 50 copies per month.

- **Low-volume copiers** (p. 65)–Copiers that produce from 10 to 45 copies per minute and up to 50,000 copies per month.

- **Mid-volume copiers** (p. 65)–Copiers that generate between 45 and 80 copies per minute and as many as 150,000 copies per month.

- **High-volume copiers** (p. 65)–Copiers capable of producing up to 150 copies per minute with monthly volumes as high as 500,000 copies.

- **Intelligent copier-printer** (p. 65)–A high-end copier capable of receiving input from other machines and can print as many as 135 pages per minute.

- **Facsimile (FAX) machine** (p. 70)–A type of copier that electronically sends an original document from one location to another via communication networks.

- **Fax broadcasting** (p. 70)–A fax that is capable of personalizing copy and transmitting it to multiple locations simultaneously.

- **Fax-on-demand** (p. 70)–Service of storing information for instant retrieval via telephone and fax.

- **Color fax** (p. 70)–Ability to scan any high resolution color image and transmit it anywhere via standard telephone lines.

- **Portable fax** (p. 70)–A telephone handset and a small fax machine which will fit in a briefcase.

- **Confidential mailbox** (p. 71)–Mailbox that provides for the confidentially of faxes.

- **Scrambled signals** (p. 71)–Signals in code used for security of faxes.

- **Artificial intelligence** (p. 71)–Using computers for tasks requiring human characteristics of intelligence, imagination, and intuition.

- **Expert systems** (p. 71)–Systems that allow the computer to be expert on a particular subject.

- **Natural language** (p. 71)–The ability to communicate with the computer in our native language.

- **Speech-recognition systems** (p. 71)–Natural language systems that understand and accept the human voice.

- **Vision systems** (p. 71)–The ability of a computer to identify features of real objects or images of objects, as in a photograph, and use this information to solve a problem.

- **Robots** (p. 71)–An intelligent robot might be one that utilizes expert systems, speech recognition, and vision technologies.

DISCUSSION ITEMS

These discussion items provide an opportunity for you to test your understanding of the chapter through discussion with your classmates and your instructor.

1. Explain the different classifications of computers.

2. Identify two computer networks. What are their functions?

3. Explain the difference between personal copiers, low-volume copiers, mid-volume, and high-volume copiers.

4. What is a fax and how is it used?

5. What is the Internet? How would you use the Internet?

6. What are some possibilities for the future of technology?

CASE STUDY

Your company provides you with copy keys for copying documents. Several times as you have been waiting for the copier, you have noticed that one of the employees is copying personal documents. The first time you noticed it you thought surely it did not happen often. Then you noticed it again the next week and three times a week later. To make matters worse, the individual is the assistant to your supervisor's boss. You know that she is considered an excellent assistant, and she seems to have a good relationship with the employees in her work group. You feel strongly that it is wrong. You realize, however, that she does not report to you and is not even in your department. Should you say something about what you have observed? If so, why and who should you talk with about the infraction?

Select one of your classmates and discuss this case. Suggest what action should be taken and explain your reasons for choosing the action.

RESPONSES TO SELF CHECK

1. List the three main categories of computers.

   Mainframe and supercomputers

   Minicomputers and superminis

   Microcomputers and supermicros

2. What is a Pentium processor?

   The Pentium processor is a type of microprocessor, which is the brain of a computer. The Pentium processor is used extensively on a PC. It contains the circuitry and components for memory, arithmetic, logic, and control operations. It is a powerful microprocessor that provides for increased speed and performance capability of the PC.

3. List six input devices.

   computer keyboards

   scanners

   touch screen monitors

   mouse and trackball

   pens and tablets

   voice

4. What are the components of the CPU?

   memory unit

   arithmetic-logic unit

   control unit

5. How are memory capacities on the computer expressed?

Memory capacities are measured in bytes or multiples of bytes. Thousand-byte units are called kilobytes; million-byte units are called megabytes; billion-byte units are called gigabytes; and trillion-byte units are called terabytes.

OFFICE TASKS

OFFICE TASK 3-1 (Objectives 1, 2, 3, and 8)

Choose one of the following tasks and write a report on your findings. Identify the local business offices that you visited or list your resources. The report is to be keyed. Print out one copy; make three additional copies on a copier duplexing it and reducing the print size. Turn in both your original and the three copies to your instructor.

1. Team with three members of your class. Visit a local office. Find out the following information:
   a. type of computer system used
   b. type of input and output devices used in the business
   c. networks utilized by the business
   d. software used for word processing, spreadsheets, and databases

2. Use an online service such as America Online, Prodigy, CompuServe, or Microsoft Internet Explorer to review articles on computers, printers, and computer networks. Two giants in the computer field have been Bill Gates of Microsoft and Andy Grove of Intel®; you might want to review some of their works.

OFFICE TASK 3-2
(Objectives 4, 5, 6, 7, and 8)

You need a new copier and fax machine in your office. Your employer has asked you to research the prices and features available on a mid-volume copier (which would be used in your office only) and a fax which is capable of broadcasting since you frequently send duplicate information to both your U.S. offices and international offices. Team with three of your classmates. Visit companies that carry copiers and faxes in your area and get the information requested or research the topic through the Internet or through periodicals such as *Managing Office Technology.* Once you have the information, compose a joint memorandum (using the form provided on Student Data Template Disk, file OT3-2) to Ms. Marquette from your team, detailing the prices and the features. Make a recommendation to Ms. Marquette, explaining why you are recommending the copier and the fax.

OFFICE TASK 3-3 (Objective 7)

You have been preparing instructions for the office manual on the formatting and composing of office reports. You have a draft copy on your computer. Access Student Data Template Disk, file OT3-3. You are now ready to prepare it in final form. The copy has not been appropriately formatted. Do so, using headings where appropriate (putting headings in all caps and underlining as appropriate); the final copy should be easy to read and clear in presentation. Correct any grammatical, punctuation, or spelling errors in the copy; use a larger typeface than was used in your draft copy. A table of contents page is to be done; the page numbers should be

Summary, p. iii

Introduction, p. 1

Findings, p. 2

Conclusions, p. 4

Recommendations, p. 6

Appendices, p. 8

If you have access to spreadsheet software include an example of a bar chart under the section on research methods. The information for the bar chart follows.

Six-Month Sales Figures
Harriet Turben: June—$35,000, July—$50,000, August—$15,000, September—$55,000, October—$40,000, November—$25,000

Josephine Alexander: June—$10,000, July—$15,000, August—$12,000, September—$14,000, October—$14,000, November—$22,000

Christopher Redding: June—$40,000, July—$35,000, August—$45,000, September—$50,000, October—$36,000, November—$60,000

If you have access to presentation software, make slides using your headings; assume that these slides will be used in a presentation about report format. Run two copies of your final report; hand in both to your instructor. As you run the copies, you determine that you have not left space for binding on the left-hand side of the report. The copy is part of an office manual and will be bound at a later date. Move the copy on the printer one-quarter inch to the left to provide for this binding space.

ENGLISH USAGE CHALLENGE DRILL

Correct the following sentences. Cite the grammar rule that is applicable to each sentence. Before you begin, refresh your memory of grammar rules by reviewing the rules on pronouns in the *Multimedia Reference for Writers* (if available to you), by reading the rules in the reference guide to this text, or by using another printed reference guide.

1. The contest winner was me.
2. May I speak to Nancy? This is her.
3. Who does Ann admire?
4. The instructor and myself had a long talk.
5. She invited my girlfriend and myself to the concert.

ASSESSMENT OF CHAPTER OBJECTIVES

Now that you have completed the chapter and the office tasks, take a few moments to review the following learning objectives. Did you achieve these objectives? Indicate your responses by answering "yes" or "no" in the blanks provided. If you were unable to accomplish these objectives, give your reason for not doing so. Your instructor may want to review your answers.

I accomplished these objectives:

1. Classify computer systems. Yes _____ No _____
   Explain how you accomplished this objective.

   _____

   _____

   _____

2. Identify computer hardware components and explain their functions. Yes _____ No _____
   Explain how you accomplished this objective.

   _____

   _____

   _____

3. Define the function of computer networks.
   Yes _____ No _____
   Explain how you accomplished this objective.

   _____

   _____

   _____

4. Identify the types of copiers available.
   Yes _____ No _____

   Explain how you accomplished this objective.

   _____

   _____

   _____

5. Explain the basic and special features of copiers.
   Yes _____ No _____

   Explain how you accomplished this objective.

   _____

   _____

   _____

6. Demonstrate a knowledge of how to maintain
   and select copiers. Yes _____ No _____

   Explain how you accomplished this objective.

   _____

   _____

   _____

7. Explain the fax process and selection criteria.
   Yes _____ No _____

   Explain how you accomplished this objective.

   _____

   _____

   _____

8. Use computers, copiers, and fax machines.
   Yes _____ No _____

   Explain how you accomplished this objective.

   _____

   _____

   _____

Provide reasons for failing to accomplish any of the
objectives.

   _____

   _____

   _____

CHAPTER 4

USING SOFTWARE

LEARNING OBJECTIVES

1. **Identify and explain various types of software programs.**
2. **Troubleshoot software problems.**
3. **Explain how to select software.**
4. **Describe how to care for software and hardware.**
5. **Use applications software in performing tasks.**

Your role as an office professional will demand that you are extremely knowledgeable about various software packages. You probably are already familiar with a word processing package and are using this package in preparing various documents for your class assignments. In addition, you may have some knowledge of spreadsheet, database, and graphics packages. This chapter is not designed to give you detailed knowledge of one software package. Such knowledge and skill must come through working daily with the package. It is designed to help you understand the broad spectrum of software packages that are available. Also, you will learn how to select and evaluate software and how to care for both software and hardware. It is expected that you will use one or two software packages which have been purchased for educational purposes by your college in completing the tasks assigned throughout this course.

Software in this chapter is divided into two main types—operating systems software and applications software. Operating systems software will not be as visible to you in your work as an office professional, but it is essential in the running of your computer. Applications software is the software that you will use daily in producing documents.

OPERATING SYSTEMS SOFTWARE

Software that controls the operating systems of your computer, keyboard, printer, mouse, and other peripheral devices is known as **operating systems software.** You are not expected to have detailed knowledge of operating systems. However, general knowledge will help you understand how your computer functions. An operating system is a program that enables your computer to read and write data to a disk, send pictures to your monitor, and accept keyboard commands. It provides the basic services for computing. For example, in the foundation of a building, there are power and plumbing hookups. You cannot cook your breakfast, take a hot shower, or watch television without these power and plumbing hookups; they are a necessary part of the building. Without an operating system, your computer is like an unfinished building. Data that you key cannot be received; data that you would like printed cannot be printed. In other words, your computer is useless without an operating system; there is no foundation. Figure 4-1 illustrates this concept.

The five basic operating systems in use are

- Windows® 95
- DOS®
- OS/2® Warp
- Windows NT®
- Novell® DOS

Because Windows and DOS are the most commonly used operating systems, the concentration here is on these two systems. OS/2 Warp, Windows NT, and Novell are mentioned briefly.

WINDOWS 95

The newest of the five operating systems given is **Windows 95.** This operating system was released in August 1995 by Microsoft and has received widespread acceptance since it was introduced.

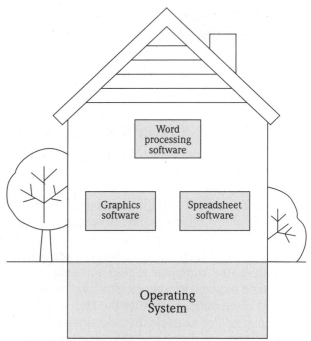

Figure 4-1 Without an operating system, your computer is useless.

Figure 4-2 A graphical user interface system uses icons.

Figure 4-3 Multitasking allows you to run more than one application at the same time.

Windows 95 uses a graphical user interface (GUI) for an efficient work environment. Remember you learned in Chapter 3 that a graphical user interface is a device that uses drop-down menus and various icons for executing commands and choosing program options. An example of a GUI is shown in Figure 4-2. To start an application, you simply click on the desired icon. With the GUI you use the mouse more than the keyboard in giving instructions to the computer. You do not have to memorize program names because Windows gives you all the programs represented by icons. Windows also enables you to multitask. You learned in Chapter 3 that multitasking means the capability to run more than one application at the same time. For example, assume that your employer has given you a letter to write. You are in the middle of writing the letter when your employer gives you new figures for you to insert in a spreadsheet document which you have previously prepared. It is to be done immediately. You can open your spreadsheet program, retrieve the appropriate table, insert the figures, run a copy, and when you are finished, a single mouse click or keystroke will take you back to your word processing document so that you may finish the letter. Figure 4-3 illustrates this concept.

DOS

DOS, a disk operating system produced by IBM, has been a widely used operating system for a number of years. It is an older system than Windows. As with Windows 95, DOS is a collection of programs that gives you control of your computer's resources. DOS uses a command-driven interface—meaning that whenever you want the computer to perform an operation you need to key in a command. Because no visual cues are on the screen, you must either memorize the commands or look them up in a book as needed. For example, using WordPerfect and DOS, you must know that to print a document,

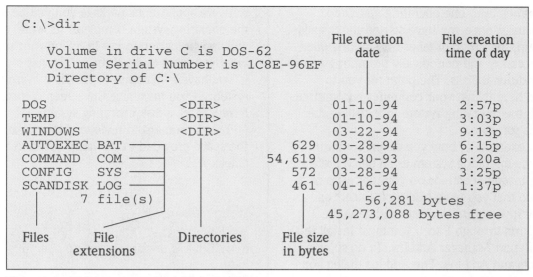

```
C:\>dir
                                        File creation    File creation
       Volume in drive C is DOS-62        date            time of day
       Volume Serial Number is 1C8E-96EF
       Directory of C:\

  DOS              <DIR>                    01-10-94        2:57p
  TEMP             <DIR>                    01-10-94        3:03p
  WINDOWS          <DIR>                    03-22-94        9:13p
  AUTOEXEC BAT                       629    03-28-94        6:15p
  COMMAND  COM                    54,619    09-30-93        6:20a
  CONFIG   SYS                       572    03-28-94        3:25p
  SCANDISK LOG                       461    04-16-94        1:37p
         7 file(s)                           56,281 bytes
                                      45,273,088 bytes free

  Files      File        Directories    File size
          extensions                    in bytes
```

Figure 4-4   DOS uses a command-driven interface.

you key shift F7. To save a document, you key F7. To center a heading, you key F6. Figure 4-4 gives a DOS screen.

OS/2 WARP

OS/2 Warp is a disk operating system also produced by IBM Corporation. It uses a graphical user interface (as does Windows 95) which allows it to handle multiple applications at the same time. For example, OS/2 may run a word processing program and a database program in different windows on the computer screen at the same time.

WINDOWS NT AND NOVELL DOS

Both Windows NT and Novell are products of Microsoft. **Windows NT** is Microsoft's high-end alternative to Windows. Currently, it is used extensively on **network servers** (any computer that shares its hard drive with the network). Although network functions vary, common network functions are communications (providing linkages to the Internet) or printing (networking several computers to one printer). Windows NT is designed to replace both DOS and Windows. It looks like Windows, but it is more reliable than Windows.

Just as Windows NT is used on network servers, so is Novell DOS. **Novell DOS** is a Microsoft disk operating system **(MS-DOS),** which is a compatible operating system that includes networking and multitasking. In the future, you may see these operating systems used on computers that are not networked.

OPERATING SYSTEM FUNCTIONS

The operating system for a microcomputer is on a floppy disk or a CD-ROM; it must be loaded into the computer before any software programs can be loaded. Once the operating system is loaded, it resides on the hard disk drive of the computer. When the computer is turned on, the operating system is loaded into the memory. The three main functions of operating systems are to

- control computer system resources;

- execute computer programs;

- manage data.

Each operating system utilizes memory and storage capacity on the computer. For example, MS-DOS 6.22 uses 512KB RAM and 6.1MB of hard drive space. OS/2 Warp uses 4MB RAM and 35MB to 50MB of hard drive space. Windows 95 uses 8MB RAM and 35MB to 50MB of hard drive.

As an office professional, you may communicate with your operating system in several ways. Several possibilities are given here.

You might need to install a new software program. While this installation in a large office is usually done by a computer technician, you may be responsible for doing so in a small office or on your home computer. Your first step is to locate the installation disk, which may be a series of floppies or a CD-ROM. You insert the disk into your floppy disk drive or the CD-ROM into the CD drive. The next step varies from one operating system to another. Usually, once you have started the installation program, the program takes over, asking questions as necessary and periodically prompting you to insert additional disks. The point for you to understand here is that your computer is communicating with the operating system in installing the applications software.

Another example of how you might communicate with the operating system as an office professional is in installing add-ins on your software package. Assume that you have Microsoft Excel® on Windows 95; you want to create and generate printed reports through Excel. You must install the View and Report Manager Add-Ins. To do so, you choose Tools and Add-Ins. The Add-Ins dialog box appears; see Figure 4-5. Then select Report Manager and View Manager from the Add-Ins Available list. Choose OK; the Report Manager and View Manager commands are added to the view menu. In adding these features, the operating system, Windows 95, has assisted you.

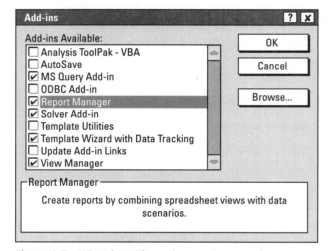

Figure 4-5　When installing software, the operating system is engaged.

To watch your operating system in action, go to a computer now and turn it on. The initial words that you see on your screen such as "hard disk installed" and "floppy disk installed" are your operating system at work. It is controlling the **booting** (the computer finding the operating system on disk and loading it) of the computer and getting it ready to receive the

software applications package you will be using. As the operating system completes its work, a screen will appear for you to use in telling your software what you want to do. If the screen has pictures on it, you have a Windows or an OS/2 Warp operating system. If you must give the screen commands, you have a DOS, a disk operating system.

Take a moment to review; give your answers in the space provided to the items given in Self Check A.

Self Check A

1. What is the purpose of an operating system?

2. Explain the difference between a DOS and a Windows operating environment?

3. Which operating system do you have on the computer you are using in class?

4. What are the three main functions of an operating system?

Check your answers with those at the end of this chapter. If you did not do well, reread the information before going on to the next section.

Chapter 3 and this chapter to this point have helped you learn about two topics that are essential to your understanding of a computer, which are:

- Hardware—The type of machinery and accessories you will be using and the basics of how these tools work.

- Operating system—The essential program that makes the computer run.

Now you are going to learn about applications software—the individual programs that let you accomplish what you intend to do with the computer: producing reports, letters, and newsletters, merging mailing lists, preparing envelopes, and preparing statistical data.

APPLICATIONS SOFTWARE

Several types of applications software are commonly used by the office professional, and new software packages are produced frequently. However, once you become proficient on one type of applications software, you will find it relatively easy to change to another software package as many of the concepts are the same or similar. For example, if you have learned how to move sections of text from one point in a document to another point by using Word-Perfect for DOS, you can quickly learn how to move text using Microsoft Word and Windows. The instructions vary, but the concept is the same. You should never be afraid to learn a new software package, and you should keep current on what is on the market.

WORD PROCESSING

The most commonly used applications software for the office professional is word processing. Word processing allows you to create letters, memorandums, reports, and numerous other documents quickly. You may produce complex documents with tables and graphics, revise the documents extensively, and print a quality product with relative ease. You may insert, delete, and rearrange text without rekeying. Word processing software has greatly improved the productivity of office professionals and has become a standard feature of the computer workstation.

Each package has its own unique features. Through word processing, the office professional can

- **create** (compose a document either by the office professional or by the employer, who then gives the document to the office professional to key);

- **edit** (make changes in a document to correct errors or improve the content of the document);

- **format** (adjust the appearance of the document by adding tabs, columns, bullets, numbering, paragraphs, and so forth);

- **store** (place the document on the hard drive or on a floppy);

- **print** (print out a paper copy of the document).

Some specialized features of word processing packages include:

- checking spelling automatically as information is input or upon the completion of a document

- creating bulleted lists and borders

- creating resumes, newsletters, and reports by using **templates** (predesigned, ready-to-use documents into which you put your own information)

- copying files, worksheets, tables, and charts from one application to another

- sending files through electronic mail

- highlighting important parts of a document with a color background (Notice Figure 4-6 which illustrates highlighting.)

- adding graphics and tables to the body of the document

- preparing envelopes and labels

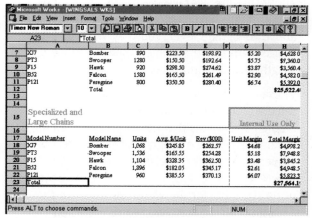

Figure 4-6   Highlighted document.

TECHNOLOGY TIP

To keep current on the software packages available, read computer periodicals such as *PC World, Byte,* and *InfoWorld* and check the Internet for information.

Chapter 4: Using Software

- displaying and printing characters in a variety of typefaces and sizes and using boldfacing, underlining, and italics

- automatically centering text, aligning the right margin, and justifying margins so that characters line up on the left as well as the right

- printing **headers** and **footers** (specified text at the top or bottom of the page)

- formatting footnotes and endnotes

- incorporating lines, boxes, and pictures within a document

- printing envelopes and mailing labels

Other features of word processing programs or add-on features which may be part of the package or added on include:

- Grammar and Style Programs. A grammar program can help you with your writing. For example, it can report possible problems such as passive verbs, pronoun errors, punctuation errors, jargon, and double negatives. The program allows you to review the error and suggestions made and then decide whether to change the text. You can even ask for a further explanation of the grammar rule. Grammar and style programs can also show overall readability of writing, sentence length, and word complexity. For example, we know that the average reading level is tenth grade. If you have written a document that is above this grade level, you may want to use words with fewer syllables and/or reduce the length of your sentences.

- Thesaurus Programs. A **thesaurus** is a book of selected words that mean the same thing (synonyms) and words that have opposite meanings (antonyms). Such a program gives you access to a powerful vocabulary electronically, as shown in Figure 4-7. For example, assume that you want to use a synonym for the word "second." In the Meanings dialog box, two words are listed—"next" or "moment," with a definition of "next" listed on the right. You can also look up new words—related or unrelated to the original word—or go back to a word you looked up earlier.

- Language Programs. These programs allow you to change the text to another language available on the program. Usually, several languages are available on each program.

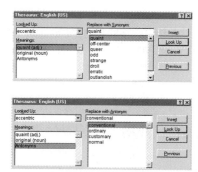

Figure 4-7   A thesaurus program gives you access to a powerful electronic vocabulary.

INTEGRATED SOFTWARE

Integrated software is a set of software that typically includes several applications within one program. Integrated packages that are used extensively include "suites" of software. These suites are special **bundles** (a software group with different functions packaged together) of software that include a word processing program and a spreadsheet program as a minimum. They may also include database management, electronic calendars, presentation/graphics, and networking programs. The programs are integrated; you can move contextual matter from one program to another quickly and easily. For example, if you are working on a word processing program, you can easily add graphics and spreadsheets to your document with integrated software.

Some of the packages available are:

- Microsoft Office 95
- Microsoft Office 97
- Lotus SmartSuite®
- Perfect Office from Novell®

SPREADSHEETS

In its simplest terms, a **spreadsheet** is a grid of rows and columns in which you enter numbers and text. With spreadsheet programs, mathematical calculations are done by the computer. Basically, a spreadsheet works in this manner. You begin by entering the raw data in the spreadsheet with formulas that indicate the types of calculations you need. For example, assume that your employer asks you to total the amount of sales of modular office units for the last six months and project the sales for the next five years using a 5 percent increase in the first year, a 6 percent increase in the second

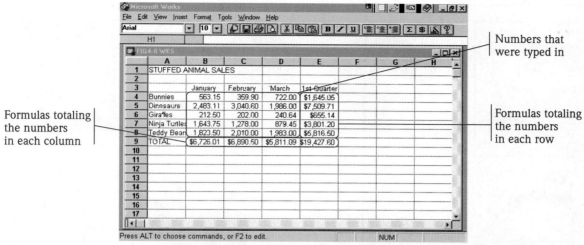

Figure 4-8   With a spreadsheet program, mathematical calculations are done by the computer.

year, and an 8 percent increase in the third through the fifth year. This fairly complex problem can be done quickly by using a spreadsheet program. The spreadsheet program will compute the projections for you after you tell the program what percentage to use in the projection. Spreadsheet programs are the computer world's number crunchers.

Now consider another advantage of a spreadsheet program. Assume that your employer has a change of mind and asks that you calculate a 6 percent increase in the first year and a 4 percent increase in the next four years. You can change the values easily and the program will recalculate the figures. Notice Figure 4-8 which shows a table done on a spreadsheet program.

The size of the spreadsheet can be quite large. Most spreadsheets contain at least 256 columns and 8,192 rows. What appears on the screen at any one time is only a small portion of the "page," usually about 8 columns and 20 rows. The work area is a movable window, which you can move sideways as well as up and down.

In addition to the spreadsheet programs that are on suites such as Microsoft Office 97, numerous other spreadsheet packages are available, including Lotus 1-2-3, Quattro Pro®, and Excel. These spreadsheets are available for both Windows and DOS operating systems.

GRAPHICS

Graphics programs allow you to show words, numbers, and data in the form of pictures. You can create the following types of artwork without being an expert:

- full-color illustrations
- headlines
- charts and graphs
- slides
- animation sequences
- logos

Once the art is created, you can modify it easily and use it in several different ways. Graphics programs produce art either by mathematical formulas called **algorithms** or by dots. If the program uses algorithms, it is called a drawing program; if the program uses dots, it is called a paint program. Both programs have certain advantages.

Drawing Programs

Drawing programs, which use algorithms, have the following advantages. They will:

- print at the highest possible **resolution** (clarity of output);
- require less room for storing a picture than a paint program picture;
- allow ease of editing.

Figure 4-9 Clip art may be used to illustrate concepts.

Paint Programs

Paint programs, which use dots, have the following advantages. They enable you to:

- control the dots, which allows for detailed editing;
- produce lifelike realism.

If you do not want to draw the illustration, you may use **clip art.** Clip art consists of illustrations that are already provided with the software package. Some examples of clip art are given in Figure 4-9.

A field that for more than a decade has used computer graphics is the **CAD/CAM**—computer-aided design/computer-aided manufacturing—field. Computers are used in this field to create three-dimensional pictures (as opposed to two-dimensional pictures which is what most graphics programs offer) of everything from toys to tools to automobiles. CAD programs allow draftspeople, architects, engineers, and technical illustrators to design with great precision. CAD programs are expensive, however, costing thousands of dollars rather than hundreds of dollars which is common for other graphics packages.

There are a number of advantages to using graphics to present data. Graphics generally can hold the attention of the reader, or any audience, more than information that is presented only in words and figures. Pictures attract and hold the eye. Also, a graph or chart can easily show a trend that may be lost in long columns of numbers. Figure 4-10 shows a color graphic.

Once you have created your document using an illustration, you very likely will want to print the document in color. If your image is to be printed on a printing press, you need to create a piece of film for each color. For example, if you are using four-color printing, you would have a film for each of the four colors. The major graphics programs allow you to create color separations, but producing the color can be difficult. Your monitor uses a different color system than the print shop color system. To get the right color is a process of trial and error; that is, seeing the results and adjusting the color as needed.

If you do not need four-color printing, you may use an easier system called **spot color.** At most art stores, you can buy a swatch book with different shades of color numbered according to a standardized Pantone® matching system (PMS) color. With a graphics program, you can specify the PMS color and be certain that the colors you see in the swatch book will match the printed piece exactly. The drawback with spot color is that you can produce only a few colors—you cannot show subtle hues of each color.

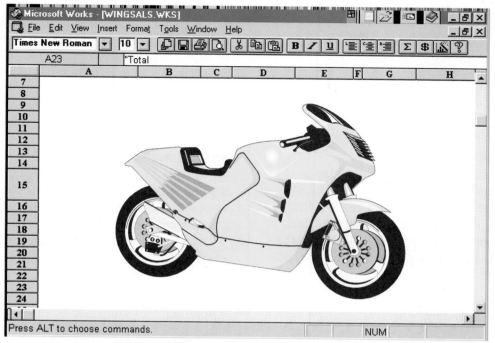

Figure 4-10   Color graphics can help the reader retain the message being delivered by the presenter.

Some of the graphics programs available are

- Adobe™ Illustrator™
- AutoCAD®
- CorelDRAW™
- Painter®

PRESENTATIONS

Presentation software allows you to use 35mm slides, flip charts, overhead transparencies, and animation with sound in presenting material. In using presentation software, you should use good presentation techniques such as the Rule of Threes.

- Tell your audience what you are going to tell them.
- Tell them.
- Tell them again what you have already told them.

You will learn more about presentation techniques in Chapter 9.

With presentation software, you can enhance your presentation by

- creating slides;
- adding company logos to slides;
- bulleting charts;
- presenting line, bar, and organization charts;
- creating color overhead transparencies;
- creating 35mm slides, using a film recorder (which is expensive), or sending the slides to a service bureau for completion;
- presenting electronic presentations by using a laptop computer and presenting on a large screen in color;
- adding sound, animation, and video clips.

Presentation software allows you to use 35mm slides.
Polaroid Corporation.

Presentation software packages available include:

- Adobe Persuasion®
- Harvard Graphics® for Windows
- PowerPoint®
- Presentations® for Windows
- Freelance Graphics® for Windows

DATABASE MANAGEMENT

A **database management program** helps you organize data in a way that allows fast and easy access to it. The program acts as an efficient filing system and an organizer of multiple types of data. For example, some of the questions that a database program can answer quickly and efficiently for businesses include:

- What was the company's best-selling product this year?
- How many customers does the company have in Japan?
- What is the inventory of a certain type of desk?
- How many applicants are interviewing for each job posting within the company?

The information needed to answer these questions may be in the computer, but it may be in spreadsheet packages, word processing packages, or even in hard copy in a file drawer. A database program enables a business to store all types of information in one central location.

Consider, for example, how an ice cream distributor may use a database program. The distributor can quickly create reports on sales to understand how each flavor of ice cream is selling and in what regions and what stores. The distributor can also look at sales by the month, the quarter, the year, or against the forecast of sales. Employees' hours can be tracked to be certain that they do not work too much overtime. Stock can be tracked so that products are available when the customer wants it.

A database program allows you to:

- locate previously entered data;
- change or delete existing data;
- select portions of data for special purposes;
- arrange data into different sequences, such as alphabetic or geographic order;
- produce reports and other printed output.

Database programs come in two basic varieties—personal data manager and programmable data managers. Personal data managers are easy-to-use programs designed to let you relate files, join two data files, record **macros** (a series of keystrokes, commands, and mouse actions that can be played back using a special key combination), and so forth. Learning a personal data manager is relatively simple; however, learning to use a programmable data manager program is demanding. You can expect to spend several days in getting started. If the process is going to be too demanding, your company may want to find a customized database package or hire a programmer to design one.

Database management programs include:

- AceFile™
- Alpha Four™
- Approach® for Windows
- FileMaker Pro for Windows®

Programmable database software includes:

- Access™
- dBase IV®
- FoxPro®—for DOS and Windows
- Paradox® for Windows

PERSONAL INFORMATION MANAGEMENT

Personal information management (PIM) software allows you to organize, track, sort, and file information related to your work. It allows you to organize your day by:

- keeping your calendar
- scheduling appointments
- managing your to-do list
- establishing ticker files
- finding phone numbers
- keeping address lists
- tracking business expenses
- keeping notes through a notepad which stores text and graphics
- accessing e-mail and messaging directories
- sharing calendars and information with other employees
- computing basic mathematical calculations

- keeping files on customers
- keeping track of your employer's schedule

   PIM software includes:

- Microsoft's Schedule Plus®
- Lotus Organizer®
- Symantec's ACT™

DESKTOP PUBLISHING

Desktop publishing allows an organization to quickly and easily produce newsletters, brochures, sales documents, booklets, and company periodicals. Today, however, word processing programs have many of the same features that desktop publishing programs have. It may not be necessary for the office professional to have a desktop publishing program; and, in fact, most office professionals will not need this capability. However, if you are working in an organization that has complex layout and color reproduction needs, desktop publishing can be the answer. Here are a few of the advantages of desktop publishing over a word processing program.

- Place multiple graphics on one page or flow text across discontinuous areas.

- Precise control over font size, type placement, and spacing between letters and lines is possible.

- Greater control with color printing is possible.

- Better management of complex, book-length projects is possible.

If a company does not have the expertise or the desire to prepare the final document in-house, the company may use desktop publishing to get documents **camera-ready** (ready to be photographed or photocopied) for printing by an outside printing company. Camera-ready copy can save a company considerable money in the printing process. Figure 4-11 depicts how a document may be prepared in-house and printed in-house on a laser printer or **outsourced** (sent outside the company) to a printer for preparing the final copy through the typesetting process.

Desktop publishing software available includes:

- PageMaker®
- QuarkXPress®
- Ventura Publisher™
- FrameMaker™

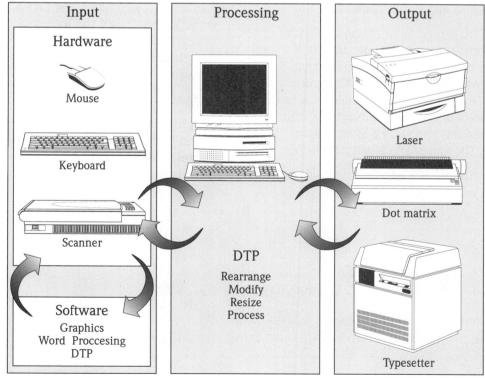

Figure 4-11   Desktop publishing process.

COMMUNICATIONS

Software that allows two or more users to communicate with each other is referred to as **communications software.** Communications software serves as the intermediary between the computer and the modem. For example, it lets you tell your modem what and when to dial, send messages to the computer on the other end of the phone line, and send and receive files. Through communications software you are able to access online services such as CompuServe®, America Online℠, and Prodigy®. You are also able to access the Internet and thus World Wide Web and other data sources available through the Internet.

Through these online services and the Internet, you can:

- Send e-mail, fax, and voice mail. Individuals within a business or across the world can communicate with each other through e-mail, voice mail, or fax machines.

- Make travel plans. Any person can have direct access to airline schedules and fares through the use of communications software. The software reports on the airline's on-time performance, uses a personalized profile to sort through flights and seating arrangements, and summarizes travel arrangements. You can also make hotel and car rental reservations and find restaurants.

- Do research. You can get information on a variety of topics. Government and legal documents, including bills currently before Congress, state and federal laws, and U.S. Supreme Court decisions are available. Other data available include the entire Library of Congress card catalog, information on museums such as the Smithsonian, and Webster's Dictionary and Roget's Thesaurus.

- Read wire service news. Up-to-date news is available from the wire services.

- Get access to a **bulletin board system (BBS).** A BBS is a computer with a modem and a reasonably large hard disk that acts as a repository for files and messages. Most BBSs run 24 hours a day; you can call whenever you need to or have the most free time. The person who owns the bulletin board is called the **system operator (sysop).** In most cases, you use a bulletin board to leave mail, to send and receive files, and to participate in ongoing conferences. Some BBSs are open to the general public; others are available only to people in a particular field. You can often find bulletin board listings in computer magazines.

- Get technical assistance. You can get advice from other users, which may be superior to what you can get at conferences, on how to handle certain technological problems.

MULTIMEDIA

Multimedia applies to a number of applications that extend the audio and video capabilities of a computer. For example, here are some things that you can do with multimedia.

- Attach voice messages to e-mail. To hear the message, the recipient clicks on the message icon.

- Produce videos.

- Run interactive training and presentation software. Such software can include animation, narration, and video sequences which you have previously learned about in the section on presentation software.

- Produce interactive materials.

To produce interactive materials, multimedia authoring software is necessary. Through these packages, you can mix text, graphics, animation, digitized sound and video clips, and music soundtracks.

COMMUNICATION TIP

Never write an e-mail message that could be personally or professionally embarrassing. No e-mail is immune from prying eyes.

Multimedia packages allow for even more sophistication in presentations than do presentation packages, because you can add sound, animation, music, and video. You can deliver your presentation in a nonlinear format to help the audience understand and retain your message. To understand what nonlinear means in this context, consider this example.

Assume that your employer is presenting information about the newest international office which has recently opened in Korea. Information is given about the size of the office, the number of employees, and the projected sales for the first year through graphs. While presenting this information in the form of graphs, your employer may click to another slide or screen in response to a question from the audience about the location of the office in Korea. There might be a series of pictures of the office and the surrounding environs. Later in the presentation, there may be an audio statement from the president of the Korean office.

Through both audio and video images, the audience's attention can be held and the information retained longer than through only an audio or audio and graphics presentation. The following photo depicts a multimedia presentation.

Multimedia programs include:

- Authorware® Professional for Windows
- IconAuthor® for Windows
- Multimedia Grasp™
- Multimedia ToolBook™

ADDITIONAL SPECIALIZED SOFTWARE

Numerous specialized software packages are available, including:

- accounting
- document management
- facility management

With multimedia, you can add sound, animation, music, and video to your presentations. *Courtesy of International Business Machines, Inc.*

- financial applications
- mail handling
- sales management
- workflow productivity

These packages allow companies to utilize computers to assist in specialized operations. For example, consider how a mail handling package works. The post office estimates that one-third of all mail is undeliverable as addressed.[1] Based on the expense of nondeliverable mail, many companies

[1]Malik, Mary S., "The Hard Facts on Mailroom Software," *Managing Office Technology* (April, 1995).

COMMUNICATION TIP

Effective presentations engage as many senses as possible. The sense of sight and sound as well as a variety of presentation aids, movement, and color are important considerations in helping the audience to retain the information presented.

Chapter 4: Using Software

are deciding they must keep their mailing lists up to date. Address correction software can effectively perform this task. Other functions of mailing software include:

- Combining mailing lists
- Verifying addresses and adding Zip+4 codes
- Determining the correct postage to be used
- Tracking and charging back postal and shipping charges to the appropriate departments within the business
- Reporting on copier use
- Collating, inserting, and labeling materials

Numerous specialized personal programs are also available. For example, you may use a financial package at home which allows you to pay your monthly bills, balance your checkbook, and record items and amounts that are deductible on your income tax.

TROUBLESHOOTING

As you work with both computer hardware and software, problems are going to occur. One of your tasks as an office professional is to be able to solve as many of your problems as possible. You need to become adept at troubleshooting. Software packages have a manual which can assist you. Specific examples are given on various problems, with tips to help you solve the problem. If the manual you received from the vendor is not adequate for you, purchase detailed manuals in your local bookstore or computer store.

Here are some general suggestions for troubleshooting.

- Know how your system works.
- Understand enough about your operating system to start the system and run a program.
- Know how the software you use should function.
- Learn to recognize text, visual, and audible clues that indicate potential problems.
- Become familiar with your program manual; keep it handy for reference purposes.
- Have patience; be willing to learn.

- Know what assistance is available to you within the company. Is a computer technician available who can help you? If not, is there an office professional who is extremely competent on the package you are using?
- Does the software company provide assistance? If so, what number do you call?

When you begin a new task, be certain you:

- Understand the task at hand. Are you trying to merge files, print color, or insert graphics?
- Know how to accomplish the task.
- Can identify the problem if one occurs. Ask: Has it ever happened before? If so, what did you do to "fix" the problem previously?

Check your manual for specific troubleshooting tips. For example, here are some troubleshooting suggestions which appear in *Using Microsoft Office for Windows 95.*

I have several lines of text that overflow to the second page of my document, but I would like them to be on the first page.

Click the Shrink to Fit button in the Preview toolbar. Magnify the document and look carefully at the changes in the text spacing and sizing. You may prefer to undo the change if the text appears to be too crowded on one page.

I have trouble setting the margins for the document with the ruler in Print Preview.

Choose File, Page Setup, and choose the Margins tab. You can type a measurement in the dialog box for the margins you want to change.

I tried to print a document and I didn't get an error message, but I don't see my document in my printer.

Verify that the correct printer is selected in the Name drop-down list box of the Print dialog box. Make sure that your printer is turned on and plugged in, and that you have paper in the printer.

To test your knowledge of the information you have been studying, respond to the items in Self Check B. Use the space provided. Once you have finished, check your answers by referring to the answers at the conclusion of the chapter.

SOFTWARE SELECTION

In addition to being knowledgeable about a particular software package and able to use that package well, you may be asked to select or have input into the selection of software your company plans to use. Here are some questions you should ask when selecting software or upgrading your software.

- Do you have the hardware requirements for the software? Do you have the memory and storage capacity needed? For example, if the program requires 8MB RAM and 50MB of hard drive space, do you have that space on your computer?

- What software support is available? Support may be in the form of tutorials (tutorials may be built into the software package or there may be a separate disk of tutorials), training sessions provided by the vendor, and/or hotline assistance. Figure 4-12 illustrates a tutorial screen.

- What documentation is available? The program should have an instruction manual that is well organized and easy to read. An index, a glossary of terms, a quick reference guide, illustrations, and examples are helpful. Visual clarity is a mark of effective documentation. There should be ample white space, pictures, and examples so that you have no trouble following the written text.

- Is the program **user friendly** (easy to understand and follow)? In answering that question, some items you should check include:

  a. Is the menu organized well and easy to understand?

  b. Are the commands logical and easy to remember? The fewer keystrokes a command takes, the better.

  c. Does the help screen really provide the help needed? The commands for displaying the help screen should be easy to remember, and the displays themselves should be easy to read. Does the help screen stay on at the top of the screen while you execute the instructions?

- Does the program offer what you need? For example, does it offer graphics? automatic correction of spelling? the ability to key a help request in your own words? an address book that manages contacts for envelopes, labels, mail merges, and connects to schedule information?

- If it has a graphics package, does the graphics package require a color monitor?

- Does the program automatically save your document to a hard disk at periodic intervals? This feature can save you considerable anguish in case of power failure or a careless move on your part.

- Is the software seller known for providing good service? You certainly may have trouble with a package after purchasing it. Will the seller assist you? Will the seller replace the software if it does not work correctly?

- Does the company who produced the software have a good reputation? Does the company provide a telephone help service?

- What is the reputation of the software? You can check with individuals who have used the software. You can also read reviews in computer periodicals such as *PC World, Byte, InfoWorld, PC Novice,* and *PC Today.*

- Will there be conversion costs? Do you have old files that must be converted to the new software? Is conversion possible, or must the files be rekeyed? Is the software compatible with other programs you use?

- How much does the software cost? Will there be productivity improvements as a result of using the software? You should do an analysis of the costs and productivity improvements before purchasing the software. How frequently is the software revised and how much do upgrades cost?

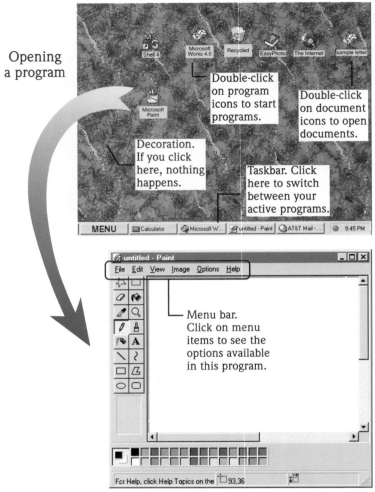

Opening
a program

Double-click
on program
icons to start
programs.

Double-click
on document
icons to open
documents.

Decoration.
If you click
here, nothing
happens.

Taskbar. Click
here to switch
between your
active programs.

Menu bar.
Click on menu
items to see the
options available
in this program.

Figure 4-12 Tutorials can assist you when learning a new software package.

- Are you going to be working with others in the office? If so, standard word processing documents will be essential. It will be necessary for you to talk with these individuals and agree on a package that will serve all of your needs.

SOFTWARE AND COMPUTER CARE

Once you have selected and purchased your software, you must take appropriate care of it. In addition, it is essential that your computer be maintained. Here are some suggestions for you in performing these functions.

SOFTWARE CARE

When working with floppy disks, you need to store and protect them properly. Carelessness can destroy untold hours of work on a floppy disk. You should always do the following:

COMMUNICATION TIP

When determining what software to use within the office, remember to get the input of others who will be using the package.

- When labeling the disk, write on the adhesive label before applying it to the disk cover. Remove old labels on a disk before applying a new label.

- Store the 3.5-inch disk in a specially designed container. Such containers keep the disks free of dust and smoke particles. One smoke particle on the surface of a disk can cause problems for the disk drive read head.

- Magnets can erase information on floppy disks, so keep them away from disks. Keep paper clips away from disks also.

- Do not store disks close to a telephone. A ringing telephone can create a magnetic field.

- Keep floppy disks away from water and other liquids. Dry them with a lint-free cloth if they should get wet.

- Keep floppy disks out of direct sunlight and away from radiators and other sources of heat.

- Write-protect a disk if it contains data that you do not want changed. On 3.5-inch disks, there is a tiny latch in the upper-right corner, which is usually closed. To write-protect the disk turn the disk over and slide the latch downward so that a small window appears in the corner of the disk.

COMPUTER CARE

Here are some tips for keeping your computer in good working order.

- Turn the monitor off when it is not being used for a long period. Most screens now have screen savers which automatically turn the monitor off if it is not used for a long period of time.

- Keep your computer clean. Dust is a problem because it causes heat buildup in the components it covers. Every so often, vacuum every horizontal surface of your computer, giving the vents special consideration.

- Keep the keyboard clean. If you need to clean the surface, put the cleaning solution on a cleaning rag and wipe the surface. Do not spray the keyboard. The best procedure is to purchase a can of compressed air to spray between the keys to remove dust. Tiny computer vacuums which are specially designed for this task can also be purchased.

- Keep the mouse clean. Use alcohol on a cotton swab to wipe the rollers. The ball inside the mouse should be cleaned with lukewarm, soapy water and dried thoroughly.

- Cover the entire computer when it is not being used for a long period. System covers (be certain you know what type of computer you have) are available from computer stores.

- Do not have food or drink near your computer. A spill of a soda or crumbs getting inside the keyboard most likely means a costly visit from a computer repairperson.

- Periodically, turn off the monitor and wipe your screen clean with a static free cleaner.

- Do not place a computer near an open window, in direct sunlight, or near a heater. Computers work best in cool temperatures, below 80°F.

- Do not smoke near a computer. Smoking adds tar and particle matter to the air. These particles can find their way into the computer.

- Periodically delete files you no longer need from your hard drive. If you think you might need the files at a later time, put them on a floppy disk. When you have purged your files, take a look at your directory structure. Having hundreds of files in one directory will slow the file-search process, which impairs the overall performance of your computer. Purge your directory also.

- Periodically defrag your drive with a **disk defragmenter**. A disk defragmenter is a utility that gathers the fragments of files that DOS has scattered across the surface of your hard disk and reassembles them, so that each file's data is contiguous (with no empty spaces between files). The defragging usually improves disk performance.

SECURITY PROCEDURES

Several steps can be taken to prevent theft or destruction of computer hardware or software. A few of these steps are listed here.

- Bolt down equipment or lock computer desks.

- **Back up** data by copying it and storing it in more than one place. Back up all material that is on the hard disk with a floppy disk.

- Invest in a surge suppressor. Fluctuations in current can damage or destroy your computer or its data. Surge suppressors come in all sizes, but you want one that is powerful enough to protect your computer. If your computer has communications capability, you want one that protects the phone/data line as well. The best suppressors have a UL 1449 rating of 330 volts.

- Invest in an uninterruptible power supply (UPS). UPSs are battery-powered boxes that give you enough power to safely shut down your system in case of a total blackout. They also protect against power surges and are a must for LAN servers and other computers where critical data is constantly updated.

- Frequently change the password or access code for individuals who have access to classified information. Figure 4-13 gives some do's and don'ts for selecting passwords.

- Password-protect your screen saver to keep your computer secure when you are away from your desk. A password prompt comes up when anyone touches your mouse or keyboard.

- Log off e-mail when you leave your desk. If you do not, anyone can read your private mail and send messages to other people in your name.

- Put confidential files in hidden directories. A hidden directory will not show up when you issue a DIR command, so only you will know where it is.

COMPUTER VIRUSES

A **computer virus** is a computer program with unauthorized instructions which are introduced without permission or knowledge of the computer user. It is called a virus because it is contagious. It can pass itself on to other programs in which it comes in contact. Viruses range from annoying but harmless creatures that pop up stupid messages on the screen to beasts that can trash all the data on your hard disk and crash your computer.

There are more than 2,000 known viruses, with new ones being born every day. Basically, viruses are of two different types.

- Boot sector viruses which reside on the part of your hard disk where the computer stores the files it needs to start up. These viruses become active each time you turn on your computer.

- Program infectors which attach themselves to any file that runs a program. These viruses are activated whenever the file is run. Program viruses can be contracted from floppies, electronic bulletin boards, and networks.

Do's and Don'ts for Selecting Passwords

Do

- Use passwords of seven characters or more.

- Change passwords often, every three months or so.

- Store a written copy of your password in a safe place, such as in a locked file cabinet away from your computer.

Don't

- Use your name or that of a family member.

- Use your phone number, street address, or other easily accessible personal information.

- Write your password on a post-it note stuck to your desk or file it in your Rolodex.

Figure 4-13

HUMAN RELATIONS TIP

Trustworthy behavior is always important in the office. Being trustworthy when working with computers means that careful attention is paid to computer care and security procedures. Being trustworthy also means keeping confidential information confidential.

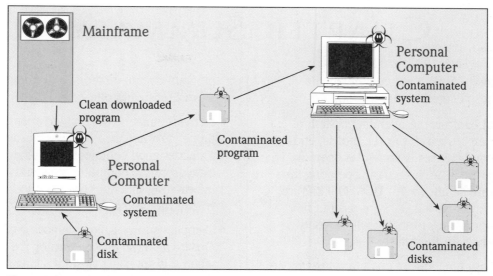

Figure 4-14   Infection from a computer virus.

Here is one example of how a computer can get a virus. A computer programmer inserts a few unauthorized instructions (either carelessly or maliciously) in a computer operating system program. The disk with the infected operating system is used and copied onto other files. The virus spreads to another disk, and the process is repeated. After the infected disk is copied a number of times, the virus can cause all data in the files affected to be erased. Notice Figure 4-14 which illustrates infection from a computer virus.

The first computer viruses crept into the world of computing in 1987. Since that time there has been a growing awareness of the need for security. Here are some suggestions on how to protect against viruses.

- Educate yourself about computer viruses.

- Make backups of your files immediately—before you have a virus. Backups are the single most important action you can take to protect against viral attack.

- **Download** only from sources you trust. Download means to receive a file from another source and transfer the information to your hard drive or receive a file via modem from a bulletin board or online service. Accept programs only from people you know and trust.

- Install an antiviral scanning program on your system. Check the options in the antivirus program to scan the hard drive during the boot process and to scan a floppy disk every time it is inserted into the system. This program will scan for viruses, letting you know if one exists.

- Ask the computer service professionals in your company to alert you when a new virus occurs; the information can be sent via e-mail.

- Do not allow programs to be loaded on your system without your authorization.

- Purchase all programs in tamper-proof packaging.

- Always boot from a write-protect disk.

- When you get a new program, write-protect the master disk before inserting it into a drive.

- When using bulletin boards and outside programs, use stand-alone computers only so that virus checks can be made routinely.

- Do not use unsolicited demo disks.

With proper care of your computer and your software, you will avoid time-consuming breakdowns, frustrations caused by the inability to get your work done, and loss of productivity.

CHAPTER SUMMARY

This summary will help you remember the important points covered in this chapter.

- Software that controls the operating system of your computer, keyboard, printer, mouse, and other peripheral devices is known as operating systems software. The three basic operating systems in use are Windows 95, DOS, OS/2 Warp. Windows NT and Novell DOS are used in networking systems; they probably will be used more extensively in the future.

- The three main functions of operating systems are to control computer system resources, execute computer programs, and manage data.

- Multiuser DOS is a multiuser, multitasking environment that allows multiple users to share a host PC with multiuser DOS software to perform multiple tasks.

- Applications software tells the computer how to perform specific tasks.

- Several types of applications software are available, including word processing, spreadsheets, graphics, database management, PIM software, desktop publishing, communications, presentation graphics, multimedia programs, integrated programs, and specialized programs.

- In selecting software, numerous items are to be taken into consideration, including hardware requirements for the software, support available, program documentation, user friendliness, vendor service, cost, and office needs.

- Software must be maintained appropriately. Proper maintenance includes storing disks in specially designed containers, keeping food and drink away from the computer area, and protecting information that does not need to be changed with write-protect tabs.

- Computers must be kept in good working order. Tips for doing so include turning the monitor off when it is not being used for a long period, keeping the keyboard clean, placing the computer properly in the workspace, not smoking next to the computer, periodically deleting files on the hard drive, and backing up files on a floppy disk when needed.

- Steps that can be taken to prevent theft of the computer and software include bolting down equipment or locking desks, backing up data, using a surge protector, and frequently changing the individual's password or access code.

- A computer virus is a computer program with unauthorized instructions. To protect against viruses, educate yourself about computer viruses, back up files immediately, download only from trustworthy sources, install an antiviral scanning program, do not allow programs to be loaded on your system without proper authorization, boot from a write-protect disk, and do not use unsolicited demo disks.

CHAPTER GLOSSARY

The following terms were introduced in this chapter. To help you review, definitions are given here.

- **Operating systems software** (p. 81)–Software that controls the operating systems of your computer, keyboard, printer, mouse, and other peripheral devices. It enables your computer to read and write data to a disk, send pictures to your monitor, and accept keyboard commands.

- **Windows 95** (p. 81)–Operating system that uses a graphical interface. System produced by Microsoft.

- **DOS** (p. 82)–A disk operating system produced by IBM which uses a command-driven system rather than an icon driver system such as Windows 95.

- **OS/2 Warp** (p. 83)–An operating system that uses a graphical interface. System produced by IBM.

- **Windows NT** (p. 83)–Microsoft's high-end alternative to Windows. Currently used most extensively on network servers.

- **Network servers** (p. 83)–Any computer that shares its hard drive with the network.

- **Novell DOS** (p. 83)–An MS-DOS compatible operating system that includes networking and multitasking.

- **MS-DOS** (p. 83)–Microsoft disk operating system.

- **Booting** (p. 84)–The computer finding the operating system on disk and loading it.

- **Create** (p. 85)–Compose a document which may be done by the office professional or the employer.

- **Edit** (p. 85)–Make changes in a document to correct errors or improve the content of the document.

- **Format** (p. 85)–Adjust the appearance of the document by adding tabs, columns, bullets, numbering, paragraphs, bolding, italics, and so forth.

- **Store** (p. 85)–Place the document on the hard drive or on a floppy.

- **Print** (p. 85)–Print out a paper copy of the document.

- **Templates** (p. 85)–Predesigned, ready-to-use documents into which you put your information.

- **Headers and footers** (p. 86)–Specified text at the top or bottom of a page.

- **Thesaurus** (p. 86)–A book of selected words that mean the same thing (synonyms) and words that have opposite meanings (antonyms).

- **Integrated software** (p. 86)–A set of software that typically includes several applications within one program.

- **Bundles** (p. 86)–A software group with different functions packaged together.

- **Spreadsheet** (p. 86)–A grid of rows and columns in which you enter numbers and text.

- **Algorithms** (p. 87)–Mathematical formulas.

- **Resolution** (p. 87)–Clarity of output.

- **Clip art** (p. 88)–Illustrations that are provided with the software package.

- **CAD/CAM** (p. 88)–Computer-aided design/computer-aided manufacturing.

- **Spot color** (p. 88)–Placing color in particular locations on an illustration; used in graphics.

- **Database management program** (p. 90)–A program that helps you organize data in a way that allows fast and easy access to it.

- **Macros** (p. 90)–A series of keystrokes, commands, and mouse actions that can be played back using a special key combination.

- **Personal information management (PIM)** (p. 90)–Software that allows you to organize, track, sort, and file information related to your work.

- **Camera-ready** (p. 91)–Material ready to be photocopied or photographed and then printed.

- **Outsourced** (p. 91)–Sending services that need to be performed outside the company to another vendor or company—one that specializes in the work to be performed.

- **Communications software** (p. 92)–Software that allows two or more users to communicate with each other.

- **Bulletin board system (BBS)** (p. 92)–A computer connected to a modem and a reasonably large hard disk that acts as a repository for files and messages.

- **System operator (sysop)** (p. 92)–A person who owns the BBS.

- **User friendly** (p. 95)–Programs that are easy to understand and follow.

- **Disk defragmenter** (p. 97)–A utility that gathers the fragments of files that DOS has scattered across the surface of your hard disk and reassembles them so that each file's data is contiguous.

- **Back up** (p. 97)–Copying data from one disk to another—from the hard drive to a floppy is a common backup method.

- **Computer virus** (p. 98)–A computer program with unauthorized instructions which are introduced without permission or knowledge of the computer user.

- **Download** (p. 99)–Receive a file from another source and transfer the information to your hard drive or receive a file via modem from a bulletin board or online service.

101

DISCUSSION ITEMS

These discussion items provide an opportunity for you to test your understanding of the chapter through discussion with your classmates and your instructor.

1. Name and explain five operating systems.
2. List five features of a word processing package.
3. Explain a thesaurus program and how it is used.
4. Give five questions that you should ask before selecting software.
5. What steps can you take to help prevent theft or destruction of computer hardware and software and data?
6. What is a computer virus? List five ways in which you may protect against a virus.

CASE STUDY

Koronet International is considering purchasing an integrated software package for the company. This package will be used in all locations, both nationally and internationally. You have been asked by Ms. Marquette to chair a committee to recommend the software package to be purchased. Ms. Marquette wants you to recommend who will be on the committee. Then, she has asked that the committee outline the process they will be using in selecting the software. She wants to approve both the committee and the software selection process before the actual work of recommending the software begins.

Select four members of your class to work with you on this project. Prepare answers to the following questions for your employer.

COMMITTEE PROCESS

1. How many members will be on the committee?
2. What criteria will you use in selecting individuals for the committee?
3. What departments or divisions of the company will be represented on the committee?
4. What will be the duration of the project?
5. How often will the committee meet?

6. Will international members be represented on the committee? If so, how will the meetings be structured?
7. What are the expectations of the committee?

SOFTWARE SELECTION PROCESS

1. What are the goals of the committee?
2. Are there guidelines that need to be followed? If so, what are they?
3. When will the recommendation be made? What format will be used in making the recommendation?
4. How will the recommendation be communicated? Is it to be communicated to individuals other than your employer?

Prepare the answers to the committee process questions in a memorandum to Ms. Marquette. Next, assume that the committee process was approved by Ms. Marquette. Prepare the answers to the software selection process in a memorandum to Ms. Marquette. The memos are to be done as a team; all team members' names should appear on the memorandums. Use the memo form on the Student Data Template Disk, file CS4. Turn in both memos to your instructor.

RESPONSES TO SELF CHECKS

SELF CHECK A

1. What is the purpose of an operating system?

   The operating system is the foundation for whatever software package you are using; without it the computer will not accept the commands you give it. An operating system is a program that enables your computer to read and write data to a disk, send pictures to your monitor, and accept keyboard commands.

2. Explain the difference between a DOS and a Windows operating environment?

   A Windows operating system uses a graphical user interface (GUI), a device that uses drop-down menus and various icons for executing commands and choosing program options. DOS uses a command-driven interface, meaning that whenever you want the computer to perform an operation you need to key in a command. There are no visual cues; you must either memorize the commands or look them up when you need them.

3. Which operating system do you have on the computer you are using in class? (If you did not know, you should have checked the computer.)

4. What are the three main functions of an operating system?

   The three main functions of an operating system are to:

   control computer system resources

   execute computer programs

   manage data

SELF CHECK B

1. What is integrated software?

   Integrated software is a set of software that typically includes several applications within one program. Integrated packages that are used extensively include "suites" of software. These suites are special bundles of software that include a word processing program and a spreadsheet program as a minimum. They may also include database management, electronic calendars, presentation/graphics, and networking programs.

2. What is the difference between graphics and presentation software?

   Graphics programs allow you to show words, numbers, and data in the form of pictures. Presentation software allows you to use 35mm slides, flip charts, overhead transparencies, and animation with sound in presenting material.

3. Define and explain how communications software is used.

   Communications software allows two or more users to communicate with each other. It serves as the intermediary between the computer and the modem. Through communications software, you are able to access online services such as CompuServe, America Online, and Prodigy. You are also able to access the Internet and the World Wide Web.

OFFICE TASKS

OFFICE TASK 4-1 (Objectives 1, 3, and 5)

With four other members of your class, visit a software store.

- Determine what operating systems are used most extensively at the present.

- Check out the types of software packages available for word processing, spreadsheet, graphics,

and desktop publishing. Also, check to see what integrated packages are available.

Do additional research by browsing the Internet and reading current computer periodicals seeking answers to the same items listed above.

Present your findings orally to the class.

OFFICE TASK 4-2 (Objective 2)

Troubleshoot the following situations using the manual that accompanies your software package. Summarize the steps that you took in a memorandum to your instructor. Use the memorandum form on Student Data Template Disk, file OT4-2.

1. The words in my document are quite large, but they don't print large.
2. Suddenly, I am lost. I guess I accidentally hit a key that I did not intend to or my mouse slipped. I need to get back to where I was in my document.
3. I can't select or change my bulleted or numbered characters.
4. I only want one line bulleted, not all of them.
5. I inserted a graphic but only part of it is there.

OFFICE TASK 4-3 (Objective 4)

With four members of your class, visit the computer services department at your school and interview the manager of the department. Ask the individual these questions:

1. How would you recommend caring for software and hardware?

2. Do you use virus protection devices? If so, what are they?
3. Do you use security precautions to help prevent theft of hardware, data, and software? If so, what are they?

Report your findings orally to the class.

OFFICE TASK 4-4 (Objective 5)

Ms. Marquette is on vacation, and the Human Resources Department needs help; you have volunteered. You are given a portion of the Human Resources Policy and Procedures Manual. You need to make the changes noted in the copy and keyboard the remainder of the document; a portion of the document is already on a disk. Load the Student Data Template Disk, file OT4-4. Key the remainder of the document, using the copy that is given on pages 105–106. Proofread the document. Print one copy. As you go to print the document, you discover that you have not left proper space for binding. Correct your margin to provide an additional one-half inch on the left-hand side.

ENGLISH USAGE CHALLENGE DRILL

Correct the following sentences. Cite the grammar rule that is applicable to each sentence. Before you begin, refresh your memory of grammar rules by reviewing the rules on use of common gender language and collective nouns.

In the past, grammatical convention specified using masculine pronouns to refer to indefinite pronouns. **For example:** *The instructor asked everyone to open his book.* Today people are more conscious that the masculine pronouns exclude women who comprise more than half the population. Correct sentences one, two, and three by replacing the masculine pronoun to include both males and

females. Check a reference source if you need help in how to make the corrections (*Multimedia Reference for Writers* or some other reference).

1. Everyone hopes that he wins the scholarship.
2. Since the technology age has resulted in a proliferation of information, a physician usually has time to read in only his specialty.
3. Each of the employees performed his job well.
   Correct these sentences.
4. The audience was cheering as they stood to applaud the speaker.
5. The class presented their report as a group.

KORONET INTERNATIONAL

Policies and Procedures

Personnel Absences

The following types of employee absences shall constitute permissible absence from duty under the conditions described; an excused absence is not applicable to supplemental employment or part-time work unless expressly provided herein.

a. Sick Leave

(1) Benefit accrual. Sick leave benefits shall accrue to full-time employees from the first day of employment, at a rate of one day per month of the employment year. No sick leave benefits shall accrues or be used under contracts for supplemental employment or part-time work.

(2) Maximum Accrual. The maximum sick leave benefits which may accrue to eligible employees shall be sixty-six (50) days. Sick leve shall be credited as earned, but may be approved by the Personnel Office beyond the accrued amount, provided that employees with less than six months service shall not be approved for more than six days' leave.

(3) Uses. Sick leave may be used only

(a) For illness of the employee;

(b) With the prior approval of the employee's supervisor, for medical or dental emergencies or appoints and when such cannot be scheduled after duty hours;

(c) For maternity leave, to the extent of accrued benefits, to be applied at the beginning of the leave period;

(d) For illness of children and other dependents living in the household. An employee may not use more than ten days of sick leave per year for this purpose.

(4) Benefit Adjustments

(a) Job-related Injury. An employee who is absent from work due to job-related injury shall be eligible for sick leave pay, provided that the sick leave pay shall be reduced by an amount equal to worker's compensation benefits paid.

(b) Disability. An employee who is absent from work due to a disability and who is covered by optional shortterm or longterm disability plans that are offered by Koronet may be eligible for disability pay under the terms and conditions of the plan.

(c) (5) Termination of Employment. Unused, accrued sick leave shall be forfeited upon termination of employment with Koronet. In the event an employee has received sick leave benefits in excess o days earned to the date of termination, there shall be deducted from such employee's final compensation check an amount equal to such excess.

b. Bereavement of Family Illness: Absence due to the death or critical illness in the immediate family of an employee (not to exceed three days at any one time) may be granted without loss of pay upon approval of the employee's supervisor. "Immediate family" means spouse, child, father, mother, brother, sister, or grandparent of the employee or other person who occupies a position of similar significance in the family of the employee.

c. Birth or Adoption of a Child: Leave may be granted for a maximum of one full day without loss of pay for an employee to be with his wife at the birth of their child or for an employee to be at the court proceeding for adoption of a child.

d. Required Court Appearance: An employee will be excused with pay for court appearance when subpoenaed as a witness. This privilege does not apply to court cases involving an employee's personal business.

e. Jury Duty: An employee may be granted leave of absence without loss pay when called for jury duty. If absence for jury duty would seriously impair the operation of Koronet, the supervisor may request the judge to defer to a later date the employee's duty. An employee called for jury duty shall immediately report such notice to his supervisor.

f. Extenuating Circumstances: For reasons not covered by other leave, an employee may be paid for

absence not to exceed two days per year. Such leave may not be accumulated from one year to the

next. Such leave is subject to approval under appropriate procedures of Koronet.

ASSESSMENT OF CHAPTER OBJECTIVES

Now that you have completed the chapter and the office tasks, take a few moments to review the following learning objectives. Did you accomplish these objectives? Indicate your responses by answering "yes" or "no" in the blanks provided. If you were unable to accomplish these objectives, give your reason for not doing so. Your instructor may want to review your answers.

I accomplished these objectives:

1. Identify and explain various types of software programs. Yes _____ No _____

   Explain how you accomplished this objective.
   _____
   _____
   _____

2. Troubleshoot software problems.
   Yes _____ No _____

   Explain how you accomplished this objective.
   _____
   _____
   _____

3. Explain how to select software.
   Yes _____ No _____

   Explain how you accomplished this objective.
   _____
   _____
   _____

4. Describe how to care for software and hardware.
   Yes _____ No _____

   Explain how you accomplished this objective.
   _____
   _____
   _____

5. Use applications software in performing tasks.
   Yes _____ No _____

   Explain how you accomplished this objective.
   _____
   _____
   _____

Provide reasons for failing to accomplish any of these objectives.
_____
_____
_____
_____

BERNICE FUJIWARA'S CASE SOLUTION

Here is how I solved the situation. I sat down and talked with my executive. I told him that I was becoming frustrated with the heavy workload. I commented that I spent an average of two and a half hours in one meeting and in transcribing my notes after the meeting. I asked if it were possible to request each division manager to e-mail me their notes on what was covered at the meeting. Most of the managers had prepared written notes to make their reports at the meeting. I told my executive that I would combine their notes into one document, edit, and print the document. I stressed that it would save time and allow me to be productive on other activities that needed to be done.

BE CAREFUL: When you notify and ask the managers to e-mail you, you may meet with some resistance. Explain to them that you would like to try this new procedure and that you have noticed that they bring notes to the meeting. Tell them that this procedure will not add to their workload; you merely want them to send you their notes. You can send a reminder before the meeting and request politely that they send you the notes. You might also e-mail them after the meeting to remind them to mark their calendars for the next meeting.

PART 2

Success Behaviors

Debra Thomas
Executive Assistant
Human Resources and Labor Relations
Traverse City Area Public Schools
Traverse City, Michigan

A Success Profile

Many factors have contributed to my success in the secretarial field, including:
- technical skills
- people skills
- education
- mentoring
- drive and ambition
- loyalty

My first priority was to develop excellent technical skills such as keyboarding, shorthand, and computer skills. While developing the technical skills necessary to obtain a position within the secretarial field, I earned an associate degree in office information systems. During this process, I was exposed to a variety of courses including government, English, mathematics, economics, and other courses which broadened my education.

Once employed, my advancement was rapid—within five years I rose from an entry-level secretary to the assistant to the CEO of a large community college. Although technical and people skills, a college degree, and hard work were necessary for success, the mentoring which I received from my supervisors was truly the key element for success. I was fortunate to work for intelligent, caring individuals who were confident and trusting of my abilities.

I graduated magna cum laude with a degree in office information systems from Oakland Community College. While working on my associate degree, I became a member of Phi Theta Kappa, a national honorary fraternity, and received the Mildred C. Storch Scholarship Award. Since college, I have continued to grow and learn on the job. I have taken advantage of numerous professional development seminars, including total quality management, time management, and diversity. Through on-the-job training, I am now proficient in Word-Perfect 6.0, Lotus, Excel, and PageMaker desktop publishing. In my role as an assistant to the CEO of a community college, I worked closely with the board of trustees. My responsibilities included attending board meetings, taking and preparing the official minutes, making travel arrangements for the board, scheduling meetings and dinners, preparing weekly mailings to the board, and numerous other responsibilities. The workload was heavy, and the job demanded consistent attention to the myriad and diverse needs of the board, plus constant attention to detail. I also was responsible for supervising one secretary. My responsibilities in my present position include scheduling interviews, maintaining degree and certification records for teachers and administrators, taking minutes during collaborative bargaining contract negotiations, and other related responsibilities.

The most enjoyable and the most stressful parts of my job are intertwined. A large part of my job consists of recording minutes for collaborative bargaining meetings to negotiating employee contracts. Although I find the meetings very interesting, it is often difficult to be clear as to the mutual agreements that are being reached. It is not unusual for a particular topic to be discussed by many people for a great length of time—as long as two hours.

Numerous individuals give a variety of input. I find it helpful when the facilitator reiterates the consensus reached. This reiteration allows me to clearly understand the agreement. I enjoy participating in the meetings and I also find them quite challenging.

I would suggest that anyone seeking a career in the office professional field be willing to continue to develop communication and human relations skills and continually update their technical skills. In addition, an individual entering the field should be willing to work hard, be reliable, and follow through on each project. I also feel that it is important to continue formal education through earning a college degree. My immediate professional goal is to be a conscientious, courteous, and caring employee.

My hobbies include physical activities which are good sources of stress relief. I enjoy swimming, skiing, and roller-blading. Having recently moved to northern Michigan, I have found it easy to enjoy a variety of physical activities. An eight-mile bike trail and public beach are within walking distance of my home which creates an environment that encourages physical exercise. I also enjoy traveling and reading.

DEBRA THOMAS'S CASE

I have prepared a case from my experiences as an office professional. Decide how you would handle the case by answering the questions at the completion of the situation. Then turn to the end of Part II (page 147) to see how I solved the case.

THE SITUATION

Early in my career as an entry-level secretary, one of my duties was to oversee college teleconferences and telecourses with a long-time employee with great technical expertise in the field. At the time I had absolutely no knowledge about this field which includes satellite coordinates, licensing, and broadcast schedules. This particular employee resented the fact that I was given responsibility for overseeing this field. As a result, our working relationship was extremely strained.

How would you handle the situation? Would you talk with the long-time employee about how he is treating you? Would you talk with your supervisor about the situation? Or, would you remain quiet?

CHAPTER 5

DEVELOPING EFFECTIVE COMMUNICATION SKILLS

LEARNING OBJECTIVES

1. **Develop an awareness and understanding of a culturally diverse workforce.**
2. **Explain the communication process.**
3. **Identify communication barriers.**
4. **Identify types of nonverbal communication.**
5. **Use effective communication techniques.**
6. **Identify types of discrimination and steps that may be taken to counter discrimination.**

Your effectiveness as an office professional by definition implies effective communication skills since the majority of the office professional's day involves contact with people. Effective communication is defined as the ability to process and exchange ideas and feelings so that the person originating the communication and the person receiving the communication clearly understand what is being communicated. Building and maintaining effective communications are never easy. This statement is particularly true today in our complex, diverse world. It is difficult enough to relate successfully to people on a daily basis who are just like us. When these people are from different cultures and backgrounds, of different ages, and from even different countries, the task becomes even more complex. In such a diverse, complex environment, discrimination may become a factor. All of us would probably quickly agree with the principle that all individuals should be afforded equal treatment and no individual should ever have to face discrimination. However, we do not live in that ideal world today and probably never will. When

we face discrimination we must understand how to effectively deal with it. This chapter also gives you some suggestions for handling discrimination.

COMPLEXITY OF COMMUNICATION

Different forces have come together today to make the complexity of our communications greater than ever before. These forces are

- our global world;
- the increasing number of foreign-born in the United States;
- the multinational nature of business;
- our technology.

OUR GLOBAL WORLD

Today, we truly live in a global world. In fact, if the earth's population was reduced to a village of 100, the population would be

- 57 Asians
- 21 Europeans
- 14 Western Hemisphere (North and South Americans)
- 8 Africans

FOREIGN-BORN POPULATION IN THE UNITED STATES

Consider the U.S. population for a moment. According to the 1990 U.S. census (done every ten years), the foreign-born population totaled a record 19.8 million, surpassing previous highs of 14 million in 1980. More than 100 languages are spoken in the school systems of New York City, Chicago, and Los Angeles. Over 31 million people speak English as their second language.

Such statistics do not mean that all Americans must speak several languages. Certainly, it is helpful to speak more than one language, but obviously we cannot learn all languages of the world. The important point is that we understand the diverse world in which we live, are sensitive to others who are struggling with learning the English language (realizing that even if someone is speaking English, their accent may make them difficult to understand), and treat all people regardless of their language with consideration and respect.

The foreign-born population in America is higher than it has ever been. *Photo by Alan Brown/Photonics.*

Our technology and the multinational nature of business add to our probabilities of communicating with people outside the United States. These contacts may be through the Internet, telephone, written documents, or face-to-face communication. Regardless of how the interaction occurs, we must be aware and respectful of the added complexities of communication due to our global contacts.

You will remember from Chapter 1 that the increased cultural and age differences in the office of the twenty-first century were discussed. You learned that your effectiveness as an office worker will depend in part on your ability to acquire the knowledge, skills, and qualities which will allow you to become a valued part of a very diverse environment. The information presented here will help you learn more about how to successfully deal with the differences you will encounter.

ASSUMPTION OF SAMENESS

Even though we know the diverse world means that people are different, we usually respond to

other individuals, no matter what their culture, as if they think and behave in the same way we do. Why? It is quite natural. Consider for a moment how you learned certain behaviors. Take a behavior that most of us learned as a child—it is dangerous or not okay to play in the street. You were probably taught this from the time you were old enough to walk. You learned this behavior because your mother, father, grandparents, or some other significant person in your life told you that it was not okay and even punished you if you were caught playing in the street.

Just as we learn not to play in the street, we learn how to function in our world by what we are taught, what we observe others doing, and how we internalize the behavior of those around us. We have no reason for believing that other people might behave differently than we do. Certainly, we have no reason for believing that other cultures might behave in different ways if we have not been around other cultures.

Another point worthy of mention about our lack of understanding of others is that most of our conditioning (learned behavior) operates subconsciously. We are not even aware that we have expectations about how people should behave based on how we behave. We might be aware through our conscious intellect that others behave differently, but this intellect is no match for what a lifetime of conditioning has taught us. To break out of this conditioning, we must develop not only an understanding of cultural differences among people in our world but also an understanding of our beliefs and conditioning. Consider now some of the cultural differences among people.

CULTURAL DIFFERENCES

Americans are considered demonstrative; generally, we show our feelings easily. If we are happy, we smile a lot. If we are sad, we seldom smile. Most of us hug each other easily; we generally do not have to know an individual intimately to hug the person. For example, if a co-worker brings you a gift for your birthday, you might respond with: "Thanks; you're great!" and grab the person in a bear hug. We are taught from an early age to make eye contact with other people. To look down at the floor while someone is talking to you can mean disrespect for the individual or signify a lack of confidence on the part of the person looking down. To take off your shoes in public or at social gatherings in America is considered poor manners.

As an American student, we learn from the time that we first enter school that class participation is important; we are taught to give our opinions. When Americans have guests for dinner, we generally accept, due to people's health needs and diets, that a guest may decline a certain food. We may feel somewhat concerned that we did not know the guest's food preference, but we would not insist that the guest eat the food after declining. American guests often bring flowers to the host; these flowers can be any color. Americans have certain concepts of time and space. For example, in America it is important to be on time for business appointments. A certain amount of space distance is maintained when talking with people; if talking to an acquaintance, we generally maintain a distance of from two to three feet. In America, an "okay" gesture is made by putting the thumb and forefinger together to form a circle, with the other fingers pointed up. Let us now take those same concepts and look at how people from other countries would view them.

Americans maintain a space distance of from two to three feet when talking with acquaintances. *Hewlett Packard.*

- In Korean culture, smiling can signal shallowness and thoughtfulness.

- In Japan, a smile may be equated with frivolous behavior.

- Asians generally do not approve of public displays of affection.

- Asians, Latin Americans, and Caribbeans avoid eye contact as a sign of respect.

- Because Asians regard teachers so highly, they find it difficult to voice their own views in class; it is almost a sign of disrespect to the teacher.

- In Java, food must be offered three times before guests can accept it; Filipinos and Koreans also frequently wait until food is offered two or three times before accepting.

- In Iran, giving someone yellow flowers means that you hate them. In Brazil purple flowers are associated with death; in China, white is the color of mourning.

- Latin Americans move very close to each other when talking; the interaction distance is much less than in America.

- In France and Mexico, being thirty minutes late to an appointment is perfectly acceptable.[1]

- In Japan, shoes should never be worn into the home unless the host insists; in Indian and Indonesian homes, if the host goes shoeless, the guest should do likewise.

- In Brazil, the gesture of the thumb and forefinger forming a circle (which means "okay" in America) is an obscene one.

---

[1]Dresser, Norine, *Multicultural Manners: New Rules of Etiquette For A Changing Society* (New York: John Wiley & Sons, 1996).

COMMUNICATION TIP

When working with someone from a different culture, commit to finding out as much as you can about the person's culture. Seek first to understand the other person.

Handshakes are the accepted greeting in most cultures.

Test your knowledge of other cultures by completing Self Check A. Compare your answers with the answers given at the end of the chapter.

CULTURALLY APPROPRIATE EXPECTATIONS

Now that you understand certain cultural differences, let us take one situation and work through it.

In your role as executive assistant at Koronet Office Furniture you have recently hired a young woman to assist you. She has only been in the United States for six months; she is from Korea. During the job interview, you noticed that she never made eye contact with you; however, you assumed that she was very nervous. She has now been on the job for one week; she continues not to make eye contact with you. Finally, in desperation and with anger, you said to her, "Please look at me when I am talking to you." She did not respond to you, but you knew from her facial expression that she was upset. The next day her eye contact was better, but she still looked down frequently. She now seems to be angry with you. You have been pleased with her work, and you want to have a good working relationship with her. What can you do? Ask yourself these questions.

- What expectations do I have? Do I expect her to behave in the same way that I do?

- Have I considered that her reaction may be culturally based?

- What do I know about her culture? If I know little, how can I find out about her culture? Can I talk with her? (In the present situation, it would probably be better to read about the Korean culture or talk with a Korean acquaintance.)

- Why did I allow myself to become upset before I understood the situation?

In the future, remind yourself not to expect people from different cultures to behave as you do. Here are some suggestions on how to educate yourself about other cultures.

- Read books of different cultures which are available in bookstores and your local library.

- Join a global "chat group" on the Internet.

- Talk with individuals from different cultures who you know at work or in other settings about their life and the differences they see in various cultures.

- Set a goal to make it one of your top priorities to develop appropriate cultural expectations.

VERBAL AND NONVERBAL COMMUNICATION

In understanding a culturally diverse workforce, you have already learned that communication is extremely important. Let us now consider both verbal and nonverbal communication in some detail. **Verbal communication** is the process of exchanging ideas and feelings through the use of words. **Nonverbal communication** is the process of exchanging ideas and feelings through the use of gestures. Both types of communication can be the sources of many misunderstandings due to people of different cultures viewing situations differently. To help you in communicating with people of other cultures in addition to people of your own culture, take a look at the process of communication and communication barriers, including nonverbal communication barriers.

THE COMMUNICATION PROCESS

As you have previously learned, communication is defined as the process of exchanging ideas and feelings through the use of words or gestures. With verbal communication, the communicator uses words; with nonverbal communication, the communicator uses gestures. All communication includes an originator, the message, the receiver, and the response.

The Originator

The **originator** is the sender of the original message. The originator transmits information, ideas, and feelings through speaking, writing, or gesturing. Although the originator is often a person, the originator may be a company, a committee, or even a nation. For example, in the advertisements you see on television about a particular product, the company is the originator of the communication.

The Message

The **message** is the idea being presented by the originator. Words are usually used in communicating the idea; but hand signals, gestures, or a combination of words and gestures may also be used. The transmission of these words or gestures usually takes the form of face-to-face exchanges, telephone conversations, voice mail, or written correspondence such as e-mail, faxes, Internet correspondence, and letters and memorandums. Other forms of transmission are radio, television, video, and cassette disk.

The Receiver

The person for whom the message is intended is the **receiver.** The receiver transfers the message into meaning. For example, if the message was, "Please send this letter out immediately," the receiver would develop a meaning based on an understanding of the words and previous knowledge of the originator. The receiver may decide that the letter should be sent out in thirty minutes, for example, or in another situation the receiver may decide that two hours is the appropriate timeframe.

The Response

The **response** (feedback) of the receiver lets the originator know whether the communication is understood. The response may be verbal or nonverbal (such as a nod of the head, a smile, or shrug of the shoulders). If the response of the receiver indicates to the originator that the communication was misunderstood, then the originator can send the message again, perhaps in a different manner. For example, in the situation of the letter to be sent out, assume the originator meant for the letter to go out within ten minutes and the receiver did not send it out for thirty minutes; as a result it missed the morning mail. In the future, the originator could frame the message in this manner: "Please get the letter out so that it will make the morning mail." Notice the communication model shown in Figure 5-1.

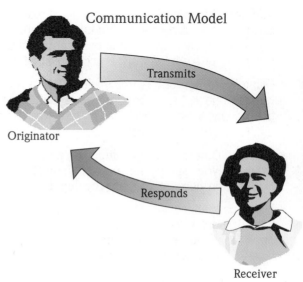

Communication Model

Transmits

Originator

Responds

Receiver

Figure 5-1   Communication model.

Each element of the communication process is important. If the originator does not clearly state the message, problems can occur. If the receiver interprets the message incorrectly and responds inappropriately, problems may also occur. Each person in the communication process has an obligation to communicate as clearly as possible, to frame the messages well, and to ask questions if the message or response is unclear.

COMMUNICATION BARRIERS

In addition to the communication problems that may occur due to cultural differences, which were mentioned in the previous section, some barriers often exist whether we are communicating with others of the same culture or of different cultures. Several of these barriers are given in Figure 5-2. Read the material given in the figure carefully. Then take a few moments to analyze the following situation and record your answers in the space provided.

When you first started to work for Koronet, you met an office assistant who works in another department. She asked you to go to lunch with her the first day; you accepted. However, you vowed that you would never do it again. She was "too chatty" in your opinion. She spent the entire lunch hour telling you the histories of numerous employees, including all the gossip about these people. You have successfully avoided her since that lunch; however, you understand that she is well respected by most of the office staff. Now, in your role as a TQM (total quality management) team member, you have to work with her. Take a few moments to look back over the communication barriers given in Figure 5-2. Were you guilty of setting up any barriers? If so, what were they?

_____

_____

_____

_____

_____

Communication Barriers

- **Hearing the Expected.** We are often guilty of sizing up an individual and then only hearing what we think that individual should say.

- **Ignoring Conflicting Information.** If you already have predetermined feelings about a subject, you tend to ignore new information on the subject. This new information may be valid, but you have made up your mind otherwise.

- **Evaluating the Source.** It is difficult for us to separate what we hear from our feelings about the person speaking. If you like the person, you tend to accept what the person says. If you dislike the person, you tend to ignore what the person is saying.

- **Viewing Things Differently.** Individuals may view the same situation in different ways. For example, if one person sees people within an office laughing and telling jokes, the person may decide that they are "goofing off," and no work is being accomplished. Another person may interpret the office as a happy place and one where work is accomplished easily in teams.

- **Using Word Barriers.** Words mean different things to different people. Even such simple words as "great," "small," "good," and "bad" are open to interpretation by the listener. In fact, communication theorists say that a word in and of itself has no meaning. A word only has the meaning given to it by the communicator. To counter word barriers, communicators must always clarify the meaning attached to words.

- **Noticing Differences in Position.** Breakdowns occur many times because of differences in position. For example, your supervisor may tell you something that you do not understand. Yet, you will not ask for clarification because you fear the supervisor may think you are stupid.

- **Listening Ineffectively.** Studies show that the average person spends 70 percent of the day communicating, with 45 percent of that communication time spent listening to others. However, listening is considered one of the weakest links in the communication process. Research studies show that most of us listen with only 25 to 50 percent efficiency. In other words, 50 to 75 percent of what we hear is never processed.

Figure 5-2

LISTENING

Listening is the complete process by which oral language, communicated by a source, is received, recognized, attended to, comprehended, and retained. The listener attends to the oral language of the source with the intent of acquiring meaning. Thus, the main components of listening are not located in the ears, just as main components of seeing are not located in the eyes. Our ears hear the sound vibrations to which we attend and comprehend; but our listening is based on our needs, desires, interests, previous experiences, and learning. Clearly, listening is a complex phenomenon involving the total individual. As we listen, our process of thought, which is composed of many separate and independent concepts, flows into ideas and emotions and affects what we hear.

BARRIERS TO EFFECTIVE LISTENING

Do you consider yourself a good listener? Complete Self Check B to determine your listening effectiveness at present. Rate yourself by answering the statements with "always," "sometimes," or "never."

How did you do? Did you recognize yourself as one of the ineffective listeners? If you are like most of us, your score can probably be improved. Improvement comes by understanding what causes poor listening and then working on effective listening techniques. Numerous characteristics produce poor listening behaviors. Consider the following ineffective listeners.

The Talker

Unfortunately, many of us are so intent on discussing what has happened to us that we have difficulty waiting for the other person to finish talking so that we can start talking. In fact, many times the eager talker will interrupt the speaker to get a point across. Such individuals absorb little of what the other person says. In addition, the talker is usually planning a story while the other person is talking.

The Attention-Faker

Have you ever talked with someone who seemed to listen to every word you said, but when it came time for the person to respond, you realized that person had not heard a word? Or, have you ever sat in a classroom and intently watched the instructor during an entire lecture but were unable to answer

---

Self Check B

Respond to the following comments by marking "always," "sometimes," or "never" after the statement.

1. When people talk to me, I find it difficult to keep my mind on the subject.

2. I listen only for facts.

3. Certain words and ideas can prejudice me against a speaker to the point that I cannot listen objectively to what is being said.

4. I can tell by a person's appearance if that person will have something worthwhile to say.

5. When someone is talking to me, I try to make the person think I am paying attention even when I am not.

6. When someone is speaking to me, I am easily distracted by outside sights and sounds.

7. I interrupt the speaker to get my point across.

8. When someone else is talking, I plan what I will say next.

9. I frequently criticize the speaker's delivery or mannerisms.

10. I use the difference between the talking time of the speaker and my own comprehension time to analyze and relate the speaker's points.

11. I am aware of the nonverbal communication of others.

12. I try to understand what the speaker is feeling as the speaker talks.

13. I ask questions when I do not understand what the speaker is saying.

---

any questions about what was said? Most of us are good at adopting an outward posture that leads the speaker to believe we are listening when actually we are thinking of something else.

The Easily Distracted

Most people speak approximately 125 words a minute, yet it is believed that the brain can process information at about 500 words a minute. Listening allows plenty of time for the mind to wander. Unless the listener is committed to hearing the speaker, it is easy to become distracted. Distraction can be in the form of **external noises** or movement, either inside or outside the room. Distractions can also be in the form of **internal noise,** such as a problem that is bothering you. You may be thinking about your problem and miss the speaker's point totally.

It is possible to miss vital information when you do not give the speaker your full attention.

The Outguesser

Have you ever known someone who would never let you finish a sentence but always finished it for you? That person may have assumed time was being saved when time is actually lost. Many times the outguesser makes an inaccurate assumption concerning your message. You, therefore, have to stop and explain that the outguesser has made a wrong assumption.

NONVERBAL COMMUNICATION

Nonverbal communication can be another barrier to effective communication. Before you consider this area, there are several cautions you must keep in mind.

- People of different cultures give different meaning to gestures; remember, you learned about some of these differences in the first sections of this chapter. You must constantly keep in mind that how you interpret gestures may not be the same as how others interpret gestures.

- Conclusions cannot be drawn from only one element of nonverbal communication. For example, a person crosses the arms because of coldness. You must take all elements of nonverbal communication as a whole, and you must be cautious about your interpretations.

Consider four elements of nonverbal communication.

The nonverbal behavior of the receiver suggests that the message is not being received.

Body Language

Various body motions or gestures can have meaning. Notice the photo above. One person is leaning forward in a chair, talking animatedly. Notice that the second individual is leaning back in his chair, frowning. Is the person with the frown accepting what the other individual is saying? Your answer was probably "no," and you are correct. The nonverbal body language signs indicate that the message is not being received. Something about the message or the speaker is blocking the individual from truly listening to what is being said.

Although body language is extremely important, one gesture alone does not have significant meaning. One gesture merely gives you a clue that something may be wrong. In evaluating body language, consider all the gestures a person makes along with what the person says. For example, when you are communicating with someone, do not make the mistake of assuming that a frown indicates that the person disagrees with what you are saying. If you are concerned about the body language, ask for an explanation. You might say something such as, "You are frowning; is there something wrong?" Such a question gives the person with whom you are talking a chance to explain the behavior.

Voice Quality

A loud tone of voice is usually associated with anger; a soft tone of voice with calmness and poise. Two people talking softly with each other usually indicates that they are at ease. The loudness or softness of the voice and the pitch of the voice are nonverbal behaviors that reveal something about an individual. A person's voice will usually be pitched higher when tense, anxious, or nervous. Also, a person usually talks faster when angry or tense. In contrast, a low pitch and a slow pace usually indicate a relaxed tone. Other forms of nonverbal voice communication include the nervous giggle; a quivering, emotional voice; a breaking, stressful voice; and a whinny (upset) voice. Voice quality is so important that individuals whose voices are important to their success or failure on the job, such as TV and radio newscasters, spend time and effort to be certain that their voice does not cause people to switch to another station. For example, a nasal voice or a very high pitched voice is irritating to the listener.

Time

Another important nonverbal communicator is time. You have already learned in the first part of this chapter that not all cultures treat time in the same way. In the United States, we have learned to treat time in certain standard ways. For example, as a student you have probably learned that turning in a paper or project late usually results in a grade penalty. In a business situation, habitually late reports or being late to work can cause an employee to be fired. An applicant who is late for a job interview may forfeit the chance to get the job.

Space

Space is also treated differently in different cultures. In the United States we have defined space expectations. For example, at home do you have a special chair that is considered yours or a special space that is considered your territory? We tend to lay claim to certain territory and defend it if someone else takes *our space,* which is defined as **territoriality.** In the office, we also use space in special ways. For example, people who have the same level or position will generally be allocated the same amount of space. The president's office will usually be larger than the vice president's office. The vice president's office will generally be larger than a supervisor's office, and so it goes in the hierarchy of the company. An administrative assistant to the president will also generally have a larger space than an administrative assistant to the vice president.

DISCRIMINATION

Often our communication is ineffective with people of different races, cultures, and ethnicities due to our own prejudices. In fact, it is such a problem in our society that it is presented here as a separate section. Unless we understand what prejudice is and how it can cause serious problems and even gross discrimination, our diverse world will be a terribly difficult place to live and work.

Prejudice is defined as a system of negative beliefs, feelings, and actions. The beliefs, feelings, and actions are based on *learned* categories of distinctions, *learned* evaluation of these categories, and a *learned* tendency to act appropriate to the beliefs and feelings held. Prejudice can hamper and even prevent communication. Prejudice can lead to acts of **discrimination** (treatment or consideration based on class or category rather than individual merit). Discrimination may occur in many forms—race or ethnicity, gender, and age are some of the most likely forms. Discrimination may also involve sexual harassment. Discrimination has been so prevalent in our society that laws have been enacted to address the issues. Title VII of the Civil Rights Act of 1964 made it illegal to discriminate on the basis of race, color, religion, sex, or national origin. Since that time, other acts have been passed which address age, disability, equal pay, and pregnancy discrimination. Figure 5-3 lists some of these acts.

RACIAL DISCRIMINATION

Racial tensions have occurred in the United States from the time the first white settlers drove out the Native Americans and set up a system of labor based on black slavery. Prejudice is based mainly on ignorance and fear. It is usually learned at an early age; changing learned attitudes is a slow process. As you have learned earlier in this chapter, in our multicultural world, individuals must accept the responsibility for changing any negative attitudes toward people of races other than their own. In our diverse world, it is not appropriate to excuse our behavior because we do not understand another culture. We must spend the time and effort to find out about that culture and to improve our communications with people of all cultures. However, our responsibility does not end there. For example, in an office situation, we have the responsibility to

Laws Governing Discrimination

These acts covering discrimination make it unlawful to discriminate against applicants, employees, or students on the basis of race, religion, color, national origin, sex, age, height, weight, marital status, disability or handicap and set out that sexual harassment will not be tolerated.

Title VI and VII of the Civil Rights Act of 1964

Title IX of the Education Amendments of 1972

Section 504 of the Rehabilitation Act of 1973

The Age Discrimination in Employment Act and the Amendments of 1986

The Americans with Disabilities Act of 1990

The Vietnam Era Veterans Readjustment Assistant Act of 1974

The Elliot Larsen Civil Rights Act

Executive Order 11246

In addition, the following acts make pay discrimination based on gender and discrimination on the basis of pregnancy, childbirth, or related medical conditions unlawful.

The Equal Pay Act. This act, a 1964 amendment to the Fair Labor Standards Act, prohibits pay discrimination because of gender. Men and women performing work in the same establishment under similar conditions must receive the same pay if their jobs require equal skill, effort, and responsibility.

The Pregnancy Discrimination Act. In 1978 this act amended Title VII to make clear that discrimination on the basis of pregnancy, childbirth, or related medical conditions is unlawful, including refusal to hire or promote pregnant women or to offer them the same fringe benefits or insurance programs.

The Family and Medical Leave Act of 1993, effective August 1993, requires private sector employees of fifty or more employees and public agencies to provide up to twelve weeks of unpaid, job protected leave to eligible employees for certain family and medical reasons. An employer must grant unpaid leave to an eligible employee for one or more of the following reasons:

- care of the employee's child (birth, or placement for adoption or foster care);
- care of the employee's spouse, son or daughter, or parent, who has a serious health condition; or,
- serious health condition that makes the employee unable to perform the job.

Figure 5-3

insist that others not let prejudice get in the way of hiring, promotions, raises, and so forth. When hiring others, any advertisements must be clear that the organization is an equal opportunity employer. In the interview process, all individuals must be treated equally. If teams are used in the interview process, the teams must be given specific criteria for the interview which include focusing on the qualifications needed for the job, not the race or ethnicity of the individual. Once individuals of different races and ethnicities have been employed, they must be given equal treatment within the organization. Competence must be the major criteria for promotion and raises. No one can be held back due to race or

HUMAN RELATIONS TIP

Every person has a responsibility to see that racial discrimination does not occur.

ethnicity. If you know that discrimination is occurring in your organization, you are responsible for reporting that discrimination to your employer or to the human resources department. All of us have the responsibility to uphold what is right and fair for all groups of people.

GENDER DISCRIMINATION

Title VII also covers gender discrimination. Employers may not advertise a job specifically for a man or woman unless the employer can prove that it is necessary that a person of a specific gender is needed. In other words, the question of gender may be asked only if it pertains to a bona fide occupational qualification; for example, a model for men's clothing. In our society today, however, we recognize that there are very few gender-specific occupations. A person may apply for any job, and the hiring decision must be based on whether the individual has the knowledge and skills needed for the job, not on whether the person is male or female.

Neither can employee pay be based on whether a person is male or female. The Equal Pay Act, a 1964 amendment to the Fair Labor Standards Act, prohibits pay discrimination because of gender. Men and women performing work in the same establishment under similar conditions must receive the same pay if their jobs require equal skill, effort, and responsibility.

The Pregnancy Discrimination Act of 1978 amended Title VII to make clear that discrimination on the basis of pregnancy, childbirth, or related medical conditions is unlawful. This act makes it illegal to refuse to hire or promote a pregnant woman or to refuse to offer pregnant women the same fringe benefits or insurance programs.

For the most part, organizations are sensitive to this issue today and take measures to ensure that gender discrimination does not occur. However, if individuals believe they are being discriminated against because of gender, it is possible to take legal action against the organization or individual engaging in such discrimination.

AGE DISCRIMINATION

No distinction can be made in age, either in the advertising or in the hiring process or once an employee is on the job. For example, an organization cannot advertise in the paper for a young person for a particular job nor can an organization specify a particular age for a position that is available. Individuals, regardless of age, must be treated equally in the advertising and hiring process. Discrimination because of age remains illegal once a person is on the job. In addition, a person cannot be dismissed because of age. Under the provisions of the Mandatory Retirement Act, an employee cannot be forced to retire before age 70. The 1986 amendments to this act eliminated the upper age limit of 70.

SEXUAL HARASSMENT

Sexual harassment has been defined by the Equal Employment Opportunity Commission (EEOC) as persistent torment arising from sexual conduct which is unwelcome by the recipient and which may be either physical or verbal in nature. Three criteria for sexual harassment are set forth.

- Submission to the sexual conduct is made either implicitly or explicitly as a condition of employment.

- Employment decisions affecting the recipient are made on the basis of the recipient's acceptance or rejection of the sexual conduct.

- The conduct has the intent or effect of substantially interfering with an individual's work performance or creates an intimidating, hostile, or offensive work environment.

Sexual harassment in the office can take many forms. It may be verbal in nature (such as suggestive comments or sexual jokes), pressure for sexual activity, unwanted body contact, or rape.

The Civil Rights Act makes the organization responsible for preventing and eliminating sexual harassment. The organization is liable for the behavior of its employees whether management is aware that sexual harassment has taken place. The organization is also responsible for the actions of nonemployees on the company's premises. Because of these liabilities, many organizations have published policy statements which make it clear to all employees that sexual harassment is a violation of the law and of company policy. These policy statements generally include a clearly defined grievance procedure so that an employee has a course of action to take if sexual harassment does occur.

RESOLUTIONS

Now that you have considered some of the errors we make in communicating and in working with people of different races, ethnicities, genders, and ages, let us concentrate on improvement strategies. How can you grow and learn so that you will be a productive employee and a contributing citizen in our diverse world?

EFFECTIVE COMMUNICATION TECHNIQUES

Because communication is so important to your performance on the job, you must constantly attempt to be a better communicator. Becoming a better communicator is a process; there is always something more that you can learn about communicating with people. Figure 5-4 gives fourteen techniques that will help you sharpen your communication skills.

CONFLICT RESOLUTION

No matter how effectively you try to communicate, conflicts will occur occasionally. When you are faced with conflict, address it. Too many people try to run from conflict. The conflict will usually not go away; it merely gets worse. Here are some suggestions for dealing with conflict.

- Identify what is causing the conflict. Is it power, resources, recognition, or acceptance? Many times our needs for these items are at the heart of the conflict.

- Determine what each person needs or wants. Ask questions to determine what the other person wants. Be willing to listen to the other person. We all feel a deep need to be understood; by satisfying that need in the other person, you may be able to lessen the conflict. If you are not understanding what the other person is saying, paraphrase what you think you hear and ask for clarification. Be open to what the other person tells you. By listening actively to the other person, your perspective may be changed.

- Identify points of agreement. Work from these points first. Then, identify the points of disagreement.

- Create a safe environment. Establish a neutral location; establish a tone that is accepting of the other person's views and feelings. Acknowledge the other person's feelings. Behind anger may be fear. Allow the other person to express personal feelings. Watch how you position yourself physically in the room. Remember, it is much harder to compete with others while sitting next to them rather than across the table or room. If you have several individuals who are involved in the conflict, a circle might be appropriate.

- Do not react. Many times individuals act too quickly when a conflict arises. It is best to step back, collect your thoughts, and try to see the situation as objectively as possible.

- Do not seek to win during a confrontation; negotiate the issues; translate the negotiation into a lasting agreement.

- Actively listen. Watch the individual's eyes; notice the body language.

- Separate people from the issue. When the people and the problem are tangled together, the problem becomes very difficult to solve. Talk in specific terms rather than in general terms.

- Do not try to project what the other person is thinking or feeling. It is dangerous to believe anyone can read the minds of others.

- If the conflict is very serious and cannot be solved by the individuals, select an intervention team. In the intervention process, establish the parameters, collect the data, frame the issues, generate alternatives, evaluate the process, and reach a solution.

COMMUNICATION TIP

When you have a customer, caller, or business associate who does not speak fluent English, paraphrase what you believe the person has said. Then ask, "Is that correct?"

Effective Communication Techniques

Because communication is so important in effective human relations, how may you communicate better? Here are several techniques that will help you become a more effective communicator.

1. Use active listening. **Active listening** means that you are involved with the speaker. You are not merely hearing what the speaker is saying; you are truly listening. Ask questions when you do not understand what the speaker is saying. Paraphrase a concept if you are having trouble, and then ask the speaker, "Is this what you mean?"

2. Get ready to listen. Stop paying attention to the miscellaneous thoughts that constantly run through your mind. Direct all your attention to the speaker.

3. Listen for facts. Use the differential time between how long it takes the speaker to say the words (an average of 125 words a minute) and how long it takes you to comprehend them (approximately 500 words a minute) to review the key ideas presented. Raise questions in your mind about the material. Relate what the speaker is saying to your own experience. Mentally repeat key ideas or associate key points with related ideas.

4. Watch for nonverbal communication. Observe the speaker's eyes, hands, and body movements. Do the nonverbal communications agree with what the speaker is saying?

5. Use mnemonic devices to remember key ideas. A **mnemonic device** is a formula, word association, or rhyme used to assist the memory. For example, if a person says that her objections to a jogging program include boredom with the activity, exhaustion in the process, and the time required, you might develop the mnemonic device of BET to remember these ideas.

6. Minimize your mental blocks and filters. All of us have certain biases and prejudices. However, if we are aware of these blocks, we can control them. You may have heard people say, "You can't talk to CPAs; they are only number crunchers" or "All athletes are stupid." In such statements, you can hear prejudices. **Stereotyping** is taking place—an entire group of people or things is being evaluated based on a perception or image held, which may be favorable or unfavorable. In this case, the image was unfavorable. Listening behaviors are improved if you become aware of your own blocks and filters, as well as the speaker's blocks and filters.

7. Use direct, simple language. Direct and simple language should be used in both speaking and writing. Never attempt to use big words and long sentences to try to impress the listener or the reader.

8. Utilize feedback. When communicating with someone, listen totally to what that person is saying, not only to the words. Remember, there are many ways to communicate; these ways include words, gestures, facial expressions, tone of voice, time, and space. If you feel that the other person does not understand what you are saying, try to explain your point in a different manner.

9. Time messages carefully. You need to be aware of what is going on in the world of the receiver. We can cause problems for ourselves by trying to communicate with someone when that person is not ready to receive our communication. Stop, look, and observe what is going on in the world of the receiver before you attempt to communicate.

10. Organize what you hear. A listener who can identify the speaker's main points and the pattern of the speaker's remarks certainly has an advantage over the listener who simply listens to the words.

11. Understand cultural differences that exist.

12. Do not expect people from different cultures to behave the same way you do.

13. Pay attention to differences in nonverbal behavior with individuals of other countries.

14. Commit to constantly increasing your communication skills.

Figure 5-4

Conflict resolution is the art of compromise.

ACTIONS AGAINST DISCRIMINATION

If you are the victim of racial, gender, or age discrimination or sexual harassment, you should take steps to see that such treatment does not continue. Here are some steps you can take.

- Know your rights. Be certain you are current on the laws that deal with your civil rights. Know your company's policies and grievance procedures.

- Keep a record of all discrimination infractions, noting the dates, incidents, and witnesses (if any).

- File a grievance with your company, if appropriate. If a grievance policy does not exist, file a complaint with your employer in the form of a memorandum describing the incidents. Identify the individuals involved in the discriminatory action and request that disciplinary action be taken.

- If your employer is not responsive to your complaint, you may file charges with the federal and state agencies that enforce civil rights laws. Check your local telephone directory for the address and telephone number of the EEOC office in your city.

- Confront the offender. Let the offender know that the behavior is unwanted and unacceptable.

- Talk to friends, co-workers, and relatives. It is important to avoid isolation and self-blame. You are not alone; discrimination does occur in the workplace.

- Consult an attorney to investigate legal alternatives.

COMMUNICATION IMPROVEMENT

If we are to develop effective relationships in the workplace, we must constantly work on communication in all forms. We must understand that our workforce is diverse, that different cultures exist, and that because of our cultures and backgrounds we view situations differently. We must work to overcome the numerous communication barriers that exist, including discriminatory barriers. We must recognize that constant attention and effort to improve communication are essential. The process of improvement must be an ongoing, ever-present one. If we are diligent in our efforts, a fairer, more effective workplace will be the result.

COMMUNICATION TIP

Be flexible and open-minded. Do not always insist on your own ideas to the exclusion of other people's ideas.

CHAPTER SUMMARY

This summary will help you remember the important points covered in this chapter.

- The majority of the office professional's day involves contact with people; thus, effective communication skills are crucial.

- Several forces contribute to the complexity of communications in our world; these forces are our global world, the increasing number of foreign-born in the United States, the multinational nature of business, and our technology.

- The foreign-born population of the United States is at a record high, with almost 20 million foreign-born according to the 1990 census.

- The "assumption of sameness" is a concept that means individuals assume other cultures are no different than their own.

- Cultural differences are great throughout our world. These cultural differences include our gestures, the food we eat, our social customs, the way we treat time and space, and the way we dress.

- If we are to be successful in our culturally diverse world, we must remind ourselves not to expect people from different cultures to behave as we do. We must begin to develop appropriate cultural expectations.

- The elements of the communication process include the originator, the message, the receiver, and the response. Each element is important.

- Communication barriers include hearing the expected, ignoring conflicting information, evaluating the source, viewing things differently, using word barriers, noticing differences in position, and listening ineffectively.

- Listening is an important part of the communication process.

- Ineffective listeners include the talker, the attention-faker, the easily distracted, and the outguesser.

- Four elements of nonverbal communication are body language, voice quality, time, and space.

- Race or ethnicity, gender, and age discrimination are some of the most likely forms of discrimination. Discrimination may also involve sexual harassment.

- Due to the prevalence of discrimination in our society a number of laws have been enacted. These laws make discrimination illegal if it is based on national origin, ethnic group, gender, creed, age, or race.

- Under the Civil Rights Act, an organization is responsible for preventing and eliminating sexual harassment.

- Effective communication techniques include active listening, getting ready to listen; listening for facts; paying attention to nonverbal communication; using mnemonic devices; minimizing mental blocks and filters; using direct, simple language; utilizing feedback; timing messages carefully; and organizing what you hear.

- Some suggestions for dealing with conflict are identify what is causing the conflict; determine what each person needs or wants; create a safe environment; do not react; do not seek to win—negotiate; actively listen; separate people from the issues; do not try to project what the other person is thinking or feeling; if the conflict cannot be solved by the individuals, select an intervention team.

- Actions that can be taken against discrimination include know your rights; keep a record of all discrimination infractions; file a grievance with the company; file charges with the federal and state agencies; confront the offender; talk to friends, co-workers, and relatives to get help and support; consult an attorney to investigate legal alternatives.

CHAPTER GLOSSARY

The following terms were introduced in this chapter. To help you review, definitions are given here.

- **Verbal communication** (p. 115)–The process of exchanging ideas and feelings through the use of words.

- **Nonverbal communication** (p. 115)–The process of exchanging ideas and feelings through the use of gestures.

- **Originator** (p. 115)–The sender of the original message.

- **Message** (p. 115)–The idea being presented by the originator.

- **Receiver** (p. 115)–The person for whom the message is intended.

- **Response** (p. 115)–The response or feedback is what the receiver does (either verbal or nonverbal) to let the originator know how the communication has been understood.

- **Listening** (p. 117)–The complete process by which oral language, communicated by a source, is received, recognized, attended to, comprehended, and retained.

- **External noise** (p. 118)–Physical sounds that stand in the way of communication; for example, loud music is external noise that may get in the way of hearing a conversation.

- **Internal noise** (p. 118)–Distractions that occur inside the listener; these distractions may come due to different backgrounds, experiences, and perceptions that cause a person to interpret a communication in a certain way or they may come from problems or issues which the listener is concerned about at the time of a communication.

- **Territoriality** (p. 119)–Laying claim to a certain space and defending that claim.

- **Prejudice** (p. 119)–A system of negative beliefs, feelings, and actions.

- **Discrimination** (p. 119)–Treatment or consideration based on class or category rather than individual merit.

- **Sexual harassment** (p. 121)–Persistent torment arising from sexual conduct which is unwelcome by the recipient and which may be either physical or verbal in nature.

- **Active listening** (p. 123, Figure 5-4)–Involvement with the speaker, listening to what is said and combining it with the listener's experiences, asking questions of the speaker, and so forth.

- **Mnemonic device** (p. 123, Figure 5-4)–A formula, word association, or rhyme used to assist the memory.

- **Stereotyping** (p. 123, Figure 5-4)–To characterize a situation or a person by a perception or image held. The perception may be favorable or unfavorable.

DISCUSSION ITEMS

These discussion items provide an opportunity for you to test your understanding of the chapter through discussion with your classmates and your instructor.

1. What is meant by the "assumption of sameness"?

2. List ten cultural differences between Americans and people who live outside the United States.

3. Identify and explain five communication barriers.

4. Explain how voice can be a nonverbal communicator.

5. List and explain five suggestions for dealing with conflict.

6. What is our responsibility in regard to all types of discrimination?

CASE STUDY

Adrian Ramos, internal auditor at Koronet, hired an auditor six months ago. The individual he hired is female; her name is Ruth Montgomery. Her entry salary was $35,000. Policy provides for a performance review after an individual has been with the agency for a period of six months. Adrian Ramos reports to George Mosher; Mr. Mosher must sign the performance review. Mr. Ramos gave the new auditor a below standard rating on the performance review. She is upset with the rating. Following the grievance procedure of the agency, Ms. Montgomery asks for an appointment with Mr. Mosher to discuss her review. Here is her view of the situation as she reports it to Mr. Mosher.

I was employed at a salary of $35,000. I discovered after I had been on the job for a month that another auditor who was hired three months before I was, a man, was brought in at a salary of $37,500. I know that his experience and education are not greater than mine. I talked with Mr. Ramos at that point about my salary, stating that I thought I should have received a higher salary. He told me

that he would "make it up to me" during the mid-year review period. Now, not only does he not recommend a salary increase for me, but he gives me a below standard rating. Never once has he said anything about my performance being below standard before my review. In fact, he has often praised me; he has told me that I am the most capable auditor he has ever hired. I am quite upset with both my salary and my review. I don't understand why this is happening. The only thing that I can think of is that Mr. Ramos is prejudiced against women. I am ready to file a gender discrimination suit unless something is done.

Answer the following questions about the case.

- Taking into consideration what you have learned in this chapter, what would you do if you were Mr. Mosher?

- Do you believe Ms. Montgomery should file a gender discrimination suit at the present time?

- What steps would you recommend Ms. Montgomery take?

RESPONSES TO SELF CHECKS

SELF CHECK A

1. True
2. True
3. False
4. True
5. True
6. False
7. True

8. True
9. True
10. False

SELF CHECK B

The most effective listener would have checked "never" on the first nine statements and "always" on the last four statements.

OFFICE TASKS

OFFICE TASK 5-1 (Objectives 1 and 6)
There is an assignment labeled "Experiencing Another Culture" on the Student Data Template Disk, file OT5-1. You are to work in teams of three or four to complete this assignment. The culmination of this project is to be a five-page, keyed paper (excluding appendices) addressing the areas specified on the template. Your team is also responsible for giving an oral report to the class of your experiences during this assignment.

OFFICE TASK 5-2 (Objectives 2 and 3)
In your position at Koronet, you have two clerical assistants who report directly to you. They are Helena Wilkerson and Fusako Goro. Fusako has been having some personal problems, which she has talked with you about. She has come in late twice during the last month. Each time Helena has made a remark (that the entire office heard) about Fusako coming in late. Fusako has not responded to Helena's remarks. Last week, Fusako called in sick, but that evening Helena saw Fusako at the grocery store. The next morning (again while the entire office listened) Helena said, "It's a shame you were sick yesterday; but you weren't so sick last night, were you?" Fusako informed her that it was none of her business. Today, Fusako was late again. When she came in Helena remarked, "I wish I were the office pet." Fusako responded in an angry tone, "Leave me alone; you aren't my boss!"

You think that Fusako will soon solve her personal problems; she has been a good employee. You want to continue to give her a chance to work out her problems and get back on track at work. You know it cannot go on indefinitely, but she has indicated that the situation should be resolved within the next three weeks. You are very concerned about Helena's actions. Helena's work is also good, but she is out of line on this matter. Fusako does not want anyone to know about her personal problems. You are beginning to feel that you cannot let the situation continue with Helena's remarks disrupting the entire office.

1. Who is the originator in this communication situation? Who is the receiver?
2. Explain the communication problem between Fusako and Helena.
3. Is there a communication problem between you and Helena? If so, what is it?
4. Should you talk to Helena and Fusako about the most recent incident? If so, what should you say?

Answer these questions in a memorandum to your instructor. Use the memorandum form on Student Data Template Disk, file OT5-2.

OFFICE TASK 5-3 (Objective 4)
With a team of three or four classmates, spend two hours at a public event noticing the nonverbal behaviors of individuals. As a group, make an oral report to the class on your findings.

OFFICE TASK 5-4 (Objective 5)
Maintain a five-day log of the time you spend speaking and listening. Do not worry about accuracy to the minute, but make a concentrated effort to record the amount of time spent on both speaking and listening. Also record the effective and ineffective behaviors you engaged in while listening and speaking. At the end of the five-day period, analyze your log. How much time did you spend speaking? How much time listening? In what effective behaviors did you engage? What ineffective behaviors occurred. Determine ways in which you can improve your communication. Write a report identifying these improved communication techniques which you plan to follow. Turn in your report to your instructor.

ENGLISH USAGE CHALLENGE DRILL

Correct the following sentences. Cite the grammar rule that is applicable to each sentence. Before you begin, refresh your memory of grammar rules by reviewing number usage in the *Multimedia Reference for Writers,* this text, or some other reference source available to you.

1. Two hundred seventy-five dollars per credit is the tuition rate for residents.

2. We have ten volunteers for Thursday evening, 12 for Friday evening, and 16 for Saturday evening.

3. The meeting will begin at two p.m.

4. The conference will be held on May 8th through May 12th.

5. We have 3 new employees in the Payroll Department and 5 new engineers in the Design Department.

ASSESSMENT OF CHAPTER OBJECTIVES

Now that you have completed the chapter and the office tasks, take a few moments to review the following learning objectives. Did you accomplish the objectives? If so, explain how in the space provided. If you were unable to accomplish these objectives, give your reason for not doing so. Your instructor may want to review your answers.

I accomplished these objectives:

1. Develop an awareness and understanding of a culturally diverse workforce. Yes _____ No _____
   Explain how you accomplished this objective
   _____
   _____
   _____

2. Explain the communication process.
   Yes _____ No _____
   Explain how you accomplished this objective.
   _____
   _____
   _____
   _____

3. Identify communication barriers.
   Yes _____ No _____
   Explain how you accomplished this objective.
   _____
   _____
   _____

4. Identify types of nonverbal communication.
   Yes _____ No _____
   Explain how you accomplished this objective.
   _____
   _____
   _____
   _____

5. Use effective communication techniques.
   Yes _____ No _____
   Explain how you accomplished this objective.
   _____
   _____
   _____

6. Identify types of discrimination and steps that may be taken to counter discrimination.
   Yes _____ No _____
   Explain how you accomplished this objective.
   _____
   _____
   _____

Provide reasons for failing to accomplish any of the objectives.
_____
_____
_____
_____
_____

CHAPTER 6

RESPONDING ETHICALLY IN THE WORK ENVIRONMENT

LEARNING OBJECTIVES

1. **Recognize the importance of ethical behavior.**
2. **Identify characteristics of an ethical organization.**
3. **Identify traits of an ethical employee.**
4. **Explain the importance of safety and health in the workplace.**

Business enterprise is the dominant institution in America and in the world, and the ethics and values of business influence our society. Highly successful business leaders are quoted in the news and their behavior is observed and often emulated by others, not only in their particular business but in the nation and the world at large.

The influence of business on society and the influence of corporate leaders on individuals, however, is not always positive. Inferior products and services, environmental pollution, unsafe working conditions, unfair treatment of employees, and various other unethical behaviors are sometimes the outcomes of poorly run businesses and leaders who misuse their power and authority. When business leadership is practiced irresponsibly, our society and individuals within it are often the losers.

BUSINESS ETHICS

Ethics is defined as a systematic study of moral conduct, duty, and judgment. Certainly, ethical behavior has always been important for organizations and individuals; however, today more and more attention is being paid to ethical concerns. Why? There are two basic answers to that question.

- One, due to the coverage given to business through television, radio, and newspapers, we are more aware of unethical practices. For example, if an airline has a crash that kills hundreds of people and the cause is faulty equipment due to improper maintenance by the airlines, the public knows it quickly due to extensive media coverage. If a food company puts a product on the market with a food additive that may cause illness or even death, the public is informed through television, radio, and newspapers. The result of such instances is public demand of improved safety and health regulations and management accountability.

- Two, technology has advanced so far today that horrendous uses of it are possible. For example, medical science has expanded to the point that ethics are of major consideration. Some of the questions we hear debated are: Does an individual have the right to determine when to die and seek assistance with death? How long should a seriously ill patient be kept alive through artificial means? How much money should be spent on health care for the indigent? With the genetic work that is being done to determine links between genetics and cancer, obesity, and so forth, is it ever "right" for parents to decide to abort a fetus? Is it ethical to insert a growth hormone into children who have no growth-hormone deficiency, but who seem to be on growth curves shorter than their parents would like? There is now a growing body of evidence that some criminal and aggressive behavior has a genetic basis. If science proves the linkage, is it "right" to abort the fetus in this situation?

Our technological communication capabilities also pose some ethical questions. With international communication occurring through the Internet and the World Wide Web, what privacy rights does the individual have? How is pornography defined in communications through the Internet? What constitutes sexual harassment over the Internet?

Obviously, these ethical questions are only a few of the issues that we are facing. As technology continues to open new vistas for all of us, ethical questions will continue to occur. The point to be made here is that great wisdom on the part of leadership in business and individuals who are employed by business is required now and in the future to face and solve the ethical issues which will confront us. An important aspect of this wisdom is **morality** (a set of ideas of right and wrong). It is important that all of us strengthen our own ethical understandings and **moral integrity** (consistently adhering to a set of ideas of right and wrong), both within the workplace and outside it.

THE ETHICAL ORGANIZATION

Ethics has become so important that it is the topic of numerous books, the subject of seminars, and the basis for consulting businesses; it is also on the minds of executives daily. A company or organization can succeed or fail due to its ethical behavior. The ethical organization has certain characteristics. Several of these characteristics are mentioned here; the scope of this book will not allow for an exhaustive treatment of the topic.

SOCIALLY AND ENVIRONMENTALLY RESPONSIBLE

Certainly, we have examples in our society when business and government have been socially and environmentally irresponsible. Chernobyl in the Ukraine, a nuclear accident which occurred in April 1986, and Three Mile Island in Pennsylvania, another nuclear accident which occurred in March 1979, are examples of dangerous incidents when chemicals have escaped into the environment and caused death and long-term health hazards for the population. Oil spills in our oceans have caused the death of fish and wildlife.

The business executive who is socially and environmentally responsible is constantly aware of the dangers that are possible in business. The responsible executive takes all possible precautions to see that the environment is not polluted. The executive

pays attention to government regulations regarding careful disposal of waste products. When building new buildings, top priority is given to cutting down as few trees as possible and protecting wetland areas and other areas that are environmentally important.

Ethical organizations are environmentally responsible.

INTERNATIONALLY AWARE

When opening businesses in other countries or buying or selling products in other countries, the ethical business organization understands the importance of learning the culture and business customs of the country. Executives must respect the differences that exist between cultures. You learned about several of these cultural differences in Chapter 5; you may want to refer back to that chapter now.

When dealing with Japanese executives, for example, the American must understand that it is a basic precept of Japanese culture to put the best face on even the worst situation. Consequently, a smile, a nod, even a spoken affirmative in business negotiations may merely mean a reluctance to disappoint. Business is also never conducted at the beginning of a meeting. There is a set ritual that includes introductions, the pouring of tea, and the exchange of business cards. In contrast, the French get right down to business matters quickly; but they may be slow in coming to decisions. Regardless of

HUMAN RELATIONS TIP

It takes courage to live consistently by a set of moral values; determine that you will do so.

Chapter 6: Responding Ethically in the Work Environment

whether the decision is good news or bad, they state their intentions unambiguously. In Latin America, you may behave as you like as long as you are comfortable with Latin ways. Eye contact must be unflinching; conversation must be nose to nose. Hugs and two-handed handshakes are common among mere acquaintances. Siesta is sacred, which means that almost all businesses, including stores and banks, close for two or three hours in early afternoon. Late arrival at meetings is customary, from a quarter of an hour to an hour or two.

HONEST

An ethical organization is honest. It makes its policies and procedures clear to both its customers and its employees. For example, its pricing policies are made clear to buyers; its product warranty is clear and upheld. Employees understand salary and promotion policies. Executives within the organization are honest. Ethical executives do not appropriate excessive and lavish perks to themselves. The ethical executive's word can be taken seriously; employees know and understand the directions of the company.

COMMITTED TO DIVERSITY

An ethical organization is concerned about equal treatment for all individuals, regardless of ethnicity, age, or gender. Minorities and women, for example, often face obstacles in the workplace that occur not because of their performance but because of their race, ethnicity, and/or gender. Individuals within the workplace, due to their own biases and prejudices, may expect minorities and women to act in certain ways and treat them accordingly. **Physically challenged** individuals (persons with a physical handicap) also often face discrimination because of their handicap.

The ethical organization ensures that such behaviors do not occur or, if they do, takes steps to stop these behaviors immediately. How? Here are some examples of effective practices within an organization that impede racial, gender, and physically challenged discrimination.

- a clearly stated policy committing to equal employment

- hiring procedures that support equal employment

- personnel departments with expertise in assisting minorities and women with special issues

- grievance policies that are clearly stated, published, and distributed to all employees

- sensitivity training for all employees in understanding how to work with diversity

- special training for people with English language deficiencies, in the form of providing tuition assistance for classes at local colleges or providing on-site sessions

- accountability to ensure that all policies in regard to diversity are understood and upheld by both management and workers

COMMITTED TO THE COMMUNITY

The ethical organization understands there is a social responsibility to the community. A business needs to work within the community to address the issues it faces. For example, the organization may

- take interns from college programs into the organization;

- provide tutors for elementary and high school students;

- engage in mentoring programs for troubled youth;

- participate in the local chamber of commerce;

- contribute to community charities;

- provide leadership for solicitation of funds for worthy causes such as disabled children, health care of the indigent, and shelters for the homeless;

- assist with art programs through providing leadership and monies.

The ethical organization is committed to the community.
Courtesy of International Business Machines, Inc.

COMMITTED TO EMPLOYEES

Employee productivity, satisfaction, and empowerment are important to the ethical organization. To assist in these areas, the ethical organization

- ensures that employees understand the goals and direction of the business;

- encourages information to be freely distributed to all employees;

- challenges employees to generate new ideas;

- accepts input from employees;

- encourages collaboration and cooperation among employees;

- commits to developing executives who are good communicators and good listeners;

- develops teams which have both the authority and the responsibility to produce a product or service. Teams have become important to business for a number of reasons, such as:

  (1) empowerment of employees and thus increased productivity,

  (2) increased employee morale,

  (3) work of organization to be done at its lowest level thus reducing the ranks of middle management, and

  (4) greater efficiency and increased profitability of the company.

COMMITTED TO PROVIDING AND MAINTAINING A SAFE AND HEALTHY ENVIRONMENT

Not only is the ethical organization committed to its employees in ways that were identified in the previous section, the ethical organization is also committed to providing and maintaining a safe and healthy environment for them. Listed are some of the necessities of this type of environment.

- The equipment is in good working order.

- The facility is well maintained.

- A no-smoking policy is enforced.

- Substance abuse is addressed.

- Employees are made aware of preventive measures for occupational illnesses such as carpal tunnel diseases.

- Measures are in place to ensure the personal safety and security of employees.

- Emergency procedures are printed and distributed to all employees.

Health and safety are discussed in greater detail later in this chapter.

VISIONARY

The visionary organization has the ability to look beyond the day-to-day activities of the organization. It knows where the organization needs to be in the next five, ten, or fifteen years. Executives within the ethical organization can help managers and employees to understand where the company will be in five, ten, or fifteen years and assist others in formulating policies and objectives that will help the company achieve its goals. The organization, through its leadership, articulates the vision of the company consistently, and constantly evaluates the daily operations of the company in relation to meeting the vision.

THE CORPORATE CULTURE

As you begin to work for an organization it is important that you understand the culture. You need to know:

- what the organization values;

- how it lives out those values;

- what is and what is not ethical behavior within the organization.

One way to help you gain this knowledge is through reading the organizational vision or mission statement. More organizations are writing these statements today than in the past. Two individuals who are prolific writers and speakers in the leadership and organizational learning field are Peter Senge and Stephen Covey. Two of their works are *Principle-Centered Leadership* (Covey) and *The Fifth Discipline* (Senge).

Both works stress the importance of developing shared visions, values, and missions within the organization if the organization is to reach its maximum productivity and potential. The mission statements of organizations usually address these three areas:

- economic well-being

- quality of life

- stakeholders

The mission statement of TDIndustries in Dallas, Texas, for example, includes as its three primary parts: service to customers, opportunities for rewarding employment, and service to the community. A portion of that mission statement is given in Figure 6-1.

Company Mission Statement

OUR MISSION IS

SERVICE TO OUR CUSTOMERS

Through high quality goods and services, and value—as determined by our customers—we must continually earn and re-earn the right to serve our customers.

OPPORTUNITIES FOR REWARDING EMPLOYMENT

A building block of our philosophy about people and business is the belief that the goals we share as a group need not conflict with the goals we seek as individuals.

SERVICE TO OUR COMMUNITIES

. . . we . . . believe we have important responsibilities as individual citizens and as a company to be involved in our communities on a volunteer basis, in addition to giving generously of our money, goods, and services.

Excerpted from the mission of TDIndustries, Dallas, Texas.

Figure 6-1

Once you know the company mission statement, it is your responsibility to behave in ways that support the mission. If you find yourself in a company in which you cannot support the mission, then it is time for you to find another job.

THE ETHICAL EMPLOYEE

Now that you have discovered some of the ethical characteristics of an organization, consider certain ethical characteristics of employees within the organization.

RESPECTFUL OF THE ORGANIZATIONAL STRUCTURE

As you have already learned, the organization today has less layers than in the past. Many organizations use teams in delivering products and services; however, there is still an organizational structure and a reporting line. Usually, an organization chart spells out the reporting structure. Being respectful of the organization means that you do not go over or around your supervisor with issues or concerns. If you have an idea that you believe will help the productivity of the office, go to your supervisor to share it. If you are having difficulty meeting a deadline on a project, let your supervisor know. If you have someone who reports to you and there are problems, let your supervisor know. Keep your supervisor informed on all significant items. The rule of *no surprises* between employee and employer is a good rule to follow.

Talk to your employer about issues you have; do not go around your employer. *Hewlett Packard.*

ACCEPTING OF CONSTRUCTIVE CRITICISM

Your supervisor is just that—your supervisor. That person has not only the right but a responsibility to help you do your job as well as possible. You should always be willing to accept constructive criticism; that is, criticism that can help you learn and grow. If your supervisor recommends that you do something differently, do not view the remarks personally. For example, assume that you have recently set up a meeting for your employer at a hotel where lunch was served. It was your first time at planning such a meeting; you thought you did a good job. After the meeting, however, your employer tells you that the room arrangement was not satisfactory and the food was not good. How do you respond to such criticism? First of all, you deal with the issues at hand. You might say, "Can we talk about it further? How should the room have been arranged? What type of meal would you suggest?" Keep an open mind;

realize that you have much to learn and that everyone makes mistakes. You might also suggest a mutual review of the arrangements before the next meeting.

Always avoid an emotional response to criticism. Try to separate the issue from the critic; realize the critic is merely concerned with the situation improving. If you respond emotionally to the critic, you will probably only succeed in upsetting yourself and possibly the person who is doing the criticizing. Do not dwell on criticism and carry it around with you. Learn what you can from the situation, determine never to make the mistake again, and then move on.

RESPECTFUL OF THE PRIVACY OF OTHERS

Respect the privacy of others within the office. If someone confides a personal matter to you, do not spread the "juicy gossip." If you have access to personnel files which contain confidential information about others, keep the information confidential. Sometimes you will be given information that is not specifically labeled "confidential," yet it should not be passed on to others. Be sensitive to the handling of this information also; do not hide behind the rationale, "But, I was not told it was confidential." Use good, common sense. Ethical conduct dictates that you are always discreet. It is good to remember the golden rule: Treat others as you would want to be treated.

The ethical employee keeps confidences confidential. *Photo by Alan Brown/Photonics Graphics.*

AWARE OF OFFICE POLITICS

Office politics are fed by networks among individuals where who you know can be more important than what you know. Favors may be handed out based on the existing networks. In the most ethical world, office politics would not exist. Unfortunately, we do not live in the most ethical world and probably never will.

So, what do you do about office politics? When you begin a new job, notice what is happening around you. Be aware of the power bases. Be aware of who knows whom and what the relationships are. Then, hold on to your own value system. Do your job to the best of your ability. Do not gossip about office politics. Use your awareness of the power bases to get your job done. In other words, do not fight a power base when you know you cannot win. Spend your energies in doing what is right. Generally, if you hold on to your values and perform your job extremely well, you will be recognized and respected for who you are.

DEPENDABLE

Do what you say you will do when you say you will do it. Do not make excuses for poor performance. Excuses are usually seen by your employer or your peers as just that—excuses. A survey done by Accountemps and reported in *From Nine to Five* polled 150 executives and asked them to list the most unusual excuses they had heard for someone being late to work or absent. Here are some of the responses.

- The wind was blowing against me.
- My favorite actress just got married—I needed time alone.
- I thought Monday was Sunday.
- I had to sort socks.
- I forgot to come to work.

In addition to providing a laugh for us, these excuses point to the ridiculousness of trying to find a reason for irresponsible actions.

HUMAN RELATIONS TIP

Do not become involved in office politics; the time and energy it takes is not worth your effort.

Chapter 6: Responding Ethically in the Work Environment

COOPERATIVE

You may have the feeling that when your particular job is finished, you need not worry about helping anyone else. However, you are an employee of the company. Just because you have completed your task, does not mean that you can sit and do nothing; there is still work to be done. Remember, that the time may come when you have more work than you can do and will need some other employee to help you. If you help someone else, do not make that person feel obligated to you. Offer your help in the spirit of cooperation and with a desire to further the interests of the entire company.

The ethical employee is willing to help others get their tasks done. *Courtesy of International Business Machines, Inc.*

To assure your failure as a professional and to always be perceived as uncooperative, follow these simple guides.

- Always have an excuse ready for why you cannot help someone else.

- Point out why the individual needs help—obviously, the individual is incompetent or lazy.

- Forget about the importance of office productivity and customer satisfaction.

- Always look out for yourself; you cannot possibly help because you have to go home early to take your sick pet to the veterinarian.

RESPECTFUL OF THE CLIENTS OR CUSTOMERS

As an office professional, you must be respectful of your clients or customers. The old adage that "the customer is always right" is so true. Stop and think about that statement for a moment. Literally, a customer may be wrong; the customer is human and makes mistakes. What the statement means, however, is that in the context of service to the customer, that customer is always right. As an office professional, you may need to listen to numerous unhappy clients or customers. Let the client or customer release any anger, and then proceed to address the issue. At times you will not be able to say "yes" to the customer. When you cannot say "yes," explain the rationale of the company. Always act as your client's advocate within the company, getting the information or providing the service (if at all possible) that your client needs. Value the client's time. Do not waste the client's time by keeping the client on the phone for an inordinate amount of time or by being late for an appointment. Deal with irate clients calmly and professionally. Do not be defensive. Treat every client or customer as a VIP (very important person). After all, they are. Without the client or customer, the company would not be in business, and you would not have a job.

Keep the customer informed. If production problems, material shortages, or other problems occur that will keep the customer from getting an order on time, tell the customer. Keep a computer file on the clients or customers with whom you work. Record important information in your file and review it if a client calls. Remember that all clients are important, whether you deal with them once a year or once a month.

You may have occasion to help entertain customers and clients. For example, you may be asked to take an out-of-town customer to dinner. If you are selected for this purpose, keep the situation on a purely professional basis. You also may occasionally receive gifts from a client or customer. Certainly, a small gift may be appropriate, and you can accept it graciously. As a matter of ethics, however, you should never accept an extremely expensive gift.

HONEST

Being honest means that the employee does not take anything that belongs to the company, is conscientious about using time wisely, and gives the company eight hours of productive work (or whatever the office hours may be) each day.

Honesty dictates that the employee NOT:

- send e-mail to family or friends on the office computer;

- take home office supplies such as paper, pens, notepads, computer paper, and printer toner;

- use the Internet for personal "chats" or research;
- use the telephone for personal calls (long-distance or local);
- use the computer for preparing personal resumes for another job;
- take extra time over the time allocated by the company for lunch or breaks;
- spend thirty minutes in the restroom repairing makeup or having coffee upon arriving at work;
- use the photocopier for personal use.

Take a few moments now to complete the following Self Check. When you have finished, check your answers with those given at the end of this chapter.

Self Check

Respond to the following statements by marking "always," "sometimes," or "never."

1. I accept constructive criticism.
2. I respect the privacy of others.
3. I become involved in office politics.
4. I am dependable.
5. I make excuses when I cannot finish a job.
6. On my job, I help others with a task if my job permits.
7. I am honest with customers.
8. I use the telephone for personal conversations.
9. I believe it is okay to accept gifts from clients.
10. I talk with my employer first about any job related issues.

ETHICS—THE CHOICE IS YOURS

Even though you consider yourself an ethical individual, you will be confronted with situations that will test your ethical stance. For example, suppose your supervisor asks you to falsify information on a monthly expense report? Would you do it, knowing that if you do not, you may be fired? What if a co-worker asks you for information in your file that is confidential, threatening to betray a personal confidence which could cause you problems if you do not do it? What would you do?

The rightness or wrongness of an action may be determined only by degree. Sometimes we rationalize our actions because they are for the greater good of the organization, they do not actually hurt anyone (or so we say), or we cannot get fired (our family needs the money).

All of us need to be able to put tough, ethical choices into a good decision-making framework. Here are some suggestions for doing so.

- Analyze the situation facing you. Write down what has happened in detail. List the sequence of the events as objectively as possible.

- Identify your concerns. What are you being asked to do? Why do you feel uncomfortable about the request? What will be the outcome of doing what you have been asked—both short- and long-range consequences? What will be the outcome of not doing what you were asked—again, both short- and long-range consequences?

- Determine the options you have.

If you are still not clear about what you should do, ask yourself these questions.

- If my actions appeared in the newspaper, would I feel okay about everyone reading what occurred?

- Is what I anticipate doing legal?

- Could I proudly tell my spouse, my parents, or my children about my actions?

HUMAN RELATIONS TIP

Deal honestly and directly with any mistakes you make. Inform the necessary people of the error; state how you will correct the error.

- Does my anticipated action match my value system? If not, what value(s) am I giving away and why?

- Will I be proud of my actions one day, one week, one year from the present?

- What will my actions say about who I am? Do my actions fit with who I think I am?

Avoid doing anything you would not want to read about in the newspaper. © *Jeff Greenberg.*

THE ETHICAL ENVIRONMENT

An ethical organization promotes an ethical environment—the two are synonymous—one without the other brings into question the sincerity of the organizational goals. What does an ethical environment mean? It means that the work spaces provided for employees promote the team concept of the company. It means that management understands that teams require a less-structured atmosphere, one that is more informal, more participatory, and more flexible. It means that management is concerned about providing a safe and healthy environment, one where the employees know that safety and health issues will be addressed and dealt with by individuals within the company. Let us take these issues as separate ones, first considering team work spaces and then safety and health issues.

TEAM WORK SPACES

Today, office space and furnishings are being refined to not only reflect the changes in management philosophy (teams, less structure, less middle management, more flexibility, downsizing) but also to reflect the technological changes. Work spaces must facilitate (not impede) high-performance work in an era of constant change. Teams require faster, clearer, more direct, and more spontaneous communication. Teaming requires a less-structured atmosphere, one

that is much more informal, participatory, and flexible. The office becomes a community with both formal and informal meeting spaces, plus private spaces.

Office furniture includes self-contained work spaces which can be opened for group interaction. *Courtesy of International Business Machines, Inc.*

Office furniture manufacturers are responding to this "new" office with a variety of furniture. One approach has been to create an environment with flexible private space and open space which is modular and mobile—tables, files, and electronic bulletin boards on wheels. This concept is illustrated in Figure 6-2.[1]

The virtual organization is another concept that is changing the way space is interpreted within the organization. You have already learned that in the virtual environment, employees are "virtually present" at the office while physically elsewhere and connected by telecommunications. Less space is needed in this virtual world, and new, nonterritorial office designs are being used which allow one space to be used by several employees at different times. Individual workers can reserve space at the time needed. This concept has given rise to such words as **hoteling, just in time,** and **free addresses,** which merely mean that employees have a space in the company or at some other location when needed, but the space is not held exclusively for the employee. It can also be easily modified for the employee's needs at any particular time.

Our global, multicultural work environment is also influencing space requirements. For example,

[1]Gunn, Ronald A. and Marilyn S. Burroughs, "Work Spaces That Work: Designing High-Performance Offices," *The Futurist* (March-April, 1996).

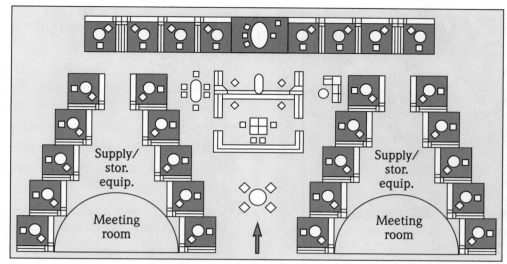

Figure 6-2   Caves and commons configuration.

in Asia, it is considered impolite to turn one's back to another person. Therefore, chairs are being designed to be angled against a wall (not a glass wall). It is anticipated that planning and furniture design concepts will become more universal, just as information technologies have become universal. For example, you might go to your company's Tokyo or London office to work as part of a team and find that the environment is very similar to the one that you have within the United States.

Generation X (the generation of people that followed the baby boomers and are now in their twenties and thirties) is also affecting the work environment. An environment that promotes productivity and high morale for Generation X includes one where there is great interaction among people and a comfortable, living-room-type setting—not a staid, constrained, hierarchy-driven design.

The thesis of this entire section is the ethical organization that holds empowered teams, productivity, and high performance as a goal translates that commitment into an environment which supports the concepts. In other words, the organization's goals are translated into actions which allow the goals to be implemented. Now let us consider the importance of safety and health in the ethical organization.

SAFETY AND HEALTH ISSUES

In 1970 the Occupational Safety and Health Act was passed to ensure American workers a safe and healthy workplace. The Occupational Safety and

Health Administration (OSHA), established by the act, was directed to encourage states to develop and operate their own job safety and health programs. OSHA requires that employers furnish a place of employment free from recognized hazards that can cause death, injury, or illness. The following is a short list of potential hazards that can be found in the office.

- frayed or loose telephone cords and electric wires
- open file and desk drawers
- wires loosely secured to the floor
- spilled beverages and food on the floor
- loose floor coverings on stairs or floors

To avoid these potential office hazards, the following details should be observed.

- Floor coverings should be durable and in good repair.
- Electrical equipment should be inspected regularly for damaged cords.
- Employees should be trained in the proper operation of equipment.
- Only one file drawer should be opened at a time.
- Employees should be instructed in procedures to follow in case of accidents. First aid kits should be readily accessible to all employees.

Always open only one file drawer at a time. *Photo by Erik Von Fischer/Photonics Graphics.*

Smoking

Studies have shown that breathing secondhand smoke is unhealthy; and nonsmokers complain of eye, nose, and throat irritations resulting from secondhand smoke. Studies also point out the linkage of secondhand smoke to emphysema and lung disease. Most businesses now have no-smoking policies which prohibit employees from smoking inside the building. If smoking is allowed, a place is designated where people may smoke; for example, a separate room for smokers.

Substance Abuse

Substance abuse is a huge problem in our society. Substance abuse refers to the use of alcohol or drugs to an extent that is debilitating for the individual using the substance. Drug and alcohol users are absent an average of two to three times more than the normal employee. Drug and alcohol users also perform at about two-thirds of their actual work potential; thus productivity in the office is lowered. Shoddy work and material waste is also evident with individuals who abuse substances. Mental and physical agility and concentration deteriorate with substance abuse. Chronic drug abuse creates wide mood swings, anxiety, depression, and anger. Employees who abuse drugs are more likely to steal equipment and materials to get money for their substance habit. Substance abusers are also over three times more likely to cause accidents. Even small quantities of drugs in the system can cause deterioration of alertness, clear mindedness, and reaction speed.

More employers today are using drug testing for employment candidates, employees, vendors, and contractors. According to the American Manage-ment Association, there has been a 277 percent increase in drug testing since 1987 due to the following factors.

- Department of Transportation and Department of Defense and state and local regulations that make testing mandatory for certain job categories.

- Court decisions permit private sector employers to test employees and job applications.

- Action by insurance carriers reduce accident liability and control health cost.

- Corporations require vendors and contractors to certify that they operate drug-free workplaces.[2]

Substance Abuse Laws

In 1988, the federal government imposed sweeping antidrug rules on private employers in an effort to curb employee substance abuse. Under the Drug-Free Workplace Act employers are responsible for.

- publishing a policy prohibiting the use of controlled substances in the workplace;

- establishing a drug-free awareness program that informs employees about the dangers of workplace drug abuse;

- informing employees that they are required as a condition of employment to abide by their employer's policy.

Carpal Tunnel Syndrome

According to an article in *From Nine to Five,* if you type rapidly on a computer keyboard, you may be striking up to 200,000 keys a day—the equivalent of your fingers walking ten miles.[3] With this type of intensity at the computer, proper techniques must be used. These techniques include appropriate keyboard usage, good posture, proper chair height, and tension releasers. Poor techniques or lack of the proper office furniture may cause **carpal tunnel syndrome** which is a condition that occurs due to the compression of a large nerve—the median nerve—as it passes through a tunnel composed of bone and ligaments in the wrist. Carpal tunnel diseases (CTDs) are considered the occupational illness of the decade. Symptoms of carpal tunnel syndrome include a gradual onset of numbness

---

[2]"Drug Testing Grows, AMA Study Finds," *Managing Office Technology* (July, 1996), 23.

[3]Lewis, Cindy, "PC Hazards Can Be Avoided," *From Nine to Five* (October, 1993).

and a tingling or burning in the thumb, index, middle, and ring fingers.

Eyestrain

Of the environmental factors affecting office personnel, eyestrain is the one that concerns workers the most according to a study done by Louis Harris & Associates, Inc. This study found that 44 percent of office workers surveyed ranked eyestrain higher than air quality and exposure to hazardous materials as their greatest health concern in the office environment.[4] Symptoms of eyestrain include visual discomfort, irritation, problems in focusing, blurring, double vision, and headaches. Some studies have found that 10 to 15 percent of video display terminal (VDT) users experience daily problems and 40 to 50 percent experience occasional problems. Eyestrain problems can be caused by uncorrected vision and long periods at the computer without breaks.

One solution to eyestrain is to reorient the employee, the workstation, and the computer so less light reflects on the computer screen. One quick way to determine the source of glare is to set up a mirror in front of the screen. If glare exists, it will be reflected in the mirror. If it is not possible to move personnel and computers, lighting controls can be used. For example, dimmers can be placed on lights which can adjust how much light floods the area. Individuals can tailor their lighting by means of a device, similar to a television remote control or through a computer system.

Fatigue

Fatigue while sitting at a VDT has to do with the type of work that is being done in addition to the time that is spent at the VDT. Some studies have found that scientists, engineers, and programmers experience less fatigue while working at a VDT than do data entry personnel. Reasons as to why this situation occurs vary. The data entry work may be more monotonous and the person entering the data may not be as involved with the subject matter as the engineer or programmer. Also, programmers are probably more tolerant of system delays and computer problems than the data entry person, because they have more knowledge of what is happening with the computer. Figure 6-3 gives some tips to assist in lessening the possibility of carpal tunnel syndrome, eyestrain, and fatigue.

---

[4]"Remove the Glare," *Managing Office Technology* (August, 1996), 22.

Health Tips

These tips will help in lessening the possibility of carpal tunnel syndrome, eyestrain, and fatigue.

- Be certain that the light on the computer screen is good—not too dark, not too light.

- Take a short rest period (ten minutes) every two or three hours.

- Stand up every half hour.

- Be certain your chair is adjusted properly for you.

- Keep your wrists flat and level when using the keyboard; key with your fingers, not your wrists. Avoid flexing or twisting wrists at odd angles. Consider using a "wrist rest" for your mouse.

- Do not rest wrists on hard edges or on wrist rests while keyboarding.

- Use good posture. When sitting at the computer, adjust the chair height and seat back so you sit erect, your body tilted slightly back. Face the computer directly; do not turn your head to one side.

- Adjust the screen height so you can hold your head at a slight downward tilt to avoid straining neck and shoulder muscles. Keep your feet flat on the floor.

- Use tension releasers. Stretch the fingers as far apart as possible; hold for five seconds, then relax. Rotate your wrists while your fingers are relaxed. Let the wrists go limp; shake them up and down, then sideways. Stretch out your arms, hold, relax, then repeat.

- Look away from the screen for a short period of time every half hour.

- If eye problems persist, get an eye examination.

- Focus on distant objects occasionally as an exercise to relieve eye muscles.

- Maintain a viewing distance of a minimum of two feet from the eye to the computer screen.

Figure 6-3

Personal Safety and Security

In most offices, it is common for employees to work overtime occasionally. These overtime hours may be in the early morning or in the evening hours. When fewer people are in the building, it is essential to take greater security precautions.

Companies have a variety of procedures to protect their employees. Security guards may be stationed at doors to monitor individuals as they enter and exit. Special badges or passes may be issued to visitors. In companies where the work has national security implications, visitors and employees may be asked to pass through gates similar to those at the airport that will detect arms or explosives. Some companies have television screens and cameras in particular locations within the company. There may be security mechanisms on doors and windows that are turned on after regular hours so that if a door is opened without using an access code an alarm will sound.

As an employee, here are some rules that you might follow to make the office environment safer when you work outside the normal business hours.

- Notify the security staff if you are working late. If you work in a high crime area, ask security to accompany you to your car when you leave work. Notify someone at your home that you are working late, and call just before you leave to let the person know that you are on your way home.

- Situate yourself near others who are working late if possible.

- Work next to a telephone and have emergency numbers handy.

- Keep all doors to your office locked while working.

- If you hear strange noises, call for help.

- Walk to your car with a group of people if possible.

- Have your car keys ready to unlock your car.

- Lock your car immediately after getting into the car.

Security of Equipment and Information

Theft can be a problem with small office equipment such as calculators and personal computers. Companies should have some type of inventory control to identify equipment that is missing; for example, serial numbers can be affixed to equipment. Information pilferage is also a concern. Computer passwords should be used for confidential information. These passwords can be changed periodically. If someone has tried to gain access to your files, most systems will let you know. Passwords should not be written down or passed on to assistants. When individuals leave the organization, their passwords should be deleted.

Emergencies

Emergencies such as fires and bomb threats may occur which demand that there be evacuation procedures. These procedures should be printed, distributed to all personnel, and personnel should be periodically reminded of the procedures. For illnesses or accidents, emergency procedures should include a list of employees who can administer first aid and phone numbers for ambulances, hospitals, and physicians. Oxygen and first aid kits should be located so that they are easily available to employees. As an employee concerned about office emergencies, you may want to take a CPR or first aid course.

ETHICAL CHANGE

We do not live in a perfect world, thus we do not live in a world in which all individuals or all organizations are ethical. If the organization is to become more ethical, then the people within the organization must understand the importance of ethics and commit to changing their unethical behaviors. Because ethics are so tied to values and values are learned at an early age, ethical change is not easy. For organizations and people who sincerely care about making their organization and the world a better place to live and work, change can occur. How? Here are some steps for producing ethical change.

- Determine what should be the organizational ethics. What is important for the organization? What will help it move forward? What is impeding the organization at the present time? Set the direction.

- Determine what changes need to occur within the organization to meet the goals which have been set. What steps should be taken? Develop an action plan.

- Define accountability. Hold people within the organization responsible for behaving ethically. Accountability means that if people are not upholding the ethical behaviors, negative consequences will result for the individuals. Punish unethical behavior.

- Reward individuals who live the ethics of the organization. Give recognition possibly in the form of awards, letters of commendation, and so forth.

- Evaluate the results. As a result of individuals living the ethical behaviors identified by the organization, is the organization a better place to work? Does it provide higher service or products to its customers? Does it contribute more to the community?

AN ETHICAL, SAFE, AND HEALTHY WORK ENVIRONMENT

Throughout this chapter you have learned the importance of working in an ethical, safe, and healthy work environment. The problems of our nation and world spill over into the work environment, and we are faced daily with ethical and environmental issues on the job. The organization for which you work has a social responsibility to help improve the conditions not only in our workplace but also in our world. You, as an office employee, also have a responsibility to help make the office and your environment a more responsible and safe place to work and live.

HUMAN RELATIONS TIP

"A small group of thoughtful, concerned citizens can change the world. Indeed, it is the only thing that ever has."—Margaret Mead

CHAPTER SUMMARY

This summary will help you remember the important points covered in this chapter.

- The importance of business ethics can be understood by observing the way that organizational ethics impact our entire society. If there is not a high standard of ethics within a business, inferior products and services, environmental pollution, unsafe working conditions, unfair treatment of employees, and various other behaviors can be the result.

- The ethical organization is socially and environmentally responsible, internationally aware, honest, committed to diversity, committed to the community, committed to employees, and visionary.

- One way to understand the corporate culture is to read its vision or mission statement.

- The ethical employee is respectful of the organizational structure, accepting of constructive criticism, respectful of the privacy of others, aware of office politics, dependable, cooperative, respectful of the clients or customers, and honest.

- Each of us must determine the rightness or wrongness of our actions or anticipated actions. By putting the possibilities in a framework which includes analyzing the situation, identifying our concerns, and determining the options open to us, we can make better ethical decisions.

- Ethical change within an organization is possible, but it demands that the organization determine its ethical position, decide what changes need to be made, hold individuals accountable for the change, reward people who live the ethics, and evaluate the results of an ethical (or nonethical) environment.

- Office space and safety and health issues impact the office environment. The ethical organization is concerned about these issues and addresses them constantly.

CHAPTER GLOSSARY

The following terms were introduced in this chapter. To help you review, definitions are given here.

- **Ethics** (p. 130)–The systematic study of moral conduct, duty, and judgment.

- **Morality** (p. 131)–A set of ideas of right and wrong.

- **Moral integrity** (p. 131)–Consistently adhering to a set of ideas of right and wrong.

- **Physically challenged** (p. 132)–Persons with a physical handicap.

- **Hoteling, just in time, and free addresses** (p. 138)–Employees have a space in the company or at some other location when needed, but the space is not held exclusively for the employee.

- **Generation X** (p. 139)–The generation of people that followed the baby boomers and are now in their twenties and thirties.

- **Substance abuse** (p. 140)–The use of alcohol or drugs to an extent that is debilitating for the individual using the substance.

- **Carpal tunnel syndrome** (p. 140)–A condition that occurs due to the compression of a large nerve, the median nerve, as it passes through a tunnel composed of bone and ligaments in the wrist.

DISCUSSION ITEMS

These discussion items provide an opportunity for you to test your understanding of the chapter through discussion with your classmates and your instructor.

1. Why is ethical behavior important for businesses?

2. List and explain six characteristics of the ethical business.

3. List and explain six characteristics of an ethical employee.

4. Why is an organizational mission or vision statement important?

5. Can ethical change occur? If so, how?

6. Why and how are office spaces different today than in the past?

CASE STUDY

Jacqueline Marquette, your supervisor at Koronet, gives her expense accounts to you each month; your responsibility is to put the information on a form and give it back to her. Once she reviews and signs it, you send it to the president for signature. Last month you noticed that Jacqueline put alcohol on the expense report (under the category of food and beverage); this month you notice the same thing has occurred. Company policy specifically states that an employee cannot be reimbursed for alcohol. You also noticed about six months ago that the same thing occurred. You believe that it is merely carelessness on the part of your supervisor; you believe in her honesty. However, you are beginning to wonder if you are engaging in unethical behavior by not calling her attention to these items. Ms. Marquette has always told you that you are responsible for knowing and adhering to the policies and procedures of the company.

• What is the problem?

• What is your role in the issue?

• Should you talk with Ms. Marquette? If so, how should you approach the topic?

• Have you been behaving ethically by not calling it to her attention? If your answer is "yes," explain your position.

RESPONSES TO SELF CHECK

The most appropriate answers are

1. Always
2. Always
3. Never
4. Always
5. Never
6. Always
7. Always
8. Never
9. Sometimes (If the gift is a small gift, it may be appropriate; each situation needs to be analyzed.)
10. Sometimes (On some issues you may not need to involve your employer, but never go around that person to a higher level.)

OFFICE TASKS

OFFICE TASK 6-1 (Objective 1)

You are to write a paper in which you examine your own values and ethics. The paper is to be from three to five pages in length. Instructions are provided on Student Data Template Disk, file OT6-1. Submit your paper to your instructor.

OFFICE TASK 6-2 (Objectives 1, 2, and 3)

With three of your classmates, interview two executives concerning the following:

- importance of ethical behavior

- characteristics of an ethical organization

- traits of ethical employees

As you are interviewing the executives, determine if their organizations have a vision or mission statement. If so, ask if you may have a copy of the statement. Present your findings to the class. Take notes carefully during the interviews so that you may accurately report your findings.

OFFICE TASK 6-3 (Objective 4)

Recently, there was a reported assault of an employee in the parking lot of the Michigan office of Koronet. This reported assault occurred at 11:05 p.m. as the employee was leaving after working overtime. The employee did not have anyone with her. The individual responsible for the assault has not been identified; the case is in the hands of the police. However, not only is there widespread fear among the employees of Koronet, but the surrounding community is also concerned about the safety of its citizens. Ms. Marquette is handling the situation internally and dealing with the media externally. She has asked for your suggestions on how the parking lot can be made safer and what type of communication needs to go to the employees. She asks that you call your TQM team together to make suggestions to her. Your TQM team meets and determines that they will meet with the security personnel to get any suggestions that they have. They will then draft "Safety Rules" for all employees who work overtime and draft a cover memo to be sent to all employees at the Michigan plant. Ms. Marquette will make the final decision as to what goes out, but she always values the work of the TQM team and uses their input extensively.

Team with your classmates (the TQM team) on this project. Draft the "Safety Rules" and a cover memo to all employees. Use the memorandum form on the Student Data Template Disk, file OT6-3.

ENGLISH USAGE CHALLENGE DRILL

Correct the following sentences. Cite the grammar rule that is applicable to each sentence. Before you begin, refresh your memory by reviewing comma rules in the *Multimedia Reference for Writers,* this text, or some other reference manual available to you.

1. When music is the topic to be discussed the group quickly begins a lively exchange of the latest light rock hits.

2. To satisfy a craving for ice cream fearful individuals will brave the worst weather.

3. For example the course does not compare favorably to a similar one at Midwestern.

4. Culture is a way of thinking feeling and believing.

5. The huge restless crowd waited patiently for the concert to begin.

Assessment of Chapter Objectives

Now that you have completed the chapter and the office tasks, take a few moments to review the following learning objectives. Did you accomplish these objectives? If so, explain how in the space provided. If you were unable to accomplish these objectives, give your reason for not doing so. Your instructor may want to review your answers.

I accomplished these objectives:

1. Recognize the importance of ethical behavior.
   Yes _____ No _____

   Explain how you accomplished this objective.

   _____

   _____

   _____

2. Identify characteristics of an ethical organization.
   Yes _____ No _____

   Explain how you accomplished this objective.

   _____

   _____

   _____

3. Identify traits of an ethical employee.
   Yes _____ No _____

   Explain how you accomplished this objective.

   _____

   _____

   _____

4. Understand the importance of safety and health in the workplace. Yes _____ No _____

   Explain how you accomplished this objective.

   _____

   _____

   _____

Provide reasons for failing to accomplish any of the objectives.

_____

_____

_____

_____

_____

DEBRA THOMAS'S CASE SOLUTION

I decided that I needed to prove to the long-time employee that I could do the job. I treated him with great respect and worked hard to learn every aspect of the field as quickly as possible. Regardless of how frustrated I became with the lack of respect and assistance I received from the employee, I continued to make every effort to maintain a warm and professional attitude toward him. Within a few months we developed an excellent working relationship. I earned his respect and even his friendship. I went the extra mile to show him that I could learn the job and do it well. The end result was a maximum level of employee service accomplished in a pleasant environment.

PART 3

Office Communications

Michelle F. MacDowell, CPS
Corporate Administrative Assistant
Halff Associates, Inc.
Dallas, Texas

A Success Profile

I attribute my success to a combination of the education I received at Bradford School of Business in Dallas, Texas, and the training I received through the many diverse positions I have been lucky enough to hold. In business school, I majored in accounting but also received strong secretarial training. I graduated at the top of my accounting class and was offered a job as a full-charge bookkeeper two weeks before I graduated. I accepted the position, and for the duration of that job I seldom used my secretarial skills.

My next position was in a small office where I was both the secretary and accountant for a CPA. My boss shared an office with another man and his secretary, who was the president of Big D Chapter of Professional Secretaries International (PSI). Through her I learned the difference between being "just a secretary" and being a true "professional secretary." I joined PSI shortly after that and then sat for the Certified Professional Secretary (CPS) exam. I passed my CPS exam in 1987.

Eventually, I had intended to get my CPA license and leave the secretarial field. However, I found more and better opportunities in the secretarial field. It was through a contact in PSI that I found my current employer, Halff Associates, Inc. I have been with Halff for seven years. As an office professional, one must have a mastery of many varied skills. Even once you have enough experience to have mastered the skills that you need to handle the constant interruptions, rushes, and

snap decisions, I have found that one cannot assume that it is going to be easy to use a position as an office professional as a springboard to a management position. It is always important to be a good ambassador for your company, while also being aware of other opportunities. Some companies are structured in a way that allow for better growth opportunities than others. It may even be possible to start your own business. As an office professional, you certainly can be placed in the right circumstances to develop the skills and the knowledge that it takes to do a variety of jobs. You merely need to determine what you want to do and have the courage to go after it.

I believe that the most crucial characteristics and skills that an office assistant must have are the ability to manage time, to be versatile, to be willing and have the desire to learn, and to have a professional attitude. By maintaining a professional attitude and giving 100 percent of your effort to everything you do, you most likely will be able to learn the required skills.

Another piece of advice, whether you believe it at this time, people who have been around awhile have much to offer. They may not do things the way you think they should be done, but you need to give their expertise the weight it deserves. Remember that everyone's ideas have value. Whether you know it or not, they have probably "been there, done that," only with a different technology. Listen to them and show respect for their knowledge. Work as a team player to achieve company goals.

Finally, decide what success is for you. The ultimate goal of reaching the top may be the very thing that keeps you from reaching the top. If your definition of success is climbing the ladder into a management position, you may not want to start out as an office professional. It does not make for an easy climb up that ladder. Reaching the top of the ladder is not always what success is about. Your definition of success will probably change as you grow. You may find that just being happy is success and enough in itself. Reevaluate your goals periodically; realign yourself with what makes you happy; and always do your best.

MICHELLE MACDOWELL'S CASE

I have prepared a case from my experiences as an office professional. Decide how you would handle the case by answering the question at the completion of the situation. Then turn to the end of Part III page 217 to see how the case was solved.

THE SITUATION

Venessa's boss, Bob, is the head of the land surveying department. The department is understaffed. They have been so busy for the last few months that Bob has had to step back into the production work that he normally delegated to the project managers under him. This has not left him enough time for sales or to manage the group, which should be the main focus of his position.

Venessa knows that Bob has a deadline for a project that he has to get out today. It is already several days late. She finds out that there is a new job on his desk that has not been assigned to anyone yet. It has been sitting there for one week already and is due in one week. She also gets several phone calls that day from clients who are checking to see what time they can expect their surveys. When Venessa checks on the status of those surveys, she finds out that they are supposed to be delivered to the clients today, but the project mangers did not find out about the jobs from Bob soon enough to finish them on time.

What can Venessa do to keep this from happening again? (Hiring more people is not an option.)

CHAPTER 7

TELECOMMUNICATIONS AND THE TELEPHONE

LEARNING OBJECTIVES

1. **Discover how information is transmitted electronically.**
2. **Describe the types of telephone systems, equipment, and features available.**
3. **Develop and use proper telephone techniques.**

Telecommunications is the electronic transmission of

- *text*
- *data*
- *voice*
- *video*
- *image (graphics and pictures)*

from one location to another. Thus, the computer and fax technology that you learned about in Chapters 5 and 6 are forms of telecommunication. The Internet and e-mail are also telecommunication vehicles. Telecommuting which you learned about in Chapter 1 is a form of telecommunication. Still another form of telecommunications is the telephone. In fact, although the telecommunications field is rapidly changing, the telephone is one piece of telecommunications equipment that has been with us since the late 1800s. Clearly, it has undergone many changes, but it is still considered one of the most important telecommunications linkages that we have. This chapter will give you an overview of telecommunications, with a brief explanation of transmission technologies. The main concentration in this chapter, however, will be on the telephone, because verbal contact with individuals both inside and outside the company through the telephone is vitally important.

TELECOMMUNICATIONS— AN OVERVIEW

As you have just learned, telecommunications is the electronic transmission of text, data, voice, video and image from one location to another. Communication in its simplest form is a transfer of information. This communication must be transferred so that all parties involved are able to receive and transmit the information. Telecommunications as we know it is determined by a combination of technology and economics. The questions become: Do we have the technological expertise and can most people afford to purchase it? The costs of new technological changes are fairly great at first but generally decrease over time. For example, in 1997 federal regulators cleared the way for the nation to switch to digital TV by 2006. The digital TV will have a crystal-clear, movie-quality picture and sound. This shift in TV is the most dramatic advance since color was introduced in the 1950s. Widescreen TV models are expected to cost at least $2,000 initially; however, as the technology becomes used more widely, the costs will decrease. Whenever new telecommunications technology becomes available, it is always the task of business to deliver it at a cost that the public can afford.

DRUMS AND SMOKE SIGNALS

Communication across distances is not a new problem. It has been of concern to people for generations. As you learned in studying history, early civilizations used drums and smoke signals to communicate with each other across the miles (see Figure 7-1). They had to devise not only the means of communicating but also what the signals from the drums and smoke signals meant in words that were understood by both parties. This concept may seem relatively simple today, but for the early civilizations, it was probably as complex a problem as telecommunications is for us. Even though our communication methods are much more sophisticated today,

151

we constantly seek to communicate across distances with ease, speed, and low cost.

Figure 7-1   Drums and smoke signals were an early form of communication.

THE TELEGRAPH AND TELEPHONE

In the nineteenth century, two inventions changed our communication patterns drastically—the telegraph transmitter and receiver invented by Samuel Morse in 1837 and the telephone invented by Alexander Graham Bell in 1876. Morse's telegraph was the first instrument to transform information into electrical form and transmit it reliably over long distances. Bell's invention of the telephone created the means by which we can maintain direct verbal communication over long distances without the use of codes. An extensive network of copper wires was constructed throughout the nation and the world to carry voice from one location to another. The voice information was also converted from its mechanical origins (vibrations in the air) to electromagnetic reproductions of the changes in air pressure. This vast hard-wired phone system is still influencing our communica-

tions system today. If cellular technology had been available in the late 1800s, the copper wire would never have been necessary. Why do we still use it today? Because it costs much less to talk on the existing system than to use a wireless system.

THE TELEVISION

The twentieth century brought the invention of television—again, a telecommunications instrument that has transformed the way we receive information. The copper wire based phone system could not handle the video requirements of television. Commercial television took care of the video needs for the masses but the system was not economically feasible for individual video needs. Coaxial cable was developed. Many homes now have two communications wiring systems, audio copper wires and coaxial video wires for cable television. Coaxial cable is also used by telephone companies, particularly for long-distance calls where it is necessary to install cable underground or beneath the ocean.

THE MICROPROCESSOR

In the early 1970s the microprocessor was invented, and data processing using computer systems that were affordable by the average citizen became a reality. These complex electronic components worked on digital principles as opposed to analog principles. The digital concept relates to binary digits and makes decisions based on combinations of two digits. The problem that exists is that computers operate on a digital system whereas almost all other telecommunications equipment uses analog signals. If computers are to be used to process information in an analog world, there must be some conversion capability. For the digital computer to send data from one computer to another through the phone system, the digital data must also be converted from parallel processed digital data (multiwire data systems) inside the computer to serial (single wire) analog telephone lines. The conversion of the information from analog to digital is one of the functions of the computer **modem** (short for modulator-demodulator, the device that enables the computer to send and receive data over the telephone lines) (Figure 7-2).

Digital Signals   Modem   Analog Signals   Modem   Digital Signals

Figure 7-2   Transmission of digital and analog signals.

FIBER OPTICS

When the technology became affordable so that many people could process data, the consumer then wanted to process both voice and video. Because a wireless system is still not economically feasible, processing video is fairly complicated. It takes a sophisticated and high-speed microprocessor to process video in real time so that it does not appear on the discriminating computer operator's monitor like an old silent movie. To carry this high-speed data transmission requires a high quality transmission line such as the expensive coaxial cable used by the television cable companies or an even better transmission system such as fiber optics. However, just as coaxial cable is expensive, so is fiber optics. Fiber installation was started in the 1970s, but due to its expense, the process has been slow. Eventually the old copper system will no longer be used. How long will it take and what will be the system? Neither answer can be given with certainty. The system may be a fiber optics system or we may find something technologically better to meet the projected future needs of the world. At this point, however, a fiberglass system is the best guess of what will be used to replace the archaic, but still functional copper wire system.

NETWORKS

Information is transmitted through the transmission technologies you have just learned about and through network linkages, which you learned about in Chapter 3. As you will recall, networks allow computers to talk to each other over distances. Recall the discussion about local area networks, metropolitan area networks, wide area networks, and the Internet. Each of these networks links computers over an established distance. The local area network provides the least distance and the Internet provides the greatest distance, with the Internet linking computers worldwide. If you do not recall the information on networks, you may want to refer back to Chapter 3 and reread the information.

By putting this information about networks with what you have just learned about transmission technologies, you begin to get an overview of some of the technical aspects of the telecommunications field. You also now have a basic understanding of some of the complexities of moving data technologically from one point to another. Let us now discuss a piece of telecommunication equipment that we use numerous times each day—the telephone.

TELEPHONES

Ever since Alexander Graham Bell made his first telephone call to Thomas Watson in 1876 with the historic words, "Mr. Watson, come here; I want you," the telephone has grown to be one of our most important means of communication. Verbal contact within the office and with business customers is so important that the employee often has a car phone and utilizes the telephones now available on planes. Also, many of us now have telephones in our personal cars, which we use to stay in contact with our families in our busy world that often involves miles of driving each day.

From the late 1800s when Alexander Graham Bell made his first call, the telephone has grown to be one of our most important means of communication. *Reproduced with permission of AT&T.*

It is easy to understand why the telephone plays such an important role; it is a fast, easy way to transmit information over long or short distances. Even though we have other ways of transmitting information quickly, such as computers and fax machines, the telephone will remain an important communication tool. Why? It adds a personal touch. Because you are able to hear the other person's voice, you can detect sincerity, happiness, and even anger. In a world in which high technology is used extensively, the telephone allows for an added dimension of humanness.

The many changes in technology, and the 1984 court order that forced AT&T® (American Telephone and Telegraph) to give up its monopoly of the industry and to divest itself of its local companies, have brought about new equipment and services provided by a number of companies, including Ameritech®, SBC® Communications, Inc., Bell Atlantic®, GTE® Corporation, AT&T®, Sprint®, MCI®, and LCI® International, Inc. to name several.

Chapter 7: Telecommunications and the Telephone

One of the newest changes in telephone technology is the use of satellites to carry signals from one telephone to another at any point in the world. In late 1998 a total of 840 satellites will be launched. The new satellites will carry calls from handheld phones and low- and high-speed digital data. Customers will include international travelers, corporate offices in international locations, and individuals in remote areas of the developing world who, today, have no access to telephones.[1] For people living in underdeveloped countries that have not changed much in a thousand years, this satellite infrastructure will create the potential for rapid economic development.

SWITCHING SYSTEMS

Calls are routed to and from the public lines of the telephone company to the private lines within a company through switching systems. These systems include key systems and **private branch exchange (PBX)** systems. Due to the continual changes in technology, the life cycle of a switching system is extremely short. It is anticipated that in the future, the life cycle will be even shorter due to continued technological advances. The two basic types of systems are key and PBX systems; however, there are no longer distinguishable dividing lines between the systems. The higher-end system is the PBX, and the lower-end is the key system. Due to computer integration, some applications that were once available only on higher-end systems are now available on lower-end systems. Some of the differences in the key system and the PBX system are given in the next section.

Two other types of telephone systems are mentioned, the central exchange (Centrex) system and single-line telephones. The Centrex system is a type of PBX system that is used extensively in businesses. The single-line telephone is used only in very small offices and in the home. Here are some of the differences in the various systems.

Key Systems

The key system is used primarily by small companies. Key systems function with a **key service unit (KSU)** which operates a maximum number of phones and lines depending on the system size. For example, a key system may handle up to eighty telephones. A key system permits the user to select an outside or an internal line. Internal lines are used for conversations within the company and for paging purposes.

Key systems may have a variety of features; for example, calls on hold can be connected to background music. A paging system linked to speakers throughout the business office can be used to notify employees of calls. Key systems have switching devices that automatically switch calls to another line if one line is busy. A key system is depicted in the following photo.

A key system. *Sprint Corporation.*

PBX Systems

The PBX system is used by large companies. This system can link up to 10,000 telephones. It may channel all incoming calls to a full-time attendant who connects the call with company extensions, or calls may be distributed automatically to extensions in the order in which they are received. Internal calls are made without attendant assistance. Outgoing calls may be made directly by employees. The employee merely dials a number such as "9" to make the connection to an outside line.

The PBX system is a sophisticated computer offering dozens of features such as

- handling multiple calls by holding one or more calls while an individual is on another line;

- providing teleconferencing capabilities where several people can hold meetings without leaving the office;

- redialing busy lines automatically;

- informing an employee that a call is waiting;

- routing calls automatically from one line to another;

- allowing an employee to answer any telephone within a certain work area;

- allowing calls to be sent to another answering point.

[1]Cook, William J., "1997 A New Space Odyssey," *U.S. News & World Report* (March 3, 1997): 45–47.

A PBX system. *AT&T Archives.*

CENTRAL EXCHANGE

Central exchange (Centrex) is a service provided by the local phone company that offers PBX-like features to a business without the business purchasing a switching system. Centrex provides **direct inward dialing (DID)** in which all calls go directly to the number dialed. Every telephone extension in the system has its own number devised by modifying the last four digits of the company's main number. If a caller does not know a particular Centrex extension number, the caller can dial the company's main number and ask the attendant to make the connection.

SINGLE-LINE TELEPHONES

Single-line telephones are used in homes and small offices. As the name implies, these telephones have only a single line available. Numerous features, however, are available, including call waiting, call forwarding, caller ID, and so forth. You will learn more about these special features later in this chapter.

SPECIAL TYPES OF EQUIPMENT

In addition to regular telephone equipment, several special types of telephone equipment are available. This equipment can assist the employee in being more productive and in providing for special needs.

Cellular Telephones

Individuals often need to maintain contact with a central location while moving between different locations. **Cellular technology** makes it possible to have a fully functional telephone in the car, the briefcase, or even a coat pocket. Cellular technology breaks a large service area down into smaller areas called cells. When a customer places a call from a mobile unit, the nearest cell or transmitting station relays it to a central computer which, in turn, directs the call into the local telephone system. When a customer leaves one cell area and enters

another, the computer automatically switches the transmission to the next nearest cell. Calls may be made anywhere in the United States, and the quality of the transmission does not lessen with distance.

Cellular phones have several useful features. They can be

- permanently installed in a car and powered by the car's electrical system;
- transportable units that are powered by separate battery packs;
- self-contained handheld units;
- adapted to include a built-in speaker phone;
- voice activated;
- totally hands-free.

Advantages of cellular phones to users include:

- flexibility
- accessibility
- efficiency
- increased productivity
- reduced stress due to being able to accomplish work while on the road

Safety can be a disadvantage if the user is not careful. Certainly, phone users must be safe drivers which means keeping their eyes on what is happening on the road. Hands-free units help with the safety factor.

A cellular phone helps the busy employee stay in contact with customers and the office. *Ameritech Cellular Services.*

Chapter 7: Telecommunications and the Telephone

Portable Pagers

Portable pagers are signaling devices that alert the holder to contact a phone number for a message. Pagers may be clipped to your pocket or belt. When someone wants to speak to you, the pager emits a sound. A phone number is displayed so that you may return the call or a short message is given. Pagers are popular for busy employees who must be away from the office frequently; through a pager, they can be reached quickly. We also use pagers personally; for example, working mothers and fathers use pagers to keep in contact with their children, and spouses may use pagers to contact each other. Pagers are a convenient and inexpensive way to contact people quickly.

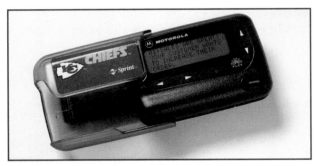

Pagers allow for quick access to individuals.
Sprint Corporation.

Cordless Telephones

Cordless telephones have a base station and a handset. The base station plugs into both the telephone jack and an electrical outlet. The handset functions as a portable telephone with a receiver and a transmitter. The handset may be carried to distances of approximately 900 feet and used as a telephone.

SpeakerPhones

Sometimes a need arises for several people in an office to talk with one or more people at another location. Speakerphones are available for such occasions. A speakerphone has a built-in transmitter and volume control that permit both sides of a telephone conversation to be amplified. A speakerphone makes it possible to consult files, take notes, or walk around the room while on the phone.

VideoPhones

Although videophone technology has been available since 1964, there was no practical application until the 1980s when Sony and Mitsubishi introduced plug-in-the-wall video telephones. These telephones, however, could send only black-and-white still images and conversation was not possible during picture transmission.

Although the technology is still not widely used, the videophone of today is very different from the videophone of the 1980s. It uses a high-speed modem that pushes sound and picture information across a phone line. A small video screen sits atop the telephone and allows you to hear and see (in color and in motion) the person or persons you have called. Privacy is guaranteed; you only have to be seen when you want to be seen. You have the controls on your telephone to allow the person on the other end of the line to see you or to block that persons's ability to see you.

A computer can also be turned into a picture phone system. The system allows one individual to view another individual through a window in one corner of the computer screen.

For use in the home, a videophone can be hooked up through a cable box to the television. This recent innovation allows family members who are at distant locations to see each other when talking and grandparents and other family members to be able to see newborn children quickly. These videophones in the home also have the capacity to operate as a security device. A motion detector on the phone can pick up someone in the home and through the use of the auto dial capacity, dial a number to let the family know that there is a possible intruder. In addition, a fire module is available that senses fire and calls the fire department.

A videophone allows for people to be seen and heard.
Courtesy of International Business Machines, Inc.

Special Telephone Features

Here is a description of some of the special features available to the telephone users.

- **Caller ID** helps you identify who is calling before you answer the phone by displaying the phone number of the person calling. You may block your number from appearing when you call someone by pressing a special key.

- **Call restriction** allows the business to eliminate unauthorized long-distance telephone calls. If an individual is authorized to make long-distance calls, that caller is given an authorization code. This code must be keyed into the telephone before the long-distance call will be processed. The telephone itself may also be programmed to not accept long-distance calls.

- **Station messages detail recording** (SMDR) allows businesses to produce detailed traffic reports by logging each incoming and outgoing call. With SMDR, managers may analyze traffic patterns to determine telephone requirements and employee workload.

- **Liquid crystal display** (LCD) allows the user to see the number dialed and records the number of minutes the individual remains on the telephone. For incoming calls, an LCD also displays the number of the incoming caller.

- **Speed dialing** allows the user to store the telephone numbers that are used most often. Once the numbers have been stored in the memory of the telephone, they may be retrieved by keying in a one- or two-digit code rather than the entire number.

- **Call forwarding** permits a telephone call to be automatically forwarded to another telephone number.

- **Call waiting** allows a call to a busy telephone to be held while a beeping tone notifies the called party that a call is waiting.

- **Automatic call back** permits a caller to give instructions to a busy station to call back as soon as the busy station is free.

- **Automatic call stacking** allows calls to arrive at a busy station and be automatically answered by a recorded wait message.

- **Identified ringing** provides distinctive ringing tones for different categories of calls. For example, internal calls may ring one long ring whereas outside calls may ring two short rings close together.

Figure 7-3

TELEPHONE FEATURES

Numerous special features are available to telephone users. Several of the features are described in Figure 7-3.

The telephone is an invaluable tool in today's business world. *Photo by Alan Brown/Photonics Graphics.*

VOICE MESSAGES

Voice messages are used widely today; and because of their wide use, it is given a separate category. Voice messages are a type of electronically stored message. The first commercial voice messaging system was installed in 1980. Today, it is a growing business, with the majority of companies using voice messaging extensively. There are two basic uses. One example of how voice messaging is used can be illustrated by the airlines industry. If you call an airlines, you get a voice message that asks you several questions. You respond to those questions by entering a number on your phone. For example, here is what you might hear:

Thank you for calling Northwest Airlines
For today's flight arrival and departure times, press 1.

To speak with an agent about reservations within the United States and Canada, press 2.
To make reservations any other place in the world, press 3.

The airlines and numerous other businesses use voice messaging to assist in routing calls to the appropriate location and thus save time for both the caller and the business.

The other basic way in which voice messaging is used is to answer individual phones within a company when those people are away from their desks. AT&T estimates that only 25 percent of all calls placed reach the person for whom they are intended on the first try. Voice messaging has become an efficient way of answering the phone when an employee is unable to do so. It allows the caller to leave a message or to be routed to another individual who can take the call. If the caller leaves a message, the individual receiving the message can then return the call as soon as possible. Here are some of the advantages of voice messaging.

- Voice messaging can make office workers more productive by eliminating repeated telephone calls when the individual called is not available.

- Voice messaging can cut down on extraneous conversation. For example, a normal phone conversation lasts four or five minutes whereas a voice message averages thirty seconds to a minute.

- Voice messaging can provide the frequent traveler with the ability to communicate with the office at any time.

- Voice messaging can cut down on internal memorandums.

- Voice messaging can speed communications by getting messages through, even with time zone differences. For example, if a user wants to send a message from California to New York at 4 p.m., the New York office will probably be closed because it is 7 p.m. in New York. With voice messaging, however, the message can be sent immediately, and the receiver can listen to it upon arriving at work the next morning or from the home office.

If voice messaging is to be effective, it must be used well. Here are some disadvantages and how to counter them.

- Voice messaging can be misused by the employee who constantly puts the phone on voice mail, even when in the office. Certainly, there may be times when it is essential to use voice messaging, for example, if a project must be done with no interruptions. However, this situation should be rare. Don't hide behind a voice messaging system. An employee can save both parties time by answering the phone when in the office.

- A voice message may be poorly designed, too long, and ineffective in routing the individual calling. A company who is designing a voice message system should check it out carefully before customers or clients use it. The voice message needs to be succinct, clearly stated, and able to route the individual to a person quickly and efficiently. With each step or set of instructions, give callers no more than four options. Keep instructions short. Try to keep them under fifteen seconds. Give the most important information—or answer the most-asked questions—first. Always state what you want the caller to do first, then the key to press. For example, "To transfer to our receptionist, press zero." If you state the action last, the caller may forget what number to press.

- A voice message may not provide for the caller to get an actual person. Be certain your system allows the caller to talk with a person as quickly as possible. No one likes to be lost in a voice message system that never allows the caller to be heard. No one likes to be held on a voice message system for a long period of time.

- The voice on a voice message may not sound pleasant. Remember, the sound and tone of your voice message greeting or message must create a favorable impression. Sometimes we speak in a monotone. It is important on a voice message to vary your vocal tone. Be careful also, of background sound when recording a message.

TELEPHONE DIRECTORIES

It is important that you are familiar with the type of information that is in a telephone directory and that you use the directory as efficiently as possible. The two distinct parts of telephone books are the white pages and the yellow pages. In large cities, these pages are in two separate directories.

White Pages

The white pages of a directory generally contain three parts. One section, the residence white pages, is an alphabetic listing of the names, addresses, and telephone numbers of individuals. The additional sections are an alphabetical listing of the names, addresses, and telephone numbers of businesses, referred to as the business white pages; and the blue pages, which are an easy reference for locating telephone numbers of local, state, and federal government offices.

Yellow Pages

The yellow pages list the names of particular businesses according to the service the business provides. For example, assume that you are interested in purchasing a computer but you are not aware of any companies in your area that sell computers. Logically, you would look under "computers" in the yellow pages. The category may be broken down as follows:

- Computers and Computer Equipment— Dealers—New

- Computers and Computer Equipment— Dealers—Used

- Computers and Computer Equipment—Renting and Leasing

- Computers and Computer Equipment—Service and Repair

Companies specializing in each area are listed alphabetically. Because the yellow pages are used as a sales mechanism for businesses, many also choose to print a large advertisement in the yellow pages giving more information about their companies.

Front Pages

If you are to use the telephone book as effectively as possible, you need to be knowledgeable about the information that is contained in the front pages. The front of the white pages contains emergency phone numbers such as police, fire, and ambulance services, with other emergency numbers such as help lines for suicide, drug, alcohol, and emotional crises. Other items in the front pages include information on renewing your driver's license and how to find an area code; a troubleshooting guide for telephone service; information and long distance services; area codes and foreign country and city codes; a time and area code

map; frequently requested government offices; and services for the physically challenged.

The front of the yellow pages contains numbers to call to get weather forecasts, national and international news, business news, stock market updates, maps of the area, educational opportunities, transit systems in the area; and information on finance, entertainment, legal services, health services, and real estate services.

METHODS OF PAYMENT

The following methods are used to pay for telephone calls.

- Direct billing—The call is billed directly to the business.

- Credit card—The call is billed to a card which is furnished by the business or to a personal card which is charged to an individual's personal phone. (Most businesses now provide their executives with credit cards that allow the executive to make calls while traveling and charge the call to the company.)

Phone credit cards are a convenient method of payment. *Sprint Corporation.*

LONG-DISTANCE SERVICES

Due to businesses becoming multinational (with locations all over the world), long-distance calls are made frequently. Various types of services are available for long-distance calling. Several are explained in this section.

Station-to-Station Direct Distance Dialing

Direct distance dialing (DDD) is an arrangement whereby it is possible to dial long-distance numbers in other parts of the United States and abroad on a station-to-station basis. Direct distance dialing is the least expensive long-distance calling method. To use DDD, it is necessary to dial a "1" plus the area code when you are charging the call to the number from which you are calling and when you are willing to talk with anyone who answers. Procedures for making a long-distance call when you are charging the call to another number or when you wish to talk with a particular individual are given later in this section. Area codes are listed at the front of the telephone book alphabetically by state (within the United States) and for selected foreign countries and cities.

If you wish to call a number in a foreign country, you key the international access code, plus the country code, city code, and the local number of the company or person. For example, to call Melbourne, Australia, you do the following:

Key

011	+	61	+	3	+	local number
(international access code)		(country code)		(city code)		

Person-to-Person Calling

Person-to-person calls are more expensive than direct number calls; however, it is sometimes essential to make such a call. Generally, the procedure for making a person-to-person call is to key "zero" plus the area code and the telephone number. When you have completed keying, the operator will come on the line and ask for calling information. You then give the name of the person you are calling.

Wide Area Telecommunications Service (WATS)

Wide area telecommunications service (WATS) is a cost-effective way to make long-distance calls if a large quantity of calls are made regularly. The fee per call is reduced as the number of long-distance calls increases. WATS also provides time-of-day and day-of-week price discounts.

800 Service

The 800 service permits an individual to call a business toll-free. Companies that use this service are listed in the telephone directory with an 800 number. Then the customer making the call is not charged a long-distance fee for the call. Charges to the company with the 800 listing are based on the number of subscribed service bands, the amount of usage, and the time at which the usage occurs. For measuring usage charges, the hours of the day and days of the week are divided into rate periods. Lower rates are in effect for the evenings and weekends.

Foreign Exchange Service

With foreign exchange service (FX), a company can obtain a local number for a plant or subsidiary of the business in a city that is remote from a company's main office and arrange for all calls to that number to be filled as local calls. For example, a company with headquarters in Michigan and a branch office in Dallas could use FX to have the Michigan number listed in the Dallas directory. Calls from Dallas to Michigan or from Michigan to Dallas would be treated as local calls. A leased line (one that the business leases from the telephone company) connects the subscriber's telephone to a central office in the foreign exchange area. Because it is a two-way service, FX permits the business subscriber to call any number in the foreign exchange area and permits people from the foreign exchange area to call the business without a long-distance number.

Time Zones

When you are placing long-distance calls to points within the United States or abroad, time zones and time differences are extremely important. For example, if you are in San Antonio, Texas (which is on Central Standard Time), you would not want to call a business in Los Angeles, California (which is on Pacific Standard Time), at 8 a.m. It would be 6 a.m. in California, and the office would not be open. Before you make any long-distance calls, be certain that you consider the possible time differences. If you are not certain of the time differences, check a time zone map. One is located in the front pages of your telephone directory. Notice Figure 7-4 which indicates the time zones and the area codes for the United States.

TELEPHONE COSTS

Businesses spend a considerable amount of money each year on telephone services. As an office professional you need to help your company conserve dollars. Here are some steps you can follow to reduce telephone costs.

- Make operator-assisted calls only when absolutely necessary.

- Do not make personal calls on company time unless it is imperative that you do so. If you must make personal calls during the workday, make them during your breaks or on your lunch hour.

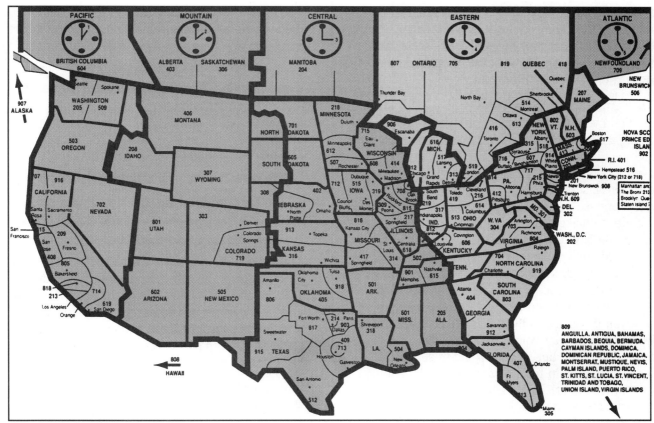

Figure 7-4   Time zone map.

- Always take messages accurately so your employer does not waste time calling an incorrect number.

- Keep a directory of frequently used numbers so that you do not waste time looking up telephone numbers. You can keep these numbers on PIM software.

- Always check time zones so that you will not call another part of the country at a time when the business is not open.

TELEPHONE TECHNIQUES

Because the telephone is an essential part of our day-to-day existence, there is no doubt you have used the telephone since you were very young. You may be thinking, "Why should I study effective telephone techniques? I already know how to use the telephone." Chances are you do make errors when using the telephone. You probably have also been the recipient of ineffective telephone techniques used by others. All of us make mistakes over the telephone. Here are some examples.

People sometimes forget that the person on the other end of the line is a human being. Somehow it is easier to be rude when you cannot see the person. Our tone of voice over the telephone often depicts

anger, irritation, and frustration. We sometimes ignore the telephone. We let it ring numerous times before answering it, or we put our voice message on and never answer the telephone. We sometimes transfer people from one department to another without handling their concerns. These are merely a few of the mistakes we make. You can no doubt add to this list of unpleasant telephone experiences. Take a few moments now to think through some of the mistakes others have made with you over the telephone and then some of your own mistakes. List these mistakes in the space provided in Self Check A.

Self Check A

- Mistakes others have made with me over the telephone include:

- Mistakes I have made with others over the telephone include:

As an office professional, it is essential that you represent your company well over the telephone. A client or customer may be gained or lost by your telephone manners. This section provides some suggestions for being more effective.

KEEP A SMILE IN YOUR VOICE

When you have customers or visitors in your office, a cheerful smile, a cup of coffee, and a magazine will usually keep the in-person callers happy, even when you have to keep them waiting. However, these services cannot be provided over the telephone, so you must rely on your voice and your manner to make the voice-to-voice contact as pleasant as the face-to-face contact.

A voice that makes the caller feel as if a smile is coming through the receiver is a winning one. How do you develop such a smile in your voice? One way is to smile as you pick up the telephone receiver. If you are smiling, it is much easier to project a smile in your voice. Treat the voice on the other end of the line as you would treat a person who is standing in front of you. Let the individual know that you are concerned. Maintain a caring attitude. Never answer the phone in a voice that is curt or rude. Do not speak in a monotone. Be expressive, much as you would when talking with someone face-to-face.

Keeping a smile on your face helps ensure a smile in your voice. *Sprint Corporation.*

Be alert to what you are saying. Sometimes when we are tired or extremely busy, we say things that we do not intend to say. A reader submitted this list of unfortunate blunders to *From 9 to 5.*[2]

- Good morning, Account Services, Lori screaming.
- You can go to any bank that is inconvenient for you.
- Thanks for holding me.
- We're open between 12 and noon.

Good for a chuckle? Yes, but similar things can happen to any of us if we are not alert at all times.

BE ATTENTIVE AND DISCREET

Listen politely to what the other person says. Do not interrupt. If the caller is unhappy about some situation, allow the caller to explain why. Most of a person's anger can be vented in telling the story. It, therefore, becomes easier to handle an unhappy person after you have listened to the problem. Use good listening skills.

- Listen for facts and feelings.
- Search for hidden or subtle meanings.
- Be patient.
- Do not evaluate.
- Try to understand what the speaker is saying, both from the words and from the tone of voice.
- Help the caller; respond to what the caller wants or asks.

Be discreet if your employer is unavailable. Carefully explain why your employer cannot answer the telephone. You may say, "Ms. Marquette is away from her office now. I expect her back in approximately an hour. May I have her call you when she returns?" Never say, "Ms. Marquette is not here yet"

---

[2]*From 9 to 5 Special Report* (1996).

COMMUNICATION TIP

To get a smile in your voice, say "cheese" to yourself as you answer the phone.

(at 10 a.m.), "She's gone for the day" (at 3 p.m.), or "She's playing tennis" (at any time during the day). A good rule to remember is be helpful, but not specific.

AVOID SLANG

It is neither businesslike nor in good taste to use slang.

Avoid	*Say*
Yeah	Certainly
OK	Yes
Un-huh	Of course
Bye-bye	Goodbye
Huh?	I beg your pardon. I did not understand. or Would you please repeat that?

TAKE MESSAGES COMPLETELY AND ACCURATELY

Incomplete messages are frustrating. Always get the necessary information. If you are not given all the information, ask the caller. Repeat the message to the caller so that you can be certain it is accurate. You need:

- the caller's name (spelled correctly). Ask that the name be spelled if you cannot understand the individual.
- company name
- telephone number (with area code if long distance)
- time of the call
- message (exactly)

Offices supply message pads for recording the information. These message pads may be in single sheets or in duplicate sheets so that the assistant has a copy of all messages. Figure 7-5 shows an example of a telephone message pad which can be very helpful for the assistant in case the executive misplaces the call.

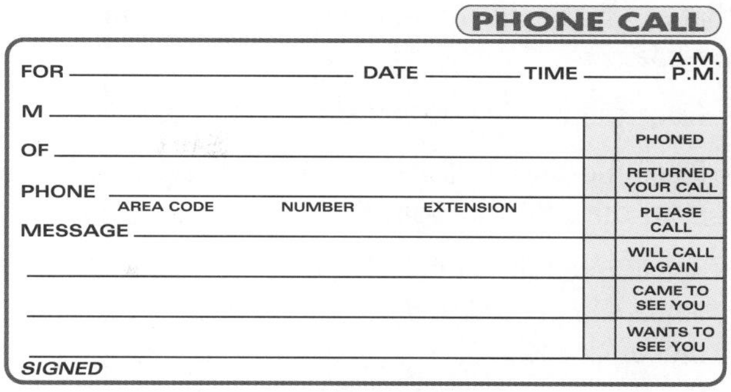
PHONE CALL
FOR ______ DATE ______ TIME ______ A.M. P.M.
M ______
OF ______ PHONED
PHONE ______ RETURNED YOUR CALL
AREA CODE NUMBER EXTENSION
MESSAGE ______ PLEASE CALL
WILL CALL AGAIN
CAME TO SEE YOU
WANTS TO SEE YOU
SIGNED

Figure 7-5 Telephone message pad.

USE THE CALLER'S NAME

It is flattering to the caller to be recognized and called by name. Frequent responses such as "Yes, Mr. Valentine, I will be happy to get the information" and "It was nice to talk with you, Ms. Keiba" indicate to callers that you know who they are and that you care about them as individuals.

ASK QUESTIONS TACTFULLY

Care should be used in asking questions. Ask only necessary questions such as "May I tell Ms. Marquette who is calling?" or "When Ms. Marquette returns, may I tell her who called?" Never ask, "Who's calling?" People are offended by such a blunt question. If your employer is not in or cannot take the call for some reason, ask about the nature of the call so that you may handle the call or refer it to someone else. For example, you may say, "If you can tell me the nature of your call, perhaps I can help you or refer you to someone who can."

SPEAK DISTINCTLY AND CLEARLY

Make sure the caller can understand what you say. You cannot speak distinctly with gum, candy, or a pencil in your mouth. Also, speak in a voice

Communication Tip

If you have regular callers who have last names that are difficult to spell, store a list of "difficult names" on your computer. Then, when the person calls, you can quickly look up the name without having to ask for the correct spelling.

that can be heard. You do not want to shout or whisper.

- Place the receiver firmly against your ear.

- Place the center of the mouthpiece about an inch from the center of your lips.

- Speak in a normal voice. Watch the speed of your voice. Do not talk too fast or too slow. Speak at a moderate rate.

HANDLE PROBLEM CALLS

Most individuals are extremely pleasant over the telephone, especially if you are courteous to them. Occasionally you may have a caller who has had a difficult day or for some other reason is unhappy. Many angry callers have been defused by an office professional taking the time to let them tell their story. Do not become emotionally involved in the situation. Remember, they are not angry with you, but rather with a situation or event.

Once you have listened to the person, try to assist the individual in getting the problem solved. This approach may mean that you suggest a solution or that you tell the person you will have someone who can solve the problem call back. It is important to not put the person on hold for a long period of time or to mishandle the call through transferring it to an individual who cannot help. Such approaches merely make the person angry again.

Sometimes you have callers who refuse to give their name. It is usually best to put such a person on hold while you tell your employer that you are unable to get the name. Your employer can then decide whether to speak to the individual.

Although you will never be able to solve all difficult situations and make all telephone callers happy, you will be able to handle most people and situations well if you remain courteous and considerate.

USE WORDS TO IDENTIFY LETTERS

Use words to identify letters in the spelling of names and places when necessary. Some letters are difficult to understand over the telephone. Figure 7-6 gives you some examples.

ENUNCIATE NUMERALS CAREFULLY

Use care in enunciating numerals. For example, when pronouncing "7" use a strong *s* and *v.* When pronouncing "9" use a strong *n,* long *i,* and a well-articulated *ne.*

Use Words to Identify Letters

A as in Alice	F as in Frank
B as in Bertha	G as in George
C as in Charles	H as in Henry
D as in David	I as in Ida
E as in Edward	J as in John

Figure 7-6

AVOID GENDER BIAS

Some people still assume that all assistants are female and all executives are male. If you answer the telephone and the voice on the other end is female, do not assume that she is an assistant and ask to speak to her employer. When addressing anyone use terms that connote respect. Do not refer to a woman as a girl, a young lady, a beautiful young thing, a gal, or any other term that can be construed as gender biased. Do not refer to a man as a boy or a guy.

KEEP A LIST OF FREQUENTLY CALLED NUMBERS

A file of frequently called numbers is an excellent time saver. For quick reference, these numbers should be kept on your computer, using some type of information management software. You may also program the most frequently used numbers into your telephone.

INCOMING CALLS

The techniques you learned in the previous section apply to all calls. Here are some special techniques for handling incoming calls correctly.

Answer Promptly

When your telephone rings, answer promptly—on the first ring if possible and certainly by the third ring. You may lose a potential customer if you are slow in answering the telephone.

Identify Yourself and Your Company

The company for which you work will usually instruct you as to how to answer the telephone. If you work in a large company, chances are that you will not be the first person to answer the telephone. The first person answering identifies the company; then the caller will ask for a specific person or department. As an administrative assistant for Ms. Marquette, you might answer,

"Ms. Marquette's office, Rebecca Martinez." If you need to identify the company, you might say, "Good morning, Koronet International."

Transfer Calls Carefully

It is frequently necessary to transfer a call to another extension. Before you transfer a call, explain to the caller why you must transfer the call. Make sure the caller is willing to be transferred. For example, you may say, "Ms. Marquette is out, but Travis Figimara can give you the information. May I transfer you to Mr. Figimara?" You may also want to give the caller the extension number of the person to whom the caller is being transferred in case the equipment malfunctions and the transfer is not completed. The caller can then call the number without having to call you again.

Be certain that you know how to transfer calls. It is extremely irritating to callers to be told that they are going to be transferred and then are disconnected due to incorrect transferring procedures.

Place Calls on Hold Only After Requesting Permission

A caller may sometimes request information which you do not have at your fingertips. It may be essential for you to check with someone else or go to the file cabinet to get information. When this happens, do not place the caller on hold without permission. You may say, "I need to pull the information from my files. Would you like to hold for a moment while I get it, or shall I call you back?" If the caller agrees to hold, try to get back to the person as soon as possible. Nothing irritates a caller more than to be left on hold. When you return to the line, let the caller know you are back by saying, "Thank you for waiting." If there has been an unavoidable delay, apologize immediately.

Handle Multiple Calls

You may have more than one telephone line that you are responsible for answering. If so, there will be occasions when you will be answering a call on one line and another line will ring. When this happens, you must remember that the caller on the second line does not know you are already on the phone. That caller is expecting to get an answer immediately. Excuse yourself politely by saying to the first caller, "May I place you on hold for a moment. I must answer another phone." Then, answer the other phone. If the other caller is going to take awhile, ask the person if you can have a

number so that you may call back as soon as you are off the first call. Then, go back to the first caller with, "Thank you for waiting." Your responsibility is to handle all calls as quickly and efficiently as possible.

Screen Calls

Many executives have one telephone number that is published for callers and an inside number that is not published. This inside number is used by the executive to make outgoing calls and may be given out to a few close friends or family. The office professional is usually expected to screen the calls that come from the published number. For example, when the executive receives a call, the office professional is expected to determine who is calling and why. The executive may refuse to take certain calls. If someone else in your company can talk with the individual, transfer the call to that person. If there is no one, let the person know courteously that your employer is not interested. One response might be, "I appreciate the information; however, Ms. Marquette is not interested in pursuing the matter at the present time."

Leave a Message When You Leave Your Desk

If you have to leave your desk, arrange for someone else to answer your telephone. You may forward it to a co-worker. Tell the co-worker who will answer your telephone, where you can be reached and the time you will be back. If your employer is also gone, tell the co-worker in general terms where your employer is and when he or she will be back. You might say, "Ms. Marquette is in a meeting and will be available around 3 p.m."

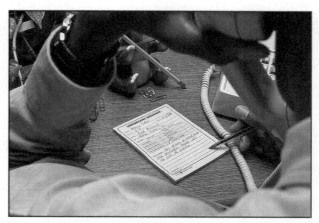

The ability to forward accurate information is an important communication skill.

Follow Through on Promises

If you make a promise to call back with additional information, do so. A broken promise can cause a canceled order or a lost customer. A kept promise can enhance a reputation for reliability and trustworthiness. Help your employer remember promises made. If you know of information that your employer has promised a customer and has not followed through, provide a tactful reminder of the need to follow through. Your employer will probably appreciate your assistance.

OUTGOING CALLS

As an office professional, you are often responsible for placing calls for your employer or for making business calls yourself. Just as incoming calls must be handled effectively, so must outgoing calls. Some tips are provided in this section.

Place Calls Properly for Your Supervisor

Supervisors usually place their own calls to save time and to create favorable impressions. You may, however, work for someone who does not wish to place calls. If so, identify your supervisor's name before you transfer the call. For example, you may say, "Ms. Marquette of Koronet International is calling." Then transfer the call to Ms. Marquette.

If your supervisor is not available or makes another call after you place one, provide some subtle training for your supervisor. For example, before you place the call you might say, "Ms. Marquette, I am going to place the call you requested to Mr. Hill. Are you going to be in for a few minutes?" It may be that your supervisor is unaware that such

habits are discourteous and irritating to the person being called.

Plan Your Call

If you are not certain of the telephone number, refer to the telephone directory. If the number is not in the directory, check with directory assistance. After checking with directory assistance, make a note of the number for future calls.

Take a few moments to plan your call before you make it. Know the purpose of your call and what you intend to say. Once you get the person on the telephone, state your purpose clearly and concisely. For example, you might say, "This is John Chin of Koronet International. I'm calling to verify your attendance at the sales meeting tomorrow at 3 p.m. in Conference Room A." Certainly, you may exchange some pleasantries with the individual you are calling. The main purpose, though, is to get your message across without wasting the time of the individual you are calling.

Place Long-Distance Calls Correctly

Although many of your calls will be local, you will also be making long-distance calls. Know what type of long-distance service you need to use. For example, if you can talk with anyone who answers or you believe the person you are calling is in the office, it is more cost efficient to place the call station-to-station. If you must talk with a particular person, and you are not certain the person is in, a person-to-person call may be more efficient. Be certain that you remember the time zone differences. You have already learned about time zones within

COMMUNICATION TIP

Always check your voice mail immediately upon returning to your desk. You cannot be at your desk to get all calls, but you can return your calls promptly.

COMMUNICATION TIP

If an individual asks you for something while you are away from your desk or office, to help jog your memory, call your voice mail and leave a reminder for yourself.

the United States. Obviously, there are also international time zones. You need to be knowledgeable of the time differences when placing calls abroad. For example, the person who places a call from New York to London must remember that when it is 11 a.m. in New York, it is 4 p.m. in London.

Self Check B

Take a few moments now to reconsider the telephone mistakes you listed in Self Check A. Now that you understand proper telephone techniques, how would you correct these errors? List the corrections you would make in the space provided. Also list other effective techniques that you are not presently using but need to use in the future.

- Corrections I would make to be more effective over the telephone:

- Effective telephone techniques which I commit to using in the future:

TELECOMMUNICATIONS—THE FUTURE

You learned at the beginning of this chapter that telecommunications is the electronic transmission of text, data, voice, video, and image from one location to another. Telecommunications is a rapidly changing field in our information age. New technology is being developed daily. This technology affects not only telephone transmission, but also the machines and the networks that we use to transmit all types of data from one location to another. It is difficult for us to even imagine the capabilities that we will have in the future.

The telephone of the future will be much more integrated with other technology than it is today. For example, there will probably be telephone services that include full-motion video, electronic mail, computing capabilities, online information services, and more on one computer screen. We will receive help in communicating internationally. A business executive might, for example, communicate in English to a Japanese executive with the translations occurring on both executives' video screens.

Consider another area you are involved in currently—education. Telecommunications is impacting the fundamental roots of education—the curriculum, the delivery methods, and the instructional models that we use. For example, the **Virtual University** is a concept that is presently being developed by any number of educational entities. Virtual means that the university does not exist at only one location and site, and is not time bound. It is not tied to a professor in a classroom at 9 or 10 a.m. Education can be delivered to any location, at any site in the world, and at any time. This delivery can be through interactive computer technology (distance learning) which allows students at one site to see and hear a professor's instruction at a very distant location and to interact with that professor and with other students at distance sites. The technology provides for instruction to be delivered directly to the company site at whatever time frame the company establishes. The term **"just-in-time"** is used in education to mean the delivery of education at the time that the employee needs to be learning it. Education can now deliver just-in-time to locations all over the world. The Internet is another appropriate vehicle for delivering instruction. By using the Internet, instruction can be delivered any place where a person has access to a computer with network and modem capabilities. These examples are merely a few of the ways in which telecommunications is causing rapid change. As individuals in this world, we need to be aware of the constant change in the telecommunications field and the impact that it has on our work and personal lives.

COMMUNICATION TIP

To save your company dollars, always check to see if an out-of-town company has an 800 number.

CHAPTER SUMMARY

This summary will help you remember the important points covered in this chapter.

- Telephones are routed to and from the public lines of the telephone company to the private lines within a company through switching systems. These systems include key systems and private branch exchange (PBX) systems.

- Centrex is a service provided by the local phone company that offers PBX-like features to a business without the business purchasing a switching system.

- Special types of telephone equipment include cellular telephones, portable pagers, speakerphones, cordless telephones, and videophones.

- Voice mail is an electronically stored message used to assist in routing calls to the appropriate location and to answer individual phones within a company when the person is not available.

- Telephone white pages contain the residence white pages, the business white pages, and the blue pages which consist of local, state, and federal government offices.

- Front pages of the telephone directory include emergency phone numbers, a troubleshooting guide for telephone service, information and long-distance services, area codes and foreign country and city codes, a time and area code map, and services for the physically challenged.

- Direct distance dialing is an arrangement whereby it is possible to dial long-distance numbers in other parts of the United States and abroad on a station-to-station basis. Direct distance dialing is the least expensive long-distance calling method. Long-distance calls also may be made person-to-person.

- WATS is a cost-effective way to make long-distance calls if a large quantity of calls are made regularly. The fee per call is reduced as the number of long-distance calls increases.

- The 800 service permits an individual to call a business toll free.

- With FX a company can obtain a local number for a plant or subsidiary of the business in a city that is remote from a company's main office and arrange for all calls to that number to be filled as local calls.

- When you are placing long-distance calls to points within the United States or abroad, time zones and time differences are extremely important.

- Effective telephone techniques include:

  keeping a smile in your voice

  being attentive and discreet

  taking messages completely and accurately

  using the caller's name

  asking questions tactfully

  speaking distinctly and clearly

  handling problem calls

  using words to identify letters

  enunciating numerals carefully

  avoiding gender bias

  keeping a list of frequently called numbers

  answering promptly

  identifying yourself and your company

  transferring calls carefully

  placing calls on hold only after requesting permission

  screening calls

  handling multiple calls effectively

  leaving the phone covered when the office assistant is not available

  following through on promises

  placing calls properly for the supervisor

  planning calls

  placing long-distance calls correctly

- The future means continual rapid changes in telecommunications, with these changes impacting many areas of our lives including how we learn.

CHAPTER GLOSSARY

The following terms were introduced in this chapter. To help you review, definitions are given here.

- **Telecommunications** (p. 151)–The electronic transmission of text, data, voice, video, and image.

- **Modem** (p. 152)–Short for modulator-demodulator, the device that enables your PC to send and receive data over the telephone lines.

- **Private branch exchange (PBX)** (p. 154)–A telephone switching system.

- **Key service unit (KSU)** (p. 154)–A key system uses a key service unit to operate a number of lines.

- **Central exchange (Centrex)** (p. 155)–A service provided by the local phone company that offers PBX-like features to a business without the business purchasing a switching system.

- **Direct inward dialing (DID)** (p. 155)–A system in which all calls go directly to the number dialed.

- **Cellular technology** (p. 155)–Breaks a large telephone service area into smaller areas called cells, which allows calls from cellular phones to go from one service area to another service area.

- **Wide area telecommunications service (WATS)** (p. 160)–A cost-effective way to make long-distance calls when a large quantity of calls are involved. Fees per call are reduced as the number of long-distance calls increases.

- **Foreign exchange service (FX)** (p. 160)–A service that allows a company to obtain a local number for a plant or subsidiary that is remote from a company's main office and arranges for all calls to that number to be filled as local calls.

- **Virtual University** (p. 167)–A university that transmits learning through technologically-mediated methods to distant locations.

- **Just-in-time** (p. 167)–Education delivered at the time the employee needs the information.

DISCUSSION ITEMS

These discussion items provide an opportunity for you to test your understanding of the chapter through discussion with your classmates and your instructor.

1. Define telecommunications. Briefly explain how data, voice, and video are transmitted from one location to another.

2. What are switching systems? List and describe the two basic types of switching systems.

3. List and explain four special types of telephone equipment.

4. List and explain eight special telephone features.

5. Give two disadvantages of voice messaging.

6. List and explain six effective telephone techniques.

CASE STUDY

Antonio Previno started to work for Koronet three weeks ago. His job includes answering the telephone in his area. You were asked by Antonio's supervisor to explain to him the company procedures for answering the telephone. These procedures state that phones are to be answered with the name of the company and the individual's name. They also state that phones are not to be left unattended, and phones are to be answered by the third ring. You were also asked by the supervisor to help him with telephone technique if you observe any problems.

You have observed that Antonio answers the telephone correctly; that is, he says the appropriate words. However, you have noticed several problems such as:

• Antonio keeps his phone on voice mail more than 50 percent of the time even though he seems to have the time to answer it.

• He tends to answer the phone in a rushed, curt manner.

• You cover Antonio's telephone when he leaves his desk. He never tells you where he is going or when he will be back.

• You overheard a manager complain because Antonio failed to write the correct telephone number on a message pad.

• Antonio does not give callers adequate information. If someone is out of the office, he says, for example, "Mr. Ueoka is out of the office now."

• Recently Antonio transferred a call to you; however, he did not tell the caller why she was being transferred. The caller was angry when you answered the phone.

You have talked with Antonio twice about these infractions. He seems to listen to what you are saying but does not change his behavior. You know that something should be done, but what? Antonio does not report to you. Should you talk with your supervisor, with Antonio's supervisor, or should you try to talk with Antonio again? Should you suggest a company workshop on telephone techniques? Explain how you would handle the situation.

OFFICE TASKS

OFFICE TASK 7-1 (Objective 1)

Work in teams on this project. Research three or four recent articles on the future directions of telecommunications. This research should include transmission technologies such as cable and satellite, networks, and the integration of telecommunications. As a team, report your findings orally to the class.

OFFICE TASK 7-2 (Objective 2)

As a team of five (four of your classmates and you), visit a technologically up-to-date office to discover the types of telephone systems, equipment, and features of the equipment used in the office. Report your findings orally to the class.

OFFICE TASK 7-3 (Objective 3)

Read the telephone responses listed. Indicate a better manner of responding. Key your answers and turn them in to your instructor.

1. Hold the line.
2. Her line is busy.
3. Call back later.
4. Ms. Marquette isn't in.
5. Ms. Marquette is playing tennis.
6. What did you say?
7. Who's this?
8. I don't know where Ms. Marquette is.
9. Your call is being transferred.
10. I am not responsible for the mistake, don't raise your voice at me.

OFFICE TASK 7-4 (Objective 3)

There are four situations on the Student Data Template Disk, file OT7-4. Access the stored file; respond to each situation. Run a copy and submit your responses to your instructor.

OFFICE TASK 7-5 (Objective 3)

Choose a member of your class to work with on this project. Call each other, re-creating situations 1, 2, and 3 in Office Task 7-4 which are on the Student Data Template Disk, file OT7-4. Complete the situations twice each, with one of you being the caller and the other the administrative assistant. Then, switch roles and replay the situations. Print out a copy of the Telephone Voice Rating Form on the Student Data Template Disk, file OT7-5. Complete the form and turn it in to your instructor.

OFFICE TASK 7-6 (Objective 3)

1. Locate telephone numbers for each of the following. Prepare the names and telephone numbers in tabular form. Turn them in to your instructor.

   - public library
   - Internal Revenue Service
   - police department
   - post office
   - city mayor's office
   - your state's employment commission
   - weather bureau
   - local radio station
   - local TV station
   - local cable company
   - local long-distance telephone company

2. Locate one company name and telephone number under each of the following categories.

Prepare the information in tabular form. Include the heading under which you found the information, plus the name and telephone number of the company. Turn the information in to your instructor.

- office supply company
- computer repair company
- certified public accountant
- company that sells copiers
- physician who specializes in cancer treatment
- automobile insurance company
- telephone equipment

OFFICE TASK 7-7 (Objective 3)

Access Student Data Template Disk, file OT7-7; there is a form used to record telephone calls. Print out four copies of the form and complete information about the calls given below. Sign your name at the bottom of each form. Hand in the forms to your instructor.

1. Ms. Marquette's husband calls at 3 p.m. and asks you to remind her to pick up her daughter at the doctor's office at 4:30.

2. Mr. Murphy calls at 10 a.m. to ask Ms. Marquette to attend a chamber of commerce meeting at Bank One tomorrow at 4 p.m.

3. Ms. Kathleen Whitson of the Gre-Pak Company, with whom Ms. Marquette has an appointment tomorrow at 11 a.m., calls at 2 p.m. to say that she has been called out of the city and will not be able to keep the appointment.

4. Mr. Chan of Hilltop, Inc. calls at 12:05 to discuss a community issue with Ms. Marquette. Mr. Chan will be out of the office from 12:30 until 3:00 p.m. today. His number is 555-1161.

ENGLISH USAGE CHALLENGE DRILL

Correct the following sentences. Cite the grammar rule that is applicable to each sentence. Before you begin, refresh your memory of grammar rules by reviewing restrictive and nonrestrictive elements, transitional and parenthetical expressions, and conjunctive adverbs in the *Multimedia Reference for Writers* (if available to you), the reference guide in this text, or some other reference guide.

1. Ruth Rogers who is in excellent physical condition enjoys swimming.

171

2. Some people, who are in excellent physical condition, enjoy swimming.

3. Her replies, that were given entirely in Spanish, amazed the visitors from Spain.

4. Individuals living in the Midwest according to studies do not have as pronounced an accent as people living in the South.

5. According to his thinking therefore the only way to overcome fear of flying is to fly.

ASSESSMENT OF CHAPTER OBJECTIVES

Now that you have completed the chapter and the office tasks, take a few moments to review the following learning objectives which you were given at the beginning of this chapter. Did you accomplish these objectives? If so, explain how in the space provided. If you were unable to accomplish these objectives, give your reason for not doing so. Your instructor may want to review your answers.

I accomplished these objectives:

1. Discover how information is transmitted electronically. Yes _____ No _____

   Explain how you accomplished this objective.

   _____

   _____

   _____

2. Describe the types of telephone systems, equipment, and features available. Yes _____ No _____

   Explain how you accomplished this objective.

   _____

   _____

   _____

3. Develop and use proper telephone techniques.
   Yes _____ No _____

   Explain how you accomplished this objective.

   _____

   _____

   _____

Provide reasons for failing to accomplish any of the objectives.

_____

_____

_____

_____

_____

LETTERS, MEMOS, AND REPORTS

LEARNING OBJECTIVES

1. **Identify the characteristics of effective correspondence.**
2. **Compose letters and memos.**
3. **Research and write a business report.**

In Chapter 5, you developed skills for communicating effectively in our multicultural workforce. You learned that if you are to be effective in your job, good verbal and nonverbal communication skills are essential. The importance of communication pervades not only our verbal communications but also our written communications. Letters, memos, e-mail, and reports comprise the major communication documents in the office. Depending on the effectiveness of the writer of these documents, goodwill or ill will for the company (and the writer) may be created. Thus, you need to add another communication skill to your list of qualifications if you are to be a truly effective office worker—the ability to compose effective business documents. This chapter will help you attain the necessary skills; practice will help you perfect these skills.

WRITTEN CORRESPONDENCE

The basic types of written messages that the office professional prepares are memorandums, e-mail, letters, and reports. As you begin your career, you may be asked to only prepare routine correspondence such as interoffice memorandums or e-mail to people within the company. As you learn more about the company and as you demonstrate to your employer your writing skills, the complexity and number of your writing assignments will probably increase. You should establish a goal now to become an excellent communicator through the written word. No matter what type of position you hold, written communication skills are invaluable to both you and the organization.

E-MAIL AND MEMORANDUMS

Correspondence to individuals within the company is written as an e-mail or a memorandum. E-mail (electronic messages) has become the interoffice memorandum of choice for many businesses due to numerous advantages.

- E-mail reaches its destination in a matter of seconds after it is sent, even if that destination is across the world.

- Multiple individuals may be sent the same message quickly, with all addressees receiving the information instantaneously.

- It is not necessary to make a hard copy (paper copy) of e-mail, thus paper is saved.

- E-mail may be filed electronically on the computer and retrieved as needed, or e-mail may be destroyed immediately after the person receiving the message reads it.

- The date and time of e-mail are automatically printed on the message so that both the writer and the recipient have a record of when it was sent.

- E-mail takes less time to write than a paper memorandum, because the writer only needs to insert the name of the receiver and own name, then write the body of the note. Also, no envelopes need to be addressed as the e-mail is sent electronically from one computer to another computer.

- When an e-mail is received, the recipient can be notified immediately of the receipt by a message which appears at the bottom of the computer screen (even if the recipient is using the computer) or an audio signal which is emitted through the computer to let the recipient know that an e-mail has been sent.

- A hard copy of the e-mail may be printed and retained in a manual file if necessary.

- An e-mail can be sent as "confidential" mail and with an "urgent" notation.

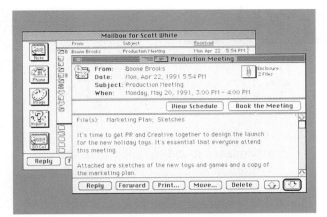

Figure 8-1   E-mail message. *Courtesy of Microsoft Corporation.*

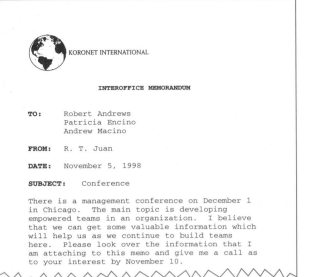

Figure 8-2   Interoffice memorandum.

Figure 8-1 gives an example of an e-mail message. The hard copy interoffice memorandum is still used, but its use has become greatly curtailed with the advent of e-mail. Generally the hard copy memorandum is written when the message is fairly long and will not fit on one computer screen. Although an e-mail can be longer than one computer screen, the general rule is that an e-mail needs to be a very short communication. When the e-mail gets several screens in length, it becomes cumbersome for the recipient to go back and forth between screens to review the message. Figure 8-2 shows a hard copy memorandum addressed to several individuals. Notice that the names of the individuals are placed in alphabetical order. You may also list the names according to rank or position, with the person holding the highest position in the company listed first. Titles are generally not used when writing memorandums. If you are addressing a memo to ten or more people, it is generally best to address it to a generic classification such as "TQM Team." When sending hard copy memorandums, specially designed envelopes are often used. These envelopes are reusable and are generally large enough that standard size stationery can be inserted without folding. An example of an interoffice envelope is show in Figure 8-3.

LETTERS

One of the first letters you may be asked to write as a beginning office professional is a routine one, such as a letter requesting information about a product. These letters are usually straightforward with the first paragraph requesting the information, the middle paragraph providing any additional infor-

INTER-DEPARTMENT DELIVERY				
NOTE—CROSS OUT ENTIRE LINE WHEN RECEIVED AND RE-USE UNTIL ALL LINES ARE FULL.				
DATE	DELIVER TO	DEPARTMENT	SENT BY	DEPARTMENT

Figure 8-3   Interoffice envelope.

mation needed, and the ending paragraph specifying the action the writer wants and expressing appreciation to the reader for responding to the request. Once you develop your employer's confidence in your skills, you may be asked to compose most of the letters in draft or in final form for the employer's signature. Whatever role you play in the composition of letters, the principles set forth in this chapter will help you be successful.

REPORTS

In addition to memorandums and letters, numerous reports are prepared in the office. These reports may be informal reports of two or three pages, or they may be formal reports containing a table of contents, the body of the report (with footnotes or endnotes), appendices, and a bibliography. You will learn more about writing reports in a later section of this chapter.

EFFECTIVE CORRESPONDENCE

If a written communication is to accomplish its goal, certain principles must be consistently maintained. These principles are presented here.

CLEAR, CONCISE, AND SIMPLE

The reader should be able to determine without a doubt the purpose of the correspondence. Writing clearly requires good organization and simple expression. Conciseness in writing means expressing the necessary information in as few words as possible. Say what you need to say without cluttering your correspondence with irrelevant information, needless words, or flowery phrases. Simple means that you use words that are easily understood; you do not try to impress the reader with your vocabulary. Here are principles to keep in mind to assist you in writing clearly, concisely, and simply.

- Keep your sentences short. Sentences should vary in structure and in length, but as an average should be no more than fifteen to twenty words. Consider the following example of a sentence that is too long and the shortened, more effective sentence.

  Long sentence: *In answer to your letter of June 12, I wish to tell you how pleased and happy I am with your asking me to speak at the meeting on July 12 and to tell you that it will give me great pleasure to speak to your group.*

  Shortened sentence: *I would be delighted to speak to your group on July 12.*

- Use the simple rather than the complex. If a shorter word can do the job, use it. Business correspondence is not the place to attempt to impress the reader with the breadth of your vocabulary. The aim of business correspondence is to get your purpose across in a simple, concise manner. Write to express rather than impress. The truly impressive writer can express complex ideas in clear, simple terms. For example, rather than "endeavor to ascertain," write "try to find out."

- Write as you speak. Ask yourself how you would say something if the reader were sitting next to you. A conversational tone is usually very appropriate. (This tone may vary in international correspondence; a section later in this chapter will help you understand some of the differences when writing internationally.)

- Edit unnecessary words. Verbosity (using too many words) weakens the message. Make sure every word is essential. Practice editing unnecessary words. You might be able to cut as much as one-half of the length of your correspondence. Consider the following example of unnecessary words.

  Excessive: *At this point in time, I must tell you that our plant will be closed due to the remodeling of our facilities. We have wanted to remodel our facilities for the last five years but have been unable to do so due to the large demands of our customers for products. We have every confidence in our ability to complete the remodeling and get your order out by July 15.*

  Concise: *Since our plant will be closed for remodeling from June 1 to June 15, your order will be shipped on July 15.*

COMMUNICATION TIP

To add crispness to your business communications, avoid redundancies such as "consensus of opinion." "Consensus" is all that is necessary.

Chapter 8: Letters, Memos, and Reports

- Use active verbs. Active verbs can bring life to your sentences by emphasizing action. For example, say "We received your order for ten modular units today" not "Your order for ten modular units was received today."

- Vary your style. Keep your writing interesting by varying your sentence structure, length, and vocabulary.

- Avoid clichés. You have probably read such phrases as, "according to our records," "at your earliest convenience," and "under separate cover." These phrases are clichés; they are overused. Notice the following clichés and the improved wording.

  Cliché: *According to our files*
  Improved: *Our files indicate*

  Cliché: *At the present time*
  Improved: *Now*

  Cliché: *In view of the fact that*
  Improved: *Because*

  Cliché: *By return mail*
  Improved: *Mail today*

  Cliché: *May I take the liberty*
  Improved: *Omit the entire phrase and make the statement.*

  Cliché: *Your kind letter*
  Improved: Omit "kind"—people, not letters, are kind.

  Cliché: *This is to inform you*
  Improved: *Omit the entire phrase and make the statement.*

COMPLETE

A business document is complete if it gives the reader the information needed so that the results intended are achieved. To help you achieve completeness in your writing, ask yourself these *W* questions:

- *Why* is the correspondence being written?

- *What* is the goal of the correspondence?

- *What* information is needed before writing the correspondence?

- *Who* needs to receive the correspondence?

- *What* information needs to be included in the correspondence?

Refer to Figure 8-4 for some examples of ineffective writing when the *W* questions were not asked and corresponding examples of effective writing when they were asked.

Use the *W* Questions

Here are some examples of ineffective writing when the "W" questions were not asked, followed by effective writing, with the "W" questions asked.

- Ineffective: Your order will be mailed soon. (When?)
- Effective: Your order will be mailed June 12.

- Ineffective: There will be a seminar on May 13. (Where and What kind of conference?)
- Effective: There will be an effective letter writing seminar in the Executive Conference Room at 2:00 p.m. on May 31.

- Ineffective: The sales meeting was canceled. (Why and When?)
- Effective: The sales meeting scheduled for May 6 at 2 p.m. has been canceled due to an unexpected meeting which Jack Edwards, sales manager, must attend. The meeting has been rescheduled for May 8 at 2 p.m.

Figure 8-4

CONSIDERATE

Being considerate in correspondence means using good human relations skills. Treat the reader with respect and friendliness and write as if you care about the reader. When dealing with people face-to-face, courtesy and consideration are necessary to develop and maintain goodwill. The same or even greater concern must be evident in written correspondence as only the written word conveys the message—a smile, a nod, or a friendly gesture cannot be seen.

Never show your anger in business correspondence. You may be extremely unhappy about a situation, but to show anger merely compounds the problem. Angry words make angry readers. Both parties can end up yelling at one another through the written word. Little is accomplished. Being considerate also means being believable. If a person is asking you something, respond to the question. If you are unable to respond, explain why. If you must respond negatively, explain why. An explanation lets others know that you are sincere.

Being considerate also means using "please" and "thank you" often. Do not be afraid to apologize when you make an error. We are all human; we all make errors. A courteous apology builds credibility and goodwill. Use the following courteous phrases often.

We appreciate . . .
Thank you for . . .
Please let me know . . .
I apologize for . . .
You were very kind to . . .
You were very nice to . . .

Courteousness in writing is just as important as being courteous in face-to-face encounters.

CORRECT

Correctness in business writing means using correct grammar and mechanics, appropriate format, and careful proofreading. Errors in writing send a message to the reader that the writer is careless or, even worse, is uneducated or lacking in intelligence.

Spelling, grammar, punctuation, capitalization, and sentence structure must be correct. To assist you in catching your errors, most word processing packages contain spelling and grammar checkers; however, there are errors that grammar and spelling packages do not detect. If you use "your" rather than "you're," for example, the error will not be detected. Thus, it is extremely important that you have good grammar and spelling skills. In addition, you must be a good proofreader to catch your errors. Proofreading tips are given in Figure 8-5.

Proofreading Tips

1. Proofread your document on the screen before you print. Scroll to the beginning of the document and use the top of the screen as a guide for your eye in reading each line.

2. Proofread a document in three steps.
   a. general appearance and format
   b. spelling and keyboarding errors
   c. punctuation, word usage, and content

3. Read from right to left for spelling and keyboarding errors.

4. Use a spell checker.

5. If possible, do not proofread a document right after keying it; let it rest while you perform some other task.

6. Pay attention to dates. Do not assume that they are correct. Check to determine that Thursday, June 18, is actually a Thursday, for example. Check the spelling of months; check the correctness of the year.

7. Do not overlook proofreading the date, subject, enclosure notation, and the names and addresses of the recipients.

8. Use the thesaurus if you are not certain a word is appropriate.

9. Watch closely for omissions of *-ed, -ing,* or *-s* at the end of words.

10. If punctuation causes you problems, check a grammatical source after you have completed all other proofreading.

11. Be consistent in the use of commas.

12. Be consistent in the use of capital letters.

13. Check numerals.

14. Be consistent in format.

15. Keep a good reference manual at your desk to look up any grammar or punctuation rules you question.

Figure 8-5

Correctness also means using the correct format. Readers expect business letters and reports to follow recommended styles and formats. Using a nonstandard format detracts from the message by drawing the reader's attention to its layout rather than its contents. Standard formats for business letters and reports are given in the reference guide.

Correctness also includes accuracy. Although you cannot be perfect all the time, you should do your best to be accurate. Get the facts before you begin the business correspondence. Check your information carefully. If you are quoting prices, be certain you have the latest price list. If you are presenting dates, confirm the dates. If you are giving sales figures, double check the figures. Verify the correct spelling of any names used in the letter.

PROMPT

The conscientious business correspondent is concerned about being on time. Prompt messages say to readers that the writer or company cares about them. Conversely, late messages convey the impression that the writer or company is indifferent to the needs of the reader or is grossly inefficient. A rule of thumb is that replies to routine letters and memorandums should be sent within three to five days. Urgent messages such as urgent e-mail or mail sent by UPS or telegram should be answered immediately (within twenty-four hours).

POSITIVE

It is easier to hear the word "yes" than to hear the word "no." It is much easier to accept a concern than it is to accept a complaint. Positivism gives the reader a favorable association with the person, service, or product. It helps the reader to respond the way the writer intends. A positive tone is set by the words that are chosen and how they are used; for example, some words possess positive qualities and other words possess negative qualities. Figure 8-6 gives some positive and negative expressions. And, even a negative statement can be written in a positive tone. For example, "Do not litter" can be changed to "Please deposit all trash in the nearest receptacle."

Positive and Negative Words

Positive	Negative
glad	sorry
immediately	whenever possible
pleasure	displeasure
inconvenient	not convenient
satisfactory	unsatisfactory
accept	reject
fortunate	unfortunate
Please let us know.	You failed to let us know.
Please send your check.	You neglected to send your check.
Your order will be shipped.	I hate to inform you.

Figure 8-6

APPROPRIATE TONE

The entire **tone** (manner of expression in writing) of the letter (whether that tone is positive or negative) is set by considering your reader first and carefully choosing your words. Establishing a positive tone at the beginning of a letter and carrying that positive tone throughout are important. In establishing a positive tone you should adhere to the concepts spelled out in the previous sections; that is,

- completeness
- conciseness
- consideration
- correctness
- promptness

COMMUNICATION TIP

When you are in the "think" phase of writing a document, do not be concerned about formatting. It can interrupt your creative thought processes. Do your formatting when you are refining the document.

In other words, as you have learned in these sections, you should write in a conversational tone—one that is appropriate for the reader. You should write to express your thoughts not to try to impress the reader. You should treat the reader with respect and friendliness; you should never show anger. Using the words "please" and "thank you" and referring to the reader by name helps the reader know that you care. Being prompt says to the reader that the writer cares. Expressing statements in a positive rather than a negative manner helps give the reader a favorable association with the writer and the business. If you carefully and consistently heed these guidelines, you will set a positive tone for the reader; in the process, you will have served your company well.

To illustrate the importance of tone, refer to Figure 8-7 which shows a letter written in a positive tone (adhering to the concepts set forth) and a letter written in a negative tone. As a reader, to which letter would you respond favorably? Notice the first letter is written from the writer's point of view. There is no consideration of the reader; in fact, the writer is almost condescending to the reader. The overall tone of the letter is very negative.

EFFECTIVE PARAGRAPHS

Effective paragraphs possess unity, varied sentence structures, and parallel construction.

Unity

A paragraph has unity when its sentences clarify or help support the main idea. All sentences in the paragraph must relate to the main idea. The sentence that contains the main idea of a paragraph is called the **topic sentence.** This sentence shapes the content of the paragraph. Notice the following paragraph; the topic sentence is the first sentence.

> There is a management conference on December 1 in Chicago. The main topic is developing empowered teams in an organization. Please look over the information that I am enclosing and give me a call as to your interest by November 10.

The topic sentence is not always the first sentence. It may be at the beginning of the paragraph, at the end of the paragraph, or it may even be implied. The point to remember here is that the topic sentence helps the writer keep focused on one main idea for the paragraph.

Coherence

A paragraph has coherence when its sentences are related to each other in content, in grammatical construction, and in choice of words. Each sentence should be written so that the paragraph flows from one thought to the next in a coherent fashion. The following sentences represent coherence in content and construction.

> Before television was invented, people were entertained by radio shows. These shows required the listener to pay careful attention to the story. Sound effects were used extensively to hold the listener's interest and to emphasize some of the details of the story. For example, a creaking door sound effect was used to represent fear; it often meant that the "intruder" was approaching.

Coherence can be achieved by repeating key words in a paragraph or using certain words for emphasis. Consider the following use of repetitive words.

> The anthropologist Elena Padilla describes life in a squalid district of New York by telling how much people know about each other—*who* is to be trusted and *who* not, *who* is defiant of the law and *who* upholds it, *who* is competent and well and informed and *who* is inept and ignorant.

During the 1996 Summer Olympics in Atlanta, Erik Brady of *USA Today* wrote this story about the gold medal gymnasts. Consider his use of the words "and" and "but" for emphasis.

> Don't even think of calling them America's Sweethearts. Throw out Teens of Tumble and Mighty Mites and Flying Princesses, too. Just call them what they are. Olympic champions. Gold medal winners. *And* some of the best athletes you will ever see . . . They are the new Beatles, and we are all finding our own favorites. Shannon, the quiet one. Two Dominiques, take your choice: the little one and the emotional one. *And* Kerri, the courageous one. *But* they aren't the Fab Four. They are the Magnificent Seven. . . . Call them cool. Call them courageous. *But* do not call them pixies or darlings. They are Olympic champions.

Notice how the writer used the conjunctions "and" and "but" to begin a sentence as emphasis. At one point, we were taught not to use conjunctions to

McBEE CONSULTING

September 18, —

Ms. Cordelia Ramsey
Office Assistant
Koronet International
3500 Division
Grand Rapids, MI 49503-3295

Dear Ms. Ramsey:

Since we at McBee Consulting are certain that you have trouble writing letters, we are having a one-day seminar on letter writing which you must not miss. We have put together a program which we know will be beneficial for you. After our seminar (as you write your next letter), you will have no trouble explaining to your reader exactly what you expect of him or her and getting what you want.

Give my office a call at 555-3046 to register. We are looking forward to your positive response to this letter.

Sincerely,

Rhonda Knowit
Training Consultant

McBEE CONSULTING

September 18, —

Ms. Cordelia Ramsey
Office Assistant
Koronet International
3500 Division
Grand Rapids, MI 49503-3295

Dear Ms. Ramsey:

Do you compose letters frequently? If so, do you sometimes find yourself at a loss for exactly what to say to let the customer know that you care about him or her while at the same time making your point clearly and concisely?

If you answered "yes" to these questions, you are certainly in the majority of those of us who write frequently. As you know, it isn't always easy to write. All of us sometimes have writer's block—we can't decide how to say what we mean and say it effectively.

Join us, along with a number of individuals who work in positions similar to yours, for a writing seminar on Tuesday, October 25, from 9 a.m. until 3 p.m. at the State Room. The cost for the day is $50—a small price to pay for hearing a noted communication theorist, Abraham Gassell, and having a chance to learn from your colleagues about their writing techniques. And, lunch is included in the price.

Just mail the enclosed card by September 28, and your name will be added to our writer's list. Hope to see you soon.

Sincerely,

Marvin Hanley
Communication Consultant

Figure 8-7 Letters with positive and negative tones.

begin sentences; however, this rule no longer holds true. In fact, according to the *Harper Dictionary of Contemporary Usage,* it is perfectly acceptable to use "and" at the beginning of a sentence. Our writing has become more informal. Another example of this informality is in the use of contractions. We have also been taught in the past not to use contractions. Again, today in most writing, contractions are considered most appropriate.

Parallel Structures

Parallel structures help you achieve coherence in a paragraph. **Parallelism** is created when grammatically equivalent forms are used within a sentence. Consider the parallel construction used in the following paragraph.

> Superstitions are *sometimes smiled at, sometimes frowned on, sometimes seen as old-fashioned,* and *sometimes seen as backwoods.* Nevertheless, they give all of us ways of moving back and forth among our different worlds—*the sacred, the secular,* and *the scientific.*

The following sentence illustrates nonparallel and parallel construction.

> Nonparallel: The position is prestigious, challenging, and *also the money isn't bad.*
> Parallel: The position offers prestige, challenge, and money.

READABILITY LEVEL

Readability is the degree of difficulty of the message. Items that contribute to a greater reading difficulty include long sentences and words with several syllables or very technical terms. Readability formulas such as the Gunning Fog Index and the Flesch-Kincaid Index provide readability indices. The higher the readability index, the less readable the message. Business messages should be written to achieve a readability index between 7 and 11. This means that what you have already learned about short words and short sentences should be

followed. You want the letter, memo, or report to be clearly understood by the reader. Obviously, if it is not understood, the message is ineffective.

Formal reports that include technical or scientific terms may have a readability index of 14 or higher due to their complexity. These reports, however, are not written for a general audience but for an audience who has the background and educational level to comprehend the report.

THE CORRESPONDENCE PLAN

To be effective, correspondence must be well planned and organized. For a formal report, it is always smart to make an outline before beginning. If you are a beginner at writing letters, you may find that making notes on a scratch pad will help you organize your thoughts. As you become more experienced in writing letters and informal reports, you may make only a mental outline of what you want to write. A formal report will always require an outline. Whatever the case, planning before writing saves you time and lessens any frustration that may occur.

The steps in the planning process include:

- determining the objective of the message;
- considering the reader; and
- gathering the facts.

DETERMINE THE OBJECTIVE

When writing letters or reports, determine your objective. Why are you writing the letter or the report? What do you hope to accomplish? Business messages generally have one of three primary objectives—to inform the reader, to request an action or information, or to persuade the reader to take action or accept an idea. Some business messages will have more than one objective. For example, the objectives may be to inform and to persuade. What does the reader need to know about the subject? Will the reader want or need background

---

COMMUNICATION TIP

If you are trying to avoid using certain words when writing, delete them from your spell checker's dictionary. Then, if you mistakenly use them, the computer will flag them, giving you an opportunity to change the word.[1]

---

[1]Communication Briefings, Blackwood, NJ.

Chapter 8: Letters, Memos, and Reports

information or support data? If your task is to persuade someone to say "yes" to an offer, consider what it would take to convince you to say "yes."

CONSIDER THE READER

Who will receive your letter or report? How much does the person receiving the document know about the subject? Is the reader familiar with technical jargon that might be used? What is the educational level of the reader? What effect will the message have on the reader? Will the reader react favorably or unfavorably to the message? How much time does the reader have? Is the reader a busy executive who prefers short, concise memos, letters, and reports? Or, does the reader need a great deal of supporting information and detail?

GATHER THE FACTS

Before you begin to write a letter or report, gather the necessary facts. If it is a letter you are writing, ask yourself the *W* questions. Who? What? Why? When? Where? For example, assume your employer asks you to find an appropriate video on building teams. Who will be viewing the video? What type of knowledge do these persons already have about teams? What vendors have videos available on team building? What price range is appropriate?

If you are writing a report, what information do you need? Where can you obtain the information? Do you need to research the subject? Where can you find the information? Is it available through library research or must you do original research? Are you responsible for making recommendations? If so, who will act on these recommendations? Are you expected to present an action plan in addition to the recommendations? Is an executive summary needed? What level of detail is important to the reader?

SEEK HELP FROM SOFTWARE PACKAGES

You have learned that the readability level should be between 7 and 11. If you are a beginning writer, you may want to check the readability level of your writing. Grammar packages generally contain one of the readability formulas such as the Gunning Fog or the Flesch-Kincaid. Within a matter of seconds, you can obtain the readability of your material.

Once you know the level at which you generally write, it is not necessary to check the readability of each piece of correspondence.

Spell checkers now appear on all word processing software. You can quickly identify misspelled words by using the spell checker; however, there are errors a spell checker will not detect such as "to" for "too," "here" for "hear," or "you" for "your." In addition to using the spell checker, you must proofread well.

Grammar programs can help you with grammatical errors. They will flag punctuation and capitalization errors; they will also let you know if you have used the passive voice excessively. A thesaurus helps you develop your vocabulary by suggesting additional words that may be used rather than the one you have used. If you are not comfortable with the word you have used, you can quickly check for other possibilities.

LETTERS AND MEMORANDUMS

Additional suggestions for writing effective letters and memorandums include classifying and organizing the message, using the "you" approach, and developing an effective beginning and ending.

CLASSIFY AND ORGANIZE THE MESSAGE

Letters and memorandums can be classified into the following four categories.

Type of Message	Anticipated Reader Reaction
Favorable	Positive
Routine	Neutral
Unfavorable	Negative
Persuasive	Interested to Indifferent

Favorable messages are those messages the reader will be pleased to receive. A favorable message might be a letter offering a job or a letter of congratulations upon receiving a promotion.

Routine messages have a neutral effect on the receiver. Most of the letters and memorandums written in business are routine messages such as requests for information, relaying information, orders and acknowledgments of receipt of information.

COMMUNICATION TIP

Do not mix metaphors; for example, roar like a cat.

KORONET INTERNATIONAL
3500 Division
Grand Rapids, MI 49503-3295

September 20, —

Mrs. Roselyn Carroll
Carroll Management Institute
52 Drayton Street, Suite 305
Fairview, NJ 07022-5739

Dear Mrs. Carroll:

Please send me information on the management conference
scheduled for November 27. Specifically, I need answers to the
following questions:

1. Will there be a session on budgeting in addition to the
    session on planning?
2. Is the conference designed for the beginning or the
    seasoned manager?
3. Is there a discount if more than one manager from a
    business attends?

Can you get this information to me by November 5? Your
conference could be an excellent addition to our training
sessions which take place in December.

Sincerely,

Jacqueline Marquette

Jacqueline Marquette
Vice President of Community Relations

GA:al

Figure 8-8   Direct letter.

Unfavorable messages will bring a negative reaction from the reader, such as a letter turning down a job applicant or a memorandum informing an employee about refusal for a promotion.

Persuasive messages attempt to get the reader to take some action. For example, a letter in which you try to convince a busy executive to speak at a local conference is a persuasive letter.

The type of message determines the organization of the letter or memorandum.

Type of Message	Organization
Favorable	Direct
Routine (neutral)	Direct
Unfavorable	Indirect
Persuasive	Indirect (persuasive approach)

Direct

If the reader's reaction to your message will be favorable or neutral, you should use the **direct approach.** Much of the routine correspondence you will write falls into this category. Examples of direct correspondence are

- letters—inquiries, requests, orders

- e-mail

- memorandums

Direct correspondence should:

1. Begin with the reason for the correspondence. If you are making a request or inquiry, state that request or inquiry.

Your cellular ad in today's newspaper caught my attention. I am interested in finding out more about these phones.

2. Continue with whatever explanation is necessary so that the reader will understand the message.

Please send me any literature you have on the various types of cellular phones and the prices of each.

3. Close the letter with a thank you for action that has been taken or a request that action be taken by a specific date.

I would appreciate having the information by September 15 so that I may make my decision and purchase a phone.

Figure 8-8 is another illustration of a direct letter. The checklist presented in Figure 8-9 will help you as you begin to write favorable and routine messages.

Indirect

When your message to the reader will cause an unfavorable reaction, your best avenue is an **indirect approach.** There are times when you have to write correspondence refusing a request or an appointment or in some way saying "no" to a person. Even so, you want the person to accept the

Favorable and Routine Message Checklist

- Did you begin the first paragraph with the reason for the correspondence?
- Did you continue with whatever explanation was necessary?
- Did you close with a thank you for action or a request that action be taken by a particular date?
- Did you use the "you" approach?
- Is the correspondence clear, concise, and simple?
- Is the correspondence complete? Did you ask the *W* questions?
- Is the correspondence considerate?
- Is the correspondence timely?
- Is the correspondence positive?
- Do the paragraphs have unity, coherence, and parallel structure?
- Is the readability level appropriate for the intended audience?
- Is the format correct?
- Did you proofread carefully?

Figure 8-9

decision and to understand that you are concerned. You want to leave the person with a positive impression. The indirect correspondence should:

1. Begin with an opening statement that is pleasant but neutral.

Your plan to build a fund for a new arts center in the community is a commendable one. I hope you are able to meet your goal.

2. Then review the circumstances and give the negative information.

Every year Koronet contributes several thousand dollars to important causes. However, even though your proposal is a worthy one, we have already expended this year's budget. If you are still in need of our help next year, please let me know. We will be happy to consider a proposal from you.

3. Close the correspondence on a pleasant and positive note.

Good luck in your efforts. Our town needs more civic-minded groups such as yours.

An example of an indirect letter is given in Figure 8-10. To help you in writing unfavorable messages, use the checklist presented in Figure 8-11.

Persuasive

The **persuasive approach** is indirect with certain special characteristics. Use the persuasive approach when you want to convince someone to do something or change an indifferent or negative reader reaction. By using this approach, you can hopefully change the reader's initial negative or indifferent attitude to a positive position. The persuasive correspondence should:

1. Begin with the **"you" approach.** This approach requires the writer to place the reader at the center of the message. Rather than using "I" or "we," the writer takes the reader's position and uses "you" frequently. You will learn more about this approach in the next section. Here is an example of an effective beginning for a persuasive approach.

Your role as an office professional is often challenging. You deal with conflict, unhappy customers, changing technology, and numerous other challenges daily. Would you like to know how to handle these challenges effectively and keep your frustration level down?

2. Continue by creating an interest and desire.

If you answered "yes" to the question, our monthly publication, *The Effective Office Professional,* will help you. It is packed with effective techniques and suggestions for handling office situations.

3. Close by asking directly for the action desired.

You may have this publication in your office each month for only $48 per year. This is such a small amount to pay for lowering your frustration level and making your job more fun. Fill in the information on the enclosed card and return it by August 15. Your early return will guarantee you one free month of the subscription. We look forward to counting you as one of our many satisfied subscribers.

USE THE "YOU" APPROACH

With the "you" approach, the reader is kept uppermost in the mind of the writer. The "you"

KORONET INTERNATIONAL
3500 Division
Grand Rapids, MI 49503-3295

September 21, —

Mr. Steven Marceau
Higgins Association
19 Belmont Avenue
Dallas, TX 75001-4839

Dear Steve:

Your invitation to speak at the conference on October 13 is an honor. Your group is a respected one, and I have enjoyed my association with it.

The demands on my time at work now are extremely heavy. In addition to a new planning process that I must implement, we have recently employed two new managers who are looking to me for assistance in learning their jobs. As you might expect, I hardly have time to "look up." As I would not want to accept your invitation without having adequate time to prepare, I must say no this time. However, if you need a speaker in the future, please don't forget me. It is always a good experience for me to speak to your group.

Have you met Ramona Stanley, our sales manager? She does an excellent presentation on listening, and she might be available to speak at your conference. Her number is 555-4378. Good luck with the program.

Sincerely,

Jacqueline Marquette

Jacqueline Marquette
Vice President of Community Relations

pjc

Figure 8-10   Indirect letter.

approach involves using **empathy** in writing. When trying to sell a product or a service, the writer must look at the benefits that the product or service will offer the reader, not the amount of sales commission the writer will receive. If the message involves something as routine as setting up a meeting, then the writer must stress the benefits of the meeting to the reader. Such writing emphasizes the "you" and "your" and deemphasizes the "I," "we," "mine," and "ours."

To carry out the "you" approach, adhere to two words of caution: Be sincere. Do not overuse the "you" approach to the point of being insincere and even dishonest. Your goal is not to flatter the reader; rather, your goal is to see the situation from the reader's point of view and to respond accordingly. Sincerity dictates that you tell it like it is. Be honest and empathetic with the reader.

Notice how the following examples of writing from the "I-we" viewpoint have been changed to

Unfavorable Message Checklist

- Did you begin with a pleasant but neutral statement?
- Did you review the circumstances and give the negative information as positively as possible?
- Did you close on a pleasant note?
- If you had to say "no" to something, did you offer an alternative if possible?
- Is the correspondence clear, concise, and simple?
- Is the correspondence complete, considerate, and correct?
- Is the correspondence prompt and positive?
- Do the paragraphs have unity, coherence, and parallel structure?
- Is the format correct?
- Did you proofread well?

Figure 8-11

the "you" viewpoint. The changes are small, yet the meaning and tone are quite different.

"I-We" viewpoint: We received your order for 100 seat belts today.

"You" viewpoint: Your order for 100 seat belts was received June 10.

"I-We" viewpoint: We sell the seat belts for $25 each.

"You" viewpoint: Your cost for the seat belts is $25.

"I-We" viewpoint: I will be glad to attend the conference.

"You" viewpoint: Thank you for asking me to attend the conference. I am delighted to accept your invitation.

Take a few moments now to check your understanding of what you have learned to this point about writing. In the Self Check, rewrite the following sentences so that they are effective.

Self Check

1. Your kind letter of October 8 was received today.

2. I wish to thank you for your recent order.

3. As per my letter of November 5, the modular furniture is unsatisfactory.

4. Please send us the information at your earliest convenience.

5. The error I made was unfortunate; your bill is $500 rather than $1500.

6. Your claim that there is an error in your bill is incorrect.

7. A preponderance of businesspersons was consulted on this esoteric matter.

8. People's propensity to consume goods is insatiable.

9. You will receive the merchandise without any more delay.

10. You will not be sorry if you buy one of our seat belts.

Check your rewrite with those given at the end of the chapter on page 194.

ENSURE MAILABILITY

Because letters represent your company to individuals outside the company, it is essential that they not only be written well but that they be free of grammatical, spelling, punctuation, and format errors. If you need a quick review on letter styles, refer to the reference guide on page 369. In the office, as you apply the techniques learned in this chapter, your employer may, on occasion, give you back a piece of correspondence, telling you that there is an error that you must correct before it can be mailed. A mailability checklist is given in Figure 8-12. Paying attention to all details on a letter will help ensure your effectiveness as an office professional.

REPORTS

The office professional's role in preparing reports will vary. You may only have the responsibility of keyboarding the report, producing the final copies, and distributing the report to the appropriate individuals. Or, your role may involve assisting with the creation of visuals for the report (charts, graphs, and so forth), doing research for your employer, and even drafting some or all portions of the report. You also may have the complete responsibility for keying the report. As you have learned earlier, many businesses today are using a team approach to solving problems within the business. If you are chairing a team, your responsibility may be to write the final report for management.

You learned in this chapter that you must plan before you write any type of correspondence. Planning includes determining the objective, considering the reader, and then gathering the facts. Once this planning has taken place, the next step is to determine how the report will be organized.

BUSINESS REPORT ORGANIZATION

Although reports may be organized in numerous ways, here are possibilities.

* direct

* indirect

* chronological

* geographical

* simple to complex

* function or product

Mailability Checklist

- Does the letter satisfy these requirements?
  Is it complete?
  Is it concise?
  Is it courteous?
  Is it accurate?
  Is it positive?
  Does it use the "you" approach?

- Is the format correct? Have you used an appropriate letter style and appropriate punctuation?

- Is the dateline appropriately placed? Is the date correct?

- Is the letter address correct? Is it appropriately placed?

- Is the salutation correct? Is it appropriately placed?

- Are the complimentary close and signature lines correct and appropriately placed?

- If there are enclosures, has such been noted on the letter?

- If there are special letter parts such as attention lines and subject lines, are they correct and appropriately placed?

- If a copy is to be sent to another individual, is it noted on the letter in the appropriate place?

- Does the envelope address match the letter address?

- Is the letter free of grammatical and punctuation errors?

- Is the letter free of any misspelled words? (Have you used a spell checker?)

- Is the letter folded and inserted in the envelope correctly.

Figure 8-12

Direct

The direct organization presents the main idea first, followed by the additional ideas, and a summary or conclusion. When a report contains routine information, the direct plan is useful. This style is used often in business.

Indirect

The indirect organization plan gives an introduction first, followed by a body, and an ending. Recommendations may be made based on the findings of the report. The indirect style is used frequently in academic settings in presenting information from a formal study which many times includes research.

Chronological

When the time sequence of events is important, a **chronological order** may be used. For example, a sales report may present information in chronological order by week, by month, or by year.

Geographical

Geographical order organizes material by location. Koronet may, for example, have its financial reports organized by location, with its U.S. offices and its international offices presented separately.

Simple to Complex

Technical material that is directed at readers with nontechnical backgrounds lends itself to a **simple to complex order.** The reader must be educated about certain concepts before understanding the more difficult concepts.

Function or Product

A business report may be organized into **function** or **product order.** As an example, a business might organize a marketing report by its products or a business school might organize its annual report by departments (functions).

Once you have determined the objective of the report, analyzed who the reader will be, and considered how the report should be arranged (classified), you must begin to consider the content of the report by:

1. Preparing a summary of what should be included in the report.

2. Gathering information for the report. If research is necessary, it is done at this point. The next section gives you some research suggestions.

3. Preparing an outline of the report. The outline may be a detailed one (for a formal report) or merely one the writer prepares to organize thoughts (for an informal report). Figure 8-13 shows a portion of an outline. Notice that no

Preparing a Business Report

I. Introduction

    A. Purpose of a Business Report

    B. Role of the Office Professional in Preparing a Business Report

II. Outline

    A. Purpose of an Outline

    B. Organization of Information

        1. Titles, headings, and subheadings

        2. Parallel structure

            a. Definition of parallel structure

            b. Example of parallel structure

Figure 8-13

main heading or subheading stands alone. For every *I*, there must be a *II*; for every *A*, there must be a *B*, and so forth. An outline should also be parallel in structure; that is, if roman numeral *I* begins with a noun, then all roman numerals must begin with a noun.

4. Drafting the report. The body of the report should have:

    a. an introduction to help the reader understand the purpose of the report;

    b. a main part which includes all the pertinent information;

    c. a conclusion or findings and recommendations to help the reader understand what should be done with the report.

Quoted material may be used in the report. If so, footnotes, endnotes, or internal citations are necessary to give proper credit to the source by citing the author of the work, the title of the work, the publishing company, year of publication date, and page number.

5. Preparing any necessary graphs, charts, and tables.

6. Reading and editing the report.

7. Making the appropriate changes and rereading the report

8. Printing and distributing the report.

RESEARCH SOURCES

If you are asked to research a report, you need to be familiar with various sources of information. Several of these sources are given here.

Government Publications

Numerous informational and statistical publications are available from the U.S. government. *The Monthly Catalog of United States Government Publications* provides a comprehensive list of all publications issued by the various governmental departments and agencies. This publication is available on a CD-ROM. Generally access to bibliographic information through CD-ROM is free; however, costs may be involved in printing. This information should be available from your school or local library. The following is a listing of a few other government publications, with a brief synopsis of what is contained in each.

- *Statistical Abstract of the United States* gives statistics concerning population, climate, employment, military affairs, banking, transportation, agriculture, and related fields.

- *Survey of Current Business* reports on the industrial and business activities of the United States.

- *Monthly Labor Review* publishes labor statistics, standards, and employment trends.

The numerous business and government publications are good sources for researching a business report.

Computer Reference Sources

Numerous computer networks exist which allow you to do research at the computer. You have already learned about the Internet and online services such as American Online, CompuServe, Prodigy, and others. Some of the topics that can be accessed over these networks include business and economic information and financial and statistical information. Complete descriptions of various databases are found in a reference book entitled *Directory of Online Databases.*

Corporate Directories

A number of corporate directories are also available, including:

- *Moody's Industrial Manual, Moody's OTC Industrial Manual, Moody's Municipal and Government Manual,* and *Moody's Handbook of Common Stocks*

- *Standard and Poor's Register of Corporations, Directors and Executives*

- *Thomas Register of American Manufacturers*

International Business Information

Numerous data are available concerning international business; a few of the publications are listed here.

- *Statistical Yearbook of the United Nations*

- *Industry and Development: Global Report*

- *World Directory of Industry and Trade Associations*

- *The World Bank Atlas*

- *Global Market Surveys*

Primary Research

At times, information from secondary sources such as those mentioned is not adequate for the task. **Primary research** (original) may be essential. There are numerous ways in which primary research may be conducted, including observational research, survey research, and experimental research. Observational research as its name implies involves collecting data through observations of an event. Survey research involves collecting data through interviews. These interviews may be face-to-face, by telephone, or by a mail questionnaire. Experimental research has generally been used in the sciences; however, it is becoming popular with business. It may involve a researcher selecting two or more sample groups and exposing these groups to treatments. For example, a business may decide to test a marketing strategy before implementing a marketing campaign. Experimental groups would be selected and the marketing strategy implemented. Based on the outcome of the research, the business would proceed with the marketing strategy, modify it, or select another marketing strategy.

PARTS OF THE REPORT

An informal report might have only one or two parts, with those parts being the body and an **executive summary.** The purpose of an executive summary is to provide the reader with a shorter, more compact version of the report. It provides a brief review of the findings of the report and makes recommendations, if appropriate. Because the busy executive may only read the summary, it should provide enough information to make a decision.

An informal report is written in a conversational style. Personal pronouns such as "I," "you," "me," "we," and "us" should be used. Contractions are also acceptable. The direct plan of organization is generally used with an informal report.

The formal report normally deals with a more complex subject, is longer than the informal report, and requires more time and preparation. Formal reports are generally written in manuscript format and contain preliminary and supplementary parts. These parts include:

- letter of transmittal

- title page

- table of contents

- list of tables and illustrations

- executive summary

- body of the report

- endnotes, footnotes, or internal citations

- bibliography or reference section

- appendix

Letter of Transmittal

Most business reports are presented to the reader with a letter of transmittal. The letter introduces the report to the reader. The purpose of the letter is to help the reader understand the nature of the report and to arouse interest in its study. If the report is one that is to be used within the organization, a cover memorandum may be prepared rather than a formal letter. The letter should use a direct style with the beginning being as simple as: "Here is the report you requested about . . ." Next, there should be a brief statement of the purpose or goal of the report. Any individual who helped with the report should be acknowledged. The close might be expressing the willingness to do additional research or suggesting future actions that might be necessary.

Title Page

The title page contains the title of the report; the writer's name, title, and department or division; and the date the report is being submitted.

Table of Contents

A table of contents lists each major section of a report and the page number of the first page of that section. A table of contents is not required; however, when a report is long, it helps the reader find particular parts of the report.

List of Tables and Illustrations

If there are numerous tables and illustrations within a report, it is appropriate to list the title of each table and illustration, with the respective page number. This procedure helps the reader to quickly locate the tables and illustrations and scan the data presented.

Executive Summary

The executive summary should include an introduction (similar to the introduction in the body of the report), the findings and any discussion of these findings, any recommendations, and a conclusion.

Body of the Report

The body is divided into the following major sections:

- introduction
- problem statement
- research methods
- findings and discussion
- recommendations (if appropriate)
- report ending

Endnotes, Footnotes, or Internal Citations

Footnotes appear at the bottom of the page where the reference is made. Endnotes are grouped at the end of the document. Internal citations appear within the context of the document.

Bibliography or Reference Section

All references used in a report should be included in a bibliography or reference section. This section includes the complete name of the author(s), the title of the book or periodical, the date of the publication, the publishing company (if the reference is a book), and page numbers (if the reference is a periodical).

Appendix

A formal report may contain an appendix which includes supporting information such as tables, statistics, and other pertinent material. Items in an appendix are lettered Appendix A, B, and so forth. The appendix is the last part of the report.

COLLABORATIVE REPORTS

You have been learning throughout this text that teams have become important in getting the work of the organization done. This team approach is also used in preparing reports, so that they become collaborative. Although working in teams and collaborating on a report can be very productive, they bring their own set of difficulties. For example, more planning time is essential when you are working with a group of people. If the planning time does not take place, there may be problems such as poor communication, role misunderstandings, procrastination, and so forth. When organizing a collaborative project, here are some items that need to be determined before the project begins.

- Identify individual roles (determine the team leader and the recordkeeper, how work will be allocated, how decisions will be made, how conflicts will be resolved, and so forth).

- Establish ground rules. These ground rules should be in writing and address such items as all individuals will contribute equally; communication will be open; listening to each other is essential; respect for each other is imperative.

- Allocate the work.

- Monitor the progress.

A collaborative report requires identifying the role that each individual will take in the report process. *Hewlett Packard.*

INTERNATIONAL CORRESPONDENCE

Throughout this course, you have been reminded of the global nature of business today and what that means for you as an office professional. Chances are great that you will be communicating in writing with individuals from various countries at some point in your career. This chapter has focused on written communication using the principles that are appropriate for U.S. firms. However, if you are writing to individuals outside the United States, you must consider the differences in culture. You learned in Chapter 5 about various cultural differences. Although these differences vary from country to country, you need to be aware and be understanding of these differences as you communicate in writing. Such knowledge and understanding can assist your employer in developing clear, concise, and appropriate communications with international businesses. Generally, it can be said that communication must be more formal than it is in the United States. In learning the particulars of the country, it is a good idea to read as extensively as possible. General principles that hold true are given in Figure 8-14, but understand that customs will vary from nation to nation just as cultural differences vary.

You learned earlier it is projected that in the future we will have computers that can automatically translate a communication into the native language of the recipient. Until these are available, however, translation can be an issue. English is the most predominant language used in the world. Even if the person receiving the communication speaks English, it may be a good idea to translate the communication into the person's native language. Translation services are available if you need one; you can find listings in the yellow pages of your telephone book.

When writing internationally, the customs and culture of the recipient must be considered. *Courtesy of International Business Machines, Inc.*

General Principles for International Written Correspondence

- Language is relatively formal; phrases such as "Very Honored Professor Dr. Fruer" and "Your honored servant" are used in some countries.

- Do not use expressions unique to the United States; do not refer to events that are common only to the United States.

- Use the dictionary meaning of a word.

- Always use the title of the individual with whom you are corresponding. First names should not be used.

- Be extremely courteous; use "thank you" and "please" often.

- Be complimentary when appropriate (but always sincere).

- Ask questions tactfully.

- Practice the art of negotiation in writing documents.

- Do not use humor; it may be misunderstood.

- Respect all customs of the country (social, religion, values, and so forth).

- Learn all you can about the country; read extensively.

- Translate correspondence into the native language of the country.

- Send business cards that are printed in the native language of the country.

Figure 8-14

CHAPTER SUMMARY

This summary will help you remember the important points covered in this chapter.

- Basic business correspondence prepared by the office professional includes memorandums, e-mail, letters, and reports.

- Effective correspondence is clear, concise, and simple. This means that the sentences are short, the vocabulary is easily understood, a conversational tone is used, unnecessary words are deleted, active verbs are used, the writing style is varied, and clichés are avoided.

- Effective correspondence is also complete, considerate, correct, prompt, and positive. The paragraphs have unity and coherence. The sentences are parallel in structure. The appropriate readability level is used. The writer gears the message at a readability index between 7 and 11.

- In planning correspondence, the writer should determine the objective, consider the reader, and gather the facts.

- Letters and memorandums can be classified as favorable, routine (neutral), unfavorable, or persuasive. If the message is favorable or routine, the direct approach is used. If the message is unfavorable or persuasive, the indirect approach is used.

- The "you" approach should be used when writing letters. This approach keeps the reader uppermost in mind. It involves using empathy in writing.

- Business report organization includes these methods: direct, indirect, chronological, geographical, simple to complex, and function or product focused.

- In researching for a business report, resource possibilities include government publications, computer reference sources, corporate directories, and international business information. Many of these resources are available through online computer databases.

- Primary research may be essential for a business report. This research may include observational research, survey research, and experimental research.

- Parts of a formal business report include the letter of transmittal, title page, table of contents, list of tables and illustrations, executive summary, body, endnotes or footnotes, bibliography, and appendix.

- Reports are often done through a collaborative process. When such occurs it is necessary to identify individual roles, establish ground rules, allocate the work, and monitor the progress.

- International correspondence is usually much more formal than correspondence written to individuals within the United States. The writer must be aware of the customs and culture of that particular country.

CHAPTER GLOSSARY

The following terms were introduced in this chapter. To help you review, definitions are given here.

- **Tone** (p. 178)–The manner of expression in writing.

- **Topic sentence** (p. 179)–The sentence that contains the main idea of a paragraph.

- **Parallelism** (p. 181)–Creating grammatically equivalent forms that are used several times.

- **Readability** (p. 181)–The degree of difficulty of the message.

- **Favorable messages** (p. 182)–Communication that the reader will be pleased to receive.

- **Routine messages** (p. 182)–Communication that has a neutral effect on the receiver.

- **Unfavorable messages** (p. 183)–Communication that will bring a negative reaction from the reader.

- **Persuasive messages** (p. 183)–Messages that attempt to get the reader to take some action.

- **Direct approach** (p. 183)–Used when the message is favorable or neutral. It begins with the reason for the correspondence, continues with any needed explanation, and closes with a thank you for the action that has been taken or a request for action at a specific time.

- **Indirect approach** (p. 183)–Used when the message is unfavorable. It begins with an opening statement that is pleasant or neutral, reviews the circumstances, gives the negative information, and closes with a pleasant and positive note.

- **Persuasive approach** (p. 184)–This approach is basically an indirect one, but it is a special kind of indirect approach that begins with the "you" approach, continues by creating an interest and desire, and closes by asking directly for the action desired.

- **The "you" approach** (p. 184)–An approach that requires the writer to place the reader at the center of the message. "You" and "your" are used frequently rather than "I" or "we."

- **Empathy** (p. 185)–Mentally entering into the feeling or spirit of a person or thing.

- **Chronological order** (p. 187)–Used in writing business reports when the time sequence of events is important.

- **Geographical order** (p. 187)–Used in writing business reports when material should be organized by location.

- **Simple to complex order** (p. 187)–Used in writing business reports when material is highly technical and readers need to be educated to a degree.

- **Function or product order** (p. 187)–Used in writing a business report when it should be arranged by function (e.g., marketing, finance) or product (e.g., office furniture, office equipment).

- **Primary research** (p. 189)–Collection of data through means such as observation, surveys, or experiments.

- **Executive summary** (p. 189)–Provides the reader with a shorter, more compact version of the report.

DISCUSSION ITEMS

These items provide an opportunity for you to test your understanding of the chapter through discussion with your classmates and instructor.

1. Cite six advantages of using e-mail rather than interoffice memorandums.
2. Explain what is meant by clear, concise, and simple when referring to effective correspondence.
3. What constitutes an effective paragraph?
4. How may letters and memorandums be classified?
5. When is the indirect approach used in writing?
6. Identify the parts of a formal business report.

CASE STUDY

One of the managers, Martin Helmholdt, asks the administrative assistant who works with him to write a letter to Ruth Hart congratulating her on becoming city manager of Dallas. Ruth worked for Mr. Helmholdt a number of years ago and moved to Dallas five years ago. The assistant has prepared a draft, but he is not pleased with the letter. He asks that you critique the letter before he gives it to Mr. Helmholdt.

Here is the draft of the letter.

Dear Ms. Hart:

I want to congratulate you on becoming City Manager of Dallas. I recognized your talent during the years that you worked for me. I know that you will do an excellent job for Dallas.

Again, my congratulations on your success.

What suggestions would you make to the assistant?

RESPONSES TO SELF CHECK

1. Your October 8 letter was received today.
2. Thank you for your recent order.
3. The modular furniture that we received on November 5 is unsatisfactory. Copies of our purchase order and your shipping statement are enclosed. Please notice as you compare the two statements that the furniture received does not match our order.
4. Please send us the information by September 14.
5. You are correct; your bill is $500 rather than $1500. A corrected bill is enclosed.
6. Your bill has been reviewed carefully by our billing department. We can find no error in the computations. Please give me a call at 555-1500 if the bill is still unclear; I will be happy to discuss the matter with you in detail.
7. A number of businesspersons were consulted on this matter.
8. People constantly consume goods.
9. You will receive the merchandise by January 10.
10. Our seat belts will be a good investment for your company.

OFFICE TASKS

OFFICE TASK 8-1 (Objective 1)

Team with two of your classmates. Collect six business letters that you have received through the mail. Any type of business letter will be acceptable. Using the effective letter characteristics given in this text, critique the letters. Pick one letter to rewrite. Present the critique orally to your class along with the rewritten letter.

OFFICE TASK 8-2 (Objective 1)

Each of the following sentences is intended to be the beginning sentence of a letter. Rewrite the sentences so they will be effective.

1. I received your order today and wanted to thank you for it.
2. Enclosed please find my check in the amount of $510.36 in payment for your Order 34560.
3. I regret to inform you that the modular furniture you ordered is no longer being manufactured.
4. This check affirms my intent to subscribe to your weekly investment publication, *Financial News.*
5. I hope you will send us your subscription renewal today.

OFFICE TASK 8-3 (Objective 2)

Ms. Marquette has been asked by Dr. Marcel Lubbers, president of Grand Haven University, to do a presentation on business ethics at a national conference for business executives scheduled on November 11 from 3 to 4:40 p.m. Koronet is having a meeting of its executive management team, both within the United States and its international locations on November 8, 9, 10, and 11. The meeting will conclude at noon on November 11. Ms. Marquette has decided to ask Travis Ueoka from the Japan office and Raphael Herrara from the Mexico office to join her, along with Katherina Schmidt from the North Carolina office. The presentation will be a panel with each participant taking approximately twenty minutes to discuss business ethics, internationally. A question and answer session will follow the presentations.

She asks you to write a memorandum to the individuals listed in the office task, asking them to participate; the memorandum may go out with your name on it; all parties have e-mail. (Because you will not be able to actually send an e-mail, use the simulated e-mail form on Student Data Template Disk, file OT8-3 in completing this assignment.)

OFFICE TASK 8-4 (Objective 3)

Team with three members of your class. Ms. Marquette asks you to research articles on business ethics, both within the United States and internationally for the November 11 panel. She has a particular interest in the ethical responsibility of the company to society. You are to check computer databases and your local library for information. Once you have completed your research, prepare a detailed summary of your findings in informal report form. The report will have an introduction (giving the research methods used), a body, and the findings. A bibliography is to be included, listing your resources (include at least three resources).

OFFICE TASK 8-5 (Objective 2)

Ms. Marquette plans to use presentation software in the ethics presentation. She will need to discuss her needs with John Valentine of the Telecommunications Department. Write a memo to him asking him to meet with Ms. Marquette on November 1 at 10 a.m. in her office. You may use e-mail. (Because you will not actually be able to send the e-mail, use the simulated e-mail form on Student Data Template Disk, file OT8-5.)

OFFICE TASK 8-6 (Objective 2)

Ms. Marquette has asked you to write a letter to Dr. Marcel Lubbers, president of Grand Haven University, 1800 College Street, Grand Haven, MI 49534, giving him the names of the individuals who will be on the panel with her. Explain the presentation format that she will use and the time that she expects each individual to take. Tell Dr. Lubbers that you will be sending him a copy of the resumes of all individuals by November 8. Ms. Marquette does not know the room number for the presentation; ask Dr. Lubbers for this information. Ms. Marquette will sign the letter. A letterhead form is available on the template on Student Data Template Disk, file OT8-6.

OFFICE TASK 8-7 (Objective 2)

You have been asked by Mr. Mike Rowse, Temporary Office Workers, 3986 Ottawa SE, Grand Rapids, MI 49501, to participate in a panel discussion on the topic of effective communications within the office. You would like to do so, but your current workload is extremely heavy. Write a letter to Mr. Rowse saying "no" to his request. Use the letterhead provided on Student Data Template Disk, file OT8-7.

OFFICE TASK 8-8 (Objective 2)

One of your friends, Monica Sanchez, has just received a promotion to office manager for Vickers Steel, 1852 Airport Drive SE, Grand Rapids, MI 49502. Write a letter of congratulations to her. Use the letterhead provided on Student Data Template Disk, file OT8-8.

OFFICE TASK 8-9 (Objective 3)

Team with three of your classmates. Write a formal report about students' use of the Internet in your school. You will need to do original research. Develop a survey instrument which asks questions similar to these: Do you use the Internet? If so, how often? How do you use the Internet? What information do you seek? Do you do research on the Internet? Do you use the Internet in any of your classes? If so, what class? Ask the approximate age of the respondents, using these categories as a checklist: 18–25, 25–40, 40–50, above 50. You may want to do the survey in the cafeteria or in the student lounge. Survey at least twelve students. Prepare the information obtained from the survey in graph form, showing the use of the Internet and other information obtained by age categories. Include the survey form as an appendix to your report. Do a title page with the title and date of the report, plus your name and the names of your team.

ENGLISH USAGE CHALLENGE DRILL

Correct the following sentences. Cite the grammar rule that is applicable to each sentence. Before you begin, refresh your memory of grammar rules by reviewing comma rules in the *Multimedia Reference for Writers,* the reference guide in this text, or some other reference manual available to you.

1. Everyone wanted to be near a television set to watch the Summer Olympics beginning July 25 1996 in Atlanta.

2. The jury listened closely to the testimony of Nelson Hemingway M.D. last week.

3. Of the gymnastic team's thirty two received gold medals.

4. Her address is 49,000 State Street.

5. The major news story during July, 1996, was the TWA plane crash.

ASSESSMENT OF CHAPTER OBJECTIVES

Now that you have completed the chapter and the office tasks, take a few moments to review the following learning objectives. Did you accomplish the objectives? If so, explain how in the space provided. If you were unable to accomplish these objectives, give your reason for not doing so. Your instructor may want to review your answers.

I accomplished these objectives:

1. Identify the characteristics of effective correspondence. Yes _____ No _____

   Explain how you accomplished this objective.
   _____
   _____
   _____

2. Compose letters and memos. Yes _____ No _____

   Explain how you accomplished this objective.
   _____
   _____
   _____

3. Research and write a business report.
   Yes _____ No _____

   Explain how you accomplished this objective.
   _____
   _____
   _____

Provide reasons for failing to accomplish any of the objectives.
_____
_____
_____

CHAPTER 9

OFFICE CALLERS AND PRESENTATIONS

LEARNING OBJECTIVES

1. **Develop effective techniques for working with office callers.**
2. **Release and expand your creativity.**
3. **Deliver effective individual and group presentations.**

In Chapter 5 you learned effective communication techniques. Throughout this course, you will have the opportunity to use these techniques as you communicate with your instructor, your classmates, and business professionals in the community as you complete certain office tasks. As you have already learned, communication is a large part of the office professional's job, whether that communication be oral or written. In Chapter 8, you began to perfect your written communication skills through composing memorandums, letters, and reports. In this chapter, you will continue to perfect your oral communication skills through learning how to receive office callers and to make effective individual and group presentations, while maximizing your own creativity. Remember that developing communication skill is an ongoing process. This course will help you learn and practice certain skills. As you enter the office world (or, if you presently have a part-time or full-time job in the office), you will continue to develop communication skills. Your understanding of and commitment to continual growth in this area will help ensure your effectiveness as an office professional.

OFFICE CALLERS

In many large organizations a receptionist greets all office visitors initially. The receptionist may keep a register in which the name of the visitor, company affiliation, nature of the visit, person the visi-tor wishes to see, and date of the visit are recorded. After obtaining this information from the visitor, the receptionist notifies the office professional that the caller has arrived. If this is a first time visit for the office caller, your job may involve going to the receptionist area and escorting the visitor to your employer's office.

In small companies, you may also serve as the receptionist. In other words, you may have the responsibility of greeting all visitors to the company and seeing that they are directed to the proper persons. Regardless of whether you work in a large or small company, here are some techniques for receiving office visitors.

KNOW YOUR SUPERVISOR'S EXPECTATIONS

In most cases, your supervisor will have definite expectations in regard to the handling of certain visitors. For example, there are usually people who will have immediate access to your supervisor's office. The president of the company, the chairperson of the board, a valuable client or customer, a distinguished civic official—these people are usually granted immediate access. Here are some questions you may ask your supervisor to learn about preferences concerning visitors.

- Are there certain persons whom you will see immediately regardless of how busy you are?

- Are there friends or relatives who call on occasion that you will see immediately?

- Are there certain persons you will not see under any circumstances? How are job applicants handled? Should they be referred to the human resources department? How are sales representatives handled? Should they be referred to the purchasing department?

- Do you want me to make introductions if you have not met the caller?

- Is there a particular time of day that you set aside for seeing callers?

GREET THE VISITOR

Even though the visitor to a large organization has usually already been greeted by the receptionist, your role as an office professional is to welcome the visitor to your office. Greet the person graciously with a simple "Good morning" or "Good afternoon." Use the visitor's name if you know it. All visitors appreciate being called by name, and it lets them know that you care enough to make an effort to remember their name.

If you have never met the visitor, it is appropriate to rise from your chair, say "Hello (or "Good morning," "Good afternoon"), I'm Eleanor Wilkerson, Ms. Marquette's administrative assistant," shake hands, and then ask the client to be seated. Your handshake should be relaxed but firm. Your handshake should never be as limp as a dishrag nor should it be so firm that the individual feels as if the knuckles are being broken. As you shake hands, look the person in the eye, smile, and say "I'm happy to meet you" or some similar cordial greeting. You always extend your hand first to the visitor. If the person seems to back off, however, do not force a handshake. Simply drop your hand back to your side, smile, and say, "I'm happy to meet you." Do not be embarrassed that the person has not offered a hand.

Greet office callers you have not met with a smile and a handshake.

Business greetings have become more informal than in the past. Sometimes they even begin with a kiss on the cheek or a hug for someone that you know well. You may find that your supervisor sometimes greets long-time acquaintances in this manner. The general rule for you as an office professional, however, is to never initiate a kiss or hug with someone entering your office. If the caller initiates it, do not recoil in surprise or embarrassment; this response is awkward for both parties. If a frequent caller to your office insists on this greeting and you are uncomfortable, you may mention it to your employer, who can politely tell the caller that you are uncomfortable with such a greeting.

You certainly might greet a co-worker who has been away from the office for a period of time with a more informal greeting such as a hug; however, always take into consideration the occasion and the setting. Never hug someone who is at a higher or lower rank in the company than you. It can look as if you are currying favor or taking advantage of someone.

In greeting international visitors, the rules change depending on the visitor's nationality. A section later in this chapter deals with the international visitor.

Always give a caller your immediate attention. It is discourteous to leave someone standing at your desk while you finish filing papers, preparing a report, or talking on the phone. If you are on the phone when a caller arrives, ask the telephone caller to hold for a moment while you greet the visitor. Tell the visitor you will be of assistance in just a moment. Return to your telephone call and finish as quickly as possible. Excuse yourself if you must answer the telephone when a caller is at your desk.

KEEP CONFIDENTIAL INFORMATION CONFIDENTIAL

If you are working on confidential information on your desk or your computer screen when a visitor arrives, be certain to cover the information so that it cannot be read by the visitor. You can tactfully handle such situations by keeping a folder readily available in which you place written information. If you have information on your computer screen, you may save it quickly and return to a blank screen. You can handle these situations very nonchalantly, while at the same time smiling and greeting the visitor appropriately.

DETERMINE PURPOSE OF VISIT

When a scheduled visitor (one with an appointment) comes to the office, you probably already know the purpose of the visit. When you receive an unscheduled visitor, however, you must find out why the person is calling. Your initial greeting may be, "Good morning (or afternoon), how may I help you?" Such a greeting gives the person a chance to respond with an introduction and the reason for the call. If the visitor does not volunteer the information you need, you must ask for it. Avoid blunt questions such as

- What is your name?

- What do you want?

- Where do you work?

Keeping a register of office visitors is a polite, proven way to get the information you need. Merely ask the visitor to record the necessary information on the register (see Figure 9-1.) Notice that there is a place for the date, time, visitor's name and affiliation, person visited, and purpose of the call. Most people regard a register of office visitors as routine procedure and usually do not object to giving the information requested. In fact, some office professionals must keep a register of the time their employer spends with clients for billing pur-

poses; for example, attorneys bill by the hour. If you use a register frequently, you will probably want to transfer the information to a computer file for ease of recall at a future date.

Another possibility for getting information about a caller is to ask for a business card which contains the person's name, position, company name, address, and telephone number. If you proceed in this manner, you will still need to get the purpose of the visit. Once you have the visitor's card, you can say, "May I tell Ms. Marquette the purpose of your visit?"

Greet visitors promptly and in a professional manner.
Courtesy of International Business Machines, Inc.

Register of Office Visitors				
Date	Time	Name and Affiliation	Person Visiting	Purpose of Call
8/9/--	10	J. Harcourt, Harcourt Glass	J. M.	Board meeting
8/9/--	11:15	P. Freeman	J. M.	Community arena
8/9/--	2:30	D. Martin	J. M.	Community arts function

Figure 9-1   Caller register.

Sometimes the visitor's purpose in seeing your supervisor is outside the scope of your supervisor's duties. You will save the visitor and your supervisor time by finding out the purpose of the visit and referring the visitor to the appropriate person. Be certain that you are considerate if it is necessary to refer the visitor to someone else. Call the office of the person to whom you are referring the visitor and explain the situation. If the person can see the visitor immediately, escort the visitor to the correct office if possible. If you are unable to leave your desk, give the visitor specific instructions on how to find the correct office. If an appointment must be made for another day, check with the visitor to set a mutually convenient time.

REMEMBER NAMES AND FACES

As you have already learned, it is always good to use a caller's name. The following pointers will help you learn names quickly.

- Listen carefully to the person's name when it is pronounced.

- If you do not understand a name, ask the person to repeat it.

- Write the name phonetically if the pronunciation is difficult.

- Use the person's name when you first learn it. For example, you might say, "I'm very happy to meet you, Mr. Aikers."

- Before the person leaves, use the name again; practice helps you get the name straight for future meetings.

- Ask the person for a business card; attach it to an index card with notations about the caller. Place the index card in a card file and refer to it often. Or, transfer the card information to your computer; make notations that will help you remember the person; for example, you might describe the person's appearance briefly—tall, wears glasses, black hair, slight build.

If you receive an office caller who has been in the office before but whose name you have forgotten, be tactful and say, "It's good to see you again." At least you will let the person know that you remember a previous visit. If the person has an appointment, however, forgetting the name is unforgivable. It is your responsibility to check all appointments each day (on both your calendar and your employer's calendar to be certain an appointment has not been scheduled without your awareness) and be certain that you know the name of the person, the reason for the appointment, whether your supervisor needs an introduction, and so forth.

MAKE THE WAIT PLEASANT

If the caller must wait, it is your job to make the wait as pleasant as possible. If coffee is available, offer the visitor a cup of coffee. Explain approximately how long the wait will be. If possible, explain the reason for the delay—particularly if the caller had an appointment. For example, you may say, "I'm extremely sorry, but Ms. Marquette had a very important, unexpected meeting; she will be available in approximately ten minutes." Such an approach lets the caller know that you are concerned but that the wait is unavoidable. Offer the visitor something to read so that the wait will not seem so long. You should have available business periodicals such as *Forbes®, Fortune®,* or *Business Week®.*

After the office caller is situated, you are free to go back to your work; you are not expected to chat. The visitor realizes that you have other duties. If the wait is longer than you anticipated, determine if the caller wants to come back later or see someone else in the company if that can be arranged.

MAKE INTRODUCTIONS

In making business introductions, follow one basic rule: the most important person is named first, regardless of gender. For example, a customer or client is more important than your supervisor, a government official is more important than your supervisor, and your supervisor is more important than a new employee who is at a lower level on the organization chart than your supervisor.

If the president of another company visits your supervisor, for example, you would say, "Mr. Poster, this is Ms. Marquette." Or, if your supervisor does not know the name of the company of the visitor, "Mr. Poster, president of Cortez Equipment, this is Ms. Marquette." Another appropriate introduction is: "Mr. Poster, I would like you to meet Ms. Marquette."

It may not always be necessary to use the titles Mr., Mrs., Miss, or Ms. In other words, you may use the first and last names of the individuals when introducing them. Be certain what your supervisor prefers; if you do not know the supervisor's preference, use the titles. Always use titles such as "Dr." or "Senator" before a person's name when applicable.

When introducing people of equal rank in business situations, the social rules for introductions apply, which are a man is introduced to a woman and a younger person is introduced to an older person.

HANDLE INTERRUPTIONS

You may need to interrupt your supervisor with a message when callers are present. Do so as unobtrusively as possible. You can knock on the door or telephone your supervisor—whichever is preferred. If you knock on the door, hand your supervisor a note; never give the information verbally to your supervisor. The caller should not be privy to the information.

There may be times when a caller overstays the time allocated. You may help your supervisor by bringing in a note or by telephoning. This approach provides your supervisor with a convenient means of letting the visitor know that other people are waiting or other responsibilities require attention.

HANDLE THE DIFFICULT CALLER

It is not always easy to be pleasant to visitors, especially those who are ill-tempered and discourteous. At such times, however, you must keep foremost in your mind your role as an ambassador of goodwill.

It is your job to find out the name of the caller and why that caller wants to see your employer. Be wary of an office caller who tries to avoid your inquiries by evasive answers such as

- It's a personal matter.

- I have reason to believe Ms. Marquette will be interested in what I have to say.

You may respond, "I'm sorry, but Ms. Marquette sees callers only by appointment. If you will tell me the purpose of your visit, I will check to see if Ms.

Marquette will be available at a later date to see you." If the caller still refuses to reveal the purpose of the visit, you may offer the caller a sheet of paper and suggest that a note be written to the executive. Then deliver the note and ask if the supervisor wishes to see the caller. If your supervisor is in a conference, you might suggest to the caller that a letter be written to your supervisor requesting an appointment.

Do not disclose specific information about the company or your supervisor to unidentified callers. If a person comes to your office and asks for specific information, your response should be, "I'm sorry; I don't have that information."

Sometimes a caller is upset or angry for reasons that have nothing to do with you or the company. Something may have happened on the way to your office that triggered the unhappiness, and the person is venting frustrations. If you are curt and further provoke the caller, the situation is aggravated. Let the caller talk. Listen. Try to understand the caller's viewpoint. Much of the anger or frustration usually is released through talking. Your role is to be even-tempered and tolerant.

COMMUNICATE WITH THE INTERNATIONAL VISITOR

If you have frequent international guests, you need to become aware of their culture and customs. Some suggestions for communicating with the international visitor follow.

Greetings

Greetings in other countries differ depending upon the country. Europeans and South Americans shake hands, although South Americans hug and kiss on the cheek (for both the same and opposite gender) when they know someone. Women in many other countries do not enjoy the status or prestige of American women. If you are greeting a woman from another country, wait for her to

---

COMMUNICATION TIP

When introducing business associates, mention something about the other person. You might say, for example, "Mr. McQuale, I would like you to meet Mr. Greer, who is the head of marketing at Phillips International and a Boston Braves fan."

extend her hand. If she does not, you can assume that women do not shake hands in her country. In Saudi Arabia you do not even acknowledge the presence of a woman. When a Saudi Arabian man is accompanied by a woman, do not even notice her unless he introduces her.

When greeting people from Asian countries, you may bow. Many Asians have accommodated to the American handshake, however, and bowing is not expected. If you do bow, follow these guidelines.

- Your hands should remain at your sides.

- Your back and neck should be held in a rigid position, with eyes looking downward.

- The person in the inferior position always bows longer and lower.

When greeting people from India, Bangladesh, and Thailand, hold your hands together in front of your chin in a prayerlike position and nod your head.

The general rule for all international callers is to never use first names. Use titles and the last name. Remember that in China, the first name is the surname, thus Zhao Xiyang is Mr. Zhao, not Mr. Xiyang.

During the greetings, your supervisor should always offer a business card. If you have one, you should also offer a business card. A business card is important with all international visitors, but with Asians, it is almost a ritual. The card is not merely handed to the individual, but it is presented. You should always receive the card gracefully, using both hands and never stuffing the card recklessly into your pocket.

Welcoming

You may have the responsibility of making arrangements for international visitors. Remember that it is always best to read about your visitor's country before the visit. Numerous books are available in local libraries and bookstores. It is a good idea to get information for you and for your supervi-

sor. You might also talk with any people within the company who have traveled to the particular country of the visitor. Being knowledgeable is the best way to avoid showing any disrespect to the visitor.

In making arrangements, follow these general guidelines.

- Meet (or have someone meet) the guest at the airport and drive the individual to the hotel. Remember that language difficulty may be a problem. You might carry a sign with the person's name on it.

- Provide a driver (if possible) while the individual is in the country.

- Arrange for complimentary food or flowers to be delivered to the visitor's hotel. Be certain, however, that you choose the appropriate food and flowers. For example, Muslims and Hindus do not drink alcoholic beverages. Do not send a person from Iran yellow flowers; it can mean that you wish the person dead. Do not send a Chinese person white flowers; white is the color of mourning.

- When arranging for dinners, respect the dietary customs of your guests. Hindus do not eat beef; Muslims and Jews do not eat pork; Muslims and Jews do not eat fish without fins.

- If the international visitor is accompanied by family, offer to arrange outings for the family.

Communicating

When talking with the international visitors, be sensitive to possible language difficulties. Do not talk in long sentences. Keep slang and **acronyms** (words formed from the initial letters of other words) out of your vocabulary. Check to be certain that you are being understood. It is appropriate to ask, "Did I explain that clearly?" However, never talk down to the person; do not assume that the

COMMUNICATION TIP

Germans often shake hands at the beginning of a business day and at the end of a business day. The French need a certain amount of general conversation before getting to the business of the day.

person knows nothing about America. Most people from other countries know more about American culture than Americans know about other cultures. Language difficulties do not equate to stupidity. In fact, you can usually be assured that the international visitor has prepared for the visit just as much as you have or maybe even more. The visitor is concerned with making a favorable impression just as you are.

GREET INTERNAL CALLERS

Co-workers are in and out of each other's offices frequently. If you have not met a co-worker, it is appropriate to stand and offer your hand when introducing yourself or being introduced. If a co-worker drops by your office for a quick question, you do not need to offer the person a seat; doing so will probably prolong the visit. However, if the person is your superior, do offer the person a seat. If you are visiting a co-worker who has a modular office rather than a standard office, you should either knock or say the person's name from the entrance to the work space in respect for the fact that it is indeed that person's space.

As a courtesy to a co-worker when visiting, knock or call the person's name from the entrance of the work space before entering. *Photo courtesy of Herman Miller, Inc.*

GREET GOVERNMENT OFFICIALS

State or federal government officials should be greeted as "Senator" or "Representative" followed by their last name. If you are introducing a legislator, the form of the introduction is to present the company person to the legislator; for example, "Senator Hackett, I would like you to meet Jennifer Farnsworth, our human resources director. Jennifer, this is Senator Hackett of Georgia."

SCHEDULE APPOINTMENTS

As an office professional, you will be responsible for scheduling appointments for your employer and for maintaining a record of the appointments your employer has scheduled. Even in our electronic age, the manual desk calendar still appears on most desks. You and your employer may have a manual desk calendar. It is a good idea to check your employer's calendar each morning to verify that both calendars contain the same information and that there are no conflicts.

In addition to the manual calendar, electronic calendaring is used extensively. Any number of software packages have calendaring functions. You learned earlier about PIM software which offers a calendar. Electronic calendars may be networked within the office so that executive calendars may be easily coordinated. For example, assume your employer asks you to schedule a meeting with several individuals within the company. You indicate to the system the names of the meeting participants and the date, time, and length of the meeting. If the meeting is going to be held on a recurring basis, the system allows you to indicate that information also. If a participant is not available at the time requested, the system will notify you. Figure 9-2 shows an electronic calendar screen.

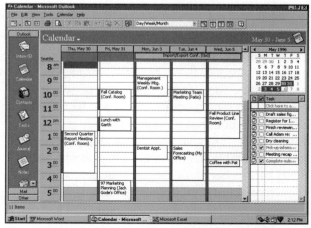

Figure 9-2 Electronic calendar. *Courtesy of Microsoft Corporation.*

CANCEL APPOINTMENTS

If your employer cannot keep an appointment, it is your responsibility to cancel it. Appointments may be canceled by a telephone call or by an e-mail (if they are internal). Be sure to give a reason for canceling the appointment and offer to reschedule. A detailed explanation is not necessary. You may say, "Ms. Marquette has been called out of town unexpectedly, and she will be unable to keep her appointment. May I schedule another appointment for next week?"

PRESENTATION SKILLS

With the team approach being used in business more and more today, office professionals frequently are expected to give presentations. These presentations may be informal ones to a small group, more formal ones to a larger group, or group presentations. Not only do you need to understand how to present, but you also need to exercise creativity in making your presentations fit the intended audience. The remainder of this chapter is devoted to helping you understand and develop your creativity and to prepare and give effective individual and group presentations.

CREATIVITY

Creativity is important for producing effective presentations, but it is also important for dealing with the constant change occurring in offices today. In fact, creativity and change are closely linked. Creativity is needed to respond successfully to change, and creativity results in change. For example, in giving presentations, you probably have a goal of educating your audience in a certain concept or idea. Assume that you are giving a presentation on developing empowered teams. Your goal is to help the audience understand the importance of teamwork and to help other individuals within their work area form teams which produce the product or service needed. In other words, through your presentation, you hope to effect change within the organization. The next few pages will be devoted to helping you understand what creativity is and how you may use it in giving presentations. A **serendipitous** (a desirable but unsought discovery by accident) benefit hopefully will be your ability to think creatively in numerous office situations.

Definition

Creativity is defined in the dictionary as "having the ability or the power to cause to exist." Creativity is a process. It is a way of thinking and of doing. It is a way of making new connections or new links. It is solving a problem in a new and different way. For example, assume that you and your colleagues are going to give a presentation. You think the presentation would be more effective if you used presentation software. You suggested it at your last planning meeting. All of them said it would be too difficult. You know it will work, but the idea does not have a chance unless you are heard. You decide that rather than trying to talk with them you will prepare one concept using presentation software and bring it to the next planning meeting. You do so; they agree that it is extremely effective and begin planning how software might be used throughout the presentation. You have used your creativity in changing individuals' minds. You did not just present your idea in one way; you thought of another way to present it, and you were successful. You brought about change.

How Creativity Works

Clearly, there are no rigid steps to becoming creative. Remember, it is a process; and a process that can be different for each individual. Here are some steps you can try to help release the creativity that already exists within you.

Self Check A

Take a few moments to get in touch with your own creativity. Assume that it is autumn and the leaves are falling. List the number of ways that you might use a falling leaf in the space provided. Even if the idea seems a little crazy to you, list it. Revolutionary new ideas can occur by this very process. Did you know that the Walkman was born because a Sony executive gave his design staff an impossibly small block of wood and told them to render a product in its image?

WAYS THAT A FALLING LEAF
MIGHT BE USED

_____

_____

How did you do? Did you come up with ideas you have never thought of before? Good for you!

Imagine the sensations you would feel if you are on a roller coaster.

Have Faith in Your Creativity. First of all, have faith in the fact that you are creative. If you have an idea about something that is different from others, do not immediately assume that you must be wrong. Try it out; your idea may be the creative spark to solving a complex problem. Always maintain a spirit of inquiry. Ask questions. Do not assume that any question you might have is too dumb to ask. Allow yourself the freedom to ask. Do not be uncomfortable when you are unsure of how something is going to turn out. Through experimenting with the unknown, a wonderfully new and creative product can occur. For example, assume that Orville and Wilbur Wright had no faith in their dream of a "flying machine." What if they had been put off by all the people who openly laughed and made jokes about their "craziness"?

Destroy Judgment. As you are trying to think through a problem or an issue, do not be judgmental. Let your thoughts flow freely. Do not discard any of them. Do not let your mind tell you that the idea is no good or ridiculous. To help you destroy judgment (which, by the way, is not easy to do), pay attention to each thought you have. Notice it; hear yourself think it. If you begin to be critical of your thought, attack the judgment. Say to yourself or even say it out loud, "Judgment—get out!" Be firm. Do not let judgment have its say.

Lest you are becoming too judgmental about the importance of creativity in business and thus this whole section of the book, know that surveys show that one of the skills wanted by businesses is creative thinking. Employers clearly understand that the most successful employees are those who can creatively solve the problems that they face within the organization. Kao, a professor in the Stanford Business School, in a book entitled *Jamming: The Road to Creativity*[1] states that creativity is so necessary in the technology world that we either "create or fail." According to Kao, we are going right through the age of information to the age of creativity. He suggests that companies should be auditing their staff to discover how many new ideas employees generate and who are the most creative people.

Look and Listen. The story is told of a businessman who heard that a Zen master (who lived at the top of a mountain) knew the three basic secrets to life. Anyone who knew these secrets would live a happy, fulfilling life. The businessman climbed for two years to get to the top of the mountain. Once there he approached the old master and asked that he tell him the secrets. The master said, "Yes, I will tell you. The first secret is pay attention. The second secret is pay attention, and the third secret is pay attention."

You may be asking, "Pay attention to what?" Pay attention to what you sense, what you think, what you hear, what you see. Pay attention to nature; pay attention to others.

---

[1] Kao, John, *Jamming: The Road to Creativity* (New York: Harper Business, 1996).

Ask Questions. Michael Ray and Rochelle Myers in their book, *Creativity in Business,* report writing down the following questions that a 4½ year old asked in less than an hour.

- What's behind a rainbow?

- What color is the inside of my brain?

- What's inside of a rock? A tree? A sausage? Bones? My throat? A spider?

- Does the sky have an end to it?

- Why are my toes in front of my feet?

We smile when we read these questions; and if you have children or younger siblings, you have probably smiled when they asked similar questions. As we grow up, somehow we do not allow ourselves to continue to ask questions. We think we should know all the answers; and obviously, we do not. Our continuing to ask questions—whatever they may be—helps us get in touch with our cre-

ativity. Do not frighten yourself at first with trying to ask big questions such as "What is the nature of humans?" Give yourself permission to ask the small and even playful questions. Ask these small (and, yes, maybe even dumb) questions of yourself. Let yourself question things you have never questioned in your adult life.

Bring Your Personal Creativity to the Office. Begin to ask questions in your work environment. Realize that through your asking and finding answers you may discover a more creative, more productive way to produce the work of the organization. As you practice thinking creatively, you will find that you have successes and then you experience the ultimate frustration. But, if you keep up the struggle, you will achieve a breakthrough. The breakthrough often comes at a higher level of creativity than before. Do not lose your creativity when problems arise. You probably need it more than ever. **Aikido** (the Japanese soft martial art) teaches that you should never meet force with force. The person who breaks harmony by attacking or being aggressive in some way fails. Rather, you should move with the person rather than struggling against him or her. By moving in the same direction of the other person you are able to effect more change than by attacking.

Consider this example of the Aikido concept in a business situation. As an office professional, your supervisor (Ms. Marquette) has become a "technocrat." Whatever the latest technology is, she has to have it; however, she never gets training for herself. She expects you to be able to solve whatever problem she is having with the latest technology she has acquired. If you cannot solve it, she gets angry. Rather than you getting angry with her, go with her. Tell her you understand how frustrating it is when she cannot solve a problem, and you are frustrated, too, when you cannot solve one. Tell her you will get help for both of you. Then, contact the service people who installed the new technology. Ask them to come and show you and your boss how to handle the problem she has just had. Then ask if they can give both of you a short course.

Now that you have learned how you might "grow" your creativity, look at how you can put creativity into action in developing and delivering presentations.

CLASSIFICATION OF PRESENTATIONS

You will probably not be giving presentations every week or maybe not even once a month; however, at times you will be expected to speak before a group. These presentations may be **impromptu** (without any advance notice), **extemporaneous** (in which you refer to notes but actually compose your thoughts and sentences as you speak), or **scripted** (in which you read a presentation that you or someone else has written).

As you mature in your job, you will probably have more occasions to speak, particularly before small groups of people. In addition, you may be active in professional organizations outside work which require you to present occasionally. Oral presentation skills can be valuable to you in a number of situations throughout your life.

THE AUDIENCE

Your presentations will be given to three basic types of audiences.

- Co-workers in your organization

- Clients and customers

- Colleagues within professional organizations to which you belong

THE PLAN

Planning means gathering and arranging your thoughts, developing your ideas, and finding a unique way to express them. Using your creativity in the process will help you put together a memorable presentation which holds the audience and allows you to get your message across.

As soon as you know that you are going to give a presentation, start a folder. Put everything in the folder as it comes to your mind—ideas, quotations, and so forth. You may even wake up in the middle of the night with an idea. Keep a pad and pencil by your bed so that you may jot down your thoughts. Sometimes the best thoughts occur in this way, and you do not want to forget them.

In the planning process, take these steps.

Begin Early

A good presentation is not prepared thirty minutes before it is given. Sometimes you may get lucky and be able to deliver a presentation with little or no preparation time, but such is a rarity. Do not tempt fate. Begin early. You might say, "I don't have the time to prepare." Then, do not agree to give the presentation. Anything worth doing is worth doing well. Beginning preparation three weeks before the presentation is to be delivered is not too soon. Also, by beginning early, you can spend a few minutes each day thinking about what you want to say, writing down your thoughts, coming back to it at a later point, and revising or discarding material if it no longer seems relevant. In other words, the brain has a chance to "mull over" the thoughts.

Determine the Purpose

Is your purpose to inform your audience? To persuade? To inform and persuade? Spend some time determining the purpose. If you do not understand the purpose of your presentation, certainly no one else will. Once you have determined the purpose, write it down in one clear, concise statement. As you prepare your presentation, review the statement frequently to keep you on track.

Analyze the Anticipated Audience

Who will the people be in the audience? For example, if it is a group of office professionals you know immediately some of their interests. You can use antidotes or stories that will have meaning for them. Find out the age of your audience. A teenage audience will be very different than an audience in its fifties and sixties. Know something about the educational level and experiences of the audience. For example, if you are giving a presentation on software, you need to know what level of expertise the audience already has. You do not want to bore them by giving them information that is too elementary nor do you want to confuse them by being too technical.

Figure 9-3 Visualize your audience.

Find out how many people will be in the audience. Will there be fifteen or fifty? Numbers do make a difference. A small audience allows greater interaction; questions can be used effectively. With a large audience, there is little chance for interaction other than possibly saving time for a question and answer period at the end, and then, a microphone in the audience is necessary so that all people can hear the questions or comments.

If you are providing handouts for the audience, you need to know the number to expect so that you can have the appropriate number of handouts. It is also a good idea to have only the exact number of chairs needed for the audience. Having to add chairs after most of the audience has arrived makes you look as if you have not prepared appropriately. If you have too many chairs in the audience, it looks like you did not have a good turnout for your presentation.

Determine the Length of the Presentation

Most presentations should be no longer than twenty minutes, with thirty to forty minutes being a maximum. Part of your task is to manage your topic; do not try to give the audience so much information that you are droning on for an hour or more. You will lose your audience; people's attention span is not that long.

Generally speaking, 175 words (or three-quarters of a keyed, double-spaced page) equals one minute of talking time. A fifteen or twenty-minute talk will be about ten to twelve keyed pages.

Gather the Material

Research the topic if necessary in the library or through the Internet or online services such as America Online. Do original research if needed. For example, you may want to let your audience know how a group feels about a particular idea. If so, you may send out a survey to a targeted group to get responses.

Construct an Outline

The outline should consist of an introduction, body, and conclusion. In the introduction you tell your audience what you are going to say. In the body you give them the information, and in the closing you remind them again of what you have said by giving a summary. In other words, you remind the audience three times of the important points of your presentation; such repetition

increases the chances that the audience will understand and remember what you have said. Figure 9-4 shows a sample outline.

Presentation Outline

I. Introduction

   A. Opening statement to gain attention

      1. Development of opening statement

      2. Supporting material

   B. Second introductory point (if needed)

II. Body

   A. First main idea

      1. First support point

      2. Second support point

   B. Second main idea

      1. First supporting point

      2. Second supporting point

   C. Third main idea

      1. First supporting point

      2. Second supporting point

III. Conclusion

   A. Summary

   B. Application or challenge and final statement

Figure 9-4

Develop an Opening

The opening should immediately get the audience's attention. You might tell a story, use a quotation, ask a question, or refer to a current event. Begin with the unexpected and the unpredictable. Also, know what you do best. If you are a good joke teller, you might open with a joke. If you are not, however, stay away from a joke like you would stay away from poison. Nothing can be worse than starting a presentation with a joke that is in poor taste and offends someone in the audience or that the audience does not think is funny. If you tell stories well, tell one. Not only should the opening get the audience's attention, but it should also help you to relax with your audience. Plan it well and stick with something you do well. When you determine how you are going to open, ask yourself these questions about your selection.

- Is there a link between the story and the presentation?

- Is it a new story or joke? You do not want to relay one that the audience has heard numerous times.

- Am I telling it as succinctly as possible? You do not want to spend one-third of your time on your opening story.

- If it is a joke, am I timing the punch line to elicit a laugh?

Use Language Well

Nothing is more disconcerting than discovering that people are asleep while you are talking. Obviously you are not getting your message across in an interesting fashion. One technique that will help you get your message across is to involve the audience. People are always interested in their own concerns. When you know who the audience will be, think about how you can establish a link with them. For example, if it is a group of office professionals, what concerns does the audience have in common. Make your major points and relate those points to experiences that both you and the audience have had.

Another helpful technique is to refer to people, not to abstractions. Use interesting facts, figures, and quotations. For example, if you are giving a motivational talk on the importance of service, here is a quote from Mother Teresa that could be used:

> "Love cannot remain by itself—it has no meaning. Love has to be put into action and that action is service."

Use the active rather than the passive voice. Do not say "It is believed . . . "; say "I believe . . . " Talk in a conversational tone. Talk with the audience, not at the audience. Use the tone you would use when sitting across the table from someone at a dinner party and you want to persuade the person. Be animated; if you do not appear to be interested in what you are saying, the audience certainly will not be. Never speak in a monotone; vary your tone of voice. Vary your expressions.

A commanding speaker is

- sincere
- credible
- concerned
- enthusiastic
- energetic
- intense
- knowledgeable

Develop an Appropriate Conclusion

The conclusion should summarize the points made in your presentation and leave the audience feeling motivated to respond in the way that you intended. Remember, it is the final impression you will make on the audience. Be forceful and positive. When summarizing, state the points in slightly different ways. You might also suggest a challenge to the audience, propose a solution to a situation, or use a compelling quote.

Write the Presentation

Once the presentation is written, put it aside for a day or two; then go back over it. Does the speech fit the anticipated audience? Does it meet the purpose? Is the opening creative? Will it get the audience's attention? Have you used stories and quotes in appropriate numbers and spaced them throughout the presentation? Remember, if you involve the audience they will learn. A well-selected story or quote can involve the audience. Is the presentation the proper length? Remember, it is better to be too brief than too long. Abraham Lincoln delivered one of the nation's most celebrated addresses (the Gettysburg Address) in less than five minutes. Do you need to rewrite any parts?

Prepare Visual Aids

When used properly, visual aids can be very effective. People remember 40 percent more when they hear and see something simultaneously. Figure 9-5 lists some of the basic steps in preparing visuals. Presentation software with its features of clip art and drawing tools can assist you in preparing visuals. Some presentation software allows you to produce video and animation. Computer-generated graphics can also be converted into slides for use with a slide projector.

Steps in Preparing Visuals

- Keep text to a minimum. Do not try to transfer information from an 8½ × 11 inch page to a visual. As a general rule, text has to be presented in 24-point type or larger to be visible. Reduce sentences to brief phrases; do not put more than three or four phrases on one visual.

- Determine how many graphics you should have. For example, you might have one graphic for every one minute of the presentation.

- Use color to enhance the graphics or to highlight the text.

- Make the aid simple and easy to grasp. Each graphic should present only a single idea.

- Make visuals consistent—typestyles should be basically the same size.

- Make certain the visual can be seen and read from all parts of the room.

- Proofread the visual carefully. Make certain there are no errors in content or in grammar.

- If you are writing or drawing on the original, use a black marking pen.

- Make certain the equipment needed is working properly.

- Practice using the visual before the presentation.

- Talk to the audience—not to the visual.

- Stand to the side of the visual when showing it.

Figure 9-5

Rehearse the Presentation

Rehearse the presentation just as you are going to give it. For example, if you will be standing at a lectern during the presentation, stand at a lecture during the rehearsal. If you are going to be using a microphone, use a microphone during the rehearsal. You also may want to have a respected colleague listen to your rehearsal and make constructive criticisms. It is a good idea to go over your presentation completely three or four times. Even though you have written the presentation, rehearsing it several times helps make it totally yours. With repeated rehearsals, the text becomes part of your memory;

you will be more at ease because you are not likely to forget an important point during the presentation.

Rehearse the presentation just as you are going to give it.
Courtesy of International Business Machines, Inc.

Control Nervousness

First of all, realize that nervousness is normal. In fact, one great fear (as shown in surveys) that individuals have is the fear of speaking before an audience. Two things you have already learned to help you control nervousness are preparation and rehearsal. A well-prepared and well-rehearsed presentation can eliminate many of your fears. You know who your audience is, what you intend to say, and how you will say it. Now, here are some other suggestions for controlling nervousness.

- Sarnoff in her book *Never Be Nervous Again* suggests saying these four sentences several times to yourself before you get up to speak.

  1. I'm glad I'm here.

  2. I'm glad you're here.

  3. I care about you.

  4. I know that I know.[2]

- While waiting to present, sit in a straight chair, carry your rib cage high, and breathe deeply. As you exhale, push the air over your lower teeth in a *ssss* sound. Focus your efforts entirely on your breathing.

- Walk around. Take a brisk walk for a minute or two.

---

[2]Sarnoff, Dorothy, *Never Be Nervous Again* (New York: Crown Publishers, Inc., 1987).

- Go off by yourself for a few minutes. Compose your thoughts.

- As you begin your presentation, walk slowly up to the lectern. Arrange your note cards; look at the audience for a few seconds and then begin.

- Realize that some nervousness can help you. You can channel this nervousness into your talk, and it will become a positive energy source which adds to your effectiveness.

- Realize that the audience is much less aware of your nervousness than you are. Also, realize that the audience is your friend; they want you to succeed.

Watch for Nonverbal Feedback from the Audience

Puzzled looks or blank stares are cues that the audience does not understand what you are saying. You may need to modify the rate of your voice or give another example or two to clarify what you mean. Smiles and nodding heads are positive reactions.

Use Body Language Effectively

Maintain eye contact with the audience. If you are in a small group, look at each individual for a period of time. When you are in a large group, use an eye sweeping motion. Sweep from one side of the room to another, concentrating for a period of time on each portion of the room. Use natural gestures. You may use your arms and hands to emphasize points. It is not a good idea, however, to constantly use arm and hand gestures. Be natural; do not perform. Speak in a normal tone of voice; vary your tone; do not speak too fast. Articulate carefully; for example, do not drop the ending *g;* say "learning" not "learnin."

Use body language effectively when giving presentations.
Apple Computers.

Dress Appropriately for the Audience

The usual dress for a woman is a suit or a dress and a suit and tie for a man. Wear something that you are comfortable in and that looks good on you. Bright colors for women are perfectly okay. Necklaces and earrings should not be too large and overwhelming. Avoid dangling earrings because their constant movement can be distracting. Rings and bracelets are appropriate, but do not wear noisy bracelets that distract from what you are saying. It is appropriate for men to wear colored shirts and bright ties. The color of the suit should look good on the person. Men should not wear gold bracelets and a number of rings; again, they are distracting to the audience. Hair for both men and women should have a well-groomed look and not be in the eyes. Having to throw your head back to get hair out of your eyes is bothersome to the audience.

Conduct a Last-Minute Check

Know how the room will be set up. Know where the lectern is going to be if you are using one. If you are using visuals, allow enough time before the presentation to check out the visuals. Be certain that you have the visuals in order.

Critique Your Presentation

After you have finished delivering the presentation, critique what happened. Either evaluate yourself or have someone else evaluate you. You may want to tape or videotape your presentation to help you in the critiquing process. You may also want to provide evaluation forms for the people in the audience. In critiquing yourself,

- Be kind to yourself. List the good with the not so good.

- Do not try to solve too many problems at once. Pick one or two things to improve each time.

- Realize evaluation is an ongoing process.

- Build yourself up by thinking of how much you have improved.

- Get feedback from other people; really listen to the feedback. If someone compliments you, believe it.

TEAM PRESENTATIONS

You have already learned that team presentations are being used extensively in business today. The techniques presented in the previous section still apply, but team presentations require collaborative planning. In addition to knowing the purpose of your presentation, the people who will be in attendance, and how long the presentation will need to be, you will need to take these additional steps.

- **Brainstorm** (sudden inspiration) what the presentation should include and how it will be presented. Refer to Figure 9-6 for techniques on brainstorming.

- Decide who will present which part of the presentation.

- Determine how you will make the transition from one speaker to another. It is usually a good idea for the speaker finishing to mention the next speaker's name.

- Practice your presentation as a group.

- If graphics are going to be used, determine who will be doing the graphics.

- Determine what the dress will be; each speaker should dress in a similar fashion. For example, if it is determined that suits will be worn, all speakers should dress accordingly.

- Determine how the group will be seated before the presentation begins and after each presentation is finished. For example, will there be a table with chairs for the speakers or will the speakers be on a stage? In what order should the speakers be sitting? It is generally a good idea to have the first speaker the closest to the podium.

Brainstorming Techniques

1. Say each idea aloud as it occurs to you.

2. Have a recorder to jot down each idea.

3. Listen attentively to others' ideas.

4. Piggyback on the ideas of others.

5. Suspend your judgment. Do not critique the ideas (either yours or others) as they are presented.

6. Encourage an uninterrupted flow of ideas.

7. Expect to be outrageous.

Figure 9-6

Brainstorming is an effective technique for planning team presentations. *Courtesy of International Business Machines, Inc.*

CHAPTER SUMMARY

This summary will help you remember the important points covered in this chapter.

- In receiving office callers, know your employer's expectations. There are some people your employer usually will see without an appointment. There also may be some people the employer will not see at all.

- Appropriate techniques for receiving office callers include:

  Greet the visitor with a handshake if you have not met previously.

  Determine the purpose of the caller's visit.

  Call the visitor by name if at all possible.

  Make the wait pleasant by offering the caller coffee and reading material.

  Introduce your supervisor to the caller if appropriate.

  Never be discourteous to callers—even to the difficult ones.

- In dealing with international guests, know their culture and customs. Use the appropriate greeting; be sensitive to language differences.

- Develop and use your creativity when preparing presentations.

- These steps will help you release your creativity:

  Have faith in your creativity.

  Destroy judgment.

  Look and listen.

  Ask questions.

  Bring your personal creativity to the office.

- In planning presentations:

  Begin early.

  Determine the purpose.

  Analyze the anticipated audience.

  Determine the length of the presentation.

  Gather the material.

  Construct an outline.

  Develop an opening.

  Use language well.

  Develop an appropriate conclusion.

  Write the presentation.

  Prepare visual aids.

  Rehearse the presentation.

  Control nervousness.

  Watch for nonverbal feedback from the audience.

  Use your body language and appearance effectively.

  Conduct a last-minute check.

  Critique your presentation.

- Team presentations require collaborative planning; this collaborative planning should include brainstorming to release the creativity of the group.

CHAPTER GLOSSARY

The following terms were introduced in this chapter. To help you review, definitions are given here.

- **Acronym** (p. 202)–A word formed from the initial letters of other words.

- **Serendipitous** (p. 204)–A desirable but unsought discovery by accident.

- **Creativity** (p. 204)–Having the ability or the power to cause to exist.

213

- **Aikido** (p. 206)–The Japanese soft martial art.

- **Impromptu** (p. 207)–A presentation without any advance notice.

- **Extemporaneous** (p. 207)–A presentation in which you refer to notes but actually compose your thoughts and sentences as you speak.

- **Scripted** (p. 207)–A presentation in which you read what you or someone else has written.

- **Brainstorm** (p. 212)–Sudden inspiration.

DISCUSSION ITEMS

These discussion items provide an opportunity for you to test your understanding of the chapter through discussion with your classmates and your instructor.

1. Explain how you would introduce Ms. Harriet Eihardt, president of Simon Manufacturing, to Ms. Marquette.

2. Explain how to deal with a difficult caller.

3. Explain how you would handle the international visitor.

4. Define creativity and give four steps for helping to release the creativity that exists within you.

5. List the planning steps involved in developing a presentation.

6. What additional steps need to be taken in preparing team presentations?

CASE STUDY

Katrina Marcell has been with Koronet International for three months as a part-time employee in your office. This morning you have been very busy preparing a report for Ms. Marquette. You asked Katrina to take all telephone calls and handle all office visitors; you shut your office door and continued to work on the report. A shabbily dressed man came in to see Ms. Marquette at 9:50. He identified himself as Jim and said that he needed to talk with Ms. Marquette immediately. Ms. Marquette was on the telephone when he came in. Katrina (in a pleasant voice) told Jim that Ms. Marquette was on the telephone and asked him to be seated. Although Katrina was pleasant to the man, she thought that he could not be very important because he was dressed so shabbily, and she wondered how she could get rid of him without bothering Ms. Marquette. She did not offer him coffee or reading material; she hoped that he would get tired of waiting and leave. After about ten minutes of waiting, Jim said, "That phone conversation is certainly long; could you let her know that I am here."

Ms. Marquette had finished her first conversation but she was now on another call. Katrina informed Jim that she could not interrupt Ms. Marquette, but that when she was off the phone, she would let him know. Finally, after fifteen more minutes (and two calls later), Katrina went in to tell Ms. Marquette that a man named Jim was outside. She told Ms. Marquette that she was sure she did not want to see the man but that she did not know how to get rid of him. Ms. Marquette became very upset. She said, "What do you mean, I won't want to see him? That is Jim Brooks—one of our most important customers. Send him in immediately." Katrina meekly did as she was told, wondering how she could redeem herself.

1. What was Katrina's original mistake?

2. How can she rectify her mistake now?

3. How should she have handled the situation?

4. What advice can you give her to avoid making such a mistake in the future?

OFFICE TASKS

OFFICE TASK 9-1 (Objective 1)

You have the following callers in your office today. How would you handle each situation? Prepare a memorandum (using the form on the Student Data Template Disk, file OT9-1) to your instructor, stating how each situation should be handled.

1. A sales representative comes in and asks for an appointment to see your supervisor; your supervisor has told you that she does not like to see sales representatives.

2. Your supervisor has been called out of town unexpectedly. Mr. Scheen (with whom your supervisor had scheduled an appointment but has failed to tell you about) shows up for his 11 a.m. appointment.

3. An associate of your supervisor comes by and asks you to set up a luncheon engagement with your supervisor. You know that your supervisor does not care for the person.

4. A woman comes in to see your supervisor. She refuses to give her name or the purpose of her visit. However, she says the matter is urgent. She seems upset.

5. Ms. Nicole Botha comes in to see your supervisor. Ms. Botha has an appointment at 11 a.m., and it is now 10:55 a.m. Your supervisor has had an extremely busy morning, and she is now in a conference that will last until 11:20 a.m.

6. A man walks into your office and asks to see your supervisor, but he does not give you his name or the company he represents.

7. R. T. Arlston is in your supervisor's office. He had an appointment at 2 p.m. It is now 3 p.m., and your supervisor has an appointment with Ms. Carol Haile. Ms. Haile has arrived.

8. George O'Casey arrives at 3 p.m. for his appointment with your supervisor. On checking your appointment book, you find that Mr. O'Casey's appointment really is for 3 p.m. tomorrow.

OFFICE TASK 9-2 (Objective 2)

Divide into groups of four or five. Decide who will be the "starter" for the group. For example, the starter may be the person with the longest hair, the bluest eyes, or the youngest person. The purpose of this activity is to learn to release your creativity. So, do not be confined to this list to determine the starter. The group may want to develop a list of its own. Once the starter is determined, that person will begin a story. As a departure point, use this starter, "Everyone knows that Dorothy (in *The Wizard of Oz*) traveled down the yellow brick road to the land of Oz. However, did you know that the land of Oz was actually on the moon and the yellow brick road was made of numerous moon crystals which glistened and even spoke to Dorothy giving her directions as she made her way to the land of Oz? In fact, these crystals sang a song in moon language that went like this: "Dorothy, Dorothy, follow this path; run with us into the unknown; you can do it, you can, you can."

Now, each person within the group adds a little known fact about Dorothy to the story. Tape record your story; play it for the class.

Once you have finished the story, members should discuss how they felt during this process. Was it difficult to be spontaneous? If so, why? Did you have trouble thinking of "little known facts"? If so, why? Listen to each other carefully. Develop a list as a group of how creativity can be encouraged and released.

OFFICE TASK 9-3 (Objective 3)

Research one of the following topics.

1. Women in Management
2. Creativity—Understanding and Releasing It
3. Diversity in the Office

Prepare a five- to ten-minute presentation to be given orally to your class. Prepare one or two visuals to use in the presentation.

OFFICE TASK 9-4 (Objective 3)

Work in groups of four or five on this team presentation. The team presentation is to be on a topic of the team's choosing. Use the brainstorming techniques listed in Figure 9-6 to brainstorm topics and how the presentation will be presented. The presentation is to be from ten to fifteen minutes in length; each team member is responsible for presenting a portion of the presentation which is to be delivered orally to the class. Notes prepared by the team for the presentation are to be given to your instructor.

ENGLISH USAGE CHALLENGE DRILL

Correct the following sentences. Cite the grammar rule that is applicable to each sentence. Before you begin, refresh your memory of grammar rules by reviewing parallelism in writing. Parallelism calls for the use of equivalent grammatical forms when expressing ideas of equal importance.

1. The automotive workers had tried pleas, threatening, and striking to make their demands known.

2. The committee discussed the petition, analyzed its major points, and the decision was made to reject it.

3. Having a solid friendship with one or two individuals can be more rewarding than the acquisition of possessions.

4. Differing expectations for a friendship not only can lead to disappointment but also to frustration and even anger.

5. Difficult supervisors not only affect their employees' performances but their personal lives may be affected as well.

ASSESSMENT OF CHAPTER OBJECTIVES

Now that you have completed the chapter and the office tasks, take a few moments to review the following learning objectives which you were given at the beginning of this chapter. Did you accomplish these objectives? If so, explain how in the space provided. If you were unable to accomplish these objectives, give your reason for not doing so. Your instructor may want to review your answers.

I accomplished these objectives:

1. Develop effective techniques for working with office callers. Yes _____ No _____

   Explain how you accomplished this objective.

   _____

   _____

   _____

2. Release and expand your creativity.
   Yes _____ No _____

   Explain how you accomplished this objective.

   _____

   _____

   _____

3. Make effective individual and group presentations. Yes _____ No _____

   Explain how you accomplished this objective.

   _____

   _____

   _____

Provide reasons for failing to accomplish any of these objectives.

   _____

   _____

   _____

   _____

   _____

MICHELLE MACDOWELL'S CASE SOLUTION

I asked my boss, and everyone else in the group who writes proposals, to give me a copy of any proposal as soon as it was written. I created a database to keep track of every proposal written. If it becomes a job, I add the job number, budget, deadline, and who is responsible for the job. I started scheduling regular production meetings for our group every two weeks. We all use this database as a guide during the production meetings to keep track of how many jobs each project manager has, if the person is going to need help to meet the deadlines, and so forth. More than anything, it helps keep new jobs from falling through the cracks. Any job that has not yet been assigned to someone is listed at the beginning of the report, and I do not let anyone out of the meeting until someone has committed to every job. I also started making daily to-do lists for my boss and asked him to add any verbal deadlines to that list as he commits to them. I check with him at the beginning and end of each day and add those commitments to my master database.

PART 4

Meetings, Conferences, and Travel

Narressa Ross Lee
Staff Assistant, Risk Management
Howard University Hospital
Washington, D.C.

A Success Profile

Success like everything else has its beginning. My early mentor was my mother, Nancy L. Ross, who was a former secretary for Howard University. From a small child, I was able to observe her unquestionable pride in her job and the professionalism she displayed on the job. I would often go to her office, watch her carefully, and ask loads of questions. Sometimes, I would sit in her chair and play my game of pretend. It was a nice, warm, fuzzy feeling for me. I was awed by the respect she received from her executive and others within the university complex. I recognized early that if I chose to follow in her footsteps, I would become a significant part of the management team responsible for the day-to-day operations of the hospital. Though I initially aspired to become an elementary teacher, I supported myself financially by working as a hospital secretary and found that I really liked it. To this day, I have continued my employment as an office professional in the healthcare setting.

Since 1969, I have been employed at Howard University Hospital, Washington, D.C., as a unit clerk, secretary, and administrative assistant in various departments—nursing, emergency room, and outpatient clinics. My present position is staff assistant for risk management, which operates like a miniature law office as an extension to the office of general counsel for the university. My education includes two years of college in the areas of education and business management. I continue to learn through classes, seminars, and workshops on subjects related to the secretarial profession. I also have taken classes sponsored by Professional Secretaries International in preparation for the CPS exam. I have been an active member of Professional Secretaries International since 1983.

An enjoyable part of work for me is to learn a new computer program that makes the job easier. I also enjoy serving as a host for special occasions, being recognized on Professional Secretaries Day, giving Halloween gifts to the pediatric patients when they visit, and participating in community health projects.

One stressor of my job is having the computer network fail and cause the delay of important insurance reports for which I am responsible. Other stressors include unreasonable deadline constraints and telephone interruptions while I am attempting to complete an assignment for someone who needs the work I am producing in order to complete another project.

For someone just beginning in the office support field, I offer this advice. Regardless of the type of employment you seek, first do your homework. Research the profession, test the waters by volunteering to help or work part-time, take a class or seminar that relates to your chosen profession to understand more about the field, and make sure the field fits your workstyle and your personal style. Though position titles in the field are ever-changing, the basic responsibilities do not change. Always do your best. However, you should realize that only a few executives will remember that you have given a quality presentation or completed a project well. Be prepared to *not* receive credit, a pat on the back, or compliments for a job well done. You can get your satisfaction in knowing that you did a job well. Learn to recognize that your role may not appear glamorous, but your job is a necessary link within a solid management team structure. We do live in the age of the computer, but computers cannot operate by themselves. Each year technology changes. The office professionals truly are important individuals who support the mission and goals of the company and stay tuned into and abreast of the ever-changing technology. Learn to feel good about representing yourself well and with style. The praises and positive benefits will come in time—you must be patient.

My hobbies and interests include assisting my aunt with her catering business, working with my daughter on special school assignments, taking long drives with my husband to visit friends in Kent Island, enjoying the sights and sounds of Washington, D.C., Maryland, and Virginia, and active participation in Professional Secretaries International.

NARRESSA ROSS LEE'S CASE

I have prepared a case from my experiences as an office professional. Decide how you would handle the case by answering the questions at the completion of the situation. Then turn to the end of Part IV (page 266) to see how the case was solved.

THE SITUATION

I work in a department that is responsible for the monthly meeting of selected members of the hospital administration. The discussions at the meeting are confidential in nature and pertain to malpractice and risk issues. On occasion, committee members interject statements that may or may not be pertinent to the subject matter. There are usually a few comments I think should not appear in the minutes. At the conclusion of the meetings, the director gives me his notes to be combined with my notes and later reviewed by others, prior to final approval of the chairman. The director does not provide assistance as to what should and what should not be in the minutes. He tells me that the minutes are a top priority.

How much of your notes should you use? Should you include all comments made? Should you use all of the director's notes, even when the notes seem to include information that is not pertinent to the subject matter?

Visas, arrangements for, 249
Visual aids, for presentation, 209
Voice messages feature, on telephone, 157–58
Voice quality, in communication, 119
Voice recognition, computer, 57
　defined, 74
von Leibniz, Gottfried Wilhelm, development of computer, 51

W

The Wall Street Journal, 16
WANs, 62
　defined, 76
WATS, 160
Web page, 62, 64
　defined, 76
Wide area networks. *See* WANs

Wide area telecommunications. *See* WATS
Windows 95, 81–82
　defined, 100
Windows NT, 83
　defined, 101
Women, stereotyping of, 7
Word processing, 85–86
Work area, organization of, 340
Work environment, 1443
Work experience, resume listing, 32–33
Work overload, stress and, 330
Work spaces, team, 138–39
Workgroup evaluation, 360–61
Working Woman, 16
Workplace. *See also* Office
　changes in, 9
　virtual, 5
Workweek, changes in, 11–12
The World Bank Atlas, 189

World Directory of Industry and Trade Associations, 189
World Wide Web, 62–64
　defined, 47
　for job information, 28–29
WORM, 59
　defined, 75
Write-one, read-many. *See* WORM
Written communication skills, 12–13
WWW. *See* World Wide Web

Z

Zones, time, map of, 161

Videoconferencing is more equipment intensive than audioconferencing or computer conferencing. *Photo courtesy of Compression Labs, Inc.*

In addition to videoconferencing, a video **downlink** also may be used in which a one-way presentation is presented to a group of people through satellite or fiber optics technology, which you learned about in Chapter 7. This type of conference is presented with a speaker at one location and audiences at locations throughout the city, state, nation, or world. For example, a president of an organization may send a state of the organization presentation to employees situated at locations throughout the world. The employees can see and hear the president, but have no chance for interaction.

Computer Conferencing

Another alternative to face-to-face meetings is **computer conferencing.** Computer conferencing requires that each participant have a computer. Individuals can stay in their offices where they have access to the necessary data and communicate with other individuals on a common issue or concern. Information can be transmitted back and forth between a number of individuals in a short time.

For example, employees of a company that has several international locations as well as locations within the United States can engage in computer conferencing with individuals throughout the company, as long as the computers are linked by networks. As you learned in Chapter 3, networks permit information to be transmitted from one computer to other computers at distant locations. Other computer conferencing opportunities exist via the Internet through such avenues as "chat lines." Through the Internet, individuals from all over the world can communicate.

Advantages and Disadvantages of Electronic Meetings

Just as there are advantages and disadvantages to face-to-face meetings, there are also advantages and disadvantages to electronic meetings.

Advantages include

- savings in travel costs, travel time, meals, and hotel rooms;
- ability to present a considerable amount of information concisely through sophisticated audio and video technology;
- ability to bring together people with expertise in a number of different areas to discuss problems of mutual concern with a minimum of effort;
- interactivity of individuals—ability to connect through audio and visual means.

Disadvantages include

- less spontaneity between individuals due to a fairly structured environment;
- more formal in nature;
- inability to see body language of all participants at any one time; inability to pick up small nuances of body language over the monitor;
- a relatively small amount of or no socialization time between participants;
- less chance for effective brainstorming on issues.

COMMUNICATION TIP

When engaged in an international videoconference, remember to respect the cultural differences of the participants.

- Coffee, lunches, and other refreshments for the participants can be costly.

- The face-to-face meeting can be harder to control because people are freer to interact with each other.

- Socializing can consume a major part of the meeting time if not controlled by the leader.

- Time can be lost through waiting on people who are five or ten minutes late.

- Individuals (particularly those who work together daily) may tend to rely on (or second) their colleagues suggestions or solutions; thus creativity can suffer.

ELECTRONIC MEETINGS

Telecommunication technology provides alternatives to face-to-face meetings through several electronic options referred to as **teleconferencing.** Teleconferencing is a general term applied to a variety of technology-assisted, two-way (interactive) communications via telephone lines, fiber optics, or microwaves. The three main types of teleconferencing are audioconferencing, videoconferencing, and computer conferencing.

Audioconferencing

Audioconferencing is a type of conference in which participants either use telephones in their offices or meet in small groups, using speakerphones. As you learned in Chapter 7, speakerphones provide hands-free communication by amplifying and projecting the voices of the speakers. If speakerphones are not used, a conference operator will assist individuals by setting up a call among a group of individuals. To set up this call, the conference operator must be contacted and given the date and time of the audioconference, and the names and numbers of the people to be connected on the call. You can check in the business pages of your telephone directory for the number of the conference operator. With either the speakerphone or conference call method, participants at different locations are linked through regular telephone lines. Advantages of audioconferencing include

- being able to assemble individuals on short notice (assuming their schedules allow);

- being able to connect individuals at any location;

- using the familiar and readily available telephone technology.

One primary disadvantage of an audioconference is the lack of visual input; however, visual input can be achieved through the use of facsimile equipment discussed in Chapter 3. For example, an ordinary fax machine may be used to transmit reports, spreadsheets, graphs, and so forth which may be necessary to discuss in the audioconference. In addition, visual messages can be written on an **electronic blackboard** (similar to a chalkboard). This blackboard has a pressure-sensitive surface. Individuals write on the surface and the information is instantly converted to signals, which are then transmitted over telephone lines. Participants in the audioconference are able to see what is written on the blackboard by viewing it on a video screen which has been set up at their locations. Participants can also add or change the visual input through an electronic blackboard that is also set up at their locations. In other words, the blackboards allow for **interactivity** (information transmitted from one location to another and acted upon by participants at any location).

Videoconferencing

Videoconferencing is a system of transmitting audio and video between individuals at distant locations thereby eliminating the need for travel. Individuals can see and hear each other on monitors in either full-motion or **still-frame** (nonmoving) pictures. Videoconferencing may occur with minimal equipment (a screen and a camera at each location) or with numerous pieces of equipment. For example, there might be color cameras to transmit pictures of people and graphics, monitors to pick up people images and graphic images, microphones and speakers for audio interaction, and facsimile units for hard copy transmission of documents. Videoconferencing is interactive; that is, participants at all locations can see and respond to other participants. Because videoconferencing is equipment-intensive, there is usually a specially equipped room. Although this room can be expensive to set up initially, there can be a cost savings to the company if videoconferencing is used frequently.

223

CHAPTER 10

PLANNING MEETINGS AND CONFERENCES

LEARNING OBJECTIVES

1. **Identify the responsibilities of the office professional for meetings and conferences.**
2. **Prepare notices for meetings.**
3. **Prepare agendas and minutes.**

Meetings are a way of life in the office. You learned about an increased emphasis on teamwork within the office, which therefore produces more meetings. Taking a conservative estimate of time spent in meetings, office professionals average four hours a week. This average increases the higher your position in the organization. Management may spend as much as 50 percent or more of each week in meetings. Obviously, these meetings are costly to business. In fact, it has been estimated that organizations spend between 7 and 15 percent of personnel budgets on meetings. Thus, it is important that the meeting time be spent as productively as possible. This chapter will help you develop the knowledge and skills to assist your supervisor in planning, organizing, and holding meetings with the purpose clearly established and the outcomes produced consistent with the purpose.

NECESSARY MEETINGS

Meetings are a good means of generating ideas, sharing information, and making decisions. Calling a meeting can be appropriate when:

- advice is needed from a group of people;
- a group needs to be involved in solving a problem or making a decision;
- an issue arises that needs clarification;
- information needs to be given to a group;
- a problem occurs, but it is not clear what it is or who is responsible for dealing with it;
- communication needs to occur quickly with a large number of people.

Meetings are a good means of generating ideas.
Photo by Alan Brown/Photonics Graphics.

UNNECESSARY MEETINGS

Unfortunately, a number of unnecessary and nonproductive meetings are held daily in organizations. These meetings generally have no clear purpose, agenda, or follow-up after the meeting. These meetings are not only a waste of individuals' time but also a waste of organizational time. We have all been to such meetings. Sometimes the major purpose of such meetings seems to be:

- to consume large quantities of coffee and doughnuts at the company's expense;
- to small talk with our co-workers;
- to get away from our desk;
- to ask others' opinions about an item that we do not have the courage to confront;
- to avoid making a decision.

Clearly, some meetings do provide for these opportunities, and are the ones that are totally unnecessary. Meetings are generally not a good idea when:

- confidential or sensitive personnel matters must be addressed;

- there is inadequate data for the meeting;

- there is insufficient time to prepare for the meeting;

- the information could be communicated by memo, fax, e-mail, or telephone;

- there is a considerable amount of anger and hostility in the group and people need time to calm down before coming together.

Figure 10-1   Participation of all participants is essential.

TYPE OF MEETING

For years meetings were traditional in nature; that is, the participants gathered in face-to-face meetings at a common location. Now, with the technology available, we have numerous choices as to the type of meeting that is held. Both the traditional meeting and the electronic meeting have certain advantages and disadvantages. By carefully ana-

lyzing the purpose of the meeting and the outcomes expected, it is usually possible to determine which type of meeting will be most appropriate.

TRADITIONAL MEETINGS

The traditional meeting where people gather for face-to-face discussion of the issue or the problem at one location has a number of advantages.

- All individuals have a chance to talk informally with the participants before, during, and after the meeting.

- The body language of the participants and their speech may be closely observed.

- People generally feel more relaxed and less formal when the meeting is face-to-face.

- If the issue to be discussed is difficult, the face-to-face meeting can provide an atmosphere that allows the attendees to more effectively deal with the issue.

- A creative, interactive group discussion is more likely in a face-to-face meeting.

- Widespread participation among group members is also more likely in a face-to-face meeting.

Some disadvantages to the face-to-face meeting are also listed here.

- Travel to and from a face-to-face meeting can be costly, particularly if this travel is from another city, state, or country. The cost is not only in the transportation to and from the meeting and hotel rooms if the meeting is long, but also the time lost in travel.

- The meeting room may be costly; or if the meeting is held within the company, finding a vacant room or tying up a room used for multiple purposes can be a problem.

HUMAN RELATIONS TIP

Schedule meetings only when absolutely necessary. A poorly structured meeting with no apparent purpose results in a waste of everyone's time, frustration for many, and unnecessary costs for the organization.

ORGANIZATIONAL MEETINGS

Several types of meetings are held within an organization. Executives usually meet often with the people who report directly to them. These meetings are generally referred to as staff meetings. Meetings are often held with customers and clients of the business. These meetings will generally consist of only two or three people. Other types of meetings within a company (which may be more formal in nature) include board meetings, committee meetings, and meetings of special task forces or project teams.

EXECUTIVE'S ROLE

The executive has certain roles in planning meetings. These roles are determining the purpose of the meeting, determining who should attend, and determining the appropriate number of attendees. The executive may work closely with the office professional in getting these tasks accomplished.

Determining the Purpose of the Meeting

Unless the office professional is calling the meeting, it is generally not the office professional's responsibility to determine the purpose of the meeting. It is always necessary, however, for the office professional to understand the purpose of the meeting so that appropriate arrangements can be made. If your supervisor does not tell you the purpose of the meeting, it is a good idea to ask. Your asking may also help your supervisor in clearly stating the purpose; in other words, it may help crystallize your supervisor's thinking regarding the meeting.

Determining Who Should Attend

The decision as to who will attend a meeting is not generally the prerogative of the office professional. However, you may be asked for input if you have worked for the company for a considerable amount of time. You may also, through total quality management initiatives, be calling a meeting yourself. In either situation, you can use the ideas presented here to help determine who should be at a meeting.

If it is a problem-solving meeting, individuals who have knowledge of the problem and who will be involved in the implementation of the solution should be at the meeting. For example, if the issue is to establish a strategic plan for the business, the top level executives of the business should be involved—the president, vice presidents, and possibly the board of trustees.

One way to think about who should be at the meeting is to consider who is most affected by the problem or issue and who can contribute to the solution. It may be a good idea from time to time to bring in an expert from outside the company to work with internal people. New people can inject new life into groups by bringing in fresh ideas and helping to break communication barriers which have formed. You also need to consider the backgrounds of the people. For example, a **heterogeneous group** (a group having dissimilar backgrounds and experiences) can often solve problems more satisfactorily than a **homogeneous group** (a group with similar backgrounds and experiences). A heterogeneous group can bring varying views to the problem and encourage creative thinking through the diversity that is present; however, an extremely heterogeneous group demands a skilled facilitator to make the meeting productive.

A heterogeneous group can bring varying views to a problem.

Determining the Number of Attendees

The ideal number in attendance is based on the purpose of the meeting and the number of people who can best achieve the purpose. The best size for a problem-solving and decision-making group is from seven to fifteen people. This size group allows for creative **synergy** (the ideas and products of a group of people developed through the interaction with each other). This size group provides enough people to generate divergent points of view and to challenge each other's thinking.

Small groups of seven people or less may be necessary at times. For example, if the purpose of the meeting is to discuss a personnel matter, the human resources director and the supervisor may be the only people in attendance. If the purpose of the meeting is to discuss a faulty product design, the product engineer, the manager of the engineering section, and the line technician may be the only people in attendance. Here are some advantages to having only a few people in a meeting.

- The participants may be assembled quicker.

- The meeting can be informal and thus provide for more spontaneity and creativity.

- Group dynamics are easier to manage.

  Here are some disadvantages of a small group.

- The points of view are limited due to the size of the group.

- There may not be sufficient ideas to create the best solution to the problem.

- The participants may not be willing to challenge each other's point of view due to the closeness of the group.

One disadvantage of a small group is that there might not be a sufficient number of ideas generated to create the best solution to a problem. *Photo by Alan Brown/Photonics Graphics.*

OFFICE PROFESSIONAL'S RESPONSIBILITIES

In planning meetings (whether they be face-to-face or some type of electronic meeting), the office professional has a number of responsibilities. As you have just learned, you must work closely with your supervisor in determining the purpose of the meeting, who will attend, and the appropriate number of attendees. You can handle other responsibilities on your own; however, you must understand your supervisor's preferences in these areas. When you first join an organization or begin to work with a different supervisor, it is essential for you to spend a significant amount of time with that supervisor before each meeting to understand needs and preferences. Once you have spent a period of time with a particular supervisor, you will begin to have less need to discuss details. It is always essential, however, that you discuss the purpose of the meeting and the general expectations. You do not want to spend unproductive time in the numerous activities which must be performed only to find that your supervisor is not pleased with the directions you have taken.

Selecting and Preparing the Room

The room can impact what happens during a meeting. You probably have attended meetings where:

- the room was too large or too small for the group;

- the participants could not be heard;

- the room was too cold or too hot;

- the lighting in the room was not adequate;

- the ventilation was poor.

Having room inadequacies may start the meeting in a negative manner. As you have learned already, meetings are expensive. When a meeting is called the arrangements should allow for maximum effectiveness from the participants. If you plan the room arrangements carefully, you can help the meeting begin in a positive way.

When you know how many people are going to attend the meeting, look for a room that is the proper size to accommodate the group. Most businesses will have several conference rooms of varying sizes available. There is usually someone that schedules the conference rooms; if so, you will need to contact this individual to reserve the room. If you have to choose between reserving a room that is too large or one that is too small, it is generally a good idea to choose the smaller room. For example, twenty people in a room that accommodates eighty people can make the group feel intimidated by the empty space. The participants may feel like they were giving a party and no one came. However, you do not want to attempt to put forty people in a room that accommodates twenty. In addition to the room being too crowded, there are usually restrictions established by the local fire department concerning how many people may occupy a room at one time. If you must take a room that is too large for the participants, try to make the room appear smaller. For example, you might set up chairs or tables in one corner of the room. If there are movable partitions, the partitions can be arranged around the space selected.

A large room may be partitioned to accommodate a smaller group. *Photo courtesy of Ventana Corporation, Tucson, AZ.*

Check the temperature controls before the meeting. Remember that bodies generate heat, so the room will be warmer with people in it. A standard rule is to aim for about 68 ° F. Be certain that you know whom to call if the temperature gets too hot or too cold during the meeting. Nothing can be worse than a hot, stuffy room or a room that is icy cold when you are trying to make important decisions.

Check the ventilation—is the airflow adequate? Is the lighting bright enough? If visuals are going to be used, can they be seen? If you have any questions about the temperature, ventilation, or lighting, you should check with the building maintenance personnel well before the meeting begins. Give them a chance to correct the problem. It is not good to call at the last minute about a problem simply because you did not plan well.

If you are selecting a room for an electronic meeting, you need to be certain that the room is large enough to accommodate the equipment needed for the meeting. The seating arrangement needs to be one in which all individuals can see the monitors, electronic blackboards, or whatever other equipment may be in use. As stated earlier, if you are arranging for a videoconference, the meeting is usually held in a room that is permanently maintained with the special equipment.

Determining the Seating Arrangement

The seating arrangement of the room depends on the objectives of the meeting. The four basic seating arrangements are rectangular, circular, U-shaped, and semicircular. Figure 10-2 shows these arrangements.

The **rectangular arrangement** allows the leader to have good control because the leader sits at the head of the table. Conversation is usually directed to the leader. The rectangular arrangement is also good if the purpose is to have individuals talk in groups of two or three. Individuals seated next to or opposite each other have a chance to discuss. If discussion is important, the table should not be too long. A long table may make communication difficult due to the inability to see the nonverbal behavior of all the participants. A long table can be particularly difficult for the leader if discussion is the purpose, because the leader may be at a distance from several of the participants.

The **circular arrangement** is effective for minimizing status positions. For example, in a circle it is difficult to determine the leader because each participant has an equal amount of space. The leader has less control in a circle than in any other arrangement. Communication channels should be fairly equal among all members because no one assumes a dominant position. The circular arrangement encourages a sense of warmth and togetherness. It is easy to make direct eye contact with everyone in the group.

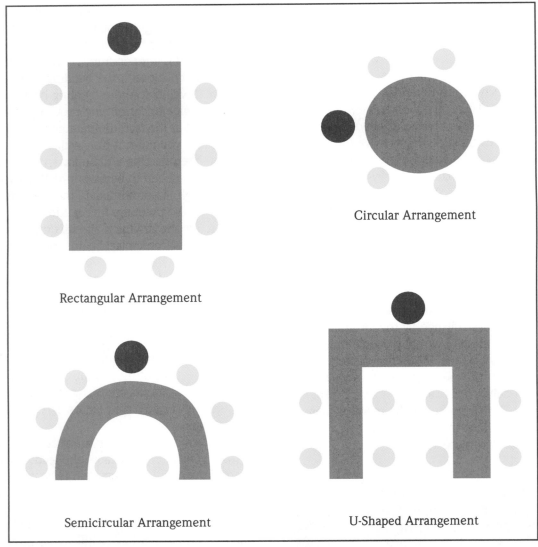

Figure 10-2   Seating arrangements.

The **U-shaped** and **semicircular arrangements** work well for small groups of six to eight members. The leader has moderate control because the leader can be positioned in a fairly dominant position. These two arrangements are also good for showing visuals because the visual can be set up at the front of the configuration. The U-shaped and semicircular arrangements are desirable for semiformal meetings, with the circular arrangement being most effective for informal meetings, and the rectangular arrangement most effective for formal meetings.

Always make certain that you have the appropriate number of chairs for the participants who will attend. You do not want to have extra chairs as it might appear that some people failed to attend. You also do not want to have too few chairs; it appears you have not planned properly.

Sending Meeting Notices

The most effective way to notify participants within an organization of a meeting is e-mail. Because most people now keep their calendars on their computers, you may quickly check to determine when the participants are available. The next most common way to inform internal participants is through an interoffice memorandum. When notifying participants of a meeting, you should include the following information.

- purpose of the meeting
- topics to be considered at the meeting
- materials that should be read before the meeting and brought to the meeting
- date of the meeting

KORONET INTERNATIONAL

M E M O R A N D U M

TO: All Managers

FROM: Jacqueline Marquette

DATE: November 12, —

SUBJECT: Meeting Notice

There will be a meeting on November 22 beginning at 9 a.m. in Conference Room A to discuss our accomplishments on our plans for this year and to review our goals and budget for next year. Please send a summary of your accomplishments to the other managers by November 20 and bring a copy to the meeting. Please plan to spend until 11 a.m. It is most important that everyone be in attendance. If you cannot attend, please call Roger Drucker by November 18.

Figure 10-3   Meeting notification.

- starting and ending times

- location

- name of the person to whom the addressee should respond and when the response should be made as to attendance

When considering the time of the meeting, it is generally best to avoid Monday mornings and meetings immediately after lunch. Meetings should generally be from one hour to no longer than two hours. If people have to sit for longer than two hours, they usually get restless and lose interest in the topic. When a meeting is two hours in length or longer, short breaks of from five to ten minutes should be given at the forty- to fifty-minute interval, depending on the participants. If you are observant, you will know when it is time for a break. Signals include lack of participation, individuals leaving the room, and even the occasional covering of the eyes with the individual's hands as if reflecting on a problem when actually the individual is "dropping off." Breaks allow people to move around a little; generally, they will return to the meeting ready to concentrate and get back to the task at hand. An example of a meeting notification is given in Figure 10-3.

It is important to begin and end meetings on time. If the meeting notice states that the meeting will begin at 9 a.m., begin sharply at 9. Do not wait for stragglers. People will soon get the message that you will start on time, and they will be there. The same holds true for ending meetings; end them on time. People will be appreciative of your being respective of their time constraints. Also by stating an ending time, the leader of the meeting is forced to help the group accomplish the objectives in the time allocated rather than dragging on for an inordinate amount of time.

As an office professional, you may also have the responsibility of following up to determine if people are planning to attend the meeting. Although you ask people to let you know, there are usually some people who do not respond. The usual method of follow-up is a call or an e-mail reminder. It is also a good idea to contact the office professionals who work for the individuals invited; they can remind their supervisors of the meeting. For your supervisor, you need to keep track of who will be at the meeting. If someone is going to be late, that needs to be noted also. You may write this information directly on a copy of the memo or e-mail that went out announcing the meeting and give this to your employer. Another alternative is to prepare a special form for noting attendees.

Preparing the Agenda

Everyone should know what to expect before coming to a meeting, and an **agenda** satisfies this requirement. An agenda is an outline of what will occur at the meeting. Participants should receive a detailed agenda at least a day, and preferably a week, before the meeting. The agenda should include the following:

- name of the meeting or group

- date of the meeting

- starting and ending time

- location

229

- order of agenda items

- person responsible for presenting the agenda item

- action expected on agenda items

- background materials (if needed)

In addition, you may also wish to allocate a particular time period for the presentation of the agenda items. Although this process is not absolutely essential, it usually does remind people of the importance of time and adhering to a schedule. If time frames are not listed, the facilitator of the meeting may need to move the meeting along. The order of the agenda items can vary. Some people feel that the most difficult items should be presented first so that participants can deal with them while they are fresh. Other people feel that the difficult items should be presented last. Find out your supervisor's preference. An agenda is shown in Figure 10-4.

Notice that the word "Action" is listed after certain agenda items. This word denotes that a decision is expected to be made. Such an approach helps participants know what is expected. If they are to make a decision, they can come prepared to do so. If a decision is not going to be made on an item, the individual in charge of the meeting needs to let the group know what will happen to the item being discussed. Is it going to be discussed again at a later date? Is it going to be referred to another group for a decision? If participants understand what is expected of them, they can be better contributors.

When sending out materials prior to a meeting, keep them as concise as possible. Most people will not spend the time to read verbose materials.

Determining the Procedures

Highly structured procedures are generally not appropriate for small committee meetings, departmental meetings, informational meetings, and other informal meetings. If it is a formal meeting, you may need to adhere to Robert's Rules of Order. For example, parliamentary procedure is essential at a meeting of the board of directors of a corporation or at an annual business meeting for a professional organization. You should become familiar with parliamentary procedures; such information can be helpful in a number of situations.

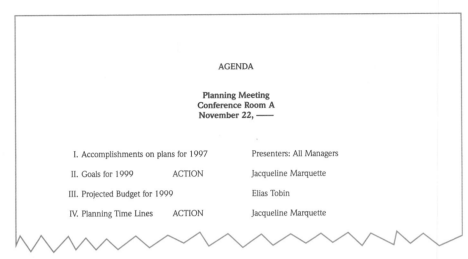

AGENDA

**Planning Meeting
Conference Room A
November 22, ——**

I. Accomplishments on plans for 1997 — Presenters: All Managers

II. Goals for 1999 — ACTION — Jacqueline Marquette

III. Projected Budget for 1999 — Elias Tobin

IV. Planning Time Lines — ACTION — Jacqueline Marquette

Figure 10-4   Meeting agenda.

Preparing Materials for the Supervisor

You should prepare a folder for each meeting your supervisor will attend or lead. The folder should include the following:

- the meeting notice with a list of the people who will be in attendance;

- materials that have been sent out before the meeting;

- notes that are needed at the meeting; and

- visuals or handouts.

If your supervisor is a participant of a meeting off site, you may also need to include directions to the location. Most large cities have detailed maps available of the city; it is usually a good idea to have one available as a handy reference. Also, maps for particular locations can now be obtained through the Internet. You merely give the address that you want and ask for a map; the computer immediately draws a map for you.

Preparing Materials for Attendees

If handouts are to be distributed during the meeting, prepare these handouts well in advance. If the handouts have several pages, it is helpful to place them in individual folders. Sometimes attendees are expected to take notes; if so, you might provide a pad of paper in the folder. Extra pencils and pens may be placed on the table or at a convenient location for the attendees in case they are needed.

Ordering Equipment

Determine what equipment, if any, is needed for the meeting. Then follow through to see that it is available. It is a good idea to make a list of the equipment needed and note on the list what arrangements have been made. List who is responsible for obtaining each item; if it is your responsibility, note that. Before the meeting begins, take your list to the room and check it against the equipment.

Ordering Food and Beverages

If it is a morning meeting, coffee or juice can be provided for the participants. Water should also be available. If it is an afternoon meeting, you may want to provide coffee and soft drinks. Do understand, however, that it is not necessary to provide beverages; find out your supervisor's preference.

For a luncheon meeting, you will probably have the responsibility of selecting the menu, calling the caterer, and arranging for the meal to be served. It is usually a good idea not to have a heavy lunch if you are expecting people to work after lunch. A salad or a light entree is more appropriate for a working lunch.

If it is a dinner meeting, you may have the responsibility for working with an outside caterer. Due to health concerns, many people do not eat red meat or eat it only sparingly. If you know the attendees, you should consider their needs. If you do not know the attendees, ask the caterer to recommend several meals, and select from one of these meals. Be certain to ask your supervisor what the budget allocation is for the meal.

If it is a dinner meeting at a hotel, you can usually expect a great deal of assistance from the hotel staff. You will usually be responsible for selecting the menu. If it is formal, you might also wish to have table decorations and place cards. It is wise to know the group when selecting the seating arrangement; you should get your supervisor's assistance here. It is never good to have two people seated next to each other who do not get along well.

Handling Duties During the Meeting

The office professional's responsibilities during the meeting are varied. You may be expected to greet the participants and to introduce individuals to each other if participants do not know each other. Your courteousness, warmth, and friendliness can go a long way toward making people feel comfortable and getting the meeting off to a good start.

Your main responsibility during the meeting will probably be to take the **minutes** (a record of the meeting). Sit near the leader so that you will be able to hear easily. You may wish to use a laptop computer while taking notes. The computer can save you time, because you can record the minutes directly on a hard drive or a disk. After the meeting is over, you can go over the notes and edit where necessary. You do not have to key the information; you already have most of the information keyed. Such an approach is faster than taking notes by hand or recording the meeting on tape and then having to key everything after the meeting.

Minutes should contain a record of all important matters presented in the meeting. You do not need to record the minutes verbatim (with the exception of motions which do need to be recorded verbatim); you do need to record all pertinent information. Include the following items in the minutes.

- date, time, and place of the meeting

- type of meeting (regular, special, monthly, etc.)

- name of the group

- name of the person presiding at the meeting

- members present and absent

- approval or correction of the minutes from the previous meeting (if necessary)

- reports of committees, officers, or individuals

- actions taken and motions made

- items on which action needs to be taken and the person responsible for taking the action

- date and time of the next meeting (if there is one)

- adjournment of the meeting

- signature of the secretary for the group (if necessary)

Minutes are not necessary for all meetings; however, they are helpful so that attendees can be reminded of what happened and any responsibilities that they might have after the meeting. Minutes are needed in the following situations.

- When decisions are made that affect a large number of people.

- In formal meetings such as board of directors' meetings.

- When attendees must act upon a list of different topics and a record is necessary for recall of the events.

- When the same type of meeting is held on a regular basis and a record is needed of the continual activities of the group.

- When meeting results need to be reported to the president of the company or any officers of the company.

Following Up After the Meeting

Your duties after the meeting include seeing that the meeting room is left in good order, preparing the minutes, and handling any other details.

Routine Tasks. The following is a list of some of the routine tasks that need to be handled after a meeting.

- Return all equipment. See that any additional tables and chairs are removed from the room. Clean up any food or beverage leftovers or notify the cleaning staff if the room needs a general cleanup.

- Write items on your calendar that may require future attention by you or your employer.

- Send out any follow-up memos that may be necessary.

- Evaluate the meeting. Review what happened; consider how you might improve the arrangements for the next meeting. Make notes for your files so that you may review these notes before the next meeting. If you have used a caterer, make notes about the effectiveness—the quality of the food, the helpfulness of the staff, and so forth.

- Keep files for all meetings for a period of time so that you may refer to them before planning the next similar meeting. It is also a good idea to keep names and telephone numbers of contact people in the files.

BOARD OF DIRECTORS MEETING
MANAGEMENT SOCIETY

Grand Rapids Chapter
November 16, —

TIME AND PLACE OF MEETING

The regular monthly meeting of the Board of Directors of the Management Society was held on November 16 at the Regent Hotel at 6:30 p.m. The meeting was called to order by the President, Ronald Anderson. All twelve board members were present.

READING OF THE MINUTES

The minutes of the October meeting were approved without reading since each member had received a copy prior to the meeting.

TREASURER'S REPORT

The treasurer's report (copy attached), showing a balance of $2,053 as of November 1, was read, received, and filed.

UNFINISHED BUSINESS

Ronald Anderson reported that he has received acceptance from H. R. Princeton to speak at the December meeting and that his picture and vitae have been turned over to the Publicity Committee.

NEW BUSINESS

Membership Committee: The application of T. A. Alexander for membership was unanimously approved.

Service Committee: It was suggested that the merit award qualifications be included in the Chapter Bulletin for the first week of December.

Program Committee: Silas Sechr, chairperson of the Speakers Bureau, reported that he and the committee are planning to increase the number of speakers at the winter seminar so that the number of programs can be expanded. Mr. Sechr asked for recommendations from the Board on program topics for the seminar. A discussion followed; it was determined that the theme of the seminar should be: Preparing Leaders for the Twenty-First Century.

Publicity Committee: Percy Atwater reported that approval on the solicitation of ads for the bulletin was received. He explained that the format of the bulletin would have to be changed to accommodate the inclusion of the ads. The Board of Directors approved the action.

ADJOURNMENT

The meeting was adjourned at 8:30 p.m.

Arthur M. Grant, Secretary

Figure 10-5   Minutes.

Minute Preparation. Minutes should be prepared and distributed within twenty-four to forty-eight hours of a meeting. Prompt preparation and distribution of minutes provide a reminder for all in attendance of what must be done before the next meeting. At certain times, nonparticipants may get copies of the minutes from a meeting. For example, if the meeting is a company board meeting, the minutes may be made available to all executives within the company.

Minutes from a meeting are shown in Figure 10-5. Although there is no set format for writing minutes, here are some general guidelines.

- Minutes may be double or single spaced. Margins should be at least one inch. If the minutes are to be placed in a bound book, the left margin should be one and one-half inches.

- Capitalize and center the heading.

- Use subject captions as paragraph headings; these subject captions usually are similar to the agenda topics.

- Minutes may be signed. Minutes of board meetings and professional organizations are generally signed. If minutes are to be signed, a signature line should be provided.

- Minutes should be stored for future reference. Minutes may be stored in hard copy form, on a disk or tape, or on microfiche. (Microfiche storage will be explained in Chapter 13.) In addition, the agenda and all pertinent materials that were presented in the meeting should be stored with the minutes.

Organizing—The Key

Regardless of your responsibilities, the key is organization. Know what you have to do and stay organized in doing it. As you begin the planning for a meeting and as you continue through the process of the meeting and the follow-up activities, constantly ask yourself the following questions.

- How can I best organize my time and efforts?

- When should each task be completed?

- Who is responsible for each activity?

- What should I discuss with my supervisor? What can I do on my own?

Self Check

Take a few moments to check your understanding of the office professional's role in planning meetings by responding to the questions below.

1. What should you consider when selecting a room for a meeting?

2. Which seating arrangements are most effective for semiformal meetings?

3. What should an agenda include?

4. What should minutes include?

How did you do? Check your answers with those provided at the end of the chapter.

LEADER'S RESPONSIBILITIES

The leader of a meeting where you are assisting generally will be your supervisor. As you work in teams within the company, however, you may be the leader occasionally. If the meeting is to go well, the leader must fulfill certain responsibilities.

Adhering to the Agenda

As you have already learned, the purpose of the meeting must be clearly established and that purpose made clear in writing to the participants when the meeting is announced. When the meeting begins, the leader should reiterate the purpose of the meeting. The leader should also let the participants know the expected outcomes. For example, if the purpose of the meeting is to establish directions for the department for the next two years, then the expected outcomes of the meeting may be to determine at least two of the directions.

If participants stray from the agenda, the leader is responsible for sensitively but firmly bringing them back to the agenda. The leader might say, "Thank you for your comments about that issue; we might want to put the issue on the agenda for a future meeting. Now, let's continue on with the department directions that we must set."

Managing Time

The leader must begin the meeting on time, even if several people are not present. Waiting for others to arrive is not fair to the individuals who have made an effort to be on time. Just as important as starting on time is ending on time. The leader must be sensitive to other time commitments made by the participants. Time frames (both beginning and ending) should have been established when the notice was sent. The leader must adhere to these time commitments.

Encouraging Participation

Before the participants are invited to the meeting, considerable thought should be given to who should be at the meeting. The people in attendance have been determined to be the best people in the organization to discuss the issues, set the directions, or solve whatever the problem may be. Once the meeting begins, the leader is responsible for seeing that all individuals participate. If, as the meeting gets under way, several people have not spoken, the leader might say, "Inez, what direction do you think we should take to satisfy our needs in the twenty-first century?" or "Juan, we haven't heard from you on this issue. What is your opinion?"

Let the participants know that you and the group value their opinions. Make it easy for everyone to contribute. Respect each comment that is made. You might make statements such as, "Thank you for that contribution," "That's a great idea," and "Thanks, can you expand on that direction? It seems as if it has possibilities for us."

A leader needs to encourage the participation of all individuals. *Courtesy of International Business Machines, Inc.*

The leader is also responsible for seeing that one or two people do not dominate the conversation, even if the contributions are excellent. The leader might say, "Diana, that is an excellent idea. Juan, how could it be implemented in your area?" or "Thanks, Diana; Juan, what do you think about the direction?"

The leader's main roles are to

- keep the participants focused on the agenda;

- encourage participation from everyone in the meeting;

- limit the domination of any one person in the meeting;

- positively reinforce all individuals for their contributions;

- keep the discussion moving toward the outcomes determined.

Reaching Decisions

The leader is responsible for helping the participants to reach a decision around the issue, prob-

lem, or direction, if a decision is needed. The leader needs to carefully assess if all alternatives have been discussed. Then the leader needs to push for a decision on the issue. For example, the leader might say, "We seem to have identified each issue and the possible solutions. Does anyone else have anything to add?" The leader then moves to resolution by saying, "Now, let's determine which solution will work best in our present situation." Once a resolution is reached, the leader can check to see if all participants agree by asking, "Now that we have reached a resolution, is everyone in the room comfortable with the resolution? Is there anything that we are overlooking? Are there land mines we haven't seen?"

Evaluating the Meeting

Generally, with informal meetings within the organization, no formal evaluation is done; however, an informal evaluation by the leader (and possibly the participants) should always be done. Many times the attendees are very forthright. They may even tell the leader that they found the meeting a waste of their time. If any attendees make such a statement or a similar statement, the leader should always seek clarification on exactly what is meant. If no participants say anything to the leader, the leader may want to ask participants individually how they felt the meeting went. In any case, the leader should ask questions such as the following of himself or herself after the meeting.

- Were the attendees participatory?

- Was the nonverbal behavior positive?

- Were the participants creative problem solvers?

- Did the participants exhibit a high energy level?

- Was the purpose of the meeting satisfied?

- Were appropriate decisions made?

- Can I improve in how I handled the issues, the people, or the meeting in general?

If the meeting is a relatively formal one, the leader may ask participants to fill out an evaluation form. If so, the office professional's role is to prepare and possibly administer the evaluation form. A meeting evaluation form is shown in Figure 10-6.

Evaluation Form

	Yes	No
1. Was the purpose of the meeting accomplished?		
2. Was the agenda received in time to prepare for the meeting?		
3. Was the room arrangement satisfactory?		
4. Did the leader help the group to accomplish the goals of the meeting?		
5. Did the leader adhere to the agenda?		
6. Were the appropriate people included in the meeting?		
7. Did all the attendees participate in the discussion?		
8. Did the attendees listen to each other?		
9. Did the leader encourage participation?		
10. Did the meeting start on time?		
11. Did the meeting end on time?		
12. Were decisions made that were consistent with the purpose of the meeting?		

Additional comments.

Figure 10-6

PARTICIPANT'S RESPONSIBILITIES

Just as a leader has responsibilities, so do the participants. Their roles are much broader than attending the meeting. Their responsibilities begin before the meeting and continue after the meeting.

Before the Meeting

Participants are responsible for reading the meeting notice, responding to it in a timely fashion, and reading any materials that are sent out before the meeting. Participants are also responsible for understanding the purpose of the meeting and analytically evaluating the materials in relation to the purpose of the meeting. Participants need to be aware that they have been asked to the meeting because the leader believes they have something to offer. Each participant must take seriously the responsibility to contribute to the success of the meeting. Contribution before the meeting means being prepared. No one appreciates the participant (or the leader) who comes to the meeting late and opens the pack of materials for the first time—clearly not having read a word before the meeting began.

During the Meeting

During the meeting, participants are responsible for

- being on time;
- adhering to the agenda;
- making contributions;
- listening thoughtfully to other participants' contributions and responding (if the individual has something to add);
- respecting the leader's role;
- not dominating the discussion;
- not being judgmental of others' comments;
- being courteous to each individual in the meeting;
- taking notes, if necessary.

It is not always easy to listen carefully to others, to not be judgmental, and to make contributions. You may really feel like making a face at the leader, excusing yourself and jogging around the block, or even taking a nap. Figure 10-7 illustrates various behaviors in meetings. We have all been in meetings when we or others have behaved similarly; however, our contributions may be the very ones that will get the meeting back on track if individuals have strayed or will help the leader to focus on the meeting. Our obligation is to stay in there—help it get better.

After the Meeting

Once the meeting is over, the participant's responsibilities do not necessarily end. The participant may be responsible for some research or action before the next meeting, or the participant may have been asked to work with one or two other people in bringing back to the next meeting a recommendation. It is important that the participant fulfill any obligations assigned during the meeting by the designated time.

Figure 10-7 Listening: a meeting *must*.

INTERNATIONAL MEETINGS

Your supervisor or you may be responsible for setting up an international meeting, either through electronic media or through a face-to-face meeting. In either situation, you cannot forget the cultural differences that exist. If the meeting is to be successful, cultural differences must be understood and respected. Otherwise, you might have an international incident occur rather than get to a resolution on an important contract or issue. International meetings are always more formal in nature. Hierarchical considerations must be known and dealt with appropriately, as well as proper greetings and amenities. Here are some suggestions for what to do and what not to do in international meetings. Remember that each culture differs. Just as you have learned throughout this course, it is important for you to do your homework before the meeting. Find out as much as you can about each culture that will be represented. Then, be sensitive to the needs of the individuals in the meeting.

- Greet each person properly. Do not let yourself ignore greetings merely because the conference is electronic. Greetings become doubly important in such a situation.

- Do not use first names of participants. Such is an American custom, but rarely appropriate in other countries.

- Recognize the leader of the other groups. For example, if the presidents of companies are involved, they should be recognized first and speak first.

- Take time for the amenities before beginning the meeting.

- Shake hands with the participants or bow if met with a bow from the international visitor.

- Dress conservatively.

- Do not ask personal questions; keep the conversation general (even at the more informal times such as over lunch).

- Disagree agreeably; it is generally offensive to flatly contradict people from another country.

- Do not use slang.

- Avoid gesturing with your hands. Many people take offense at such gestures.

- Watch your body language; remember that body language is different in various cultures; make certain you do not communicate things you do not mean through your body language.

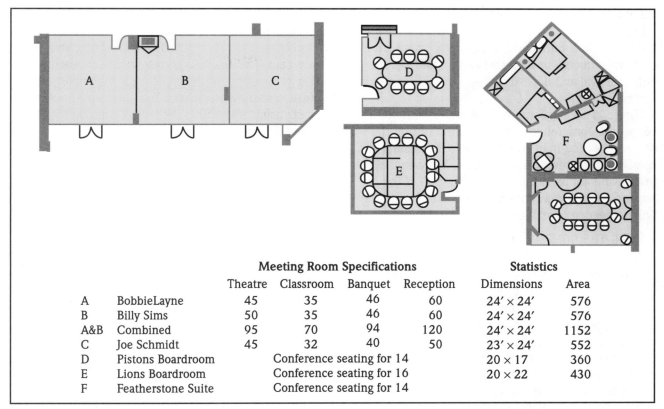

Meeting Room Specifications | **Statistics**

		Theatre	Classroom	Banquet	Reception	Dimensions	Area
A	BobbieLayne	45	35	46	60	24′ × 24′	576
B	Billy Sims	50	35	46	60	24′ × 24′	576
A&B	Combined	95	70	94	120	24′ × 24′	1152
C	Joe Schmidt	45	32	40	50	23′ × 24′	552
D	Pistons Boardroom		Conference seating for 14			20 × 17	360
E	Lions Boardroom		Conference seating for 16			20 × 22	430
F	Featherstone Suite		Conference seating for 14				

Figure 10-8 Hotel floor plan.

- Use an interpreter if necessary.

- Do not mistake a courteous answer for the truth—"Yes" does not always mean "yes" and "no" may not mean "no."

- Remember and respect the hierarchical nature of many countries.

CONFERENCES

A conference is much larger in scope and number of participants than a meeting. Many executives belong to professional organizations such as the American Management Association or other associations in their particular fields such as accounting, engineering, or human resources. These organizations generally hold at least one major conference each year. Most companies encourage their executives to participate in conferences as a means of broadening their knowledge. Your role as an office professional may be to assist your supervisor in planning a conference.

As an office professional, you may be a member of Professional Secretaries International, the National Association of Legal Secretaries, the Amer-

ican Association of Medical Assistants, or some other similar organization. Through such organizations you may get involved in attending or helping to plan some of their conferences.

BEFORE THE CONFERENCE

Preparing for a regional or national conference takes months of work. Good planning will ensure a smooth, successful conference; poor planning will result in a disorganized, ineffective conference. One major responsibility in planning a conference is to determine the location and meeting facilities for the conference. Contact the chamber of commerce in the city being considered; ask for information about the city and appropriate conference facilities. Request conference planning guides from the hotels and conference centers that give floor plans of the facilities, dining and catering services, price list of rooms, meeting rooms, and meals. Notice Figure 10-8 which shows a portion of a hotel floor plan. Once the city and hotel have been selected, detailed arrangements need to be made for meeting rooms, guest rooms, meals and so forth.

Presenters must be contacted and travel and lodging arrangements must be made before the conference. If you are responsible for making the arrangements for a presenter, you should determine the type of accommodations required—room (single or double, queen- or king-size bed), flight preferences, arrival and departure times, rental car needs, and so forth.

There is usually some type of preregistration before the conference and registration during the conference. You may be responsible for mailing and receiving the preregistration forms. You also may be responsible for assisting with registration at the conference. If the conference is large, several people will be needed to staff the registration tables.

DURING THE CONFERENCE

Your responsibilities during the conference may include running errands, assisting in getting messages to participants, and being on hand to help solve any problems that may occur. Other responsibilities may include checking room arrangements, equipment needs, meal arrangements, and so forth. At a conference, you are a representative of the company for which you work or the organization; you should present an outstanding public relations image at all times. Keep a smile on your face and handle even the most difficult situations with **aplomb** (self-assurance).

AFTER THE CONFERENCE

After the conference, your basic duties involve cleanup and follow-up. These responsibilities may include seeing that all equipment is returned, pre-

senters are assisted with transportation to the airport, letters of appreciation are sent to presenters and others, expense reports are filled out, and bills are paid. You may also be responsible for seeing that the proceedings of the conference are published and mailed to the participants. You will usually not be responsible for writing the report, but you may be responsible for working with the conference reporters in assembling and mailing the report. At some conferences, tapes are made of sessions and these tapes are available (for a fee) for attendees.

If others have worked with you on the conference, call a meeting to evaluate the conference. Ask questions such as the following.

- What went right?
- What went wrong?
- Was the facility adequate?
- Was the registration process smooth?
- Were the meals good and served on time?
- Were the presenters effective?

A formal evaluation is usually done of the conference by the attendees. This evaluation may be of the total conference or of the individual sessions.

Keep a record of your evaluation so that you may refer to it before the next conference. Also keep your files containing information about conference preparation. These files can be valuable in planning future conferences.

CHAPTER SUMMARY

This summary will help you remember the important points covered in the chapter.

- Management spends as much as 50 percent or more of each week in meetings. Due to the frequency and cost of meetings, it is important that meeting time be spent as productively as possible.

- Meetings are a good means of generating ideas; however, a number of unnecessary and nonproductive meetings are held daily in organizations. Meetings are not a good idea when confidential or sensitive personnel matters must be addressed; when inadequate data are available; when there is insufficient time to prepare for the meeting; when information could be communicated by memo, fax, or e-mail; or when there is a considerable amount of anger or hostility in the group.

- Meetings may be face-to-face or electronic through audioconferencing, videoconferencing, or computer conferencing.

- The executive's roles in meeting preparation usually involve determining the purpose of the meeting, determining who should attend, and determining the number of attendees. The office professional may assist with these roles.

- The office professional's roles (in consultation with the executive) include:

  selecting and preparing the room

  determining the seating arrangement

  sending meeting notices

  preparing the agenda

  determining the procedures

  preparing materials for the supervisor

  preparing materials for the attendees

  ordering equipment

  ordering food and beverages

  handling duties during the meeting

  following up after the meeting

  preparing minutes

  organizing

- The leader's responsibilities during the meeting include:

  adhering to the agenda

  managing time

  encouraging participation

  reaching decisions

  evaluating the meeting

- The participant's responsibilities during the meeting include:

  reading material before the meeting

  being on time

  adhering to the agenda

  making thoughtful contributions

  listening to other participants

  carrying out any responsibilities assigned during the meeting

- In planning and conducting international meetings, the leader and office professional should become familiar with the customs and culture of the participants.

- A conference is much larger in scope and number of participants than a meeting. The office professional may be involved in helping to plan a conference, carrying out duties during the conference such as helping to solve individual problems, running errands, assisting with registration, and so forth. After the conference the office professional may be involved with writing letters of appreciation, filling out expense reports, paying bills, and numerous other follow-up activities.

CHAPTER GLOSSARY

The following terms were introduced in this chapter. To help you review, definitions are given here.

- **Teleconferencing** (p. 223)–A general term applied to a variety of technology-assisted, two-way (interactive) communications via telephone lines, fiber optics, or microwaves.

- **Audioconferencing** (p. 223)–A type of conference in which participants either use telephones in their offices or meet in small groups, using speakerphones.

- **Electronic blackboard** (p. 223)–A board with a pressure-sensitive surface; individuals write on the surface and the information is instantly converted to signals, which are then transmitted over telephone lines.

- **Interactivity** (p. 223)–Information that can be transmitted from one location to another and acted on by participants at any location; this information transmission may be in the form of participants talking with each other across long-distance locations.

- **Videoconferencing** (p. 223)–A system of transmitting audio and video between individuals at distant locations thereby eliminating the need for travel.

- **Still-frame** (p. 223)–A term to describe nonmoving pictures.

- **Downlink** (p. 224)–Sending information from one location to another through a satellite or fiber optics technology.

- **Computer conferencing** (p. 224)–A conference in which each participant is linked via a computer.

- **Heterogeneous group** (p. 225)–A group having dissimilar backgrounds and experiences.

- **Homogeneous group** (p. 225)–A group with similar backgrounds and experiences.

- **Synergy** (p. 225)–The ideas and products of a group of people developed through the interaction with each other.

- **Rectangular arrangement** (p. 227)–A rectangular table where participants in a meeting are seated; the leader sits at the head of the table and has control.

- **Circular arrangement** (p. 227)–A circular arrangement of chairs in a meeting; no one assumes a dominant position.

- **U-shaped arrangement** (p. 228)–A U-shaped arrangement of tables for participants in a meeting; the leader assumes a fairly dominant position.

- **Semicircular arrangement** (p. 228)–A semicircular arrangement of chairs for participants in a meeting; the leader assumes a fairly dominant position.

- **Agenda** (p. 229)–An outline of what will occur at a meeting.

- **Minutes** (p. 232)–A record of the meeting.

- **Aplomb** (p. 238)–Self-assurance.

DISCUSSION ITEMS

These discussion items provide an opportunity for you to test your understanding of the chapter through discussion with your classmates and instructor.

1. When is a meeting unnecessary?

2. List and define three types of electronic meetings.

3. Why should the office professional understand the purpose of a meeting?

4. List ten responsibilities that an office professional has when meetings are being held.

5. What should minutes contain?

6. What should be taken into consideration when conducting an international meeting?

CASE STUDY

Koronet is planning an electronic meeting for its Michigan, Texas, North Carolina, California, Japan, Korea, and Mexico executives. The meeting is being held to discuss the directions of the company for the twenty-first century. You have been asked to coordinate with these offices on agenda items. Once you receive the agenda items, you will be working with Ms. Marquette to get out the necessary materials and the agenda. You have contacted the appropriate office professional at each location to discuss these details. To date, you have heard from the Texas, North Carolina, and California offices with their agenda items. You have heard nothing from the Japan, Korea, and Mexico offices. You have asked for the agenda through e-mail on three different occasions, with no response. The meeting is one month off, and you are becoming anxious. You know that you must get the agenda out soon. You hate to go to Ms. Marquette with the situation, but you do not know how to handle it. What should you do?

RESPONSES TO SELF CHECK

1. When selecting a meeting room, you should consider the size of room, arrangement of room, appropriate number of chairs, temperature of the room, ventilation, and any equipment needed.

2. The U-shaped and semicircular arrangements are the most effective for semiformal meetings.

3. An agenda should include:

   name of the meeting or the group

   date of the meeting

   starting and ending time

   location

   order of agenda items

   person responsible for presenting the agenda item

   action expected on agenda items

   background materials (if necessary)

4. Minutes should include:

   date, time, and place of the meeting

   type of meeting

   name of group

   name of person presiding

   members present and absent

   approval or correction of minutes from previous meeting

   reports of committees, officers, or individuals

   actions taken and motions made

   items on which action needs to be taken and the person responsible for taking the action

   date and time of the next meeting

   adjournment of the meeting

   signature of the secretary for the group

OFFICE TASKS

OFFICE TASK 10-1 (Objectives 1, 2, and 3)

Ms. Marquette is planning a meeting with nonprofit groups and several large businesses within the Grand Rapids community to consider ways in which the groups might work together to establish a learning community that meets the needs of the citizens within the area. The issues that eventually will be addressed by the learning community include: welfare, job training, transportation, and crime. The nonprofit groups who will be involved in this meeting are Department of Social Services, the Grand Rapids Foundation, the Grand Rapids Chamber of Commerce, the Hispanic Coalition, and the Native American Council. The businesses are Koronet International, Clinton Health Care, Clark Associates, Inc., Godwin Tools, and Lowell Granite.

The first meeting will be an organizational one in which a mission statement for the group will be developed and the goals for the first year of operation will be established. The meeting will be held on Thursday, November 15, beginning with lunch, continuing until 4 p.m., and beginning at 8:30 a.m. on Friday, November 16, with breakfast and continuing until 11 a.m. You are responsible for sending out the letters inviting the participants to the meeting, preparing the agenda for the two-day meeting, and making arrangements for lunch on November 15 and breakfast on November 16. Ms. Marquette has asked that you check the Internet for any references to learning communities that have been set up by other community leaders.

The agenda on November 15 will include a welcome to the group from Ms. Marquette, lunch, introduction of the participants, and then a videoconference with Dr. Peter Sigman, who has been working with learning communities for a period of time. Dr. Sigman will be in Chicago; the participants at the meeting will have a chance to interact with him after his presentation. The remainder of Thursday afternoon will be devoted to writing a mission statement for the group. On Friday morning, the group will begin to develop the goals for the first year. Ms. Marquette will facilitate the mission and goal sessions. It is anticipated that there will be approximately thirty people in attendance.

Work with two of your classmates on this assignment. Do the following:

1. Refer back to the section in Chapter 10 on the office professional's responsibilities in assisting with meetings. Make a list of the things that must be done. Include menus for lunch and breakfast.

2. Prepare a copy of any articles that you might have found on the Internet concerning learning communities; turn these articles in to your instructor with the remainder of this assignment.

3. Draft a letter inviting the nonprofits and businesses to the meeting and also list the agenda; give the draft to your supervisor for approval. The meeting will be held in the Board Conference Room at Koronet. (In this case, the supervisor will be your instructor.) Once your instructor has approved the letter and the agenda, prepare letters and envelopes to the people who are to be invited. Include the agenda for the two days. Addresses are given on the Student Data Template Disk, file OT10-1. Letterhead is provided on the Student Data Template Disk, file OT10-1B. (Use the mail merge capability on your software to prepare the letters and envelopes.)

OFFICE TASK 10-2 (Objective 3)

Attend a meeting of a professional organization—either a club of which you are a member at school or some other organization. Take notes at the meeting and key your notes in the form of minutes. Turn in the minutes to your instructor.

ENGLISH USAGE CHALLENGE DRILL

Correct the spelling errors in the following sentences. Cite the spelling rule that is applicable to each sentence. Before you begin, refresh your memory of spelling rules by reviewing them in the *Multimedia Reference for Writers* (if available to you) or by reading the rules in the reference guide to this text or some other reference guide.

1. The cieling of the room needs some paint.
2. The speech is forgetable.
3. Happyness can be a state of mind; one that has to be worked at to be achieved.
4. The beachs on the shores of Lake Michigan are beautiful.
5. The office stationary is 75 percent cotton content.

ASSESSMENT OF CHAPTER OBJECTIVES

Now that you have completed the chapter and the office tasks, take a few moments to review the following learning objectives that you were given at the beginning of this chapter. Did you accomplish these objectives? If so, explain how in the space provided. If you were unable to accomplish these objectives, give your reason for not doing so. Your instructor may want to review your answers.

I accomplished these objectives.

1. Identify the responsibilities of the office professional for meetings and conferences.
   Yes _____ No _____
   Explain how you accomplished this objective.
   _____
   _____
   _____

2. Prepare notices for meetings.
   Yes _____ No _____
   Explain how you accomplished this objective.
   _____
   _____
   _____

3. Prepare agendas and minutes.
   Yes _____ No _____
   Explain how you accomplished this objective.
   _____
   _____
   _____

Provide reasons for failing to accomplish any of the objectives.
   _____
   _____
   _____
   _____
   _____

MAKING TRAVEL ARRANGEMENTS

LEARNING OBJECTIVES

1. **Make travel arrangements.**
2. **Prepare itineraries.**
3. **Describe the duties to be performed when the executive is traveling and when the executive returns.**
4. **Prepare expense reports.**

Travel is a way of life for most business executives and with our global economy, the travel may be within the United States or international. As you have already learned, many U.S. businesses now have subsidiaries abroad. Conversely, a number of companies abroad have subsidiaries in the United States. Both the United States and other countries take advantage of land, labor, and technical expertise available in other parts of the world in making decisions as to where a product is produced. Markets today are also international. Thus, a company such as Toyota (a Japanese firm) locates plants within the United States due to the large car market that is here. Therefore, due to the global nature of our economy, it is not unusual for an executive to make trips abroad for business purposes. As an office professional, you also may travel occasionally. For example, you may be asked to attend an occasional conference designed to assist you in performing your job better. If you are working for a company who has subsidiaries abroad, you may have the opportunity to work for a period of time in one of the international locations.

To handle travel arrangements effectively, you must become familiar with the types of services available. This chapter will help you understand the options you have when making the necessary arrangements. It also will help you know how to handle the other responsibilities associated with travel.

DOMESTIC TRAVEL

Because time is an extremely important commodity for the busy executive, almost all travel is done by air. The executive usually does not have the additional time that is required to go by car or by rail. Thus, the concentration in this section is on air travel. Car and train travel are given a limited amount of attention.

AIR TRAVEL

An air traveler today can fly across the United States from New York to California in approximately five hours of flight time. (Since New York is on Eastern Standard Time and California is on Pacific Standard Time, there is a difference in clock time of eight hours.) During the time on the plane, the traveler can use the time productively through the technology that is available. For example, the executive might catch up on office correspondence by writing letters and memorandums on a laptop computer. The executive can make any telephone calls necessary by using the plane telephone which is available at the person's seat. Once the executive is on the ground, correspondence can be sent back to the office via a modem, a fax, or by mail. Thus, air travel not only saves travel time but it also allows the executive to continue to be productive.

The executive may use time productively while traveling.
© 1997, PhotoDisc Inc.

Flight Classifications

The three classes of flight are first class, business class, and coach. Some flights offer all three classes. Other flights offer first class and coach, while still others offer business class and coach. All large planes offer first class and coach; several offer business class also. Some smaller planes such as commuter flights, which fly shorter distances, have only coach or business class and coach.

First-Class Accommodations. First-class accommodations are the most expensive of the three classes and the most luxurious. The seats are wider and farther apart, and services are greater. For example, the quantity and quality of food offered is better. More attention is paid to presentation of food. Cloth napkins, tablecloths, silverware, and china dinnerware are used. Alcoholic beverages are offered without additional cost. Some airlines allow you to eat the meal at any time you ask. Headsets for listening to music are provided, and the seats generally recline. There is also more leg room. There are more flight attendants per customer than in coach or business, which allow for greater attention to be given to the individual flyer. First-class customers are allowed to board first and to exit first. Attendants take coats and hang them up for the customer; they also store parcels in overhead bins.

Business-Class Accommodations. Business-class accommodations are slightly more expensive than coach. The business-class section is located in front of the coach class if first class is not offered, or directly behind first class. Accommodations may include more spacious seating than coach, complimentary alcoholic beverages, headsets for listening to music, recliner seats, more leg room, and better food than coach class.

Coach-Class Accommodations. Coach-class accommodations provide snacks, soft drinks, fruit juice, tea or coffee, and meals at no additional charge. However, seats are closer together and fewer flight attendants are available to serve the needs of the customers. Food is served with plastic plates and dinnerware and paper napkins. Because there are fewer flight attendants, meals and other services are slower in delivery than in first class.

Company-Owned Planes

Large companies may have their own plane or fleet of planes if the amount of travel within the company makes it advantageous to do so. These planes are generally flown by pilots employed by

In order to decrease travel costs, many airlines offer coach-class accommodations. *Courtesy of Southwest Airlines.*

the company; the planes are housed at a local airport. When an executive is flying in a company-owned plane, that person may be driven to the airport by a company employee and picked up at the airport on returning from the trip.

Special Services

Several special services are provided by airlines and airports. For example, an airline may have a shuttle service which runs from a location in the downtown area or from various strategic locations across the city. Tickets can often be purchased at these shuttle locations through self-ticketing machines or through airline employees on duty. The shuttle will take the customer to the departure gate and then pick the customer up at the airport and return the customer to the shuttle location. Vehicle parking is provided at the shuttle location.

Airports also offer parking for a fee. Generally, some type of covered parking is available close to the airport (this is the most expensive on a daily rate basis). Other parking locations are provided at locations some distance from the airport, and a shuttle service is provided to take you to your departure gate and to return you to your car after your trip.

In addition, in large cities, private parking services are available in proximity to the airport. The traveler drives to the parking service and leaves the car. The parking service takes the traveler to the airline terminal via a van. Upon returning to the airport, the traveler is picked up by one of the parking service vans and returned to the car. These services are reasonably priced and can help the traveler get to the airport without much hassle.

Changes or Cancellations

Occasionally, it may be necessary to cancel or change flight reservations. If you have purchased an initial flight through some type of special fare, however, you may be charged a penalty for changing the flight. When arranging for a special fare, be certain to ask if the flight may be canceled or changed. Sometimes your money is not returned on a special fare if you cancel. If your employer is prone to make frequent changes, it might be wise to seek fares that do not have a penalty for changes. Even though they may be more expensive initially, you may save money over the penalty rate charged.

Ground Transportation

Once the executive arrives at the destination, some type of ground transportation is generally necessary. That transportation may be as simple as taking a taxi or shuttle service to the hotel. It is a good idea to check taxi costs and the availability of shuttle services in making the travel arrangements. Some hotels provide free shuttle service to and from the airport. Shuttle services are also available from private vendors which are generally less expensive than taxi service. Limousine service is also available at many airports, with the cost being approximately the same as taxi service.

If it is necessary for the executive to attend meetings at several locations during the stay, renting a car may be the most economical and convenient method of ground transportation. Toll-free numbers for car rental agencies are listed in the telephone directory, or cars may be rented through the airlines or travel agent. Cars may also be rented through the Internet; more information is given later in the chapter. When renting a car, specify the make and model of car preferred and the date and time the car will be picked up and returned.

When arriving at the destination airport, the executive picks up the car from the rental desk (generally located next to the baggage claim area). The cost of a rental car is determined by a daily rate plus an amount for each mile driven or by a daily rate with unlimited mileage. Company policy may dictate that the executive rent a car no larger than mid-size. Prices from rental agencies are determined by the size of the car, with the classifications being full-size (the most expensive), mid-size (middle price range), and economy (the least expensive available). Insurance is available upon rental of the car. (The insurance is not mandatory if the executive has outside coverage through a business or personal policy.) The executive will be asked about a preference to carry extended types of insurance coverage. Authorization forms will be filled out by personnel at the rental agency; the executive must sign the forms.

The car will have a full tank of gas when it is rented. It is usually a good idea to fill the car with gas before returning it because the rental agency will charge for gas (generally at a higher price than can be obtained at a local gas station) if the tank is not full when returned. The executive usually carries a company credit card; this card can be used for the purchase of gas and for the car rental agency. Special credit cards are also issued by the major car rental agencies. Some companies prefer to deal with only one car rental agency, and they will provide the executives with a credit card from this agency. Most car rental agencies will provide maps of the area and assist in planning the best route to the destination. They also will supply information about hotels, restaurants, and tourist attractions in the area.

CAR TRAVEL

If traveling only a few hundred miles, the executive may prefer to travel by car. Most top level-executives have cars furnished by the company, with gasoline expenses paid by the company. Other executives are generally reimbursed on a per mile basis for any job-related travel. Your responsibilities for a trip by car may include determining the best route to follow, making hotel reservations, and identifying restaurants along the way. Computer programs are available to help you with these responsibilities, or you may obtain information through the American Automobile Association (AAA®). The executive must be an AAA member; however, membership is extremely inexpensive. The telephone number of your local AAA is listed in your telephone directory. The office will provide maps that show recommended routes to the location and the location of restaurants and motels along the route.

RAIL TRAVEL

Rail travel is also an option for the executive if the trip is a fairly short distance. Certainly, travel by train is more time consuming than by air; but it has the advantage over car travel of allowing the executive the freedom to work during the trip. The executive may use a laptop computer, just as can be done on a plane. Train stations are most often centrally located within a city, and their fares are usually less expensive than airfares. First-class and sleeping accommodations are available on trains, with coach accommodations for more economical travel. Dining cars are also available; meals are delivered in first-class accommodations. To find out about train travel in your area, look under "Railroads" in the yellow pages or call Amtrak®.

OFFICE SERVICES

The executive may need office services while away. These services are available at most hotels in large cities. The services include access to computers, printers, office supplies, fax equipment, and even secretarial assistance. When services are not available at the hotel, most concierges can find assistance for the traveler. Some car rental agencies also provide office services.

INTERNATIONAL TRAVEL

As you learned earlier, many businesses now have interests in other countries; these interests may be subsidiaries of the firm, separate firms, or partnerships with firms in other countries. Whatever the interests may be, travel abroad is becoming quite common for executives in many companies.

CULTURAL DIFFERENCES

Travelers need to be knowledgeable and sensitive to the customs and culture of the countries they are visiting. Information about other countries may be obtained from a variety of sources.

- Consulates of the country to be visited usually have printed materials available, and they are also willing to answer questions about the customs and culture. (Look in the Yellow Pages under "Consulates" for listings.)

- Travel books which are available at libraries or bookstores generally have information about customs and business practices.

- Books specifically about doing business with the particular country that will be visited are also available at libraries and bookstores.

- The company may provide seminars or local colleges and universities often provide short courses on doing business with particular countries.

You may also want to refer back to Chapter 5 where cultural differences were discussed.

Here are some general rules that apply to international travel.

- Learn the appropriate greeting for the country you will be visiting.

- Learn how to say "please" and "thank you" in the language of the country.

- Have your business cards printed with both your name and the company name in English and in the language of the country you are visiting.

- Never criticize the people or the customs of the country. Show appreciation for the music, art, and culture of the country.

- Remember that business is generally more formal in other countries than in the United States.

- Dress appropriately, which generally means business suits for men and conservative dresses or suits for women. Dress in some United States companies is more casual than ever before. However, when traveling internationally, casual

COMMUNICATION TIP

When your supervisor brings back business cards from an international trip, file the cards according to the name of the trip. For example, if the trip is to Japan, set up a card file with the first card following the Japan tab having the date of the trip and the places visited. Place the business cards behind this card.[1]

---

[1]Rhodes, Karen, "Arrange Business Cards by Encounter," *From Nine to Five* (July 22, 1996).

business dress does not imply a professional image. It may be seen as sloppy dress or failure; casual dress is rarely accepted. In addition to dressing in conservative business suits or dresses, it is also important to be well groomed.

- Eat the food that is offered you; do not ask what you are being served; show appreciation to your host.

- Be courteous and respectful at all times.

APPOINTMENTS

If you are involved in setting up appointments or meetings for the executive, remember the time zone differences. **Jet lag** (a term used for the feeling of exhaustion after a trip abroad) can greatly restrict an executive's effectiveness. Because it takes the body about a day for each time zone crossed to adapt to the new environment, it is a good idea to give the executive an extra day before meetings begin to recover from the trip.

If the executive does not have the luxury of a full day before scheduling appointments, there are some techniques that will generally help with jet lag. For example, if you are traveling west, postpone the time you usually go to bed by two or three hours for two days before your flight. If you are traveling east, try to retire a couple of hours earlier than usual. At the same time, you can also start shifting your meal times in the direction of those of your destination city. Your body clock will not be fully adapted to the new time cycle when you land, but you will have made a start in the right direction. Also, it is best not to schedule appointments the day the executive returns from the trip due to the necessity of contending with the time zone changes upon returning to the United States.

BUSINESS GIFTS

Generally it is appropriate to take a gift, particularly if it is your first time to meet the officials from the business you are visiting. The gift should be small—a nice pen or some memento that is representative of the United States. However, be aware of customs and taboos when giving gifts as it is easy to offend without knowing it.

INTERNATIONAL AIR TRAVEL

International air travel is basically the same as domestic air travel. Classes of flight are first class and coach, with business class available on some international flights. Weight and size restrictions for luggage may vary slightly from one airline to another. When traveling abroad, it is essential that you arrive at the airport earlier than normal; most airlines suggest that you arrive at least an hour before the flight. This gives you time to check in, which is more involved than in traveling within the United States.

PASSPORTS

A **passport** is an official government document that certifies the identity and citizenship of an individual and grants the person permission to travel abroad. A passport is required in most countries outside the United States. Check with your local travel agent to determine if the country being visited requires a passport; for example, Canada and Mexico do not require a passport, and there are a few other limited exceptions. Even if a country does not require a passport, it is a good idea to have one as proof of citizenship is required.

A passport certifies the identity and citizenship of an individual and is necessary for almost all international travel. © 1996, PhotoDisc Inc.

Passport application forms can be obtained from a travel agency, a passport office, or the post office. You can find your local passport office telephone number by looking under "United States Government, Passport Information" in the blue pages (if you live in a large city that has blue pages in the directory) or in the yellow pages under "Passports." To obtain a passport for the first time, you must appear in person before an agent of the passport office and present the following items.

- a completed application

- proof of U.S. citizenship through a certified copy of a birth certificate, baptismal certificate, or certificate of naturalization (If such proof is not available, the applicant must submit both a notice that no birth record exists and secondary evidence such as census records, family Bibles, school records, or affidavits of persons with personal knowledge of the applicant's birth.)

- proof of identification through such documents as a driver's license

- two signed duplicate photographs taken by a photographer within the past six months

- passport fee

A passport is valid for ten years from the date of issue. As soon as the passport is received, it should be signed. It is not valid until it is signed. Also, the information in the front pages should be filled out, which includes the address of the bearer and names to be contacted in case of an emergency. While traveling abroad, the passport should always be carried by the traveler; it should never be left in a hotel room.

VISAS

A **visa** is a document granted by a government abroad which permits a traveler to enter and travel within a particular country. A visa usually appears as a stamped notation on a passport indicating that the bearer may enter the country for a certain period of time.

CURRENCY

Money can be exchanged from certain banks and currency exchange offices for the currency of the country being visited before leaving the United States. The rate of exchange for various countries is published in the newspaper. The executive may exchange only a small amount of money in the United States and exchange additional money when arriving at the country of destination. If the foreign currency has not been used by the end of the trip, it may be exchanged for U.S. currency. It is always a good idea to be aware of the exchange rates before going to the country and to pay attention to the exchange rates once in the country. Exchange rates may not be the same; for example, the exchange rate at a bank may be more favorable to you than the exchange rate at the airport.

HEALTH PRECAUTIONS

Before leaving for a country abroad, it is smart to check with a physician concerning any medications or vaccinations needed. The environmental factors are usually different from those experienced in the United States; and it is easy to develop some type of illness as a result of food, water, or the particular climate of the country. A physician may prescribe medications that can be taken to relieve stomach-related illnesses or colds. Also, when traveling to certain countries, it may be necessary to get vaccinations before leaving the United States.

Travel agencies also have information as to possible health precautions. In some countries, it is important that you not drink the water unless it has been boiled or purified in some manner. Another health precaution may be not eating any type of raw fruit or vegetable unless it has been peeled.

LOCAL TRANSPORTATION ARRANGEMENTS

Local arrangements within the country may include hotel, car, and rail accommodations. The hotel arrangements generally are made before arrival in the country; however, car and rail arrangements may be made after arriving.

Hotel Reservations

Hotel reservations can be made through a travel agent or through an airline at no additional cost. Hotel reservations may also be made over the Internet. A continental breakfast is often included in the hotel charge. If secretarial assistance or meeting rooms are needed at a hotel, a travel agent can arrange for these services, or they can be made directly to the hotel. Direct arrangements may be difficult, however, particularly when there is a language difference. When making hotel reservations, it is important to let the hotel reservations clerk know if the executive will arrive late. You simply ask the hotel to guarantee the room for late arrival; this procedure ensures that the hotel room is not released to someone else if the executive is arriving late in the evening.

Many hotels offer varying degrees of assistance for the business traveler.

Car Rental

Cars are readily available for rent; a travel agency can arrange the rental for the traveler, or it may be done once the executive arrives in the country. In most countries, a U.S. driver's license is sufficient. You may obtain an international driver's license from AAA. It is important that the traveler get appropriate insurance. It is also important that the traveler become familiar with the driving regulations of the country. Conditions are often quite different from those in the United States; for example, the steering wheel may be mounted on a different side of the car or the speed limits may differ.

Rail Transportation

Many countries have excellent rail service (particularly in Europe). Service is provided relatively inexpensively and frequently. A traveler can get from one city in Europe to another in a relatively short time with a limited amount of inconvenience. Underground rail transportation within cities such as London is also quite good and is an inexpensive way to travel. Bus transportation within large cities (again, particularly in Europe) is also generally good and inexpensive.

TRAVEL ARRANGEMENTS

How travel arrangements are made depends on the company where you work. Many companies have a travel agent that they use to schedule all travel for the company. This agency becomes knowledgeable about the needs of the company and can then provide the unique services they require.

Some companies have their own travel department. When the executive plans to travel, the office professional contacts the travel department, giving the personnel there the necessary information. Other companies, particularly small ones, ask that individuals make their own travel arrangements. Now, by using the Internet, you can find the least expensive flights available at any point in time and can also make hotel and car reservations. Whatever method the company uses, as an office professional you will have a role in making the arrangements.

Before the executive takes the first trip (whether that trip is by plane, car, or rail), have a talk with the person about travel preferences. If you are to be an effective agent, you must have the following information.

- dates and times of travel

- cities to be visited

- hotel preferences—price range, number of nights, single or double room, size of bed (full, queen, king), smoking or nonsmoking room

- car rental—type of car, size, make, model; number of days of usage; pickup and drop off locations

- reimbursement—How is the executive to be reimbursed for travel expenses? (Remind the executive to keep all receipts that are required.) Is there a set **per diem** (per day) for meals or total travel expenses? Is a travel advance needed? If so, how much? Is it necessary to have the travel approved before the executive leaves on the trip? If so, who approves the travel?

- arrangements for transportation to airport or train station—Will the executive drive? Take a taxi or shuttle service?

- appointments—Are there appointments to be made? With whom? When? Where?

- materials—Are materials needed for the trip? If so, what and how many copies? Are any office supplies or equipment needed such as disks and a laptop computer? Are additional business cards needed?

- person in charge—Who will be in charge while the executive is away?

- correspondence—How will correspondence be handled while the executive is away?

- phone calls—How are phone calls to be handled in the executive's absence?

- executive's credit card number or company account number for charging tickets, hotel, car rental, and so forth

If the executive is traveling by air, you need to have the following additional information.

- preferred airlines (if the executive has a preference), with **frequent flyer** number (A frequent flyer program is an incentive program offered by most airlines that provides a variety of awards. Awards may include upgrading from coach to first class and free airline tickets after the accumulation of a certain number of mileage points.)

- type of flight—Is the flight to be direct (if possible) or is the employer willing to change planes? (In many instances, particularly if you live in a large city, direct flights from one location to another are possible. If the employer is concerned with saving money, less expensive flights are sometimes available if the executive is willing to change planes. The downside of changing planes is the hassle of getting from one flight to another and the increase in the travel time due to going an indirect route to the location.)

- class of flight—first class, business class, or coach

- preference as to aisle or window seat

- food preferences (low calorie meals, low cholesterol meals, salt-free meals, and other special needs are available upon request)

- ticket delivery—Are tickets to be sent to the business? Picked up at the airport? Mailed? Sent by courier?

- time line for arriving at airport—thirty minutes before the flight departs is standard arrival time for domestic flights and one hour is standard for international flights

If the executive is traveling by rail, you will also need to know the following:

- type of accommodations—coach or first class

- sleeping accommodations—If traveling on the train for more than one day, does the executive want sleeping accommodations?

- ticket delivery—How will tickets be obtained? Are they to be picked up at the train station, mailed, or delivered?

It is a good idea to set up a folder when the executive first tells you about the plans for a trip. You can then place all notes and information relating to the trip in the folder. It is available for instant referral when needed.

TRAVEL AGENCIES

Travel agencies will perform complete travel services for the company; that is, schedule the flight, obtain tickets, make hotel reservations, arrange car rental, and perform specialized services which the executive may need such as obtaining work space or meeting space at the destination. The agency will see that airline tickets are delivered to your business. Their service also includes providing an **itinerary** which gives flight numbers, arrival and departure times of flights, hotel reservations, and car rental. Figure 11-1 shows an itinerary prepared

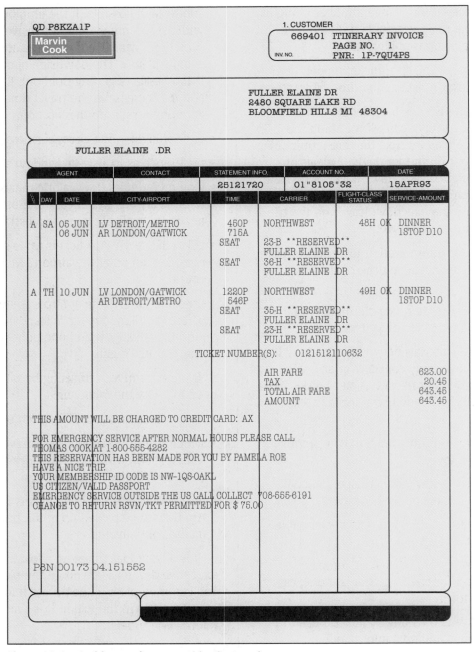

Figure 11-1 An itinerary is prepared by the travel agency.

by a travel agency. Also, travel agencies (through the use of computer software) can give you a list of all airlines leaving at the approximate time the executive wishes to travel and provide an analysis of the lowest fare. Figure 11-2 illustrates the type of information that can be provided. The travel agency usually will bill the company directly for the tickets and other arrangements. Travel agencies do not charge the business for their service. They receive

commissions from airlines, hotels, and other service industries when services are sold.

It is a good idea to ask the travel agency to determine the least expensive flight available. Companies are cost conscious; they want to keep travel costs as low as possible. Because airlines are so competitive today, there may be reduced fares available on a particular airline. If this airline is not one that the executive normally uses, ask about an

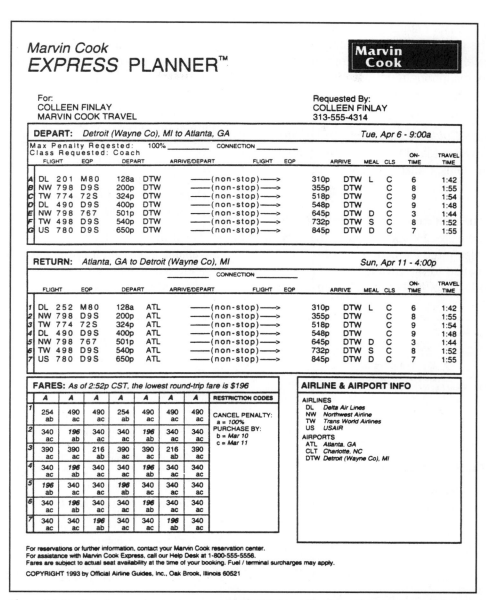

Figure 11-2 Travel agencies have access to flight information through computer software.

interest in getting a lower fare rate. There may also be reduced rates if the executive travels over a weekend; however, the reduced rate has to be considered in light of any additional hotel rooms and meals which may be added due to a longer stay. The reduced fare, considering other costs, may not prove to be cost effective.

ARRANGEMENTS BY THE OFFICE PROFESSIONAL

If the executive does not wish to work with a travel agency, you have the responsibility of calling the airlines, hotels, and car rental agencies directly; or, you may choose to use the Internet to determine the best fares available. (More information will be given about the Internet in the next section.) It is a good idea to use comparison shopping when making these arrangements; you will want to call several airlines, hotels, and car rental agencies to get the best quotes on prices and services available.

Several sources are available to you if you are making the arrangements yourself, including

- *Official Airline Guide* published by Official Airline Guides, Inc. (a hard copy and an electronic copy are available)—The guide provides information on fares, schedules, aircraft, and other services.

- *OAG Business Travel Planner for North America*—The guide provides information on hotel and motel listings, such as ratings, prices, number of rooms, phone numbers, and amenities such as health clubs, fax service, meeting rooms, and so forth.

- *Official Railway Guide, North American Edition*—This guide provides schedules of all railway lines in the United States, Canada, and Mexico.

E-TICKETS

Tickets may be sent from the airlines by e-mail. These tickets are called *E-Tickets*. The actual tickets are held in an electronic file by the airlines. Boarding passes are issued to the traveler upon arrival at the airport. An E-Ticket is shown in Figure 11-3.

RESERVATIONS THROUGH THE INTERNET

More people today are using the Internet to make airline reservations, book hotels, and reserve rental cars. Airlines, hotels, and travel agents are providing online services to computer-knowledgeable individuals who wish to handle the arrangements themselves. For travel companies, the Internet has become a profitable source of clients. According to an article in *Fortune,* AMR™ Corporation sold 1.6 million tickets online in 1995.[2]

Here are some of the advantages of making travel arrangements on the Internet.

- Virtual travel agents are convenient as they are available at any hour of the day or night and on weekends; credit cards are taken by e-mail; tickets are sent by overnight mail at no extra charge.

NORTHWEST E-TICKET™

38905 West Six Mile Road • Livonia, MI 48152

Customer Itinerary and Receipt

| Flight Confirmation Number: | Z7MHWQ |
| Original Booking Date: | 12FEB97 |

Thank you for choosing Northwest's **E-TICKET**. This is your travel itinerary and receipt. Your actual tickets are held in an electronic file in our Reservation system. Boarding passes for your flight will be issued when you check-in. For your protection, picture identification or the credit card used as payment will be required at check-in.

If you are unable to use your **E-TICKET** or if your travel plans change, please call Northwest at 1-800-555-2525. For automated flight arrival and departure information please call 1-800-555-1818.

RICHARD CALKINS
2519 RIVEREDGE DR SE
GRAND RAPIDS MI 49546-7450

NAME(S):	TICKET NUMBER	WORLDPERKS ACCT.	SPECIAL SERVICES
RICHARD MR CALKINS	0122125404656	058328631	
PATSY MRS CALKINS	0122125404658		

ITINERARY:

DAY	DATE	FLIGHT NUMBER		DEPART FROM		DEPART TIME	ARRIVE AT		ARRIVAL TIME	MEAL SVC	SEAT		EQP
Thu	13MAR	0625	Q	GRAND RAPIDS	GRR	440P	DETROIT	DTW	530P				727
Thu	13MAR	0861	Q	DETROIT	DTW	640P	MEMPHIS	MEM	740P	Snack	20C,	21C	727
Thu	13MAR	1421	Q	MEMPHIS	MEM	805P	LITTLE ROCK	LIT	850P		19B,	19C	727
Mon	17MAR	0202	Q	LITTLE ROCK	LIT	715A	MEMPHIS	MEM	755A		11D,	11E	727
Mon	17MAR	0290	Q	MEMPHIS	MEM	845A	DETROIT	DTW	1135A	Snack			75R
Mon	17MAR	1202	Q	DETROIT	DTW	1205P	GRAND RAPIDS	GRR	1254P		20D,	20E	D95

Please present this document for curbside check-in. Photo identification or the credit card used as payment will be required for check-in. Please be at the departure gate at least 15 minutes before scheduled departure.

Figure 11-3   E-Ticket.

---

[2]Gunther, Marc, "Travel Planning in Cyberspace," *Fortune* (September, 1996), 187–188.

- The fare beater feature seeks out the lowest fares.

- Some of the websites offer pictures and videos of the site.

- Special price breaks are offered through some airlines by alerting individuals (who have signed up for a special service) to seats available that would otherwise be empty.

Presently, making travel arrangements on the Internet also has some disadvantages, namely there is no one-stop travel service. You have to check at a number of different websites, which can be time consuming and frustrating. It is anticipated that services will improve greatly in the near future. In fact, with the rate of change that is occurring on the Internet, by the time you are reading this material, such a one-stop shop will probably be available.

Here are some Internet addresses that will help you in locating travel services.

- **Travelocity™—website: http://www.travelocity.com—offers airline tickets**

- **PCTravel™—website: http://www.pctravel.com—offers airlines tickets**

- **Internet Travel Network—website: http://www.itn.net—offers plane, hotel, and car bookings**

- **Flifo℠—website: http://www.flifo.com—offers airline tickets**

- **American Airlines™—website: http://www.americanair.com—offers tickets and frequent flyer information**

- **Northwest Airlines®—website: http://www.nwa.com—offers tickets**

- **Travelweb℠—website: http://www.travelweb.com—offers airline tickets and hotel bookings**

- **Global Network Navigator—Using a Web browser, search for Global Network Navigator. You will find numerous hypertext travel essays which provide links to other websites for global travel information.**

- **Travel Weekly On Line—website: http://www.traveler.net/two/—offers information on travel-related topics such as tours, cruises, world sites, hotels, air travel, railroads, and services.**

This website also offers a system called Map Quest which allows you to create a custom map for the executive's appointments while on the trip.

- **USA Today® Weather—Using a Web browser, search for USA Today Weather. You will find several websites which provide weather information on U.S. cities as well as many international locations. Five-day forecasts are listed, with visuals. You may print out the forecast and include a copy for the executive.**

RESPONSIBILITIES BEFORE THE TRIP

In addition to the duties already mentioned that you have in assisting the executive with travel arrangements, other responsibilities include

- preparing a complete itinerary

- obtaining travel funds

- preparing materials for the trip

- checking the calendar

- understanding how matters are to be handled while the executive is away

- confirming appointments

PREPARE THE ITINERARY

Once you have determined where and when the executive wants to travel and after you have made the appropriate travel arrangements, you need to prepare an itinerary. The itinerary, a detailed outline of the trip, is a record of all trip arrangements for you and the executive. An itinerary should include information on flight numbers, airports, departure and arrival times, hotel arrangements, car rental information, appointments, and any other pertinent information. You have already learned that a travel agency will provide an itinerary that includes flight, hotel, and car information. They do not have the information on appointments and other special information. The executive needs to have an itinerary that will be reflective of all activities on the trip.

You will want to prepare multiple copies of the itinerary, specifically for

- the executive;

- the executive's family;

- the person who will be in charge while the executive is away;

- your files.

Figure 11-4 shows an itinerary. The time zones are given on the itinerary because the executive is traveling from one time zone to another. Of course, if the executive is not changing time zones, it is not necessary to list them.

OBTAIN TRAVEL FUNDS

The travel policies of companies differ in relation to how funds for trips are handled. Usually, the airline tickets are charged directly to the company. Hotel, meals, and car rental may be charged on a credit card provided by the company and for which the company is billed directly. Another practice is for the individual to get a cash advance to cover all expenses of the trip. To do so, the individual fills out a travel form before going on the trip, indicating how much money will be needed for the hotel,

meals, and so forth. This money is then obtained before the trip is taken. Still another practice is for the executive to pay the expenses with personal money or credit card and be reimbursed by the company upon returning from the trip. Most company policies require receipts to be turned in for expenses above a small amount.

If traveling abroad, the executive may take traveler's checks. Traveler's checks may be purchased from most local banks and travel agencies. However, because credit cards are readily acceptable in almost all international locations, it may be easier to use a credit card. The executive may want to take a limited amount of money in traveler's checks. They come with two receipts that serve as records of the check's serial numbers. One copy of the receipt should be kept in the files at the office and the other copy should be given to the executive. If checks are lost, the individual may be reimbursed by producing the receipt. The receipts should be kept separately from the checks.

Itinerary for Paul Forrest

March 5-6, ——

Trip to San Francisco

Monday, March 5 (Dallas to San Francisco)

CST Leave Dallas—DFW Regional Airport, American Flight 55; tickets are in briefcase.	9:30 a.m.
PST Arrive San Francisco—San Francisco International Airport; arrangements have been made for car at Hertz; hotel reservations are at the Airport Hilton, telephone: 555-3100.	10:30 a.m.
PST Appointment with Peter Nelson of Nelson & Nelson in his office, 1214 Harwood Avenue, telephone: 555-5418; correspondence file in briefcase.	2:00 p.m.

Tuesday, March 6 (San Francisco to Dallas)

PST Appointment with Roger Hall of San Francisco office;reports in briefcase.	10:00 a.m.
PST Appointment with Carla Hampton of San Francisco office; reports in briefcase.	2:00 p.m.
PST Leave San Francisco International Airport on American Flight 43.	5:00 p.m.
CST Arrive Dallas—DFW Regional Airport.	10:00 p.m.

Figure 11-4   A detailed itinerary is prepared by the office professional.

PREPARE AND ORGANIZE MATERIALS

Any number of items may be needed for the trip. If it is an international trip, items such as passports, medications, business cards, and small gifts to present to company executives abroad may be necessary. Whether the trip is domestic or international, usually several items must be prepared, such as reports for meetings and presentation materials.

Here is a list of items that may be included in the briefcase.

- plane tickets

- itinerary

- credit cards, traveler's checks

- hotel confirmation

- special materials for appointments

- presentation notes

- office equipment and supplies (laptop and disks)

- reading materials

- business cards

- passport (for international trips)

The executive may also want to take a laptop computer. If so, make sure that files and programs needed are loaded on the computer. As you have already learned, the executive may wish to use the laptop on the plane. During take off and landing, the attendants may ask that computers not be used as there is a possibility of the computer interfering with instrument landing (if it becomes necessary).

CHECK THE CALENDAR

Check your employer's electronic and desk calendars and your calendars to see if any appointments have been scheduled for the period in which the executive will be gone. If so, find out if they are to be canceled or if someone else in the company will handle them. Then notify the people involved. Also check other files such as tickler files or pending files to see if there are matters that should be handled before the executive leaves.

The office professional must check the executive's calendar before scheduling a trip to be certain that all appointments previously scheduled can be rescheduled or canceled.
Photo by Mimi Ostendorf/Photonics Graphics.

KNOW HOW MATTERS ARE TO BE HANDLED

Find out who will be in charge during your employer's absence. Check to see if your employer is expecting any important papers that should be forwarded. Be sure you understand how to handle the incoming mail; for example, your employer may want you to refer all mail that must be answered immediately to another executive within the office. Or, your employer may ask that you answer the routine mail (signing the employer's name with your initials) and refer the nonroutine mail to the designated executive.

COMMUNICATION TIP

Prepare a folder to be placed in the executive's briefcase for the special materials that are to be taken on a trip; label the folder appropriately. Be certain that you make the necessary copies of all information needed.

Chapter 11: Making Travel Arrangements

CONFIRM APPOINTMENTS FOR THE TRIP

Write or call persons whom the executive plans to see during the trip to confirm the appointments. It is wise to do this before preparing the itinerary. Get correct addresses and directions from the hotel to the location of all meetings. Make a note of these addresses and directions on the itinerary.

RESPONSIBILITIES WHILE THE EXECUTIVE IS AWAY

You may be tempted to tell yourself that you have worked hard in getting the executive ready for the trip, packed, and off, so you deserve a little time off. Such is not the case. It may be a more relaxed pace for you while the executive is away, but there are certain responsibilities that you have. Here are a few of them.

MESSAGES

Executives often call in on a daily basis while they are on trips. If possible, it is a good idea to determine the time of day the executive may be calling so that you can have all messages and items of importance ready to discuss. Always keep messages and correspondence that are urgent in a certain place on your desk so that you may refer to them quickly.

CORRESPONDENCE

It is important that correspondence be kept up-to-date. You may be responsible for seeing that all mail is given to the person in charge; you may also be required to assist the person in answering the mail. You may have the responsibility for answering routine correspondence. If so, keep a copy of the correspondence, along with your answer, for your employer to review upon return. So that your employer will be apprised of the visitors and telephone callers, you may wish to keep a log. Figure 11-5 shows such a log.

DECISIONS

You have the responsibility of making wise decisions within the scope of your responsibility during the executive's absence. You should know which matters to refer to someone else in the company and which matters to refer directly to the executive through a telephone call or fax. Certainly, you do not want to place an excessive number of calls to the traveling executive, but there may be matters that the executive must be informed of immediately.

APPOINTMENTS

You will probably need to set up appointments for persons who want to see the executive upon return from the trip. Remember, when you are setting up the appointments, the executive will

---

COMMUNICATION TIP

While the executive is away, keep the person who is in charge apprised of all happenings. Just as you do not want your employer surprised, you also do not want the person in charge during your employer's absence to be surprised.

| | VISITORS AND TELEPHONE CALLS | | | |
| | February 5-6, —— | | | |
Date/Time	Visitor	Telephone	Reason for Call	Action
February 5	Reese Vaughn		Crime in community	He set up an appointment 9 a.m., Feb. 10
February 5	Kathleen Steel	555-5118	Civic Theatre	Will call Feb. 8
February 6	Clara Campbell Consolidated Investments		Investments	Set up appt. 10 a.m., Feb.11

Figure 11-5 A telephone and visitors' log.

probably already have a full day of work in the office to handle on the first day back. Thus, it is not a good idea to schedule appointments for that day. If you must do so, however, remember to schedule as few appointments as possible and keep the timing convenient for the executive.

PLANS AND ORGANIZATION

The slower work pace that generally occurs while the executive is traveling gives you the time to plan and organize your work. Perhaps you have needed to organize your desk, clean out the files, prepare new labels for folders, plan your work for the next two weeks, or catch up on your professional reading. While the executive is gone, you have the opportunity to do so. It is important that you use the time wisely; planning and organizing is definitely a wise use of your time.

RESPONSIBILITIES WHEN THE EXECUTIVE RETURNS

When the executive returns, a number of tasks must be handled. Correspondence must be sent, expense reports must be prepared, and telephone calls must be returned. You will also need to bring the executive up-to-date on what happened during the absence.

CORRESPONDENCE

The executive will probably need to write several follow-up letters as a result of the trip. Thank you letters are often sent. As a result of the contacts made, information on products or services may be sent to customers. The executive may give you a short explanation of what needs to be said and ask that you write or draft the correspondence. The executive

COMMUNICATION TIP

Answer all correspondence and handle all visitors and telephone callers in a timely manner.

KORONET INTERNATIONAL

REIMBURSEMENT REQUEST

REQUEST NUMBER 3337

Soc. Sec. No. _____

Name _____

Date _____

AMOUNT TO BE PAID

Conference ☐
Miscellaneous Expense ☐
Professional Activities ☐
11-000-3822-0000-0 Advance ☐

ADVANCEMENT (IF ANY)_____
TYPE OF LEAVE_____

Date	Itemization of Expenses	Names and/or Business Relat.	Amount	Account Number

I certify that this is a true report of my expenses.   **ATTACH ALL RECEIPTS**

Employee Signature _____ Date _____

I approve of the reimbursement of these expenditures

Supervisor's Signature _____ Date _____

Financial Services Approval _____ Date _____

YELLOW-Financial Services   WHITE-Accounts Payable   PINK-Employee

Figure 11-6   Expense Report form.

may also need to answer certain correspondence that has accumulated during the absence.

EXPENSE REPORTS

Regardless of whether the executive received funds in advance from the company or used personal funds and is due reimbursement, careful records must be kept of all expenses. Most companies require receipts for hotels, registration fees, car rental, plane tickets, and other major expenses. The traveler's word is usually taken for meals, taxi fares, and tips.

Expense forms are provided by the company and should be filled in correctly with the amounts totaled. An example of an expense report is shown in Figure 11-6. You should complete the expense report carefully, double-checking all figures and totals. You should also be sure that the necessary receipts are attached and that the figures on the expense report match the figures on the receipts.

FEEDBACK MEETING

It is a good idea to have a feedback meeting after the trip with the executive. At this time, you can provide the necessary information as to what happened at the office during the time away. You can also go over with the executive the appointments set up, telephone calls and correspondence received, and other items which should be called to the executive's attention.

CHAPTER SUMMARY

This summary will help you remember the important points covered in this chapter.

- The three classes of flight are first class, business class, and coach.

- First-class accommodations are the most expensive and the most luxurious, offering wider seats, more leg room, better food, better service, and no charge for alcoholic beverages.

- Business-class accommodations are slightly more expensive than coach and offer more spacious seating, complimentary alcoholic beverages, headset, recliner seats, and more leg room.

- Coach-class accommodations provide snacks, soft drinks, fruit juice, tea or coffee, and meals at no additional charge. Seats are closer together and less service is provided. Coach class is the least expensive class.

- In addition to flying, the executive may go by car or rail. The AAA can provide information for car travel and the appropriate railroad can provide information about rail travel.

- When traveling internationally, the executive needs to be sensitive to different customs and cultures. The executive should take business cards printed with the name of the individual and the company printed both in English and in the language of the country being visited.

- Jet lag can be a factor in international travel; it should be considered when setting up appointments.

- Small business gifts are appropriate for individuals when traveling abroad.

- A passport is necessary when traveling to countries other than Canada or Mexico.

- Before leaving for a country abroad, it is smart to check with a physician concerning any health problems that may occur due to the food, water, or climate of the country.

- Rail and bus transportation is generally quite satisfactory in Europe.

- In helping the executive to schedule travel, the office professional must know the dates and times of travel, the cities to be visited, hotel preferences, car rental preferences, appointments to be scheduled, materials needed, and so forth.

- If the executive is traveling by air, the office professional must know the preferred airlines, the class of flight, preferences as to aisle or window seat, meal preferences, and so forth.

- Arrangements for travel can be made through travel agencies or by the office professional through calling the airlines, hotel, and car rental agency directly or by making the reservations on the Internet.

- The office professional has several responsibilities before the trip, including getting the tickets, preparing an itinerary, obtaining travel funds, preparing materials for the trip, checking the calendar, understanding how matters are to be handled while the executive is away, and confirming appointments.

- While the executive is away, the office professional should handle correspondence, appointments, and messages; and plan and organize work if there are slack times.

- When the executive returns, the office professional must help with the correspondence, prepare the expense report, and make the executive aware of what has happened during the absence.

CHAPTER GLOSSARY

The following terms were introduced in this chapter. To help you review, definitions are given here.

- **First-class accommodations** (p. 245)–Refer to the classes of flight on an airlines; they are the most expensive of the three classes and the most luxurious.

- **Business-class accommodations** (p. 245)–Slightly more expensive than coach and less expensive than first class; business class is located in front of the coach class or directly behind first class.

- **Coach-class accommodations** (p. 245)–The least expensive of the three classes of flight; the seats are closer together, there is less leg room, and the service is not as good as in first class or business class.

- **Jet lag** (p. 248)–A term used for the feeling of exhaustion after a trip abroad.

- **Passport** (p. 248)–An official government document that certifies the identity and citizenship of an individual and grants the person permission to travel abroad.

- **Visa** (p. 249)–A document granted by a government abroad which permits a traveler to enter and travel within a particular country.

- **Per diem** (p. 251)–Literally means "per day"; it is used in conjunction with how much a company is willing to reimburse an individual for travel.

- **Frequent flyer** (p. 251)–An incentive program offered by most airlines that provides a variety of awards. Awards may include upgrading from coach to first class and free airline tickets after the accumulation of a certain number of mileage points.

- **Itinerary** (p. 251)–A detailed outline of the trip showing all trip arrangements, including flight numbers, airports, departure and arrival times, hotel arrangements, car rental information, appointments, and so forth.

DISCUSSION ITEMS

These discussion items provide an opportunity for you to test your understanding of the chapter through discussion with your classmates and your instructor.

1. List and explain the three main classes of domestic flights.

2. When traveling internationally, list eight general rules that apply.

3. What services does a travel agency provide?

4. What are some of the advantages of making travel arrangements over the Internet?

5. List four responsibilities of the office professional during trip preparation.

6. What responsibilities does the office assistant have when the executive returns?

CASE STUDY

Ms. Marquette recently took a trip to the North Carolina office. You were responsible for making the travel arrangements. You used a travel agency in making the arrangements. However, Koronet has not been happy with the travel agency they have been using. Ms. Marquette asked you to try another travel agency for this trip. You had not used the travel agency in the past. You gave the travel agency information on the flight times, car rental and hotel accommodations. You prepared all the materials necessary for the trip; everything seemed to be in order.

Ms. Marquette's flight left at 8 a.m. You had a doctor's appointment on the day of her travel and did not get into the office until noon. You failed to mention to Ms. Marquette that you would not be in the office; however, you did make arrangements for the office to be covered. When you arrived at the office, the employee who was covering for you told you that Ms. Marquette had called in to get car rental information. The car rental agency had no reservations for her. The employee told Ms.

Marquette that she did not know anything about the reservations and that you were not in. She told you that Ms. Marquette seemed a little upset when she called. One day later, Ms. Marquette called the office to ask about the calls while she had been gone. You were at lunch; once again the employee who answered the phone could not help her. When you returned from lunch, you tried to call Ms. Marquette to give her the information but she was not available. You did not leave a message at the hotel.

When Ms. Marquette returned from the trip, she told you that she was not pleased with what happened. She was nice about it, but you could tell that she was upset. Answer these questions about the situation.

- How can you avoid the same occurrences on a future trip?

- What should you tell Ms. Marquette?

- What were the errors you made in the situation?

RESPONSES TO SELF CHECK

1. Contributions to the increase in international travel include the global economy, countries taking advantage of land, labor, and technical expertise available in all parts of the world, international markets, and technology.

2. You may find information concerning customs and cultures of other countries through consulates of the country to be visited, travel books, books about the particular country, and seminars and short courses offered at local colleges.

3. Six general rules that apply to international travel are to be listed (any six of the eight may be listed).

   - Learn the appropriate greeting for the country you will be visiting.

   - Learn how to say "please" and "thank you" in the language of the country.

   - Have your business cards printed with both your name and the company name in English and in the language of the country you are visiting.

   - Never criticize the people or the customs of the country. Show appreciation for the music, art, and culture of the country.

   - Remember that business is generally more formal in other countries than it is in the United States.

   - Dress appropriately, which generally means business suits for men and conservative dresses or suits for women. Always be well groomed.

   - Eat the food that is offered you; do not ask what you are being served; show appreciation to your host.

   - Be courteous and respectful at all times.

4. Because it generally takes the body about a day for each time zone crossed to adapt to the new environment, it is a good idea to give the executive an extra day before meetings begin to recover from the trip.

5. Business cards should be given to all representatives of companies; the cards should be printed in English and in the language of the country being visited.

OFFICE TASKS

OFFICE TASK 11-1 (Objectives 1 and 2)
Choose a team of two other people to work with on this project. Ms. Marquette is traveling to Koronet's office in Seoul, Korea, on November 11 through November 16. This is Ms. Marquette's first visit to this office. She asks that you help her with researching the customs and culture before the trip. Check three resources on the customs and culture of Korea, specifically tied to the business culture. Then make flight arrangements and hotel arrangements. She will be picked up at the airport by Chikara Hayashi, Executive Vice President, Korea Office of Koronet; she will not need a car. She wants to leave in the morning on November 11; she wants to return sometime November 16, preferably in the morning. She will fly first class; she wants low calorie meals. She wants a hotel that has good accommodations, with a queen size bed, no smoking, and exercise facilities. Ms. Marquette does not speak Korean. Her appointments while she is in Korea include the following:

November 13	9 a.m.	Akeo Matsumi
	2 p.m.	Danjiro Umezaki
November 15	10 a.m.	Jun Kato
	1 p.m.	Kazumori Soga

Make travel arrangements by using the Internet if you have access. If you do not have access to the Internet, a travel schedule is listed on the Student Data Template Disk, file OT11-1; determine the most appropriate arrangements. Prepare a travel itinerary, listing the appointments. Note the number of hours on the itinerary for travel time; also note the time differences from Michigan to Japan. Turn in the itinerary to your instructor. Present the Korean custom and cultural differences which you found in an oral report to the class.

OFFICE TASK 11-2 (Objectives 3 and 4)
Answer the following questions about the travel assignment you received in Office Task 11-1.

1. What are your responsibilities in preparing Ms. Marquette for the trip to Korea?

2. What are your responsibilities while Ms. Marquette is away?

When Ms. Marquette returns, she gives you the following expenses. Prepare her expense report.

- Flight (first class)—$5,389 (This expense was billed to Koronet; however, it must be shown on the travel expense report. The amount will be listed and then deducted, with a notation that it was billed to the company.)

- Hotel for five nights at $195 per night

- Meals:
  $35 for November 12
  $70 for November 13
  $225 for November 14 (Ms. Marquette took two clients to dinner.)
  $75 for November 15

- Health Club
  $20 for November 12
  $40 for November 13
  $20 for November 14

- Taxi
  $25 for November 12
  $30 for November 13
  $35 for November 14

Prepare an expense report using the form given on the Student Data Template Disk, file OT11-2.

OFFICE TASK 11-3 (Objective 4)

Using the expenses from OT11-2, create a spreadsheet that can be used to record and calculate monthly travel expenses. After creating the spreadsheet, plug in the figures for the trip in OT11-2 and the following figures for previous trips. Turn in your spreadsheet to your instructor.

September 10–14 Texas Business Trip for Ms. Marquette

Flight:	$350
Hotel:	$615
Meals:	$325
Miscellaneous: Tips, taxi, etc.:	$ 55

October 16–19 North Carolina Business Trip

Flight:	$475
Hotel:	$486
Meals:	$160
Miscellaneous:	$ 35

ENGLISH USAGE CHALLENGE DRILL

Correct the following sentences. Cite the grammar rule that is applicable to each sentence. Before you begin, refresh your memory of grammar rules by reviewing semicolon and colon punctuation rules.

1. The First Wives' Club was both funny and poignant I laughed and cried in the movie.

2. When an item is worth having, there is generally a price to pay, and the price is often hard work and sacrifice.

3. If you want to lose weight, you need to give up three things eating fatty snacks, eating large portions of food at meal times, and being a couch potato.

4. I use this quotation from Theodore Roosevelt frequently when making speeches, "It is not the critic who counts, not the man who points out how the strong man stumbled, or where the doer of deeds could have done them better. The credit belongs to the man who is actually in the arena; whose face is marred by dust and sweat and blood; who strives valiantly; who errs and comes short again and again; who knows the great enthusiasms, the great devotions, and spends himself in a worthy cause; who, at best, knows in the end the triumph of high achievement; and who, at the worst, if he fails, at least fails while daring greatly, so that his place shall never be with those cold and timid souls who know neither victory nor defeat."

5. The students' demands included the following better food in the cafeteria, free parking, and less markup on textbooks in the bookstore.

ASSESSMENT OF CHAPTER OBJECTIVES

Now that you have completed the chapter and the office tasks, take a few moments to review the following learning objectives which you were given at the beginning of this chapter. Did you accomplish these objectives? If so, explain how in the space provided. If you were unable to accomplish these objectives, give your reason for not doing so. Your instructor may want to review your answers.

I accomplished these objectives:

1. Make travel arrangements. Yes _____ No _____
   Explain how you accomplished this objective.

   _____

   _____

   _____

2. Prepare itineraries. Yes _____ No _____

   Explain how you accomplished this objective.

   _____

   _____

   _____

3. Describe the duties to be performed when the executive is traveling and when the executive returns. Yes _____ No _____

   Explain how you accomplished this objective.

   _____

   _____

   _____

4. Prepare expense reports. Yes _____ No _____

   Explain how you accomplished this objective.

   _____

   _____

   _____

Provide reasons for failing to accomplish any of the objectives.

   _____

   _____

   _____

   _____

NARRESSA ROSS LEE'S CASE SOLUTION

Using our computer network, I typed my notes and entered his notes (highlighting his) directly under mine in areas where differences were evident. I provided him a hardcopy of the notes and also let him know that the minutes were on the network. I asked him to review any discrepancies between the two sets of notes and let me know where I should change the notes. I did not include items that I felt were not pertinent to the meeting; I told him that I had the complete comments if he felt certain items needed to be added.

NOTE: The computer network saves time and permits the director access to the document for changes. It also eliminates printing the document a multitude of times prior to making changes. You should always keep your notes so that you may check any discrepancies. In this situation, the director and I have a good working relationship which has been built over time. If you work for someone who is very autocratic or has not developed a level of trust in you, you would probably have to handle this situation differently. For example, you might prepare the minutes, using the director's notes only, and verbally note to the director that there are some differences between your notes and his notes. This approach leaves the door open for the director to ask for your input.

266

PART 5

Mail and Records Management

Linda Hardaker
Personal Assistant
Steelcase Australia
Sidney, Australia

A Success Profile

I attribute my success to being at the right place at the right time; and, at the same time, having my skills recognized. I inherited my mother's organizational philosophy—A place for everything and everything in its place. My organizational skills have definitely contributed to my success in the office professional field. In addition, a retentive memory helps, which I have and use daily.

I completed my formal educational training at the age of 16 after receiving excellent passes in both English and math. On a scale of 1 to 5, I received a 1 for English and a 2 for math. I started work in a bank and remained with them for two years. This was the grounding for other jobs I have held that have varied from manager of a jeans shop, to merchandising, and then back to a bank where I remained for five years as a branch manager. Each job provided me with a variety of skills that I now use in my current role as personal assistant to the managing director of our company.

What is the most enjoyable part of my job? That's tough to answer. There is not one thing that stands out as being fun; it is more the job as a whole and the satisfaction I get from helping people. Every day is different; and for me, that's what keeps me interested. I also believe that your job is what you make of it yourself, and I work with a terrific bunch of people who are totally focused on working as a team.

What is the most stressful part of my job? Unrealistic demands and unhappy customers. I am the only administrative person in our office, and there are times when everyone wants me to do something at the same time. I have to prioritize my work and be extremely organized. Also, it is stressful when I have to handle phone calls from customers who are waiting for one of our products and have been given unrealistic dates of when the product will be ready by our sales people. These telephone calls demand that I listen well to the customer and handle the situation tactfully.

What advice would I give someone just beginning in the office professional field? It is important to continue to learn. I am a firm believer of a hands-on approach to learning. I think you absorb knowledge much faster if you learn while doing. Also, it is important to develop a "customer service" orientation. The customers of a business are extremely important; without them, the business would fail. Employees need to understand this philosophy and treat all people as valued customers. Computer and keyboarding skills are very important, as is the ability to remember names and phone numbers. Learning can also take place through attending professional meetings and seminars. My company is a member of the American Chamber of Commerce, and I regularly attend the networking evenings with other secretaries and personal assistants. It's a great place for industry contacts, and you meet a lot of nice people as well.

I am an extremely athletic individual. I jog five kilometers every morning and attend aerobic classes regularly. I play netball and have recently joined a mixed touch football side (football without tackle). I live one hundred meters from the beach so I spend hours in the surf on a weekend or relaxing on the beach with a good book. I also enjoy snow skiing every winter. I am currently renovating a house that needs a lot of "tender loving care," and enjoy the challenges that it brings.

LINDA HARDAKER'S CASE

Here is a case I prepared from my varied experiences as a personal assistant. Decide how you would handle the case by answering the question at the end of the situation. Then turn to the end of Part 5 (page 325) to see how I solved the case.

turn to the end of Part 5 (page 325) to see how I solved the case.

THE SITUATION

You are in charge of booking travel for the entire company. All the executives have different preferences—from the airline they like to fly, to their seating preferences, to the food they eat. When they are away you receive numerous phone calls from other colleagues looking for them. Where are they? In what hotel are they staying? Do you have the phone and fax number of the hotel? How long will they be away? You spend half your day just answering their questions and giving out details, not to mention the time it takes to make the booking in the first place, with frequent flyer numbers and hotel memberships.

How can you maximize your time better?

CHAPTER 12

HANDLING THE OFFICE MAIL

LEARNING OBJECTIVES

1. **Identify classes of mail and determine which class should be used when preparing outgoing mail.**
2. **Identify and explain how special mail services are used.**
3. **Process both incoming and outgoing mail effectively.**
4. **Recognize the importance of recycling paper.**
5. **Cite mailroom trends.**

The information age in which we live is generating more mail than ever before. Americans mail over half a billion letters, parcels, and magazines every day. Mail volume has increased over 300 percent in the past two decades.[1] Technology allows us to produce all types of correspondence easily and quickly. Technology also allows us to access and maintain mailing lists which include the names of individuals worldwide. In other words, technology contributes to our increased use of mail, and this trend is expected to increase in the future.

The cost of handling mail is a significant expense to business. In fact, mail expenditures have grown to 9.2 percent of total operating expenses at the average **Fortune 500** *(the largest 500 companies in the United States).[2] If mail is not handled as expeditiously as possible, thousands and even millions of dollars can be lost by the company. In addition, the failure to address mail properly, to maintain up-to-date mailing lists, and to use the proper postage can result in both increased postal costs and increased delivery time.*

---

[1]Group I Software, "Address Accuracy Delivers Greater Benefits," *Managing Office Technology* (April, 1995), 34.
[2]Malik, Mary S, "The Hard Facts on Mailroom Software," *Managing Office Technology* (April, 1995), 31.

As an office professional, your mail duties usually include preparing the incoming mail for your employer to review and preparing the outgoing correspondence to be mailed. In addition to the traditional paper mail that you process, you will also be involved in processing electronic messages such as e-mail and fax mail. This chapter will help you to learn how to process mail effectively.

MAIL SERVICES

The main provider of mail services in this country is the United States Postal Service (USPS), which is a governmental entity. For many years, the USPS was almost the only provider. Today we have a number of private carriers who do a huge amount of business yearly. These private carriers include

- United Parcel Service (UPS) and Federal Express® (FedEx)—carrier companies that deliver mail all over the nation

- messenger or courier services that deliver mail within a city location

- Mail Boxes Etc.® and other similar companies—businesses that will package your mail and make arrangements to have it sent to any location you desire

Regular and special mail services provided by the USPS, private mail services, and international mail are presented in the next section.

Mail may be delivered by courier service. © *Jeff Greenberg.*

POSTAL SERVICE CLASSIFICATIONS

Domestic mail (mail delivered within the United States) is divided into the following classes.

- first-class mail
- priority mail
- express mail
- second-class mail
- third-class mail
- fourth-class mail
- official mail

First-Class Mail

Although we think of first-class mail as basically letters and other types of business correspondence, any type of mail that weighs eleven ounces or less may be sent first class if you pay the appropriate postage. If you use an envelope larger than a standard No. 10 envelope, be certain to clearly mark "first class" on the envelope in the area below the stamp.

Priority Mail

First-class mail that weighs more than eleven ounces is sent as **priority mail.** Priority mail cannot exceed seventy pounds in weight, and the maximum size for any item is 108 inches in combined length and **girth** (measurement around the thickest part). Packages sent by priority mail are given preferential handling and are shipped by air or by selected ground transportation. Priority mail should be designated on both the front and back of the envelope or the package so that it will not be handled as third-class mail.

Express Mail

Express mail is a fast, reliable service for sending both letters and packages. There are several types of express mail offered.

- Express Mail/Post Office to Addressee. Mail deposited by a designated time (usually 5 p.m.) is delivered by noon the next day between all major business markets and by 3 p.m. in other markets, including weekends and holidays.

- Express Mail/Post Office to Post Office. Mail deposited by a designated time at your local post office is delivered by 10 a.m. to more than 6,400 post office locations nationwide. The addressee then picks up the letter at the post office.

- Express Mail/Custom Designed Service. This service is tailored for customers who have regularly scheduled, time-sensitive mailings. Delivery will be made anywhere in the United States within twenty-four hours every day of the year.

- Express Mail/Same Day Airport Service. Customers may take letters or packages to the airport mail facility (AMF); the correspondence is then sent by the next available flight to the destination airport.

- Express Mail/Second Day Service. Mail deposited by the time designated by the USPS (usually 5 p.m.) is delivered by 3 p.m. the second day after mailing, including weekends and holidays.

- Express Mail/International Service. International service to more than 200 countries is offered through express mail international service. The service is available for regular, scheduled shipments that benefit from customized processing and transportation. On-demand service may be used if the destinations and shipping time vary.

- Express Mail/COD Service. Collect on delivery service allows the USPS user to rush merchandise to customers who order by mail or telephone and request fast delivery. Fees for the service are based on the amount of money to be collected. The USPS collects cash or a check payable to the mailer, and then mails, by first-class mail, the money collected.

A portion of a rate chart for express mail is shown in Figure 12-1.

Second-Class Mail

Second-class mail is used by newspapers and periodical publishers who meet certain postal requirements. These publishers and news agents must obtain special authorization from the USPS to mail materials at the second-class rate. Publications mailed by the public are charged the applicable priority mail, express mail, or single-piece first-, third-, or fourth-class rate.

Third-Class Mail

Third-class mail, sometimes called advertising mail, may be used by anyone, but is used most often by large mailers. Mail that weighs less than sixteen ounces and is not classified as first- or second-class mail is considered third-class mail. This mail generally includes printed materials and

UNITED STATES POSTAL SERVICE®

EXPRESS MAIL

RATEFOLD

Notice 123 Effective July 1, 1996

Weight Not Over (lbs.)	Same Day Airport	Custom Designed	Next Day & Second Day PO to PO	Next Day & Second Day PO to Addressee	Weight Not Over (lbs.)	Same Day Airport	Custom Designed	Next Day & Second Day PO to PO	Next Day & Second Day PO to Addressee
1/2	$9.00	$9.45	$10.25	$10.75					
1	10.50	14.00	12.05	15.00	36	$47.20	$57.55	$55.60	$58.65
2 [1]	10.50	14.00	12.05	15.00	37	48.10	58.65	56.70	59.70
3	11.95	16.15	14.20	17.25	38	49.10	59.80	57.85	60.85
4	13.05	18.30	16.35	19.40	39	50.00	60.85	58.90	61.95
5	14.15	20.45	18.50	21.55	40	50.90	62.00	60.05	63.05
6	15.30	24.30	22.35	25.40	41	51.90	63.05	61.15	64.15
7	16.40	25.40	23.45	26.45	42	52.80	64.20	62.25	65.30
8	17.55	26.50	24.55	27.60	43	53.75	65.35	63.40	66.40
9	18.70	27.60	25.65	28.65	44	54.70	66.40	64.50	67.50
10	19.75	28.75	26.80	29.80	45	55.60	67.55	65.60	68.65
11	20.90	29.80	27.85	30.90	46	56.55	68.65	66.70	69.70
12	22.05	30.95	29.00	32.00	47	57.50	69.75	67.80	70.85
13	23.15	32.00	30.10	33.10	48	58.45	70.85	68.90	71.95
14	24.30	33.15	31.20	34.25	49	59.35	72.00	70.05	73.05
15	25.40	34.25	32.30	35.30	50	60.30	73.05	71.10	74.15
16	26.50	35.35	33.45	36.45	51	61.25	74.20	72.25	75.30
17	27.65	36.50	34.55	37.60	52	62.15	75.30	73.35	76.35
18	28.80	37.60	35.65	38.65	53	63.15	76.40	74.45	77.50
19	29.90	38.70	36.75	39.80	54	64.05	77.55	75.60	78.60
20	31.00	39.80	37.85	40.90	55	65.00	78.60	76.70	79.70
21	32.15	40.95	39.00	42.00	56	65.95	79.75	77.80	80.85
22	33.25	42.00	40.05	43.10	57	66.85	80.85	78.90	81.90
23	34.40	43.15	41.20	44.25	58	67.80	81.95	80.05	83.05
24	35.55	44.25	42.30	45.30	59	68.75	83.15	81.20	84.25
25	36.60	45.35	43.40	46.45	60	69.65	84.45	82.50	85.55
26	37.75	46.45	44.50	47.50	61	70.65	85.85	83.90	86.95
27	38.75	47.55	45.65	48.65	62	71.55	87.15	85.20	88.25
28	39.70	48.65	46.70	49.75	63	72.45	88.45	86.50	89.55
29	40.65	49.80	47.85	50.85	64	73.45	89.85	87.90	90.95
30	41.60	50.90	49.00	52.00	65	74.35	91.15	89.20	92.25
31	42.50	52.00	50.05	53.10	66	75.30	92.55	90.60	93.65
32	43.45	53.15	51.20	54.20	67	76.25	93.85	91.90	94.95
33	44.40	54.20	52.25	55.30	68	77.15	95.25	93.30	96.35
34	45.30	55.35	53.40	56.45	69	78.10	96.55	94.60	97.65
35	46.30	56.45	54.50	57.50	70	79.05	97.85	95.90	98.95

[1] The 2-pound rate is charged for matter sent in a "flat rate" envelope provided by the USPS.

Figure 12-1   Rate chart for express mail.

packages. Two rate structures are available for this class—a single-piece rate and a bulk rate. Bulk rate often is used by companies when they are sending large quantities of identical pieces to different addresses.

Occasionally, there may be a need to combine classes of mail; for example, you might want to send a book to a customer and enclose a letter. This can be done by attaching a No. 10 envelope to the package. The package requires postage at the third-class rate, and the letter requires postage at the first-class rate. The entire package, however, is treated as third-class mail by the post office.

Fourth-Class Mail

Fourth-class mail, also referred to as parcel post, includes all mailable matter not in first-, second-, or third-class mail weighing sixteen ounces or more.

Packages weighing sixteen ounces or more that are not marked "priority mail" are considered fourth-class mail. The amount of postage for fourth-class mail depends on its destination and its size and weight. The destination charge is determined according to the eight delivery zones in the United States. A zone chart for parcel post rates is available at your local post office. A portion of a postage rate chart is shown in Figure 12-2.

Official Mail

Federal government offices send official mail without affixing postage. There are two categories of official mail—**franked** and **penalty mail.** Franked mail must have a real or facsimile signature of the sender in place of the stamp and the words "official business" on the address side. Only a few persons, such as members of Congress, are authorized to use this special mail service. The correspondence that congressional members send must relate to official government business. Postage for franked mail is paid quarterly in a lump sum to the USPS. Post offices serving the district offices of members of Congress and other congressional officials entitled to use the franking privilege record the number of pieces of originating franked mail, the dollar value of fees for originating the special service, and the postage due. Penalty mail is used for official government correspondence. It is marked "official business" and "penalty for private use." Figure 12-3 illustrates franked mail.

SPECIAL MAIL SERVICES

In addition to knowing the various classifications of mail, you should also be familiar with special postal services. Such services, when used appropriately, can enable you to be more efficient in processing outgoing mail.

Registered Mail

Registered mail provides protection and evidence of receipt for first-class and priority mail. When this service is used, the post office guarantees delivery and, if the mail is lost, becomes responsible to the sender for the declared value of the mail up to $25,000.

United States Postal Service

STANDARD MAIL (B)

1 & 2	3	4	5	6	7	8	Weight Not Over (lbs.)
$2.63	$2.79	$2.87	$2.95	$2.95	$2.95	$2.95	2
2.76	3.00	3.34	3.68	3.95	3.95	3.95	3
2.87	3.20	3.78	4.68	4.95	4.95	4.95	4
2.97	3.38	4.10	5.19	5.56	5.95	5.95	5
3.07	3.55	4.39	5.67	6.90	7.75	7.95	6
3.16	3.71	4.67	6.11	7.51	9.15	9.75	7
3.26	3.85	4.91	6.53	8.08	9.94	11.55	8
3.33	3.99	5.16	6.92	8.62	10.65	12.95	9
3.42	4.12	5.38	7.29	9.12	11.31	14.00	10
3.49	4.25	5.59	7.63	9.59	11.93	15.05	11
3.57	4.37	5.79	7.96	10.03	12.52	16.10	12
3.64	4.47	5.98	8.26	10.45	13.07	17.15	13
3.71	4.59	6.16	8.55	10.84	13.59	18.20	14
3.77	4.69	6.34	8.82	11.22	14.08	19.25	15
3.83	4.79	6.50	9.09	11.58	14.55	20.30	16
3.90	4.88	6.66	9.33	11.92	15.00	21.35	17
3.95	4.97	6.81	9.58	12.24	15.42	22.40	18
4.02	5.06	6.95	9.80	12.55	15.83	23.25	19
4.07	5.14	7.08	10.01	12.84	16.21	23.84	20
4.12	5.23	7.21	10.23	13.12	16.59	24.41	21
4.18	5.30	7.34	10.43	13.39	16.94	24.96	22
4.23	5.39	7.47	10.62	13.66	17.28	25.47	23
4.27	5.46	7.58	10.80	13.90	17.60	25.97	24
4.32	5.53	7.70	10.98	14.14	17.91	26.45	25
4.37	5.60	7.81	11.15	14.37	18.21	26.91	26
4.42	5.67	7.91	11.31	14.59	18.50	27.34	27
4.46	5.74	8.02	11.47	14.81	18.78	27.77	28
4.51	5.81	8.12	11.63	15.01	19.05	28.17	29
4.55	5.87	8.21	11.78	15.20	19.30	28.57	30
4.60	5.92	8.31	11.92	15.39	19.55	28.94	31
4.64	5.99	8.40	12.06	15.58	19.79	29.30	32
4.68	6.05	8.49	12.20	15.76	20.02	29.66	33
4.72	6.10	8.57	12.32	15.94	20.24	30.00	34
4.76	6.16	8.66	12.45	16.11	20.46	30.33	35

Inter-BMC / ASF Parcel Post
Machinable Parcels
No Discount No Surcharge
Zone

Figure 12-2   Rate chart for fourth-class mail.

Certified Mail

For materials that have no monetary value but for which you need a record of delivery, certified mail may be used; however, it may be used only for first-class and priority mail. No insurance coverage is provided. You receive a receipt when you mail the item. The post office delivers the certified mail, obtains the addressee's signature, and keeps a record of the date the material was delivered. A receipt for certified mail is shown in Figure 12-4.

COD Mail

You may send goods by **COD mail** (collect on delivery). This service allows the mailer to collect the price of goods and postage on merchandise ordered by the addressee when it is delivered.

Insured Mail

You can obtain payment for mail that has been lost or damaged if you have it insured through the USPS. The post office will issue you a receipt for the item to be insured. If an insured item is lost or damaged, you will receive payment in the amount of your insurance.

Return Receipt

For a small, additional fee, a return receipt showing the signature of the recipient and the date received will be furnished to the mailer. This

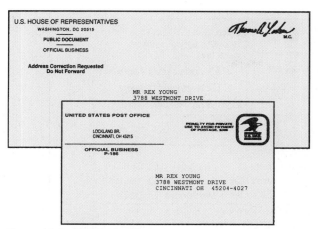

Figure 12-3   Franked mail.

service is available only for express mail, certified mail, COD mail, registered mail, and mail insured for more than $50. Notice the return receipt form in Figure 12-5.

Certificate of Mailing

A certificate of mailing is a receipt showing that a piece of mail has been received by the post office. The sender fills in the information required on the certificate, attaches the appropriate postage, and hands the certificate to the postal clerk with the piece of mail. The clerk cancels the postage and hands the certificate back to the sender as evidence that the piece of mail was received at the post office. A small fee is charged by the post office for handling the certificate.

Special Delivery

Special delivery ensures that mail is delivered beyond the regular post office hours. For example, special delivery is delivered even on Sundays and holidays. The service is available for all classes of mail except express mail. There is a fee in addition to the regular postage.

Special Handling

Special handling provides for the expeditious handling of third- and fourth-class mail. The fee for this service depends on the weight of each item; however, it is a relatively expensive service. It may be less expensive to send the item first class than to ask for special handling.

Recall of Mail

Mail that has been deposited at a post office or in a collection box can be recalled by the sender. You

P 264 262 206

US Postal Service
Receipt for Certified Mail
No Insurance Coverage Provided.
Do not use for International Mail *(See reverse)*

Sent to	
Street & Number	
Post Office, State, & ZIP Code	
Postage	$
Certified Fee	
Special Delivery Fee	
Restricted Delivery Fee	
Return Receipt Showing to Whom & Date Delivered	
Return Receipt Showing to Whom, Date, & Addressee's Address	
TOTAL Postage & Fees	$
Postmark or Date	

PS Form **3800**, April 1995

Fold at line over top of envelope to the right of the return address

CERTIFIED

P 264 262 206

MAIL

Figure 12-4   Receipt for certified mail.

must notify the post office from which the item was mailed as quickly as possible. You will be asked to complete a form entitled "Sender's Application for Recall of Mail." You must provide identification to prove that you are the sender. You will also be charged a fee for this service.

Change of Address

If the business is moving, the post office must be notified by letter or by a post office form. The old and new addresses and the date when the new address is effective must be given. Correspondents should be notified of a new address promptly by

275

```
┌─────────────────────────────────────────────────────────────────────────────────────┐
│          │ SENDER:                                                    │ I also wish to receive the │        │
│          │ ■ Complete items 1 and/or 2 for additional services.       │ following services (for an │        │
│  side?   │ ■ Complete items 3, 4a, and 4b.                            │ extra fee):                │        │
│          │ ■ Print your name and address on the reverse of this form  │  1. ☐ Addressee's Address  │        │
│          │   so that we can return this card to you.                  │                            │        │
│ reverse  │ ■ Attach this form to the front of the mailpiece, or on    │  2. ☐ Restricted Delivery  │        │
│          │   the back if space does not permit.                       │                            │        │
│   the    │ ■ Write "Return Receipt Requested" on the mailpiece below  │ Consult postmaster for fee.│        │
│          │   the article number.                                      │                            │        │
│    on    │ ■ The Return Receipt will show to whom the article was     │                            │        │
│          │   delivered and the date delivered.                        │                            │        │
└─────────────────────────────────────────────────────────────────────────────────────┘
```

SENDER:
- Complete items 1 and/or 2 for additional services.
- Complete items 3, 4a, and 4b.
- Print your name and address on the reverse of this form so that we can return this card to you.
- Attach this form to the front of the mailpiece, or on the back if space does not permit.
- Write *"Return Receipt Requested"* on the mailpiece below the article number.
- The Return Receipt will show to whom the article was delivered and the date delivered.

I also wish to receive the following services (for an extra fee):
 1. ☐ Addressee's Address
 2. ☐ Restricted Delivery
Consult postmaster for fee.

3. Article Addressed to:

4a. Article Number

4b. Service Type
☐ Registered   ☐ Certified
☐ Express Mail   ☐ Insured
☐ Return Receipt for Merchandise ☐ COD

7. Date of Delivery

5. Received By: *(Print Name)*

8. Addressee's Address *(Only if requested and fee is paid)*

6. Signature: *(Addressee or Agent)*
X

PS Form **3811**, December 1994   Domestic Return Receipt

Is your RETURN ADDRESS completed on the reverse side?

Thank you for using Return Receipt Service.

Figure 12-5   Return receipt form.

special notices. The post office supplies new address cards free of charge for personal and business use.

Mail for the Handicapped

Materials that are for the use of the blind or others who cannot read regularly printed matter can be mailed free of charge. Individuals must be certified as unable to see normal reading material. Certain other restrictions may apply; you should check with your local post office for details.

PRIVATE MAIL SERVICES

As mentioned earlier, several private companies across the United States offer mail services. Some of the services provided by these companies include.

- ground service which reaches every address throughout the forty-eight contiguous states;

- second day air service for all addresses in the fifty states and Puerto Rico with guaranteed on-time delivery;

- three day delivery within the forty-eight contiguous states, and next day air to every address within the United States and Puerto Rico.

Here is an example of some of the services offered by Federal Express (FedEx). Similar services are offered by United Parcel Service (UPS®), Purolator®, Airborne Express, and other private carriers.

Self Check

Take a few moments now to check your understanding of what you have learned to this point about USPS classifications of mail. Respond to the following questions:

1. What is priority mail?

2. List five classes of express mail.

3. What classes of mail can be sent registered?

4. Who may use second-class mail?

5. What is meant by franked mail?

How did you do? Check your answers with those provided at the end of this chapter. If you did not do very well, you might want to reread the first part of this chapter to gain a better understanding of classes of mail.

FEDEX

- FedEx Priority Overnight—delivery by 10:30 a.m. the next business day to thousands of cities and by noon the next business day to most other areas within the United States.

- FedEx Standard Overnight—delivery by 3 p.m. the next business day to thousands of cities and by 4:30 p.m. the next business day to most other areas.

- FedEx 2Day—delivery by 4:30 p.m. the second business day to virtually all of the continental United States.

- FedEx SameDay—urgent mail and packages are sent to the addressee the same day they are received by FedEx.

- Freight may also be sent overnight for delivery the next day or through 2Day Freight for delivery the second business day.

- FedEx International Priority Freight—may be shipped internationally and received the second business day. FedEx also provides next day delivery from Washington, D.C., and New York City to major world trading centers through FedEx International Priority Plus.

- Packages may be tracked at any point in their journey by calling FedEx.

- Money-Back Guarantee—if a shipment arrives late or FedEx can not tell you the status of the shipment, you may request a refund or credit for your transportation charges.

Some of these companies have same-day package pickups via the World Wide Web. This electronic pickup is available in most major metropolitan areas of the United States. Through the WWW packages may also be tracked, shipping costs calculated, transit times determined, and service information obtained. The UPS web site is http://www.ups.com.

Most large cities have messenger or courier service available within the city. For example, if you wish to have a document delivered to a customer across town, you may call the messenger service for pickup of the document and immediate delivery to the receiver.

In addition, a number of private companies such as Mail Boxes Etc. and Pak Mail® provide packing and shipping services for businesses and individuals. These companies will pack the material, ship it, insure it, and make certain that it reaches its final destination anywhere in the world. These businesses also will stuff envelopes, meter mail, accept CODs, and hold and forward your mail while you are away.

INTERNATIONAL MAIL

International postal service falls into three categories—**LC mail, AO mail,** and **CP mail.** An explanation of these categories is given here.

LC, AO, and CP Mail

LC mail (an abbreviation of the French words, lettres and cartes) consists of letters, letter packages, aerogrammes, and postcards. Aerogrammes are air letter sheets which can be folded into the form of an envelope and sealed. **AO** mail (an abbreviation for the French words, autres objets) includes printed matter, books, and sheet music, small packages, and publishers' periodicals. **CP** mail (an abbreviation for the French words, colis postaux) is parcel post. Parcel post mail resembles domestic fourth-class mail. Packages or any other articles that are not required to be mailed at letter rates can be sent as parcel post. Parcel post is the only class of mail that can be insured.

Special Services

International special services are similar to domestic special services. These services include registered mail, insured mail, return receipts, special delivery, and special handling. COD and certified mail are not available for international items. Express mail international service (EMS) provides delivery internationally from any location in the United States. This service is available on a demand basis when shipments cannot be made on a regular basis. There is no service guarantee (postage refunded if delivery is not made or attempted according to the publicized time lines) as there is with domestic express mail.

ELECTRONIC MESSAGES

The basic electronic messages that you will send as an office professional are e-mail and fax. You learned about fax messages in Chapter 3 and e-mail in Chapter 8. Information about sending and receiving e-mail and fax messages is given here. Another type of electronic message that you may infrequently send is a telegram. As you know, the telegraph transmitter and receiver was invented in 1837; however, telegrams are still sent occasionally today. Usually a telegram is sent if the writer wants to emphasize the urgency of the correspondence or for congratulatory purposes.

E-MAIL

E-mail is used extensively in interoffice correspondence today; it has almost replaced the hard copy memorandum. E-mail is also used internationally. Through online services such as America Online, e-mail addresses may be obtained and then mail sent to anyone on the Internet who has an e-mail address.

When sending an e-mail, you must know the access code of the individual who is to receive the message. Using the procedures designated by the e-mail software package you are using, you get into the system. Then, from the main menu of the package, you select "mail a document" or some similar statement to send a message. From that point, the message is keyed just as you would key any message on a computer. You also have the ability to designate whether the mail being sent is urgent or confidential. Notice that the display screen shown in Figure 12-6 has "urgent" listed at the bottom of the screen. The sender merely responds "yes" to these items on the computer to designate urgent or confidential mail.

To receive a message, you follow the procedures set out in the software package which you are using. Most software packages now alert you to when you have e-mail. For example, if your computer is turned on, there will be an audio sound and a flashing message at the bottom of your screen telling you that you have an e-mail and the name of the sender. Once you read the e-mail, you either reply to the mail, electronically file it, forward it, read and then delete it, or a combination of these. Notice the notations at the bottom of the e-mail

```
MSGS: NEW 0              DEC 29, 98  3:00 PM           DOCUMENT:
                         REPLY TO A MESSAGE

TO: Adams, Anita
BC: (YOURSELF)

SUBJECT: Human Resource System
ORIGINAL MESSAGE TEXT:

    I would like to review your progress on the documentation and
    training material for this system. Thanks.

REPLY TEXT:

    I will have the material you requested on Monday, Jan. 5.
    Are you free that day?

CERTIFIED? (Y/N)  N
FILE THIS REPLY? (Y/N)  N

CONFIDENTIAL? (Y/N)  N     ACTING FOR:
URGENT? (Y/N)  N     EXECUTE? (Y/N)  Y
```

Figure 12-6   Sending e-mail.

message in Figure 12-7 which give you options that you have in receiving the e-mail. You may also print out a hard copy of the e-mail if you need it. Generally, it is more efficient to leave the e-mail in electronic form. Occasionally, you will need to go into the e-mail file box and delete messages that you no longer need.

Most of the time, your supervisor will send and receive his or her own e-mail documents. Clearly, it saves both of you time if your supervisor does so. There may be occasions, though, that you will be asked to read the supervisor's e-mail; for example, if the executive is out of town and carries a laptop, e-mail messages may be picked up while on the trip. If your supervisor does not carry a laptop, you may be asked to read the e-mail and let your supervisor know of any urgent items. Because no person is allowed access to someone else's e-mail without authorization to maintain confidentiality, you will have to be assigned a password giving you the authority to retrieve the mail.

TECHNOLOGY TIP

Use e-mail to save your company money on paper products.

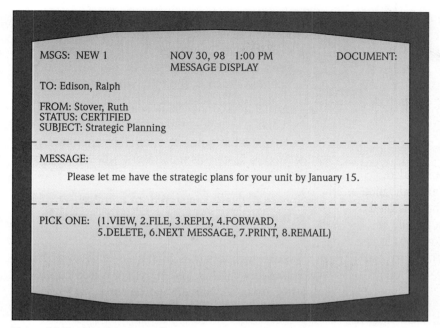

```
MSGS: NEW 1          NOV 30, 98  1:00 PM          DOCUMENT:
                      MESSAGE DISPLAY

TO: Edison, Ralph

FROM: Stover, Ruth
STATUS: CERTIFIED
SUBJECT: Strategic Planning
- - - - - - - - - - - - - - - - - - - - - - - - - - - - - - - - - - - -
MESSAGE:
     Please let me have the strategic plans for your unit by January 15.

- - - - - - - - - - - - - - - - - - - - - - - - - - - - - - - - - - - -
PICK ONE:  (1.VIEW, 2.FILE, 3.REPLY, 4.FORWARD,
            5.DELETE, 6.NEXT MESSAGE, 7.PRINT, 8.REMAIL)
```

Figure 12-7   Receiving e-mail.

FAX DOCUMENTS

You may have a fax machine in your office area or there may be a fax machine located in a common area used by several offices. When sending a fax, you must have the fax number of the individual. When faxing information within the local area, the fax number is the telephone number. When faxing outside the local area, the area code plus the telephone number becomes the fax number. You prepare a fax cover sheet with the name and company of the person receiving the fax, the name and company of the sender of the fax, the fax number of the receiver, and the number of pages being sent. The fax number is keyed into the machine, and the fax is sent to the individual.

When a fax is being sent to you, the machine will emit an audio sound to let you know that copy is coming. Once a fax is received, it should be immediately delivered to the addressee, as speed of delivery is one of the reasons for using the fax. You can assume that all fax messages take top priority unless your employer tells you otherwise.

TELEGRAMS

Telegrams can be sent any time of the day or night. Western Union® guarantees delivery of telegrams to major U.S. cities within five hours by messenger (if a delivery service is available in the area) or two hours by telephone. The minimum charge is based on fifteen words, excluding the address and signature. An additional charge is made for each additional word.

INCOMING MAIL

In large offices the mail comes into a central mailroom where it is sorted according to the company's departments. In addition to sorting, the mailroom may offer additional services such as opening the mail. If the mail is opened, it is not taken from the envelope, as the envelope may have important information that the receiver needs to note. Mail that is opened in mailrooms is done through automatic mail openers which not only open the mail, but also count

Mail is received through electronic means such as a fax machine. *Photo by Alan Brown/Photonics Graphics.*

In most companies, mail is sorted in a central mailroom before it is distributed to various departments.

the number of pieces of mail. This counting process helps a company when it is analyzing mail costs. Mail generally is delivered twice each day (in the morning and the afternoon), with these times fairly set so employees can know when to expect the mail. The methods of delivery vary, including delivery by

- a mailroom attendant;
- pick up at the mail room by the office professional;
- an electronic car—a self-powered, unattended, robotlike cart which uses a photoelectric guidance system to follow invisible chemical paths painted on carpeting, floor tile, or other surfaces may be used. The cart is programmed to make stops at particular locations, where the office professional can retrieve the mail from the cart. Notice the following photo of an electronic mail cart.

An electronic cart may be used to deliver mail within the office. *Bell & Howell Mailmobile Company.*

In small offices, the post office may deliver mail directly to the office or a mailbox may be maintained at the post office. In such an office, you may have the responsibility for picking up the mail.

SORTING

Once you receive the mail in your office or department, you must do a preliminary mail sort. If several individuals are in the department, sort the mail according to the person addressed. An alpha-betical sorter is handy if you are sorting mail for a number of individuals. Once the mail is sorted, place the mail for each individual into separate stacks.

When this preliminary sort is completed, sort each person's mail in the following order.

- Personal and confidential. Mail that is marked personal or confidential on the outside of the envelope should not be opened by the office professional. Place this mail to one side so that you do not inadvertently open it.

- Special delivery, registered, or certified. This mail is important and should be placed so that the individual to whom it is addressed will see it first.

- Regular business mail (first-class mail). Mail from customers, clients, and suppliers is also considered important and should be sorted so that it receives top priority.

- Interoffice communications. Generally, this mail is received in an interoffice envelope that is distinctive in its design and color.

- Advertisements and circulars (third-class mail). This mail is relatively unimportant and can be handled after the other correspondence is answered.

- Newspapers, magazines, and catalogs (second-class mail). These materials should be placed at the bottom of the correspondence stack because they may be read at the executive's convenience.

OPENING

Mail may be opened in the mailroom (as you have previously learned) or it may be opened in the individual's office. Mail opened in an individual's office is usually opened by hand, using an envelope opener. When opening mail, follow these procedures.

- Have the supplies that you need readily available. These supplies include an envelope opener, a date and time stamp, routing and action slips, a stapler, paper clips, and a pen or pencil.

COMMUNICATION TIP

Set aside a certain time each day for processing incoming mail.

- Before opening an envelope, tap the lower edge of the envelope on the desk so that the contents will fall to the bottom and will not be cut when the envelope is opened.

- Place the envelopes face down with all flaps in the same direction.

- Open the correspondence by using a hand envelope opener or running them through a mail-opening machine.

- Empty each envelope. Carefully check to see that everything has been removed.

- Fasten any enclosures to the letter. Attach any small enclosures to the front of the correspondence. Enclosures larger than the correspondence should be attached to the back.

- Mend any torn paper with tape.

- If a personal or confidential letter is opened by mistake, do not remove it from the envelope. Write "opened by mistake" on the front of the envelope, add your initials, and reseal the envelope with tape.

- Stack the envelopes on the desk in the same order as the opened mail in case it is necessary to refer to the envelopes. It is a good practice to save all envelopes for at least one day in case they should be needed for reference; then the envelopes may be thrown away.

KEEPING SELECTED ENVELOPES

Certain envelopes should be retained. Keep the envelope when one or more of the following situations exist.

- An envelope with an incorrect address—You or your supervisor may want to call attention to this fact when answering the correspondence.

- A letter with no return address—The envelope usually will have the return address.

- A letter written on letterhead with a different return address than that written on the envelope—For example, a person may write a letter on a hotel's letterhead and write the business address on the envelope.

- A letter without a signature—The envelope may contain the writer's name.

- An envelope that has a postmark that differs significantly from the date on the document—The document date may be compared with the postmark date to determine the delay in receiving the document.

- A letter specifying an enclosure that is not enclosed—Write "no enclosure" on the letter and attach the envelope.

- A letter containing a bid, an offer, or an acceptance of a contract—The postmark date may be needed as legal evidence.

DATE AND TIME STAMPING

Date and time stamping is an important step in handling incoming mail. After the mail has been opened and inspected, the stack of documents in each mail category is turned face up. Each item in a stack is stamped in the upper left-hand corner to show the date and time received. A hand stamp usually prints the word "received" and the date. You must set a hand stamp each day to show the current date. Machines can be used for date and time stamping. Most date and time stamping machines have a clock that automatically gives the date and exact time the letter was stamped.

There are several reasons why it is important to date and time stamp mail. The main reason is that it furnishes a record of when the correspondence was received; for example, a letter may arrive too late to handle the matter mentioned in the letter. Therefore, the stamped date of receipt is a recorded confirmation of the day the letter was received and of the resultant inability to take care of the matter. Or, the correspondence may not be dated. The date stamped on the letter, therefore, shows approximately when the correspondence was written.

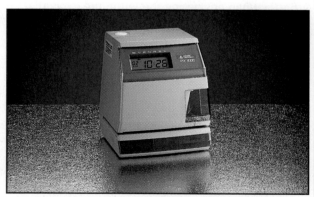

Date and time stamping provides a record of the receipt of correspondence. *Courtesy of Amano Cincinnati, Inc.*

READING AND ANNOTATING

Busy executives need as much help as they can get with the large amount of mail that crosses their desks each day. As an office professional, you can help by scanning the mail for the executive and noting important parts of the correspondence. You might underline the important words and phrases with a colored pen or pencil.

The next step is to **annotate** (making notations about previous action taken or facts that will assist the reader). You may annotate by writing notes in the margin of the correspondence or by using post-it notes. The advantage of post-it notes is that the notes may be peeled off and destroyed when you and the executive are through with them. If an enclosure is missing from the letter, make the annotation. If a bill is received, check the computations. Note any discrepancies by annotating. If the correspondence refers to a previous piece of correspondence written by the executive, pull the previous correspondence and attach it to the new correspondence. Note that the previous correspondence is being attached. Annotations may also be used to remind the executive of a previous commitment. For example, the executive might have agreed to have lunch with the individual writing; when answering the letter, the executive may want to refer to the lunch plans. Figure 12-8 shows a date and time stamped, annotated letter.

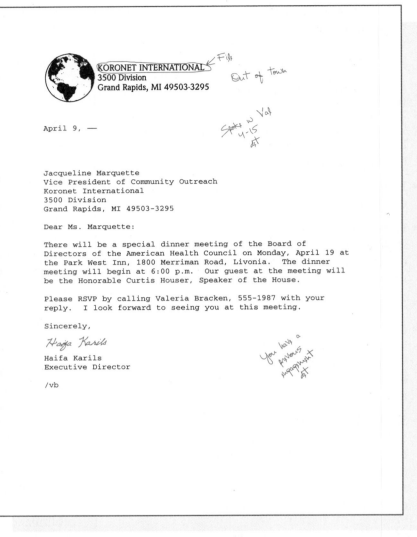

Figure 12-8 Date and time stamped, annotated letter.

ORGANIZING AND PRESENTING

After you have completed the preliminary mail sorts and have opened, date and time stamped, read, and annotated, you are ready to do a final sort. Here is one arrangement that may be used.

COMMUNICATION TIP

Be thrifty in your underlining. Underlining too much defeats the purpose—which is to save the executive time.

Routing Request

Please...

- ☐ Review
- ☐ Handle
- ☐ Approve
- ☐ Forward
- ☐ Return
- ☐ Keep
- ☐ Recycle

To: _____

_____

_____

_____

From: _____

Subject: _____

Date: _____

Figure 12-9   Routing slip.

- Immediate action. This category consists of mail that must be handled on the day of receipt or shortly thereafter.

- Routine correspondence. Such mail would include memorandums and other mail that are not urgent in nature.

- Informational mail. Periodicals, newspapers, advertisements, and other types of mail which do not require answering but are for the executive's reading should be included here.

After you have organized the mail, you are ready to place it in folders with labels indicating the categories established. It is a good practice to color code the folders; for example, the immediate action folder might be red, the routine correspondence folder might be blue, and the informational folder might be yellow. Color coding helps the executive see at a glance what mail needs to be handled first. Folders also help maintain the confidentiality of mail; for example, someone walking into the executive's office cannot read the material easily because it is in folders. The folders should be placed on the desk in a predetermined area. Usually the executive has an inbox for mail. Whatever the procedure, it should be one that meets the executive's needs.

The executive may also ask that you present the mail two times a day. For example, if outside mail is received in the morning and afternoon, the executive may ask that you organize and present it approximately thirty minutes after the mail is received.

You may handle a large portion of the mail yourself. The executive may not need to see it. This is especially true if you have been working for the company and the executive for a period of time and are familiar with the procedures and the executive's style. However, never throw mail away (even what you might consider "junk" mail) unless you have a clear agreement with the executive that you may make decisions in this regard.

ROUTING MAIL

At times it is important that more than one person read a piece of correspondence. If so, you may make photocopies of the correspondence and send a copy to each individual on the list; or you may route the correspondence to all individuals by the use of a routing slip. The basic question to ask when determining whether to make photocopies is: Is it urgent that all individuals receive the information contained in the correspondence immediately? If the answer is "yes," it is best to photocopy. If the answer is "no," it generally is best to use a routing slip, particularly if the correspondence is lengthy. You save copying costs by routing. A routing slip is shown in Figure 12-9. This routing slip is a commercially prepared example. You may design and prepare your own. For example, if you are routing correspondence to the same individuals frequently, you may want to design one that has the individuals' names already printed on it.

HANDLING MAIL DURING THE EXECUTIVE'S ABSENCE

You learned in Chapter 11 that one of your responsibilities while the executive is traveling is to handle the mail. In handling the mail while the executive is away, you need to follow these general guidelines.

- Before the executive leaves, discuss exactly how the mail should be handled; be specific in your questions so that you are clear. Mistakes in handling mail can be costly to the company.

- When urgent mail comes in, be certain that it is handled immediately according to the executive's directions; for example, you may give it immediately to the person who is in charge or you may fax it to the executive.

- Answer mail that falls within your area of responsibility in a timely manner.

- Maintain mail that has been answered (with the answer attached) in a separate folder; the executive may want to review it upon return.

- Maintain mail that can wait for the executive's return in a separate folder. Retrieve any correspondence that has previously been written that will be needed when reviewing the mail; place this correspondence in the folder also.

OUTGOING MAIL

An office professional's responsibilities for handling outgoing mail will vary. The office professional in a large company is responsible for preparing the mail for processing by mailroom employees. Mailroom employees determine postage requirements, affix postage, seal the correspondence, and sort for the USPS. In a small company, the office professional usually has responsibility for both preparing and processing the mail for the USPS. Whether you work in a large or small company, there are certain responsibilities that you have for outgoing mail. These responsibilities are given in the next section.

PREPARING CORRESPONDENCE FOR MAILING

Just as inappropriate or careless handling of incoming mail can cost the company thousands of dollars, so can mishandling outgoing mail be costly. You should follow these procedures carefully before mailing correspondence.

- Address the envelopes carefully. Check to see that the envelope address and the letter address are identical. If you are using a mail merge program with your software, you only key the address once. Therefore, your task is to be certain that the address is keyed correctly the first time. Check it carefully against your records to be certain that it is correct. If an address of a company has been changed, be certain that you correct your mailing list.

- Check each letter or memorandum to see that it is signed.

- See that any special mailing notations are keyed both on the letter and on the envelope.

- Make certain that all enclosures are included. When an enclosure is smaller than the letter, staple it to the front of the letter in the upper left corner.

- If enclosures that are too large to be sent with the letter are sent in a separate large envelope, be sure that the address on the large envelope is also correct. Mark the large envelope with the appropriate class of mail. If, for example, the enclosures are to go first class, indicate that on the envelope.

- Place all interoffice correspondence in appropriate envelopes with the name and department of the addressee listed on the envelope.

- If a mailroom employee applies postage and seals your mail, neatly stack your correspondence for the employee who picks it up.

ADHERING TO AUTOMATION REQUIREMENTS

As an office professional, you are responsible for seeing that outgoing mail is properly prepared for automated sorting equipment. The USPS uses automated equipment designed to handle the steadily growing volume of mail. Much of the sorting of letter size mail in large post offices is accomplished by a person operating a semiautomatic **letter-sorting machine (LSM)**. The operator strikes a combination of keys according to the zip code in the mailing address, and the envelope is quickly processed for delivery to its destination. Envelopes that are not legible or that do not contain a zip code are removed for hand sorting, which takes longer to process.

Companies are using automation to decrease the cost of processing mail. *Courtesy of Hunt Manufacturing Company.*

Two automated pieces of equipment installed in large post offices throughout the country are the **optical character recognition (OCR)** and **bar code sorter (BCS)** machines. The initial sort may be made with the OCR, which reads the address with its electronic eye and prints a series of short vertical lines at the bottom of the envelope. The lines or bar codes resemble the **unit price code (UPC)** on the items you purchase at the grocery store. Once the bar code is imprinted by the OCR, the envelopes are put through a final sort on the BCS.

Some companies preprint a bar code on their correspondence; you may do so quickly and easily with a software package. For example, many utility companies print a bar code at the bottom of the return envelope. If you have not noticed this bar code, you might check the return envelope received with your next utility bill. An envelope with a bar code is shown in Figure 12-10. Envelopes that have a preprinted bar code are not read by the OCR but are sorted by the BCS.

Figure 12-10   Envelope with a bar code.

In devising the five-digit code, the United States and its possessions were divided into ten geographic areas. Each area consists of three or more states or possessions and each has been assigned a number between 0 and 9. The national area is the first digit of the zip code. The remaining four numbers in the five-digit code also designate areas of the country. For example, in the zip code number 45237, the *4* designates the national area. The *5* designates a subdivision within the region. The *2* designates a section center, and the *37* designates a specific post office or delivery area within a multiple zip coded city. The zip code 45237 is a delivery area in Cincinnati, Ohio.

The ZIP+4 is an expanded designation to improve service. The additional four digits further identify the destination of correspondence and per-

mit even greater mailing productivity. When addressing envelopes or packages using the ZIP+4 code, the following guidelines should be used.

- Key the address in all caps.

- Key an attention line as the second line of the address.

- Key any special notations to the USPS such as "registered" and "special delivery" below the stamp, three lines above the address in all caps.

- Key any on-receipt notations such as "confidential" or "hold for arrival" a triple space below the return address, three spaces from the envelope's left edge.

- No punctuation should be used except the hyphen in the zip code.

- For best results, the address should be printed in black, preferably on white paper.

Figure 12-11 shows a correctly addressed envelope.

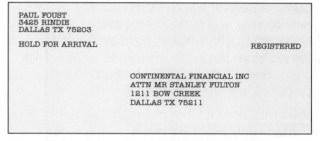

Figure 12-11   An envelope correctly addressed for automated processing.

SEALING AND STAMPING

If you work in a medium to large office, you usually are not responsible for sealing and stamping the mail. The outgoing mail is sent to a mailroom where sealing and stamping are done with automated equipment. If you work in a small office, you may seal and stamp envelopes using a postage meter. Envelopes are fed into the meter and are stacked, sealed, weighed, meter stamped, and counted in one continuous operation. The metered mail imprint serves as postage payment, a postmark, and a cancellation mark. A postage meter either prints directly on envelopes or on adhesive strips which can then be affixed to packages.

Another possibility in a small office is to seal and stamp mail manually. To seal a number of envelopes quickly, place them in a row on the desk with the flaps facing up. Run a moist sponge across the flaps and press down the flap for each envelope. You may also save time by purchasing stamps in rolls. Place the envelopes to be stamped face up on the desk. If you are using self-adhesive stamps, pull the stamp and place it on the envelope. When using stamps that must be moistened, before detaching the stamp from the roll, pass the stamp over a moist sponge, place it on an envelope, and then detach the stamp from the roll. Self-adhesive stamps may also be purchased in sheets if you prefer. These stamps are a little more difficult to handle when stamping several pieces of correspondence at once in that they must be peeled off the paper to which they are attached; however, because they do not have to be moistened, you may prefer these stamps.

ESTABLISHING A SCHEDULE

If it is your responsibility to get the mail to the post office, determine how often and at what times the local post office dispatches the mail. Outgoing mail can be delivered more quickly if it is deposited before the established collection times. If you are sending your mail to the central mail department to be processed, there will be times established that the mailroom is sending the mail to the U.S. post office. Find out these times, so your mail can be processed in a timely manner.

MAINTAINING MAILING LISTS

Most companies have correspondence that they send to a certain group of individuals. As an office professional, it is your responsibility to see that a current mailing list is maintained. Periodic updating of addresses is essential. It is also essential to add new names to the mailing list occasionally. By maintaining your mailing lists on your computer, you can update them quickly and easily. Address labels and envelopes can be printed from the mailing lists. If you do not have an envelope feeder on your printer, you may want to get one. You can print envelopes without a feeder; however, a feeder makes it easier to do so. If you are sending out large envelopes (such as 10×13), you will want to use labels; this size envelope is so bulky that it is difficult to feed through the printer.

PROCESSING MAIL USING SOFTWARE PROGRAMS

You have already learned that companies are spending more of their operational dollars on pro-

cessing mail. Because of the increased expenditures, they are concerned that their dollars are not being used as efficiently as possible. The post office estimates that one-third of all mail is undeliverable as addressed.[3] Software can assist you in maintaining and printing correct addresses. In addition, software can help you with a number of other functions that can reduce the costs of handling mail. Here are some of the advantages of using mailing software.

- address verification—By using a program available on CD-ROM, you can compare every address in your mailing list with the current USPS nationwide address database. If the address is valid, the software will standardize the address to USPS requirements and put on the correct ZIP+4 code.

- duplicate checking programs—These programs will find duplicates of names with spelling variations. They can also find duplicates that use nicknames and when the first and last names are switched.

- presort—Mailing list management software will incorporate the presort rules and check for size and weight restrictions, presort your mail, and print your labels in presorted order. With mailing list software, you can also print the USPS POSTNET bar code on all of your labels or envelopes, which is another cost-saving measure.

- carrier route coded mail—To qualify for carrier route discounts, you need a carrier route code number on the label and at least ten pieces per carrier route. Mailing list management software can affix the carrier route code to your mailing list and then presort it.[4]

- track costs—Software can track mailing costs back to each department and even notify the department when the mail budget is overrun.

- track carriers and determine costs—Software allows companies to determine which carrier is used most often for deliveries and determine whether the USPS is giving you the best rate available.

---

[3]Malik, Mary S, "The Hard Facts on Mailroom Software," *Managing Office Technology* (April, 1995), 31.
[4]Melissa, Raymond F., "Direct Mail Software Saves Printing and Postage," *Managing Office Technology* (April, 1995), 39–41.

PAPER RECYCLING

You have learned that rather than traditional mail decreasing in our Information Age, it has increased. An increasing amount of paper products are being used. More trees are being cut down to produce paper. Nearly 76 percent of municipal waste generated in the United States today is buried in landfills, but the landfills are closing at the rate of one per day. There is a shortage of available land to establish more landfills. One ton of recycled paper saves three cubic yards of landfill space, seventeen trees, 7,000 gallons of water, and 4,100 kWh of energy (enough to heat an average home for six months). At least 75 percent of all office waste is made up of paper, and about 40 percent of all solid waste is paper or paper products.[5]

Most businesses are now taking a look at how they can reduce the use of paper in the office, and they must continue to do so. For example, using e-mail for interoffice mail is one way to reduce paper costs. When a multipage document is to be printed, printing on both sides of the paper is another way to reduce mailing costs. Still another way is to control the number of copies made of documents. Rather than printing that extra document just in case it is needed, office professionals need to be taught to print only the exact number needed.

DOCUMENT SHREDDING

Shredders may also be used to recycle paper. For example, shipping departments spend several hundred dollars per week on pellets for packing. By shredding used paper and using it for packaging, a company not only addresses environmental concerns but also saves money.

Another advantage to shredding paper is that sensitive and confidential documents can be destroyed. When this type of information is not shredded, it may get in the hands of individuals who can use it for less than honorable purposes. A Hartford, Connecticut newspaper ran a front page article, startling a resident of a nearby town by naming him and saying, "We know where you work, how much you earn, your Social Security number and the amount you recently borrowed to buy your new Dodge® Caravan." The article continued, "We know all this because your banker left the information in the trash where anyone had access to it."[6] Unless sensitive and confidential documents are shredded, there is no guarantee that the information is secure.

Shredding may be done in-house through shredders which can be purchased for $1,000 or less. Or, the shredding may be done by **outsourcing** (contracting the work out to a company specializing in the work needed) to a company whose business is to shred documents. When determining whether to shed internally or to outsource, a company must look carefully at the costs of both alternatives.

As an office professional, you need to be committed to doing your part in reducing the amount of paper that is used. You should continually analyze how you are using paper. Are you using only what is essential? Are you using paperless methods when appropriate?

---

[5]Stevens, D. P., "Paper Cuts Profits, Wastes Resources," *From Nine to Five* (July, 1994).

[6]Carey, Rick, "Shredding: Information-Sensitive Precaution," *Managing Office Technology* (June, 1996).

COMMUNICATION TIP

Use recycled paper whenever possible.

COMMUNICATION TIP

Use the back of discarded paper for writing notes.

MAILROOM TRENDS

Although you will probably not work in a large mailroom, understanding the trends in this area will help you understand what you need to consider as you deal with mail in your own particular department of a business. Here are a few trends for the future.

- a paperless mailroom—In the not-too-distant future, an almost paperless processing mailroom is envisioned. Incoming mail will be processed for distribution via computer imaging and the integration of fax and e-mail into an electronic communication system.

- outsourcing—Outsourcing of mail operations is a direction for large companies. As more companies downsize, they make decisions to outsource particular parts of the company. Outsourcing can save the company money and provide the service more effectively.

- Mail classification reform—The 1996 Mail Classification Reform put in place some of the most sweeping changes in mail in the last century. Under classification reform, all automation rate mail will require:

  a. properly addressed, 100 percent valid delivery point, bar coded mail;

  b. software to develop and maintain all mailing lists, with all addresses cleansed every month;

  c. bar codes for tray and sack labels.[7]

---

[7]"Mailroom Automation Is Today's Necessity," *Managing Office Technology* (August, 1996), 30.

Mailers who conform to these standards can reduce their postage rates significantly.

- increased usage of computer software and hardware—The advances taking place in technology promise additional computer software and hardware which will increase the efficiency of mailrooms to an even greater degree. For example, according to post office surveys, more than 30 percent of all mail pieces have misspelled street or city names, improper state abbreviations, missing or incorrect zip codes, or other inaccurate or incomplete information that can slow delivery.[8] With software, addresses can be checked against a CD-ROM database of U.S. addresses. Misspellings and mistakes can be corrected and the complete nine-digit zip code added. It is anticipated that software will continue to be developed to increase mailroom efficiency.

- continual training of mailroom personnel—Increased computer capabilities demand continual training for mailroom personnel; to keep pace, employees will have to be willing to accept change and be willing to continue to learn.

---

[8]*Ibid.,* 31.

CHAPTER SUMMARY

This summary will help you remember the important points in this chapter.

- Domestic mail may be classified by: first-class, priority, express, second-class, third-class, fourth-class, and official.

- First-class mail is any type of mail that weighs eleven ounces or less on which the appropriate postage is paid.

- Priority mail is first class that weighs more than eleven ounces and does not exceed seventy pounds in weight and 108 inches in combined length and girth.

- Express mail is a fast, reliable service for sending both letters and packages.

- Second-class mail is used by newspaper and periodical publishers who meet certain postal requirements.

- Third-class mail is mail that weighs less than sixteen ounces and is not classified as first- or second-class mail.

- Fourth-class mail is mail that weighs more than sixteen ounces.

- Official mail is that used by federal government offices.

- Special mail services include registered mail, certified mail, COD mail, insured mail, certificates

of mailing, special delivery, special handling, recall of mail, change of address, and mail for the handicapped.

- Private mail services provide delivery across the United States and to certain countries abroad quickly.

- International mail is classified as LC mail, AO mail, and CP mail.

- Electronic mail includes e-mail, fax, and also the telegram.

- The office professional's responsibilities for handling incoming mail include sorting, opening, keeping selected envelopes, date and time stamping, reading and annotating, organizing and presenting, routing mail, and handling mail during the executive's absence.

- The office professional's responsibilities for handling outgoing mail include preparing correspondence for mailing, adhering to automation requirements, sealing and stamping, establishing a mailing schedule, maintaining mailing lists, and processing mail using software.

- To save costs and our environment, recycling should be a part of the objectives of each office.

- The mailroom of the future may be paperless, outsourced, and technology oriented.

CHAPTER GLOSSARY

The following terms were introduced in this chapter. To help you review, definitions are given here.

- **Fortune 500** (p. 271)–The largest 500 companies in the United States.

- **Priority mail** (p. 272)–First-class mail that weighs more than eleven ounces, does not exceed seventy pounds in weight, with the maximum size

for any item no more than 108 inches in combined length and girth.

- **Girth** (p. 272)–Measurement around the thickest part of an object.

- **Franked mail** (p. 273)–A category of official mail in which the real or facsimile signature of the sender appears in place of the stamp and the words "Official Business" appear on the address side.

- **Penalty mail** (p. 273)–Mail used for official government correspondence which is marked "Official Business" and "Penalty for Private Use."

- **COD mail** (p. 274)–Collect on delivery.

- **LC mail** (p. 277)–An abbreviation of the French words, lettres and cartes; international mail consisting of letters, aerogrammes, and postcards.

- **AO mail** (p. 277)–An abbreviation for the French words, autres objets; international mail consisting of printed matter, books, small packages, and so forth.

- **CP mail** (p. 277)–An abbreviation for the French words, colis postaux; international mail that is parcel post.

- **Annotate** (p. 282)–Making notations about previous action taken or facts that will assist the reader on correspondence.

- **Letter-sorting machine (LSM)** (p. 284)–Sorts mail in large post offices.

- **Optical character recognition (OCR)** (p. 285)–A sorting machine that reads the address with its electronic eye and prints a series of short vertical lines at the bottom of the envelope.

- **Bar code sorter (BCS)** (p. 285)–Another sorting machine used by most large post offices.

- **Unit price code (UPC)** (p. 285)–Used on items purchased at the grocery store, for example.

- **Outsourcing** (p. 287)–Contracting the work out to a company specializing in the area.

DISCUSSION ITEMS

These items provide an opportunity for you to test your understanding of the chapter through discussion with your classmates and instructor.

1. List and explain the classes of domestic mail.

2. What types of services do private mail services offer? When would you use a private mail service?

3. How should mail be sorted?

4. What is meant by organizing and presenting mail to the executive?

5. What are the office professional's responsibilities in preparing outgoing mail?

6. What are the projected trends for the mailroom of the future?

CASE STUDY

Roger Martin is a clerk in the mailroom. He has been with the company for six months. He seems like a nice young man who is eager to succeed on his job, but he has made several mistakes that you have noticed. You have also heard other employees complain about the errors he is making. You have noticed the following mistakes.

- You had a very important item to mail, and you requested that it be insured for $500. Roger failed to have the package insured.

- You asked that a piece of correspondence be sent "return receipt requested." Roger did not request the receipt.

- Roger picks up mail from you in the morning and in the afternoon. On several occasions, he has inadvertently left your outgoing mail at other desks in the building. The employees at these desks have returned the mail to you.

- One afternoon this week, Roger was one hour late picking up the mail. That meant that you had to take an important piece of correspondence that Ms. Marquette had requested be sent Express Mail/Post Office to Addressee to the post office if it was to make the 5 p.m. deadline set by the post office. Ms. Marquette was not happy; she needed you in the office for some additional assignments.

- On two mornings this week (and on several previous occasions), Roger has missed you on his mail run; he has neither picked up your outgoing mail nor brought you the incoming mail.

Each time Roger has made a mistake, you have talked with him about the error. He has been extremely apologetic and has made the excuse that he still has a lot to learn. The last time you called a mistake to his attention, however, he seemed to be quite defensive about the mistake. What should you do now?

RESPONSES TO SELF CHECK

1. Priority mail is first-class mail that weighs more than eleven ounces and cannot exceed seventy pounds in weight, with the maximum size for any item being 108 inches in combined length and girth.

2. The classes of express mail are Express Mail/Post Office to Addressee, Express Mail/Post Office to Post Office, Express Mail/Custom Designed Service, Express Mail/Same Day Airport Service, Express Mail/Second Day Service, Express Mail/International Service, Express Mail/COD Service.

3. First-class and priority mail can be sent registered.

4. Publishers and news agents who have special authorization from the USPS may send second-class mail.

5. Franked mail is federal government mail which has the real or facsimile signature of the sender in place of the stamp and the words "official business" on the address side.

OFFICE TASKS

OFFICE TASK 12-1 (Objectives 1 and 2)

Indicate the class of mail or special service that should be used in sending the items listed here.

1. newspaper
2. periodical
3. booklet that weighs fifteen ounces
4. catalog that weighs twenty-four ounces
5. important letter that weighs fourteen ounces
6. important package that has a value of $5,000
7. two books with a value of $50
8. letter for which Ms. Marquette wants proof that it has reached its destination
9. package that weighs ten pounds and is valued at $150; the receiver is to pay for the goods upon receipt
10. letter that is to get to the addressee by noon the next day
11. you missent a piece of correspondence; you need to retrieve it from the post office
12. piece of correspondence that needs to be received in Japan within two days
13. Ms. Marquette gives you correspondence on Friday that must get to the addressee by Saturday.
14. Your company is moving; what needs to be done so that mail will be forwarded?

OFFICE TASK 12-2 (Objective 3)

Retrieve Student Data Template Disk, file OT12-2. It contains a mailing list of thirty names and a letter that is to be sent to the names on the list. In addition, add the eight names given in the following mailing list. There are a few changes to be made to the letter. The session has been moved to March 21. The session will be held in the Galaxy Room of Koronet International. Once you have made the changes, prepare letters for the thirty-eight individuals and use the mail merge feature to address envelopes for the letters. Print out a copy of the new mailing list; it is to be placed in alphabetical order. Sign the letters for Ms. Marquette with your initials under the signature, fold them, and place them in the envelopes. Bundle the thirty-eight envelopes together in alphabetical order; place one copy of the letter on top of the envelopes. Submit the package to your instructor. Letterhead is available on OT12-2B; you will need to print 38 copies of the letterhead that will be used when you print the letters.

Mary Thayer, Hunt Manufacturing Corporation, 3345 Edna SE, Grand Rapids 49546

Wayne Tuftee, Robinson Drugs, 2798 Lowell SE, Grand Rapids 49502

Lynn Knouf, Manley Roofing, 323 Harcourt NE, Grand Rapids 49502

Jack Knoper, Kaczmarski Services, Inc., 2520 Normandy NE, Grand Rapids 49502

Jackson MacDonald, Soft Warehouse, 850 Powell NW, Grand Rapids 49503

Bruce Englers, Bell Atlantic Business Systems, 7620 Lime Hollow SE, Grand Rapids 49546

Richard Espinosa, Dodds Grocery, 2370 Valleywood SE, Grand Rapids 49546

Theodore Ethridge, Computers Unlimited, 5135 28th Street NE, Grand Rapids 49501

OFFICE TASK 12-3 (Objective 3)

The following is a list of Ms. Marquette's incoming mail which you are to handle. Explain how you would sort and place items in folders. Prepare a list of the mail as it is to be arranged, listing the folder you would place it in. If there are problems, explain how you would handle them.

1. confidential letter to Ms. Marquette
2. *The Wall Street Journal*
3. new product advertisement
4. letter addressed with enclosures
5. certified letter
6. interoffice memorandum
7. catalog of computer supplies
8. letter with no letterhead address
9. letter stating that there is a check enclosed; no check is enclosed
10. letter that refers to a letter written two weeks ago by Ms. Marquette
11. special delivery letter
12. *U.S. News & World Report*

OFFICE TASK 12-4 (Objectives 4 and 5)

Team with two of your classmates on this task. Read two recent articles on recycling and two on mailroom trends. Report your findings to the class in an oral report.

ENGLISH USAGE CHALLENGE DRILL

Correct the following sentences. Cite the grammar rule that is applicable to each sentence. Before you begin, refresh your memory of commonly misused words by reviewing these words in the *Multimedia Reference for Writers,* this text, or some other reference manual available to you.

1. I shall be happy to assist you in anyway I can.
2. She was pleased to discover that her dog was alright.
3. The advise received from the counselor was helpful in finding a job.
4. The affect of the decision was negative.
5. The dentist's office was further than I thought.

ASSESSMENT OF CHAPTER OBJECTIVES

Now that you have completed the chapter and the office tasks, take a few moments to review the following learning objectives. Did you accomplish the objectives? If so, explain how in the space provided. If you were unable to accomplish the objectives, give your reason for not doing so. Your instructor may want to review your answers.

I accomplished these objectives:

1. Identify classes of mail and determine which class should be used when preparing outgoing mail. Yes _____ No _____

   Explain how you accomplished this objective.

   _____
   _____
   _____

2. Identify and explain how special mail services are used. Yes _____ No _____

   Explain how you accomplished this objective.

   _____
   _____
   _____

3. Process both incoming and outgoing mail effectively. Yes _____ No _____

   Explain how you accomplished this objective.

   _____
   _____
   _____

4. Recognize the importance of recycling paper. Yes _____ No _____

   Explain how you accomplished this objective.

   _____
   _____
   _____

5. Cite mailroom trends. Yes _____ No _____

   Explain how you accomplished this objective.

   _____
   _____
   _____

Provide reasons for failing to accomplish any of the objectives.

   _____
   _____
   _____
   _____
   _____
   _____

CHAPTER 13

MANAGING DOCUMENTS

LEARNING OBJECTIVES

1. **Identify the types of document management systems.**
2. **Define the office professional's role in document management.**
3. **Learn and use the basic filing rules.**
4. **Identify and use various storage methods.**
5. **Follow proper storage procedures.**
6. **Identify and use document retrieval systems.**

As an office professional, a major part of your job is managing and maintaining the various office documents that are produced. Today, this portion of your job is a complex one.

In most offices, three types of document management systems are used—manual (paper), electronic, and image. You may be responsible for managing and maintaining portions of all three; for example, you may file incoming documents manually in their paper form in a four-drawer file cabinet, you may store all documents originating in your office electronically—on disks, and you may store vital documents (those documents that are important to the company and cannot be destroyed) on microfiche (an image system). You may be expected to establish systems for all three types of documents which include their proper storage and instant retrieval when needed.

One big complaint of executives is that it is often difficult and sometimes impossible to find essential information when it is needed. This inability to find a document quickly is not only a frustrating process but also costly. It can cost the company hundreds of dollars to find one piece of information that has been misplaced or thousands of dollars (and even a valuable client) if the information cannot be found. On the other side of this equation is the office professional who consistently sees a "mountain" of documents each week which must be properly stored. The enormity of the documents and the tedious nature of the process can be frustrating for the office professional. An understanding of document management procedures and techniques can simplify the process for you and allow you to become known as the office professional who can locate needed materials instantly— a skill that can make you invaluable to your supervisor and the company. This chapter will help you learn the basics of document management. Your task then as you continue to grow and learn is to keep current on new developments in the field.

DOCUMENT MANAGEMENT DEFINED

A **document** is any type of recorded information, whether that information has been recorded in letter form, report form, as a spreadsheet, as a blueprint, or in any number of other forms. Documents contain information about an organization—its functions, policies, procedures, decisions, and operations. Figure 13-1 illustrates several types of documents.

Document management is the systematic control of documents from the creation of the document to its final disposition. For a document management system to function, there must be information, equipment, and people. Information is generated by many sources and may appear on paper, cassette, videotape, disk, microfilm, and in other paper or electronic forms. Equipment in a document management system includes the hardware used in processing documents. People include the necessary personnel to get the right document to the right person at the lowest cost.

Figure 13-1   A document may be stored in paper, electronic, or image form.

DOCUMENT MANAGEMENT SYSTEMS

A **document management system** includes

- inputting data;
- processing the data through integration with other data, modifying, editing, deleting, and sorting;
- outputting the data;
- storing and retrieving the data.

This process may involve either a manual, an electronic, or image system. These processes are shown graphically in Figures 13-2 and 13-3. More information about each of these processes is given in the next sections.

ELECTRONIC SYSTEMS

Electronic data management systems use software to organize, store, and retrieve data. This software is referred to as **database software.** A **database** is a collection of records organized in related files. Here are some examples of what database software can do.

- Use data input previously in new ways. Assume that you work for a firm of attorneys. The firm is large, with a client base (both active and inactive) of 5,000 names. If you enter this client base in a database management program, you can quickly create mailing labels, personalized documents, and billing records.
- File automatically. Every time you add a new client or change a phone number or address, the database program will do your filing for you in whatever filing arrangement you have chosen—alphabetic, geographic, numeric, or by subject.

- Gather calculations quickly. If you bill by the hour, you can set up the database program to compute the hourly charges for each individual client. You can also set up the database program to record telephone charges and other types of charges. You can then print out this revenue and cost information by client, by attorney, or by the total firm. You can also print an invoice for the individual client.

Relational database programs let you store information in separate files and assemble related pieces to use together as needed. The following is a list of some database software programs.

- dBase IV
- Access
- FoxPro
- Paradox
- FileMaker Pro
- AceFile
- Alpha Four

IMAGE SYSTEMS

Image systems are divided into two types—those that convert documents to digital images stored on optical disks and those that store on **microforms**—(microfilm, microfiche, or aperture cards). Both the optical disk and microforms are shown in the following photo.

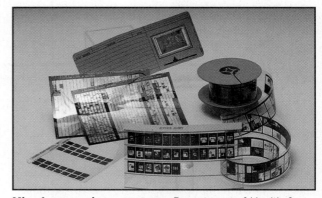

Microforms are image systems. *Department of Health & Human Services/Social Security Administration.*

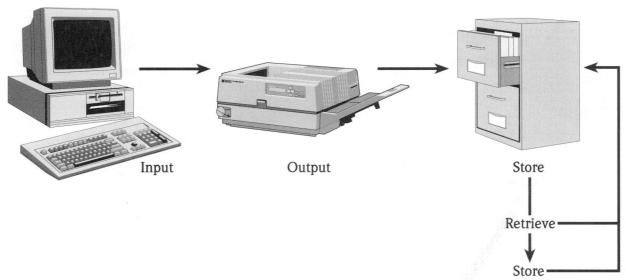

Figure 13-2   Manual document management system.

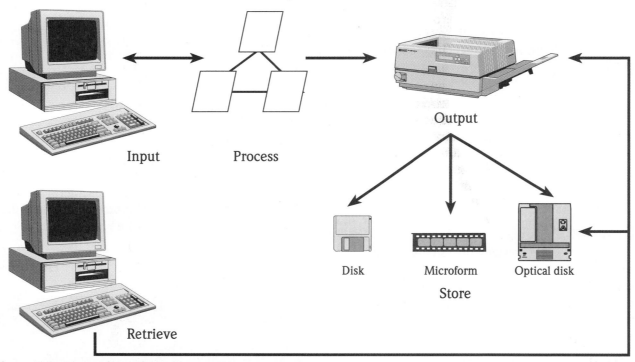

Figure 13-3   Electronic and image document management system.

Imaging System Using Optical Disk

The image system that stores on optical disks is a relatively new system. This system can convert all types of documents (letters, forms, drawings, maps, charts, and photographs) to digitized electronic data which is stored on an optical disk. The optical disk may be a write-once/ready-many (WORM) disk if there is no need to change the data on the disk; this type of disk is also called a CD-ROM (read-only memory). If there is a need to change the data in any way, an erasable disk may be used. Generally, there will be no need to change the data because

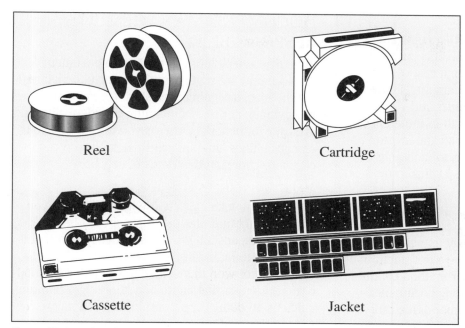

Reel

Cartridge

Cassette

Jacket

Figure 13-4 Microfilm packages.

storage methods are shown in Figure 13-4.

Microfiche. Microfiche is a sheet of film containing a series of images arranged in a grid pattern. Microfiche is usually shortened to "fiche" (pronounced "feesh"). Fiche permits direct access to any record without having to advance a roll of film to the appropriate location. Ultrafiche is a variation of microfiche, and contains more frames or images than a microfiche.

Aperture Cards. An aperture card is a standard punched card with a window (aperture) cut in it over which a portion of film is mounted. This card may contain one or several images.

Film Conversion and Processing. Although some companies photograph records in-house, many hire outside firms to convert documents to microform. As an office professional, you may have the responsibility of getting the documents ready for filming. All paper clips and staples must be removed from the records. Attachments to records such as routing slips and envelopes must also be removed. Documents should be batched and placed in sequential order.

the information consists of a file which has been completed; for example, personnel records for former employees or financial statements.

Microform Imaging System

Microforms provide an efficient and cost-effective method of storage. You probably have had some experience with microforms as you have done research in the library. For example, periodicals several years old are often stored on some type of microform. If you request the periodical, you generally are given a microfilm which you must then place in a viewer to read.

Microfilm. Microfilm is a roll of film containing a series of frames or images much like a movie film. In filming, the size of the document is reduced to make it fit the film. When it is viewed by the user, it is magnified on a screen.

Microfilm may be stored on reels or in cartridges, cassettes, or jackets. Reels are desirable for storing large volumes of records that do not require frequent changes. Microfilm on reels requires threading through a machine when it is being used. Microfilm on cartridges and cassettes requires no threading and is thus easier to use. Still another method of storing microfilm is by cutting it into strips and placing the film in a jacket. The jacket storage method allows portions of a film to be updated easily, because a strip of film can be removed and replaced with a new strip. These

INTEGRATION OF ELECTRONIC AND IMAGE SYSTEMS

Electronic and image system technologies have come together in the form of computer output microfilm, computer input microfilm, and computer-aided retrieval, and optical disks.

Computer Output Microfilm

One result of using the computer in conjunction with micrographics is **computer output microfilm (COM).** With the COM process, information from the computer is sent directly to microfilm, never being printed on paper.

Computer Input Microfilm

Computer input microfilm (CIM) is COM in reverse. Data on microfilm are converted into computer-readable data for use by the computer. With CIM, it becomes possible to use microfilm as a long-term storage device rather than using tapes or disks.

Computer-Aided Retrieval

Computer-aided retrieval (CAR) systems are designed to solve two common problems encountered in document systems—the high cost of storage and the difficulty of finding documents. Drawing on a combination of micrographics and computer technology, CAR can result in more effective and economical approaches to document storage and retrieval. With CAR, access to randomly filed documents on microforms are facilitated by the use of the computer.

MANUAL SYSTEMS

Although we have the technology (explained in the previous sections) to never store a document in its paper form, the manual or paper method continues to be a primary method of storing documents. One merely has to look at the number of file cabinets that are still evident in offices today to understand the validity of this statement. It is anticipated that we will continue to store paper documents in large numbers. The storage of paper documents demands that the office professional understand the basics of document management, the most efficient and effective procedures, and the proper supplies and equipment to be used.

ADVANTAGES OF DOCUMENT MANAGEMENT SYSTEMS

Here are a few of the benefits that a well-organized and well-managed document management system brings to a business.

- reduction of staff time spent searching the files for misplaced documents

- quick and easy retrieval of information needed in making management decisions

- financial savings through systems that provide the most efficient and effective methods of storage of materials

- protection and storage of information needed in perpetuity by the business

- trained personnel who understand the importance of records and the need for effective systems and procedures

- efficient use of space by maintaining records in the most appropriate form and determining the proper equipment for storage

DOCUMENT MANAGEMENT RESPONSIBILITIES

Your responsibilities in relation to document management are significant. They include maintaining the files, designing files, storing documents, retrieving materials, maintaining confidentiality, and disposing of materials. Unless you understand your responsibilities and perform them well, you can cost your company thousands of dollars.

MAINTAINING FILES

When you take a position with a company, you will no doubt find files that have already been set up. Your responsibility is to learn the system that is in use and to maintain the files. If you find that the system is not working well, you may (after a period of time) suggest that another system might be more efficient. In doing so, be certain that you have a solid understanding of not only the present system but also the system you are recommending.

DESIGNING FILES

If your organization is changing the filing system, you may be asked for input. You may be asked for advice on the type of document management system to use, appropriate software, and supplies and equipment. You also may be given the freedom to design a new filing system for your particular office or department. If your knowledge is not current, you may wish to obtain information from the following sources.

- Association of Records Managers and Administrators, International
  4200 Somerset Drive
  Suite 215
  Prairie Village, KS 66208
  Phone: 913-341-3808

- Association for Information and Image Management, International
  1100 Wayne Avenue, Suite 1100
  Silver Spring, MD 20910
  Phone: 301-587-8202

STORING AND RETRIEVING MATERIALS

Whether you are using electronic, image, or paper document systems, you will be responsible for storing materials so that they can be easily and quickly retrieved. This storage and retrieval demands that you have a knowledge of indexing rules, document storage methods, and storage procedures. This information will be presented in the next section of this text.

MAINTAINING CONFIDENTIALITY

The office professional is responsible for maintaining the confidentiality of materials in the files. The degree of confidentiality varies with the document. Some documents may be highly secret whereas others are not. There should be a company policy in regard to the access of confidential materials. If none exists, you should discuss with your supervisor how confidential materials should be handled.

DISPOSING OF MATERIALS

It is essential that files be purged on an established schedule, whether these files be electronic, image, or paper. If files are inactive, you do not want to take up space in file cabinets or on some type of electronic medium when the material is not being used. For example, your office may have established a procedure of purging files every six months. If there is no established procedure, you should determine one in consultation with your supervisor. Caution should always be exercised in disposing of materials; guidelines should be clearly stated and followed. You will learn more about disposal later in this chapter.

INDEXING RULES

To store and retrieve records effectively, a set of rules must be followed. The Association of Records Managers and Administrators (ARMA) has published a standard set of rules for filing documents. These rules include alphabetic indexing and cross-referencing. These same rules are used whether you are working with an electronic, image, or a manual system.

If you are presently working in an office or when you begin your office career, you may find that the indexing rules your company uses are slightly different from the ones presented in this text. At times companies may deviate from these rules for reasons that support their own internal needs. At other times, it may simply mean that the individuals setting up the filing system were not aware of the most recent indexing rules. You might want to call attention to the differences if they are significant. If you do so, wait until your supervisor has come to respect your competence.

ALPHABETIC INDEXING

The rules in this chapter are compatible with ARMA's *Alphabetic Filing Rules.*

Rule 1: Indexing Order of Units

A. Personal Names. A personal name is indexed in the following manner.

- The surname (last name) is the key unit.
- The given name (first name) or initial is the second unit.
- The middle name or initial is the third unit.

If determining the surname is difficult, consider the last name as the surname. A unit consisting of only an initial precedes a unit that consists of a complete name beginning with the same letter—*nothing comes before something.* Punctuation is omitted. See Table 13-1 (Rule 1A) for examples of indexing personal names.

B. Business Names. Business names are indexed as written, using letterheads or trademarks as guides. Each word in a business name is a separate unit. Business names containing personal names are indexed as written. See Table 13-1 (Rule 1B) for examples of indexing business names.

Rule 2: Minor Words and Symbols in Business Names

Articles, prepositions, conjunctions, and symbols are considered separate indexing units. Symbols are considered as spelled in full. When the word "the" appears as the first word of a business name, it is considered the last indexing unit.

Examples of articles, prepositions, conjunctions, and symbols that are commonly found in business names are given here. See Table 13-1 (Rule 2) for examples of indexing minor words and symbols in business names.

Articles:	a, an, the
Prepositions:	at, in, out, on, off, by, to, with, for, of, over
Conjunctions:	and, but, or, nor
Symbols:	&, #, $, %

Rule 3: Punctuation and Possessives

All punctuation is disregarded when indexing personal and business names. Commas, periods, hyphens, apostrophes, dashes, exclamation points,

Examples of Rule 1A

Index Order of Units in Personal Names

Name	Key Unit	Unit 2	Unit 3
Walter Kingscott	KINGSCOTT	WALTER	
Walter A. Kingscott	KINGSCOTT	WALTER	A
Walter Andrew Kingscott	KINGSCOTT	WALTER	ANDREW

Examples of Rule 1B

Index Order of Units in Business Names

Name	Key Unit	Unit 2	Unit 3	Unit 4
Beaumont Health Center	BEAUMONT	HEALTH	CENTER	
Beaver Creek Golf Club	BEAVER	CREEK	GOLF	CLUB
Chuck Beaver Pharmacy	CHUCK	BEAVER	PHARMACY	

Examples of Rule 2

Index Order of Units in Minor Words and Symbols in Business Names

Name	Key Unit	Unit 2	Unit 3	Unit 4	Unit 5
A Bit of Honey	A	BIT	OF	HONEY	
At Home Laundry	AT	HOME	LAUNDRY		
The $ and ¢ Shop	DOLLARS	AND	CENTS	SHOP	THE

Examples of Rule 3

Index Order of Units with Punctuation and Possessives in Personal and Business Names

Name	Key Unit	Unit 2	Unit 3	Unit 4
A-Z Video Company	A	Z	VIDEO	COMPANY
Abbey's Grooming	ABBEYS	GROOMING		
North/South Printing	NORTHSOUTH	PRINTING		

Examples of Rule 4

Index Order of Units for Single Letters and Abbreviations in Business and Personal Names

Name	Key Unit	Unit 2	Unit 3	Unit 4
J. V. Hildebrand	HILDEBRAND	J	V	
Jas. W. Hildebrand	HILDEBRAND	JAS	W	
Wm. R. Hildebrand	HILDEBRAND	WM	R	
J K of Texas	J	K	OF	TEXAS
KRLD Television	KRLD	TELEVISION		
U.S.A. Motors	USA	MOTORS		

Table 13-1   Examples of indexing rules 1–7.

Examples of Rule 5A

Index Order of Units for Titles and Suffixes in Personal Names

Name	Key Unit	Unit 2	Unit 3	Unit 4
Father James	FATHER	JAMES		
S. R. Harrold II	HARROLD	S	R	II
S. R. Harrold III	HARROLD	S	R	II
S. R. Harrold, Jr.	HARROLD	S	R	JR
S. R. Harrold, Sr.	HARROLD	S	R	SR
Frederick Johns, MD	JOHNS	FREDERICK	MD	
Ms. Helen Johns	JOHNS	HELEN	MS	

Examples of Rule 5B

Index Order of Units for Titles and Suffixes in Business Names

Name	Key Unit	Unit 2	Unit 3
Doctors' Hospital	DOCTORS	HOSPITAL	
Dr. Pepper Bottling	DR	PEPPER	BOTTLING

Examples of Rule 6

Index Order of Units for Prefixes in Personal and Business Names

Name	Key Unit	Unit 2	Unit 3	Unit 4
Paul Alan LaFaver	LAFAVER	PAUL	ALAN	
MacDugal's Meat Market	MACDUGALS	MEAT	MARKET	
McDouglas & Edwards	MCDOUGLAS	AND	EDWARDS	
Mary Lou St. Marie	STMARIE	MARY	LOU	

Examples of Rule 7

Index Order of Units for Numbers in Business Names

Name	Key Unit	Unit 2	Unit 3	Unit 4
4-Cent Copy Center	4	CENT	COPY	CENTER
4th Street Garage	4	STREET	GARAGE	
400-410 Daniels Court	400	DANIELS	COURT	
Four Seasons Health Spa	Four	SEASONS	HEALTH	SPA
Highway 30 Café	HIGHWAY	30	CAFÉ	
Highway Service Station	HIGHWAY	SERVICE	STATION	

Table 13-1 *(Continued)*

question marks, quotation marks, and slash marks (/) are disregarded, and names are indexed as written. See Table 13-1 (Rule 3) for examples of punctuation and possessives in indexing.

Rule 4: Single Letters and Abbreviations

A. Personal Names. Initials in personal names are considered separate indexing units. Abbreviations of personal names (Wm., Jos., Thos.) and nicknames (Liz, Bill) are indexed as they are written.

B. Business Names. Single letters in business and organization names are indexed as written. If there is a space between single letters, index each letter as a separate unit. An acronym (a word formed from the first or first few letters of several words) is indexed as one unit, regardless of punctuation or spelling. Abbreviated words (Mfg., Corp., Inc.) and abbreviated names (IBM, GM) are indexed as one unit regardless of punctuation or spacing. Radio and television station call letters are indexed as one unit. See Table 13-1 (Rule 4) for examples of single letters and abbreviations in indexing.

Rule 5: Titles and Suffixes

A. Personal Names. A title before a name (Dr., Miss, Mr., Mrs., Ms., Prof.), a seniority suffix (II, III, Jr., Sr.), or a professional suffix (DDS, MD, PhD) after a name is the last indexing unit. Numeric suffixes (II, III) are filed before alphabetic suffixes (Jr., Sr.). If a name contains both a title and a suffix, the title is the last unit. Royal and religious titles followed by either a given name or a surname only (Father John) are indexed and filed as written. See Table 13-1 (Rule 5A) for examples of titles and suffixes for personal names.

B. Business Names. Titles in business names are filed as written. See Table 13-1 (Rule 5B) for examples of titles and suffixes in business names.

Rule 6: Prefixes—Articles and Particles

A foreign article or particle in a personal or business name is combined with the part of the name following it to form a single indexing unit. The indexing order is not affected by a space between a prefix and the rest of the name, and the space is disregarded when indexing.

Examples of articles and particles are: a la, D', Da, De, Del, De la, Des, El, Fitz, L', La, Las, Le, Lo, Los, Mac, Mc, Saint, San, Santa, St., Ste., Ten, Van, Van der, Von, Von der. See Table 13-1 (Rule 6) for examples of prefixes.

Rule 7: Numbers in Business Names

Numbers spelled out in business names (for example, *Seven Seas Restaurant*) are filed alphabetically. Numbers written in digit form are filed before alphabetic letters or words (*B4 Photographers* comes before *Beleau Building Co.*). Names with numbers written in digits in the first units are filed in ascending order (lowest to highest) before alphabetic names (*229 Club, 534 Shop, Bank of Chicago*). Arabic numerals are filed before Roman numerals (2, 3, II, III).

Names with inclusive numbers (33–37) are arranged by the first digit(s) only (*33*). Names with numbers appearing in other than the first position (*Pier 36 Café*) are filed alphabetically and immediately before a similar name without a number (*Pier and Port Café).*

When indexing numbers written in digit form that contain st, d, and *th* (*1st, 2d, 3d, 4th*), ignore the letter endings and consider only the digits (*1, 2, 3, 4*). See Table 13-1 (Rule 7) for examples of numbers in business names.

Rule 8: Organizations and Institutions

Banks and other financial institutions, clubs, colleges, hospitals, hotels, lodges, magazines, motels, museums, newspapers, religious institutions, schools, unions, universities, and other organizations and institutions are indexed and filed according to the names written on their letterheads. See Table 13-2 (Rule 8) for examples of organizations and institutions as indexing units.

Rule 9: Identical Names

When personal names and names of businesses, institutions, and organizations are identical, including titles as explained in Table 13-1 (Rule 5), filing order is determined by the addresses. Compare addresses in the following order.

- city names
- state or province names (if city names are identical)
- street names, including avenue, boulevard, drive, street (if city and state names are identical)

  a. When the first units of street names are written in digits (*18th Street*), the names are filed in ascending numeric order and placed together before alphabetic street names.

  b. Street names with compass directions are considered as written (*South Park Avenue*). Numbers after compass directions are considered before alphabetic names (*East 8th, East Main, Sandusky, SE Eighth, Southeast Eighth*).

- house and building numbers (if city, state, and street names are identical)

  a. House and building numbers written as figures (*912 Riverside Terrace*) are considered in ascending numeric order and placed together before alphabetic building names (*The Riverside Terrace*).

  b. If a street address and a building name are included in an address, disregard the building name.

  c. Zip codes are not considered in determining filing order. See Table 13-2 (Rule 9) for examples of identical names.

Rule 10: Government Names

Government names are indexed first by the name of the governmental unit—country, state, county, or city. Next, index the distinctive name of the department, bureau, office, or board. The words "Office of," "Bureau of," and so forth, are separate indexing units if they are part of the official name. Note: If "of" is not part of the office name as written, it is not added.

A. Federal. The first three indexing units of a United States (federal) government agency name are *United States Government.* See Table 13-2 (Rule 10A) for examples of federal government names as indexing units.

B. State and Local. The first indexing units are the names of the state, province, county, parish, city, town, township, or village. Next, index the most

distinctive name of the department, board, bureau, office, government, or political division. The words "State of," "County of," "Department of," "Board of," and so forth are added only if needed for clarity and only if they are in the official name. They are considered separate indexing units. See Table 13-2 (Rule 10B) for examples of state and local government names.

C. Foreign. The distinctive English name is the first indexing unit for foreign government names. This is followed, if needed and if it is in the official name, by the remainder of the formal name of the government. Branches, departments, and divisions follow in order by their distinctive names. States, colonies, provinces, cities, and other divisions of foreign governments are followed by their distinctive or official names as spelled in English. See Table 13-2 (Rule 10C) for examples of foreign government names.

CROSS-REFERENCING

Cross-referencing is an aid used to find a document that may be called for by a name, subject, or geographic location other than the one selected for storage of the document. Here are some rules for cross-referencing personal and business names.

A. Personal Names. Cross-references should be prepared for the following types of personal names.

1. Unusual names. When it is difficult to determine the last name, index the last name first on the original record. Prepare a cross-reference with the first name indexed first.

Original	*Cross-Reference*
Andrew Scott	Scott Andrew
	See Andrew Scott

2. Hyphenated surnames.

Original	*Cross-Reference*
Sue Loaring-Clark	Clark Sue Loaring
	See Loaringclark Sue

3. Similar names. "See also" cross-references are prepared for all possible spellings.

Baier	Bauer	Bayer
See also	See also	See also
Bauer, Bayer	Bayer, Baier	Baier, Bauer

Examples of Rule 8

Index Order of Units for Organizations and Institutions

Name	Key Unit	Unit 2	Unit 3	Unit 4
Bank of DeSoto	BANK	OF	DESOTO	
First United Christian Church	FIRST	UNITED	CHRISTIAN	CHURCH
Horace Mann Elementary School	HORACE	MANN	ELEMENTARY	SCHOOL

Examples of Rule 9

Index Order of Units for Identical Names

Name	Key Unit	Unit 2	Unit 3	Unit 4	Unit 5	Unit 6	Unit 7
Liz Bowman 212 Luther Dallas, Texas	BOWMAN	LIZ	DALLAS	TEXAS			
Liz Bowman 818 Oak San Diego, CA	BOWMAN	LIZ	SAN DIEGO	CALIFORNIA			
Brother's Pizza 1120 14 Street Detroit, Michigan	BROTHERS	PIZZA	DETROIT	MICHIGAN	14		
Brother's Pizza 8010 Apple Street Detroit, Michigan	BROTHERS	PIZZA	DETROIT	MICHIGAN	APPLE		
Brown Computers 500 Forrest Building Detroit, Michigan	BROWN	COMPUTERS	DETROIT	MICHIGAN	500	FORREST	
Brown Computers Five Hundred Building Detroit, Michigan	BROWN	COMPUTERS	DETROIT	MICHIGAN	FIVE	HUNDRED	
Elder Market 213 Arch Street Troy, Michigan	ELDER	MARKET	TROY	MICHIGAN	213	ARCH	STREET
Elder Market 944 Arch Street Troy, Michigan	ELDER	MARKET	TROY	MICHIGAN	944	ARCH	STREET

Table 13-2 Examples of indexing rules 8–10.

Examples of Rule 10A

Index Order of Units for Federal Government Names
(Units 1, 2, and 3 are UNITED STATES GOVERNMENT for each example)

Name	Unit 4	Unit 5	Unit 6	Unit 7	Unit 8	Unit 9	Unit 10	Unit 11
General Services Administration Federal Protection and Safety	GENERAL	SERVICES	ADMINISTRATION	FEDERAL	PROTECTION	AND	SAFETY	
Health and Human Services Department Social Security Administration	HEALTH	AND	HUMAN	SERVICES	DEPARTMENT	SOCIAL	SECURITY	ADMINISTRATION
Internal Revenue Service Department of the Treasury	TREASURY	DEPARTMENT	OF	THE	INTERNAL	REVENUE	SERVICE	

Examples of Rule 10B

Index Order of Units for Local Government Names

Name	Key Unit	Unit 2	Unit 3	Unit 4	Unit 5	Unit 6
Department of Commerce State of Alabama Montgomery, Alabama	ALABAMA	STATE	OF	COMMERCE	DEPARTMENT	OF
Leon County Department of Public Welfare Tallahassee, Florida	LEON	COUNTY	PUBLIC	WELFARE	DEPARTMENT	OF

Examples of Rule 10c

Index Order of Units for Foreign Government Names

Name	Key Unit	Unit 2	Unit 3
Canada	CANADA	DOMINION	OF
Polska Rzecapospolita Ludowa	POLISH	PEOPLES	REPUBLIC
Estados Unidos Mexicanos	UNITED	MEXICAN	STATES

Table 13-2   *(Continued)*

B. Business Names. Cross-references should be prepared for the following types of business names.

1. Compound names. When a business name includes two or more individual surnames, prepare a cross-reference for each surname other than the first.

Original	*Cross-Reference*
Peat Marwick and Main	Marwick Main and Peat
	See Peat Marwick and Main
	Main Peat and Marwick
	See Peat Marwick and Main

2. Abbreviations and Acronyms. When a business is commonly known by an abbreviation or an acronym, a cross-reference is prepared for the full name.

Original	*Cross-Reference*
YMCA	Young Mens Christian Association

3. Changed names. When a business changes its name, a cross-reference is prepared for the former name and all records are filed under the new name.

Original	*Cross-Reference*
US Air	Allegheny Airlines
	See US Air

4. Foreign Business Names. The name of a foreign business is often spelled in the foreign language. The English translation should be written on the document, and the document stored under the English spelling. A cross-reference should be placed under the foreign spelling.

Original	*Cross-Reference*
French Republic	Republique Francaise

DOCUMENT STORAGE METHODS

As you have already learned, records may be stored in electronic, image, or manual (paper) form. The same storage classification system can be used in whatever manner the document is stored. Because it will be easier for you to understand a concept by illustrating it through a manual storage system, the illustrations given in this section reflect manual systems.

Document storage methods (sometimes called filing methods) are the manner in which records are classified for storage. These systems are:

Self Check

Take time to see if you understand the indexing rules by determining the key unit and the second, third, and fourth units in the following names. Write your answers in the space provided. Once you complete the exercise, check your answers with the correct ones given at the end of this chapter.

	Unit		
Key	*2*	*3*	*4*

1. Henry Hubert Bowers, Jr.

2. Roger Alan Le Feve

3. 500 Cafeteria

4. The 500, Inc.

5. Z. T. Glasier, III

6. Air Port Taxi Company

7. Northwest Shore Boat Rentals

8. By the Beach Café

9. Andrea's Florist

10. A Touch of Class

11. D&W Food Market

12. Horace Mann Elementary School

13. Department of Labor

14. Department of Commerce, State of Tennessee

- alphabetic
- subject
- numeric
- geographic

A company may use only one method of storage, two or three methods, or all the methods. The method used depends on how documents need to be located; for example, a company may use the alphabetic method in the central files department and the subject method within certain offices. An executive whose work consists of projects will want to keep the materials for each individual project filed in one folder. A subject system provides for this need. A law firm, who assigns numbers to cases, will use the numeric system for all case files.

ALPHABETIC METHOD

The **alphabetic method** uses letters of the alphabet to determine the order in which the names of people and companies are filed. This method is the most common method used and is found in one form or another in every office. With the alphabetic method, the name of the company, the person, or the organization addressed determines the filing order of outgoing documents. The name of the originator (company, individual, or organization) determines the filing order of incoming documents. Figure 13-5 shows an alphabetic file. Documents are filed according to the basic alphabetic filing rules.

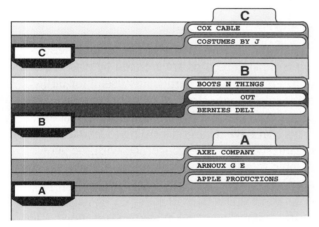

Figure 13-5   Alphabetic file.

SUBJECT METHOD

When using a **subject method,** documents are filed according to the subject of the material. Subject filing is used to some extent in all offices. An illustration of a subject file is shown in Figure 13-6.

Although subject order is useful and necessary in certain situations, it is the most difficult classification to maintain. Each document must be read completely to determine the subject—a time-consuming process. It is a difficult method to control, because one person may read a document and determine that the subject is one thing, and another person may read it and decide that the subject is something entirely different. For example, one person

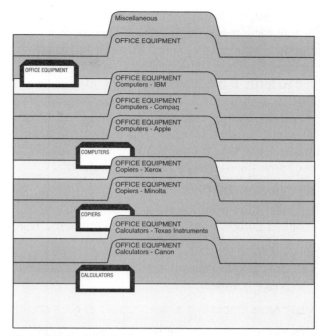

Figure 13-6   Subject file.

classifying documents concerning personnel grievances may determine that the subject is *Grievances* whereas another person may determine that the subject is *Personnel—Grievances.*

Because of this difficulty in determining subjects, a necessary part of subject storage is an index. An index is a list of all subjects under which a document may be stored. Without an index it is almost impossible for the subject storage method to function satisfactorily. The index should be kept current as new subjects are added and old ones eliminated. When new subjects are added, the index provides guidance to avoid the duplication of subjects.

The index to the Yellow Pages of the telephone directory is a good example of a subject index. Take a few moments to look at your Yellow Pages now. Notice the index that precedes the directory. The index gives you the subject areas. If this subject area is not where the information is located, the user is given the correct subject area. Note the following examples.

Advertising Art & Layout Service
    See Artists—Commercial; Graphic Designers
Doctors
    See Chiropractic Physicians; Clinics; Dentists; Hospitals; Optometry, Physicians & Surgeons, M.D; Physicians & Surgeons—DO; Physicians & Surgeons—Podiatrists

One major advantage of the subject method is that all records about one subject are grouped together; for example, notice that all dentists are grouped together, all hospitals are grouped together, and so forth. If this information were filed using a straight alphabetic method, each individual dentist would be listed by name and each individual hospital would be listed by name. Obviously, such a system is not a help in finding information if you do not know the name of a hospital or a dentist.

NUMERIC METHOD

Under the **numeric method,** documents are assigned numbers and filed by those numbers. The numeric method is particularly useful to

- insurance companies that keep records according to policy numbers;

- law firms that assign a case number to each client;

- real estate agencies that list properties by code numbers.

The numeric file has four basic parts.

- a numeric file

- an alphabetic general file

- a file containing the names of the clients, customers, and companies with the number that has been assigned to the individual or company

- a file containing a list of the numbers that have been used

In practice the numeric method works in the following way.

1. When a document is ready to be filed, the file containing the names of the clients and customers is consulted to get the number of the particular client or customer.

2. The number established is placed on the document; the document is placed in the numeric file.

3. If the client or customer is new and no number is established, the document may be placed in the alphabetic file until the client or customer has enough documents to open an individual numeric file.

4. If it is necessary to establish a new numeric file, the file containing the list of numbers is consulted to determine the next number to be used.

Figure 13-7 illustrates the numeric method in a manual system.

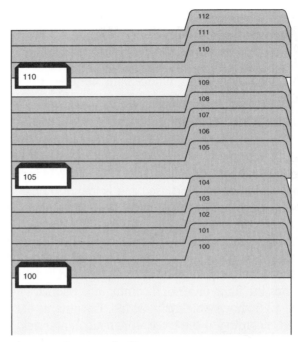

Figure 13-7   Numeric file.

GEOGRAPHIC METHOD

The **geographic method** is an arrangement in which related records are grouped by place or location. This method is particularly useful for utility companies where street names and numbers are of primary importance in troubleshooting; real estate firms that have listings according to land areas; sales organizations that are concerned with the geographic location of the customers; and government agencies that file records by state, county, or other geographic division.

In a manual geographic file by state and city, file guides are used to indicate the state and city; file folders are arranged alphabetically behind the guides by company or individual. Notice Figure 13-8 which shows a manual geographic arrangement.

MANUAL DOCUMENT STORAGE PROCEDURES

After you have determined the storage method or combination of storage methods (alphabetic, numeric, subject, or geographic) to be used, the next step is to get the material ready for storage. Here are the steps you should follow in storing records.

INSPECT

Incoming documents must never be stored until they have been reviewed and acted upon (if necessary) by someone in authority. Before sorting any

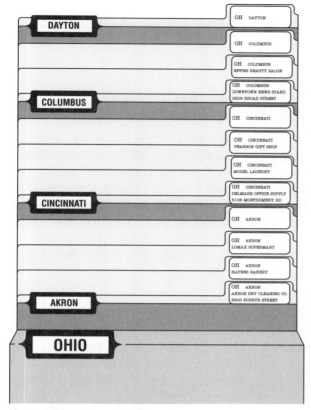

Figure 13-8   Geographic file.

incoming correspondence, be certain to **inspect** the correspondence for a release mark. This mark may be your supervisor's initials, a file stamp and the office professional's initials, a code or check mark, or some other agreed upon designation. Outgoing correspondence does not need a release mark because the original copy has been written by your employer or you. Do not store the copy until the original has been signed, as changes may need to be made.

INDEX

To **index** a document is to determine where it is to be stored. In alphabetic storage, indexing means determining the name that is to be used. On incoming documents, the most likely name to use is in the letterhead. On outgoing documents, the most likely name to use is in the address.

In a subject arrangement, indexing means determining the most important subject discussed in the document. If there are two subjects, the document should be stored under one subject and cross-referenced under the other. In a geographic arrangement, the location to be used must be determined. When using the numeric method, the name and number to be used must be determined.

CODE

To **code** is to mark the document by the name, subject, location, or number that was determined in the process of indexing. The document may be coded by writing the correct indexing units on the top right of the document in pencil. By coding in pencil, the indexing unit may be changed if there is a need to do so at a later point. Coding is important as it saves time in the refiling process. When a paper has been removed from the files and must be refiled, the office professional does not have to reread the document.

CROSS-REFERENCE

For correspondence that can be filed under more than one name, a **cross-reference** should be prepared. For example, if a company that you have been doing business with changes its name from *Heun and Miller Corporation* to *Corvell, Heun, and Miller Corporation,* you will want to cross-reference the document under *Heun and Miller Corporation,* at least until everyone in the office is aware that the name has changed. Without cross-referencing, material from this company could be misplaced.

One method of cross-referencing is to prepare a cross-reference sheet as shown in Figure 13-9. Notice in the figure that *Heun and Miller Corporation* appears in all caps under "Name or Subject" on the cross-reference sheet. *Corvell, Heun, and Miller Corporation* appears in all caps under "See Name or Subject."

Cross Reference Sheet

Name or Subject

  HEUN AND MILLER

  CORPORATION

_____

File No. _____

Date _____

Regarding OFFICE FURNITURE

See

Name or Subject _____

  CORVELL, HEUN, AND MILLER

  CORPORATION

Figure 13-9   Cross-reference sheet.

Another method of cross-referencing is to make a copy of the document, filing the original in the main file and the copy in the cross-reference file. An advantage of using the photocopying method is that if the document is looked for by the cross-referenced name first, it is not necessary to go from the cross-reference file to the regular file to obtain the document.

SORT

To **sort** is to arrange materials in the order in which they are to be filed. Sorting should be done daily or twice per day if the filing load is heavy. When sorting materials, a sorter can be used to quickly and efficiently handle the task. The letters of the alphabet appear on the sections of the sorter. Papers can be filed in each section. If papers are needed before they are actually stored in a file cabinet, they may be quickly retrieved because they have been placed in alphabetical order.

STORE

To **store** is to actually place materials into a folder. When storing materials, place the top of the document face forward at the left edge of the file folder. If you have more than one paper for a folder, the most recent date is placed on top. In other words, the papers are filed chronologically within the folder. Small items should be taped to a regular size sheet of paper. Large items should be neatly folded. No more than fifty sheets should be placed in a single folder. Set up another folder when you accumulate more than fifty sheets in one folder. Label the first folder with the name of the file and the dates that the file encompasses. For example:

Heun and Miller, 9-98 to 12-98. Label the added folder in the following manner: *Heun and Miller, 1-1999 to present.*

MANUAL DOCUMENT RETRIEVAL, RETENTION, TRANSFER, AND DISPOSAL

In all filing systems (manual, electronic, and image), it is important to be able to retrieve documents, retain them for the useful life of the document, and transfer or dispose of the document at the appropriate time to reduce the size of the active files. Manual system retrieval, retention, and transfer will be explained here. Electronic and image system retrieval, retention, and transfer will be discussed later in this chapter.

DOCUMENT RETRIEVAL

Once documents have been filed, the next step is to be able to find them quickly and efficiently. If a record is taken from a file, it is necessary to indicate what was taken and when it will be returned. Charge-out procedures provide a system for retrieving documents taken from the files.

The charge-out procedure may be a requisition form, an out guide, or an out folder. Using any of the procedures, the office professional will need to put the appropriate information on the form when the document or folder is taken. That information includes the name or subject of the file or document, the date on the material, the person who took the material, and the date taken. When the material is returned, the document is placed in the file, and the requisition form, the out guide, or the

---

COMMUNICATION TIP

Do not leave papers to be filed lying on your desk; either place them in a sorter or in the file cabinet daily. Remember the old adage: A place for everything and everything in its place.

HUMAN RELATIONS TIP

Use a rotary file to remember a client or your supervisor's birthday and other important information.

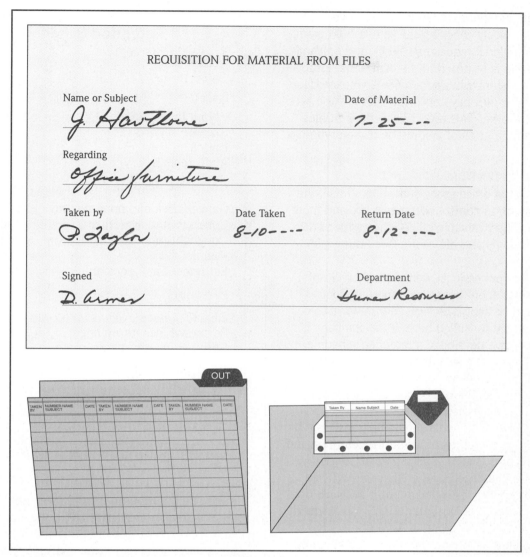

REQUISITION FOR MATERIAL FROM FILES

Name or Subject: *J. Hawthorne*

Date of Material: *7-25---*

Regarding: *Office furniture*

Taken by: *P. Taylor*

Date Taken: *8-10----*

Return Date: *8-12----*

Signed: *D. Armes*

Department: *Human Resources*

Figure 13-10   Requisition, out guide, and out folder.

out folder removed. The date the document is returned is marked on the form. Figure 13-10 illustrates a requisition, out guide, and an out folder.

Most businesses maintain certain documents that are confidential. It is the responsibility of the office professional to see that these documents are not released without proper authority. The authority may be the signature of an executive of the company.

Paper documents may be tracked through electronic processes; for example, software is available that includes capabilities for tracking color coded and bar coded file labels. Here is how the system works. Requests for files are sent to the location maintaining the files. The files are pulled and automatically charged out to the requesting departments with a bar code scanner. Personnel then deliver the files. Such a tracking system allows document

TECHNOLOGY TIP

Keep an office map on your computer of where various information is filed within your department. Distribute this office map to your co-workers.

management personnel to know where a file is at any time by quickly checking the software program. Once the individual requesting the file has finished with it, the file is returned to the central file location. Such a system will also provide a weekly report showing which files have not been moved for a certain period of time. This report helps prevent files from becoming buried or lost by the person who has the file.

DOCUMENT RETENTION

As the cost of office space continues to rise, the need for retention control becomes more and more important. Filling valuable office space with unnecessary documents and file cabinets is not a viable option.

As an office professional, you probably will not make decisions about how long important documents should be kept. The legal counsel for a company is generally consulted here. If the company is large, it may have developed a retention schedule. Figure 13-11 shows a sample portion of a retention schedule. If the company does not have a records retention schedule, the office professional should check with the supervisor before making any decisions about how documents should be transferred or destroyed. One useful reference on the retention and legality of records is the *Guide to Record Retention Requirements* published by the National Archives and Records Service. This document is available from the Superintendent of Documents, U.S. Government Printing Office, Washington, DC 20402.

Retention and destruction of files have taken on additional importance with the approval in December 1993 of the Revised Rule 26 of the Federal Rules of Civil Procedure. Revised Rule 26 requires organizations to make available all relevant records that must be kept in compliance with prevailing statutes and regulations. Delay or failure to find information makes an organization vulnerable to financial loss and adverse legal judgments. Disposal becomes important because records kept past legal retention and disposal periods can be a liability.

To understand more about retention control, consider the following categories into which documents can be classified.

Vital Documents

Documents that cannot be replaced and should never be destroyed are called **vital documents.** These documents are essential to the effective, con-

Retention Schedule

Accounting

Document	Retention in Years
Payroll (time cards)	3
Expense reports	6
Payroll	8
Audit reports	8

Corporate Records

Capital stock and bond records	Indefinitely
Contracts and agreements	Indefinitely
Copyrights and trademarks	Indefinitely
Patents	Indefinitely
Retirement and pension records	Indefinitely

Personnel

Disability and sick benefit records	6
Personnel files (terminated)	6
Withholding tax statements	6

Purchasing and Sales

Requisitions	3
Sales invoices	3
Sales contracts	3

Figure 13-11   Retention schedule.

tinued operation of the organization. Some examples of vital documents are corporate charters, deeds, tax returns, constitutions and bylaws, insurance policies, procedures manuals, audited financial statements, patents, and copyrights.

Important Documents

Documents that are necessary to an orderly continuation of the business and are replaceable only with considerable expenditure of time and money are known as **important documents.** Such documents may be transferred to inactive storage but are not destroyed. Examples of important documents are financial statements, operating and statistical documents, physical inventories, bank statements, and board minutes.

Useful Documents

Useful documents are those that are useful for the smooth, effective operation of the organization. Such documents are replaceable, but their loss involves delay or inconvenience to the organization.

These documents may be transferred to inactive files or destroyed after a certain period of time. Examples include letters, memorandums, reports, and bank records.

Nonessential Documents

Documents that have no future value to the organization are considered **nonessential documents.** Once the purpose for which they were created has been fulfilled, they may be destroyed. For example, a memorandum which is written to arrange a meeting generally has no value once the meeting has occurred.

DOCUMENT TRANSFER

At some point in the life of a document, you either decide to destroy it, retain it permanently, or transfer it to inactive storage. Two common methods of transfer are perpetual and periodic.

Documents may be transferred on a perpetual or periodic basis.

Perpetual Transfer

With the perpetual method, documents are continuously transferred from the active to the inactive files. The advantage of this method is that all files are kept current, because any inactive material is immediately transferred to storage. The perpetual transfer method works well in offices where jobs are completed by units; for example, when a lawyer finishes a case, the file is complete and probably will not need to be referred to at all or certainly not frequently. It can therefore be transferred to the inactive files.

When distinguishing between active and inactive documents, the following categories should be used.

- Active documents. These types of documents are used three or more times a month and should be kept in an accessible area.

- Inactive documents. These documents are used less than fifteen times a year and may be stored in less accessible areas than active documents.

- Archive documents. These documents have historical value to the organization and are preserved permanently.

Periodic Transfer

With periodic transfer, active documents are transferred to inactive status at the end of a stated period of time; for example, you may transfer documents that are over six months old to the inactive file and maintain documents that are less than six months old in the active file. Every six months, you follow this procedure.

DOCUMENT DISPOSAL

Documents that no longer have any use should be destroyed. If the material is not confidential, it may be disposed of by simply dropping it in a basket, with the paper being recycled. When the information is confidential, however, it should be destroyed by shredding. Shredders that cut the

---

COMMUNICATION TIP

Files generally should not contain material that is over six months old. Move older files to storage so that space can be freed up for more current materials.

paper into confetti-like strips are common pieces of equipment in offices.

MISPLACED AND LOST DOCUMENTS

Although you may be very careful in your filing, documents do occasionally get misplaced and even lost. When they do, here are some tips to help you find the document and suggestions about how to handle a lost document.

The misplacement of documents can be prevented through careful file management. *Photo by Alan Brown/Photonics Graphics.*

Misplaced Documents

- Look in the folder immediately in front of and immediately behind the correct folder.

- Look between folders.

- Look in the "General" folder.

- Check to see if the paper has slipped to the bottom of the file drawer.

- Look completely through the correct folder because a record may be placed out of chronological sequence.

- Look for the second, third, or succeeding units of a name rather than for the key unit.

- Check for misfiling due to misread letters; for example, C for G, K for H, and so forth.

- Check for alternative spellings of words; for example, McDonald or MacDonald.

- Check for the transposition of numbers.

- Look in a related subject file.

- Look on your desk and your supervisor's desk.

Lost Documents

If you are unable to find a document, try to reconstruct as much of it as you can by asking your employer about the contents and rekeying the information. Key the words "replacing lost document" at the top of the document and store it in its correct place within the file.

MANUAL SUPPLIES AND EQUIPMENT

When using a manual system, it is usually the responsibility of the office professional to determine the type of supplies needed and to order these supplies. The office professional may also be involved in recommending the type of equipment to use.

BASIC FILING SUPPLIES

Basic manual filing supplies include file folders, suspension folders, file guides, and labels.

File Folders

A file folder is generally manila, either 8½-by-11 inches or 8½-by-14 inches in size. Other colors of folders are available including blue, yellow and brown. The filing designation for the correspondence placed in the folder is keyed on a label which is then affixed to the tab of the folder. Folders are made with tabs of various widths, called **cuts.** The cuts are straight cut, one-half cut, one-third cut, and one-fifth cut. These cuts are illustrated in Figure 13-12. File folders may be purchased with these cuts in various positions. For example, if you are buying one-third cut folders, you may want to have

COMMUNICATION TIP

Coding papers properly can cut down on misfiled documents; it is a good idea to code papers using a colored pen.

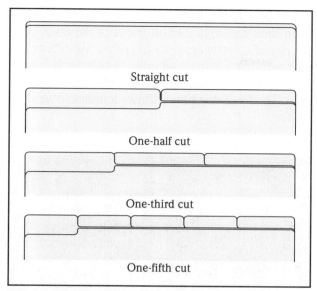

Figure 13-12   Folder cuts.

Straight cut

One-half cut

One-third cut

One-fifth cut

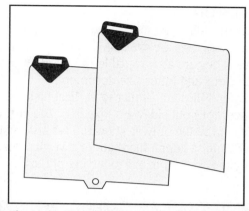

Figure 13-13   File guide.

all the tabs in first position. Or, you may want to have tabs in first, second, and third position. By choosing tabs in three positions, you are able to see the file caption on three folders at once.

Suspension Folders

In addition to standard file folders, suspension folders are available. These folders are sometimes called hanging file folders because small metal rods are attached to the folders allowing them to hang on the sides of the file drawer. Plastic tabs and insertable labels are used with the folders. These tabs and labels may be placed in any position using the precut slots on the folder.

File Guides

A file guide is usually made of heavy pressboard and is used to separate the file drawer into various sections. Each guide has a tab on which is printed a name, a number, or a letter representing a section of the file drawer in accordance with the filing system. Guides with hollow tabs in which labels are inserted are also available. The filing designation is keyed on the label and inserted in the table. Figure 13-13 shows one type of file guide. Guides are always placed in front of the file folders.

File Folder Labels

File folder labels may be purchased in various configurations including continuous folder strips, separate strips, rolls in boxes, or on pressure-

sensitive adhesive labels. Different colored labels can speed up the process of filing and finding records and eliminate much misfiling. It is easy to spot a colored label that has been misfiled—that color stands out from the other colors that surround it.

Some of the ways in which colored labels may be used are

- to designate a particular subject (e.g., green labels may designate budget items, blue labels personnel items);

- to indicate geographic divisions of the country;

- to designate particular sections of the file.

When preparing labels for files, consistency should be observed in keying them. The following are some suggestions.

- Key label captions in all capital letters with no punctuation.

- Begin the caption two spaces from the left edge of the label. Key any additional information five spaces to the right.

- Always key the name on the label in correct indexing order.

- Use the same style of labels on all folders. For example, if you decide to use labels with color strips, be consistent; if you decide to use colored labels, be consistent.

- Key wraparound sidetab labels for lateral file cabinets both above and below the color bar separator so that the information is readable from both sides.

EQUIPMENT

Vertical files are the conventional storage cabinet. These files are available in one to five drawer sizes. They are also available in sizes to accommodate cards and letter size documents.

Lateral files are similar to vertical files except the drawer rolls out sideways, exposing the entire contents of the file drawer at once. Less aisle space is needed for a lateral file than for a vertical file. A lateral file is shown in the following photos.

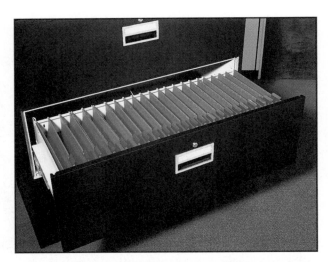

Lateral files use less space than vertical files. *Photos courtesy of Kardex Systems, Inc., Marietta, OH.*

Movable aisle systems consist of modular units of open shelf files mounted on tracks in the floor. Files are placed directly against each other. Wheels or rails permit the individual units to be moved apart for access. The movable racks are electrically powered. The following photo shows a movable aisle system.

Movable aisle systems provide for storing numerous files in a relatively small space. *Courtesy of Kardex Systems, Inc., Marietta, OH.*

Because these movable systems take less space than standard files, they are being used more frequently. Features that provide safety for both file contents and the people who work with them are of top priority for companies using the system. Movable systems may be manual, mechanical, or electrical. Manual systems are small, with two to four carriages. They require no power; the user merely pushes the files apart. Mechanical systems operate by turning a crank. Electrical systems move carriages with motors. Protection devices are available for all systems. The most basic device is a key-operated carriage lock that prevents the system from rolling on the rails. Another safety device is a

---

COMMUNICATION TIP

To keep your desk clean and improve your organization, keep a small file stand beside your desk. Place all ongoing projects and pending files (in order of importance) on this stand. You can quickly retrieve the important work without having to rummage through numerous papers on your desk.

strip that runs the length of the file cabinet at floor level. Pressure of more than a few ounces stops cabinet movement. Still another safety device is an infrared photoelectric beam. If a person or object breaks the beam, the system stops movement. When the person or object is no longer breaking the beam, the system resets itself.

To ensure safety of materials, users may have a badge which is swiped through a badge reader to allow entrance to the system, or users may enter a password code. Some systems can be fitted with locking doors.

ELECTRONIC AND IMAGE STORAGE, RETRIEVAL, RETENTION, TRANSFER, AND DISPOSAL

The document storage methods which were introduced previously in this chapter (alphabetic, subject, geographic, and numeric) are applicable to electronic and image storage systems as well as manual systems. In other words, it is still essential to establish a system as to how you will file documents, whether that be alphabetic, subject, geographic, numeric, or even a combination system.

ELECTRONIC SYSTEMS

Electronic systems generally use database software which you learned about in the first part of this chapter. Companies may choose to set up their own filing system. Whether the company uses database software or establishes its own system, the concepts are similar.

The first step in setting up a database is to choose the fields; that is, to determine how you want to sort the records—in alphabetical order, by zip code, by geographic location, by case number, by telephone number, and so forth. Any information you want to sort by must be kept in a field by itself; for example, if you want to sort your records alphabetically by last name, the first name, middle name, and last name are all considered separate fields.

If you need to pull information from several files, you will need to use a relational database program. This program will enable you to store information in two or more files, and combine data from fields in different files for queries and reports.

Indexing is an important step in setting up a database program. Indexes contain copies of the contents of important fields in every record. Assume that you have set up an alphabetic file of all personnel. The fields that you have set up are the names of the employees, the dates of employment, ages, addresses, and salaries. You **query** (ask) the file for all employees who make more than $50,000 per year. The software searches the index first and then calls up the actual records themselves. This method is much faster than searching the entire data file for all matches.

Decentralized and Centralized Storage

Decentralized storage refers to information that is stored by each office professional on disks or tapes. **Centralized storage** is one in which computers are linked through a network and files on the network can be accessed through the centralized electronic storage system. The network may be a LAN (local area network) or WAN (wide area network), for example. The centralized storage is generally where a database management program is used.

Most businesses use a combination of centralized and decentralized systems. As an office professional, you will generally store the documents you key on a disk. These documents may be reports, spreadsheets, letters, and other types of documents. There is no need for other individuals to access your files. When setting up your decentralized electronic filing system, you file the information on disks or tapes by using the alphabetic, subject, numeric, or geographic method. For example, assume you determine that you will use the alphabetic method, combined with the subject method. You work for three executives. You decide that you will use subdirectories for each executive. You have a letter written to H. R. Westveer; Michael Khirallah is the originator. You index, code, and store the letter in the following manner.

HRW92599/MK (HRW—name of addressee, 92599—date, MK—originator)

You should also label each disk with a general classification. For example, in the illustration just given, you would label the disk "Letters." Here is where the subject method comes in; the labeling by "Letters" is a subject classification. Mark the disk with the date of the first letter. You would then follow this same procedure for other documents; for example, label a "Report" disk and index, code, and store reports according to the alphabetic, subject, geographic, or numeric method. Assume that you decided to use a subject system for reports. You key a report entitled "Projected Sales for 2000" for Michael Khirallah. Your report would be indexed, coded, and stored in the following manner.

Sales10598/MK (Sales—abbreviated report title, 10598—date, MK—originator)

Retention, Transfer, and Disposal

The retention, disposal, and possible transfer of records within an electronic system must be planned. There must be a deliberate effort to go into the electronic files at scheduled intervals to review and purge the contents. A good practice would be to set up a system based on types of records (vital, important, useful, and nonessential). Just as you would set up retention schedules in a manual system, you would also set up retention schedules for an electronic system. These retention schedules should be published so that all appropriate personnel will understand when purging should take place. It is important to destroy outdated documents, not only to clear the disk or tape to provide for other documents but also to prevent any legal complications. For example, if a company fails to purge documents after the legal retention period has expired, the documents can be subpoenaed in court cases. You learned earlier about Revised Rule 26, which makes records kept past legal retention and disposal periods open for subpoena. A company could incur legal liability which would not have occurred if the electronic files had been purged. Companies should seek legal counsel in setting up their retention and disposal procedures. Once the policy is established, the requirements can be built into the document management system. Retention schedules can be imposed on documents based on content. Sensitive subjects can be identified and appropriate measures taken to handle the document, whether the document is kept on disk or a microform.

As an office professional, you will be responsible for purging your decentralized electronic files, in consultation with your supervisor. You and your supervisor may decide to purge all letters in excess of six months old. You may also decide to purge all e-mail over a month old.

IMAGE

As you learned earlier in this chapter, you can convert paper-based or electronic documents to images that can be stored on an optical disk or a microform. The general rule is to not store on a microform unless you are going to keep the document for a long time; for example, personnel records are kept for former employees of a company. The human resources department may choose to place the records on a microform, as they will be kept indefinitely but are rarely accessed. Microforms contain thousands of documents within a small amount of space. For example, up to 400 pages can be contained in an aperture card at a reduction ratio of 160 to 1.

Retrieval

Retrieval from an optical disk is extremely fast. The retrieval is similar to the retrieval of an item on a tape or cassette. You merely key in the necessary information and the retrieval occurs instantly.

To retrieve a microform, you must place it in a projector called a reader or viewer. A reader displays the microform in an enlarged form on a screen so that it can be read easily. The typical reader is a desktop unit designed to accept a specific microform such as microfiche or microfilm. There are multimedia readers, however, designed to accept two or more different types of microforms. Readers are also available in a variety of magnifications determined by the reduction ratio of the microform and the size of the viewing screen. Portable readers are also available which are lighter in weight and less expensive than desktop readers.

Often a person viewing a microform needs a paper copy of the document. This copy may be obtained through the use of a reader-printer. The microform is inserted in the reader-printer and each image is portrayed on the viewing screen. If the viewer desires a hard copy, pushing a button on the machine can produce a copy in seconds. A reader-printer is shown in the photo on page 319.

TECHNOLOGY TIP

Purge your e-mail after reading it unless you need to refer to it again.

A reader-printer is used to view and print a microform.
Courtesy of Eastman Kodak Company.

Comparison of Optical Disk and Microform Storage

Figure 13-14 lists several advantages and disadvantages of storage on optical disks and microforms.

DOCUMENT MANAGEMENT SOFTWARE

You learned earlier in this chapter about software that is available for tracking manual system files. Software is also available for tracking electronic and image files. Here are some of the features of document management software.

- log in documents
- track files, active and inactive (both on and off premise)
- provide an inventory of all records
- follow up on overdue files
- generate activity reports by department and user

Advantages and Disadvantages of Storage on Opitcal Disk and Microforms

Optical Disk Advantages

- Rapid random access.
- Large database of documents can be retained online for longer period of time.
- Copies made from original are of equal quality to the original.
- Large number of records can be reproduced easily.
- Information can be transferred to other media such as film or magnetic tape, over telecommunication lines, including FAX or networks.
- Excellent for high-activity records.
- Easily updated, deleted, or annotated.
- Multiple windows possible for viewing more than one document.

Optical Disk Disadvantages

- Few standards established.
- Heavy reliance on software high maintenance costs.
- Equipment costly.
- Multiple access can slow retrieval rate.

Micrographics Advantages

- Documents accessed through use of computer (CAR).
- Economical to use and reproduce; easy to make copies.
- Computer output microfilm can be reproduced quickly and inexpensively.
- Can be legally substituted for the original in most cases.
- Ideal storage media for inactive, low retrieval records.
- Equipment price reasonable.
- Standards are well established at state, national, and international levels.
- Can be portable.

Micrographics Disadvantages

- Single frame access, linear on roll film.
- Must be stored in a controlled environment.
- Updating or annotating is difficult.

Figure 13-14

- generate records retention and disposal guidelines

- track revisions of documents in progress

- record time for client billing or departmental charge-backs

DOCUMENT MANAGEMENT TRENDS

As technological advances continue, you can expect some of the following trends in document management for the future.

- The continued integration of both microform and electronic technologies, with systems that scan and film documents simultaneously. The document can then be maintained in its electronic form during the high-activity phase and in microform in its low-activity phase.

- Greater use of imaging systems to decrease the use of paper in the office and allow almost error-free storage, retrieval, and retention.

- The use of document management technology to handle information on the World Wide Web—update information, keep documents safe, check documents in and out, allow users to interact with disparate sources of information in complex ways.

- Greater use of outsourcing. Presently, businesses often outsource the storage of inactive records; for example, paying an outsourcing company to film and store microforms. In the future it is anticipated that more firms will outsource their entire document operation. Firms who outsource are reporting cost savings and greater efficiency (eliminating lost and misplaced records) through the services of a firm specializing in document management.

- Merger of computer systems staff with records and information management. Such a merger allows businesses to more effectively perform work, because both departments will have a better understanding of the entire process of document creation and management.

- Greater use of document management software.

- Greater use of more versatile equipment such as movable filing equipment.

CHAPTER SUMMARY

This summary will help you remember the important points covered in this chapter.

- A document is any type of recorded information, whether that information has been recorded in letter form, report form, as a spreadsheet, as a blueprint, or in any number of other forms.

- Document management is the systematic control of documents from the creation of the document to its final disposition.

- Document management systems may be manual, electronic, or image.

- One type of image system uses microforms. These microforms may be microfilm, microfiche, or aperture cards.

- The integration of electronic and image systems has been made possible through the use of COM, CIM, and CAR.

- The office professional's document management responsibilities include maintaining files, designing files, storing and retrieving materials, maintaining confidentiality, and disposing of materials.

- Indexing rules must be followed when filing documents; these rules have been set by the Association of Records Managers and Administrators, International.

- Document storage methods include the alphabetic method, subject method, numeric method, and geographic method.

- Manual storage procedures include inspecting, indexing, coding, cross-referencing, sorting, and storing.

- Documents may be divided into the following categories for determining disposition: vital documents, important documents, useful documents, and nonessential documents.

- Methods of transfer include perpetual and periodic.

- Electronic document storage methods often use database software in a centralized storage environment.

- In a decentralized electronic storage environment, the office professional generally sets up the storage system.

- Both optical disks and microforms are used in image document systems.

- Document management trends include continued integration of both microform and electronic technologies, greater use of imaging systems, the use of document management technology to handle information on the Web, greater use of outsourcing, the merger of computer systems staff with records and information management, greater use of document management software, and greater use of more versatile equipment.

CHAPTER GLOSSARY

The following terms were introduced in this chapter. To help you review, definitions are given here.

- **Document** (p. 294)–Any type of recorded information.

- **Document management** (p. 294)–The systematic control of documents from the creation of the document to its final disposition.

- **Document management system** (p. 295)– A document management system includes inputting data; processing the data through integration with other data, modifying, editing, deleting, and sorting; outputting the data; and storing and retrieving the data.

- **Database software** (p. 295)–Software that is used to organize, store, and retrieve data.

- **Database** (p. 295)–A collection of records organized in related files.

- **Relational database programs** (p. 295)–Allow the user to store information in separate files and assemble related pieces to use together.

- **Microforms** (p. 295)–Microfilm, microfiche, or aperture cards.

- **Microfilm** (p. 297)–A roll of film containing a series of frames or images.

- **Microfiche** (p. 297)–A sheet of film containing a series of images arranged in a grid pattern.

- **Aperture card** (p. 297)–A standard punched card with a window cut in it over which a portion of film is mounted.

- **Computer output microfilm (COM)** (p. 297)–A process where information from the computer is sent directly to microfilm.

- **Computer input microfilm (CIM)** (p. 297)–A process where data on microfilm are converted into computer-readable data for use by the computer.

- **Computer-aided retrieval (CAR)** (p. 298)–A process that accesses documents on microforms through the use of the computer.

- **Alphabetic method** (p. 307)–A process of filing that uses the letters of the alphabet to determine the order in which the names of people and companies are filed.

- **Subject method** (p. 307)–A process of filing in which documents are filed according to the subject of the material.

- **Numeric method** (p. 308)–A process of filing in which documents are assigned numbers and filed by those numbers.

- **Geographic method** (p. 308)–A process of filing in which documents are grouped by place or location.

- **Inspect** (p. 309)–Checking for a release mark on a document before filing it.

- **Index** (p. 309)–The process of determining where a document is to be stored.

- **Code** (p. 309)–The marking of the document by the name, subject, location, or number that was determined in the process of indexing.

- **Cross-reference** (p. 309)–An aid used to find a document that may be called for by a name, subject, or geographic location other than the one selected for storage of the document.

- **Sort** (p. 310)–The arrangement of materials in the order in which they are to be filed.

- **Store** (p. 310)–The actual placement of materials into a folder.

- **Vital documents** (p. 312)–Documents that cannot be replaced and should never be destroyed.

- **Important documents** (p. 312)–Documents that are necessary to an orderly continuation of the business and are replaceable only with considerable expenditure of time and money.

- **Useful documents** (p. 312)–Documents that are useful for the smooth, effective operation of the organization.

- **Nonessential documents** (p. 313)–Documents that have no future value to the organization.

- **Cuts** (p. 314)–Tabs of various widths, found on file folders.

- **Query** (p. 317)–Ask.

- **Decentralized storage** (p. 317)–Information that is stored by each office professional on disks or tapes.

- **Centralized storage** (p. 317)–Storage in which computers are linked through a network and files on the network can be accessed through the centralized electronic storage system.

DISCUSSION ITEMS

These discussion items provide an opportunity for you to test your understanding of the chapter through discussions with your classmates and your instructor.

1. Identify the types of document management systems.

2. What is the office professional's role in document management?

3. Identify and explain four document storage methods.

4. Define and explain proper manual storage procedures.

5. Explain the significance of indexes in a database program.

6. What are some of the features of document management software?

CASE STUDY

You enjoy the document management function of your job. You pride yourself on being able to set up files appropriately and find documents immediately upon request. In fact, Ms. Marquette has often praised your ability. She has told you that you have "an amazing ability to find anything in a moment's notice."

One of your co-workers, Lisa, never gets her filing done. She constantly complains about how much she has to do and has asked you on several occasions to help her. You do not mind helping out,

but you believe she wastes her time. You feel she is an ineffective employee. On two separate occasions, however, you have helped her with her filing. On the last occasion, you worked for almost three days helping her get her files up to date. Now she is behind again and wants your help. You do not believe you should be doing your job and her job, too. The tension is building between the two of you. You do not want to cause any problems in the office. How should you handle the situation?

RESPONSES TO SELF CHECK

Key Unit	Unit 2	Unit 3	Unit 4
1. Bowers	Henry	Hubert	Jr
2. LeFeve	Roger	Alan	
3. 500	Cafeteria		
4. 500	Inc	The	
5. Glasier	Z	T	III
6. Air	Port	Taxi	Company
7. Northwest	Shore	Boat	Rentals
8. By	the	Beach	Café
9. Andreas	Florist		
10. A	Touch	of	Class
11. D	and	W	Food
12. Horace	Mann	Elementary	School
13. United	States	Government	Labor
14. Tennessee	State	of	Commerce

OFFICE TASKS

OFFICE TASK 13-1 (Objectives 1, 2, and 4)

Team with three of your classmates on this task. Interview one office professional concerning document management. Ask the following questions. Report your findings orally to the class.

1. What document management systems do you use (manual, electronic, image, or a combination of these systems)?

2. What storage methods do you use (alphabetic, subject, numeric, geographic, or a combination of these methods)?

3. What is your role in document management?

4. Do you use document management software? If so, what packages?

5. Does your company have a records retention schedule? If so, may I have a copy?

6. What portion of document management is the most difficult for you?

7. Do you have suggestions for the beginning office professional as to how to handle document management?

OFFICE TASK 13-2 (Objective 3)

Load Student Data Template Disk, file OT13-2. For each group of names, indicate the indexing units and the order of filing. The correct response is given for the first group as an example. Key your responses and turn them in to your instructor.

OFFICE TASK 13-3 (Objectives 3 and 4)

Load Student Data Template Disk, file OT13-3. Key the list in proper alphabetic sequence.

Print out and hand in a copy of your work to your instructor.

OFFICE TASK 13-4 (Objectives 3, 4, and 5)

Load Student Data Template Disk, file OT13-4. Key the list in proper alphabetic sequence. Print out a copy of your work.

Next, key the list in proper geographic sequence. Print out a copy of your work. Hand in both printouts to your instructor.

OFFICE TASK 13-5 (Objectives 3, 4, and 5)

Load Student Data Template Disk, file OT13-5. Indicate the subject you would use in storing the correspondence listed. Place your answers to the right of the items. Print out and hand in your answers to your instructor.

OFFICE TASK 13-6 (Objectives 3, 4, 5, and 6)

Assume that Koronet switches from a manual to an electronic document system. Create a database and enter the customers from Student Data Template Disk OT13-4. Add a field for the zip code. Also add a field for the customer number; the number is listed in parentheses to the left of the name. Retrieve the list by zip code; print out a copy of the list. Next, retrieve the list by customer number; print out a copy of the list. Turn in both printouts to your instructor.

OFFICE TASK 13-7 (Objective 6)

Visit your college or public library. Locate two articles on international business on microforms. Print out one copy of these articles; turn in your printouts to your instructor.

ENGLISH USAGE CHALLENGE DRILL

Correct the following sentences. Cite the grammar rule that is applicable to each sentence. Before you begin, refresh your memory of grammar rules by reviewing subject and verb agreement.

1. The number of senior citizens in the area have increased in the last ten years.

2. A number of employees has called in ill with flu symptoms.

3. One of the guests were the 100th visitor to the new theme park.

4. The Canary Islands have been their favorite vacation site for several years.

5. The Hawaiian Islands has something which is unique on each island.

ASSESSMENT OF CHAPTER OBJECTIVES

Now that you have completed the chapter and the office tasks, take a few moments to review the following learning objectives which you were given at the beginning of this chapter. Did you accomplish these objectives? If so, explain how in the space provided. If you were unable to accomplish these objectives, give your reason for not doing so. Your instructor may want to review your answers.

I accomplished these objectives:

1. Identify the types of document management systems. Yes _____ No _____

   Explain how you accomplished this objective.

   _____

   _____

   _____

2. Define the office professional's role in document management. Yes _____ No _____

   Explain how you accomplished this objective.

   _____

   _____

   _____

3. Learn and use the basic filing rules. Yes _____ No _____

   Explain how you accomplished this objective.

   _____

   _____

   _____

4. Identify and use various storage methods. Yes _____ No _____

   Explain how you accomplished this objective.

   _____

   _____

   _____

5. Follow proper storage procedures. Yes _____ No _____

   Explain how you accomplished this objective.

   _____

   _____

   _____

6. Identify and use document retrieval systems. Yes _____ No _____

   Explain how you accomplished this objective.

   _____

   _____

   _____

Provide reasons for failing to accomplish any of the objectives.

_____

_____

_____

LINDA HARDAKER'S CASE SOLUTION

I had all existing executives fill in a travel profile that I gave directly to the travel company that does our bookings. I also had this profile included in the induction manual for new employees. This meant that I saved time on the phone to the travel agent, because that person had all the information loaded onto the computer. Once the booking was made, I entered the travel itinerary onto the computer and e-mailed it to the secretary or administration manager of each location as well as other appropriate executives. The phone finally stopped going crazy every time someone was away, and everyone was happy because they had the appropriate contact details at their fingertips.

NOTE: This type of information should never be given out to customers or clients unless under instruction by the traveler.

PART 6

Career
Advancement

Finley A. Lanier, Jr.
Lead Coordinator
Sherwin-Williams Company
Cleveland, Ohio

A Success Profile

I attribute my success to my extensive high school and business college training with a heavy degree of experience in the workplace. To make it in the office environment, one must have a clear head, a positive attitude, a neat and clean appearance, and a desire to achieve the highest standard of professionalism.

My educational background includes some college and business college. I have served as a secretary and office professional for many years in various places, including my tour with the United States Marine Corps, which was a rewarding experience. Also, I continue to attend numerous seminars to better educate myself. Many of these seminars are offered by Professional Secretaries International and the National Association of Executive Secretaries/Assistants.

The most enjoyable part of my job is sitting with the executives of my company and critiquing an issue that has gone well in planning and implementation, and seeing the contributions that I have made to the project.

The most stressful part of my job is on those occasions when I cannot seem to get anything accomplished no matter how hard I try. Sometimes I cannot get the information I need to relay to those with whom I work in time to offset unnecessary problems later.

Sometimes individuals think that the information they have is not adequate to pass along.

For someone just starting out in the office professional field, I would suggest several things.
- Possess a service attitude.
- Treat others the way you want to be treated.
- Learn all you can about the job you are doing and something about the related jobs as well. An office professional must wear many hats and cover the territory masterfully.
- Read as much as you can about situations that arise and seek guidance to help produce a successful solution.

My interests and hobbies are varied, but I particularly love music. I am a musician by trade. I teach piano, keyboard, organ, and theory. I am also the organist and choirmaster at the church I attend.

I belong to a number of professional organizations. I hold several offices and serve on two advisory boards—one for a vocational school and another for a community college. I am a past president of the local chapter of Professional Secretaries International and served the Ohio Division of PSI as its corresponding secretary and editor of the division newsletter. I belong to the Cleveland Chapter of Gospel Music Workshop of America. I serve nationally as tenor section leader for the T. G. Fraizer Memorial Chorale.

FINLEY A. LANIER, JR.'S CASE

Here is a case I have prepared from my varied experiences as an administrative assistant. Decide how you would handle the situation. Then turn to the end of Part VI (page 365) to see how I solved the situation.

THE SITUATION

I was given a time frame of four days to put a 1,500-piece packet mailing to a field of persons. My role was to organize the project, make the decisions as to how it should be done, and get it out the door within four days. I was given minimal instruction as to the job.

What should I have determined before I began the job? How should I have gone about meeting this almost impossible time frame? What skills were necessary to get the job done?

328

MANAGING STRESS AND TIME

LEARNING OBJECTIVES

1. **Define the causes of stress.**
2. **Identify stress reducers.**
3. **Implement stress controls.**
4. **Determine the importance of utilizing time well.**
5. **Identify time wasters.**
6. **Establish effective time management techniques.**

The Information Age in which we live is producing greater stress in individuals than ever before. The price for this increased level of stress is high for both the individual and the organization. Every week millions of people take medication for stress-related symptoms. Physical problems which can be the result of stress include ulcers, headaches, high blood pressure, and even heart disease. Job stress costs American businesses billions each year in absenteeism, lost productivity, accidents, and medical insurance. Businesses in the United States are seeing an increased level of employee stress rather than a decreased level.

A major cause of stress is poor management of time. Some errors Americans make include

- *trying to do too much in too little time;*

- *wasting time and becoming frustrated due to lack of productivity;*

- *not establishing appropriate priorities.*

Stress and time management go hand in hand, with each contributing to the other. If we are stressed out, we cannot manage our time well; if we do not manage our time well, we become stressed out. This chapter can be extremely beneficial to you in helping you to understand how to reduce stress and manage your time.

STRESS—A MAJOR MALADY

As knowledge continues to expand rapidly and ever changing technology becomes the rule rather than the exception, we are constantly having to learn new ways of performing our jobs. As businesses **downsize** (reduce the number of employees) and **rightsize** (determine the most efficient and effective number of employees and organizational structure), we may lose our jobs and even change our careers. As the **virtual office** (an office created at any place and at any time through the use of technology) becomes a reality for more employees, we must adjust to working in very different conditions than in the past—often by ourselves. Such situations force us to not only deal with change but also to embrace it if we are going to be successful workers in the twenty-first century. These occurrences can and often do contribute to stress.

Stress is the body's response to a demand placed upon it. Our wants, needs, and desires are derived from stress of some kind. Stress cannot be avoided; and in fact, we would not want to avoid all stress. If you never felt a need to achieve, you would not go to school. If you never felt a need to contribute, you would not accept a challenging job. Stress can and does have a positive impact on our lives. When stress becomes chronic, however, it becomes a negative factor for our health. **Chronic stress** occurs when a distressful situation is prolonged with no rest or recuperation for the body; it can cause physical and emotional problems. The chemicals produced within our bodies by chronic stress can cause high blood pressure, cardiovascular disease, migraine headaches, and other disorders. Emotional problems which may be caused by chronic stress include **burnout,** depression, withdrawal, loss of self-esteem, and deep-seated anger.

CAUSES OF STRESS

In addition to the change factors in our society that can cause stress, some other common causes of negative stress are given here.

329

Work Overload

Productivity is a key word in all businesses today. To compete in an international market, businesses are experiencing the need to be more productive, while at the same time reducing costs. Employees are often expected to produce more in less time and with a greater degree of accuracy than ever before. Employees find themselves working long hours and getting more exhausted.

Department of Labor statistics reveal that the amount of time Americans are spending on their jobs has risen steadily over the past two decades.[1]

The amount of time Americans are spending at work has risen over the past two decades. © 1995, PhotoDisc Inc.

---

[1]Davidson, Jeff, *The Complete Idiot's Guide to Managing Your Time* (New York: Alpha Books, 1995), 4.

Dual-Career Families

In the majority of families today, both parents work. The pressures of the job must be balanced against spending time with children and juggling the demands of grocery shopping, housework, and other responsibilities.

Single-Parent Families

The divorce rate in America continues to be high. Single-parent homes are prevalent. Many times the responsibility for rearing children falls on one parent. These responsibilities, along with having to make sufficient money to meet the needs of the family, can cause stress.

Elderly Family Members

Americans are also living longer than ever before, and many times this long life means that families include elderly members who must have special time and care. Or, the breadwinners of the family must devote time and energy to assisting elderly parents in adapting to new surroundings in a special home and illnesses that cause immobility and loss of mental functioning.

Economic Pressures

Even in dual-career families it is sometimes difficult to balance the budget. Individuals may work longer hours or take second jobs to bring in additional money for household needs.

COMMUNICATION TIP

Set up "job jars" for each member of your family. Determine tasks that must get done for the week on Sunday prior to the start of the workweek. Assign tasks to each family member, with the time it must be done. Or, make the assignment of tasks a family activity where each member volunteers for certain duties.

COMMUNICATION TIP

Look for ways to simplify your life. Make double or triple portions of meals; freeze the extras for use at a later time.

People sometimes take second jobs to bring in additional money for their families. © *Jeff Greenberg.*

Distressing Work Conditions

Personality conflicts sometimes occur within the office. Co-workers can be unhappy in their personal lives, and this unhappiness can manifest itself on the job. You may be the innocent party who has to face an unhappy individual each day, never really knowing in what kind of mood you will find this person. You may also encounter a difficult supervisor—one who is neither consistent nor considerate. These situations can cause stress.

STRESS REDUCERS

Although we can never avoid all negative stress, it is important that negative stress not be experienced for extended periods of time. Healthy individuals must find ways to get rid of the negative stress so that their bodies will not be damaged. Here are some stress reducers for you to practice.

Balance Work and Play

Often times people comment that they work a fifty-, sixty-, or even seventy-hour week; and the statement may be made with a sense of pride. If people are working such long hours, are they producing a large amount of work? Do they have demanding and challenging jobs? Are they appreciated and respected for their work contributions? Not necessarily. We know that there is a relationship between hours worked and productivity. Of course, individuals differ in the number of productive hours they can work; however, studies have shown that productivity decreases after extended periods of time. Most of us realize immediately when we are not being productive. When we

become fatigued, the amount of work we produce goes down; and our error rate goes up. Such symptoms are signals that it is time for us to slow down and take a break.

We actually can gain new energy by taking time to play. Maslow, a noted psychologist, talks about letting the child in us live. Too often as adults we have forgotten how to relax and, with complete abandon, enjoy the world around us. Some individuals writing in the field of creative energy urge us to take "joy breaks"—to actually stop for two to five minutes to play when we feel overtired or nonproductive. We might even have toys at our desk. Here are some examples of toys you might have.

- Tickle Me Elmo

- Silly Putty®

- Slinky

- A Nerf® ball

These toys are small enough to be kept in your desk. Just a few minutes of working the putty, moving the slinky back and forth, or tickling Elmo can do much to release stress through relaxation and laughter.

Companies across corporate America are realizing how important it is that employees take time to laugh. Companies such as AT&T, IBM, Honda®, and Monsanto™ have used humor consultants to help create joyful communities. Business issues that face people today such as downsizing, international competition, increasing workloads, and technological change are driving this move. Companies are realizing that if their employees are going to be productive and happy they must be helped to use humor in the workplace. Studies have shown that humor can increase productivity, decrease absenteeism, and lead to better job satisfaction. Stanford University researcher William Fry has found that laughing 100 times a day is equivalent to ten minutes of exercise on a rowing machine. A good, hearty laugh pumps air into the lungs, increases oxygen intake, and causes muscles to relax. Laughter can even cause blood pressure to drop. After a hearty laugh a person enters a deep state of relaxation which can last as long as forty-five minutes.[2]

---

[2]Atkins, Andrea, "Laughing Matters," *World Traveler* (November, 1996), 53–56.

Chapter 14: Managing Stress and Time

Another method of quickly reducing tension is a short exercise break. You might keep athletic shoes at your desk and during a break, spend five or ten minutes climbing stairs or walking briskly. Such physical activity allows you to release built up tensions, to open blocked thinking, and to trigger creative ideas.

Self Check A

Take a few moments now to write down in the space provided several things that are fun for you and that you can do at the office during a two- to five-minute break from your job.

_____

_____

_____

_____

_____

How did you do? Were you able to come up with five or six items?

Distinguish Between Achievement and Perfection

Perfectionism can be defined as a propensity for setting extremely high standards and being displeased with anything else. Many of us are taught that it is important to do everything perfectly. Certainly, it is important to achieve and to do things well; however, no human being can be perfect. To blame oneself continually for not doing everything extremely well is to engage in energy-draining behavior. In fact, mistakes can even be beneficial. Thomas Edison was asked one time how he came to hold so many patents. He answered that he dared to make more mistakes than ten other people

and he had learned from each of them. Edison knew that the creative process involves trial and error—failure and success. Unless we are willing to risk failure, we will never grow and learn.

Self Check B

Are you a perfectionist? Do you believe that everything you do must be done extremely well? Read and respond to the following statements by checking the appropriate blank.

	Yes	No
• If I do not do something well, I feel like I am a failure.	___	___
• When I make a mistake, I spend many hours rethinking how I might have done better.	___	___
• I have a reputation of being someone who is hard to please.	___	___
• When I am playing a sport (tennis, golf, baseball), I get angry with myself if I do not play my best game.	___	___
• I will not start a project unless I know everything about it.	___	___
• I do not like to try new things.	___	___
• I lose patience with others when they do not do things well.	___	___
• I expect every piece of work I produce to be perfect.	___	___

If you responded positively to these statements, you have probably bought into a negative, perfectionist pattern of behavior. Begin now to rethink how you view yourself and your work.

COMMUNICATION TIP

Do not worry about things you cannot control.

Recognize Your Limits

It is most important that you recognize when you are working too hard. We have different energy levels; you may be able to work ten hours a day quite successfully. Your friend may be able to work only eight hours a day. How do you know when you are working too hard? Become familiar with these symptoms of stress.

- anxiety
- headaches
- panic attacks
- muscular neck pain
- insomnia
- jaw pain
- phobias

If you identify with these symptoms, seek help. Most insurance programs provide for therapy sessions with psychologists or psychiatrists. These trained individuals can help you discover the causes of your stress and how you can alleviate them. You might want to check with your family physician for sources of assistance.

Exercise

Cardiovascular specialists have found that regular exercise can lower blood pressure, decrease fats in the blood, reduce joint stiffness, control appetite, and decrease fatigue. Exercise changes the chemistry in the body, getting rid of toxins and producing endorphins and other hormones which increase creativity and silence negative self-talk. You will be more patient, calmer, more receptive to others, and a better listener after twenty to thirty minutes of aerobic exercise.

What type of exercise should you do? There are many exercises that are good for your body—swimming, walking, and bicycling, to name a few. Participate in an exercise that you enjoy. What time of day should you exercise? It depends on you. You may find it better to exercise in the morning. Or, noon or evening may prove better for you. Whatever time you choose, numerous helps are available to you. You may choose to exercise with a video or with a television program. You may join a health club or the Y; these clubs usually open as early as 5:30 a.m. and close as late as 11 p.m. or 12 midnight. It is important that you determine a regular time of day that you will exercise and then do it. It is also important to exercise regularly. Most experts suggest three to five times a week for a period of thirty minutes to one hour. When you begin exercising, go slowly. Train your body; do not strain it. If you have any medical problems, consult your doctor about the type of exercise that is best for you.

An hour of exercise five days per week can reduce stress.
© 1995, PhotoDisc Inc.

HUMAN RELATIONS TIP

Make taking care of yourself the top priority.

Eat Right

What you eat or do not eat affects your overall health. Excessive intake of fat, sugar, salt, and caffeine contributes to poor health and to certain diseases such as hypertension and heart disease. Six ounces of coffee contain 180 milligrams of caffeine; six ounces of tea contain 70 milligrams; and twelve ounces of cola contain 45 milligrams.

Excessive amounts of caffeine can cause an individual to exhibit the same clinical symptoms as an individual suffering from anxiety. Unfortunately, many of us turn to junk food (candy, chips, and other types of munchies) to relieve stress. Rather than releasing stress, eating junk food increases stress; and the high calorie and fat content of junk food also contributes to being overweight.

The average American consumes more than 126 pounds of sugar a year. Excessive sugar consumption can lead to an increase in triglyceride levels in the blood which can cause cardiovascular disease. Too much salt can lead to an increase in blood pressure and to the development of hypertension. The wisest course of action for an individual is to lower the intake of fat, sugar, salt, and caffeine in the diet.

Your diet should include plenty of fresh fruits and vegetables. Drinking six to eight glasses of water a day is also very healthy. Whole grain breads and high fiber are good for your body. Maintaining a balanced, healthy diet will help keep your energy level high and your stress level low.

Get Enough Sleep

A survey done by *Prevention* magazine showed that 40 percent of adult Americans suffer from stress every day of their lives and find that they can sleep no more than six hours a night.[3] What is enough sleep? It all depends on you; however, the general rule is at least seven hours, with many people needing eight hours, and some even needing nine hours. You need to get enough sleep to function effectively.

Manage Your Time

There are only so many hours in a day. None of us can make the day longer, but we can manage ourselves in relation to the time we have so that we use our time well. As you have learned, stress and time management are closely linked. The mismanagement of time can contribute to stress. Because time management is extremely important, the remainder of this chapter is devoted to helping you understand how to manage your time more effectively.

[3]Davidson, Jeff, *The Complete Idiot's Guide to Managing Your Time* (New York: Alpha Books, 1995), 80.

HUMAN RELATIONS TIP
Do not drink beverages containing caffeine at least six hours before retiring.

HUMAN RELATIONS TIP
Drinking a glass of milk before you retire can help you sleep.

HUMAN RELATIONS TIP
Reading can also relax you and get you ready for sleep.

TIME MANAGEMENT

Time management is really a misnomer, because none of us can control the hours in the day. Time is finite; we cannot make it increase or decrease by managing it; but we can learn how to manage the way we use our time. Thus, **time management** really means the way in which we manage ourselves and our tasks in relation to the time that we have in a day, a week, or a year.

An electronic day planner is an effective time management tool. © 1997, PhotoDisc Inc.

TIME DEFINED

Time is a resource, but it is a unique resource. It cannot be bought, sold, borrowed, rented, saved, or manufactured. It can be spent, and it is the only resource that must be spent the minute it is received. Every one of us receives the same amount of time to spend each day; we all have twenty-four hours each day to manage in relation to our professional and personal goals. We cannot speed up the clock or slow it down. Time passes at the same rate each minute, hour, and day. The difficulty in time management occurs as we try to manage ourselves in relation to finite time that we have. Many of us do not even understand how we are spending our

time. We do not understand our time wasters, and we certainly are not taking steps to manage ourselves more effectively in relation to our time. Many of us have not realized that once we have wasted time, it is gone. It cannot be replaced.

TIME WASTERS

Before you begin to analyze how you might do a more effective job in managing yourself in relation to your time, look at some of the common time wasters. You will probably find that you have been guilty of most of these behaviors.

Ineffective Communication

As an office professional, you will communicate both orally and in writing with people in the office—your employer and co-workers—and outside the office—customers and clients. It is important that the lines of communication between you and others are open and easily understood. Think of the time you will waste if you write a letter incorrectly because you misunderstood the instructions from your employer. Or, think of the profits the company may lose if you make a customer unhappy and lose an account as a result of misunderstood communication.

Poor Telephone Usage

The telephone becomes a time waster when it is not used properly. Here are some of the mistakes made which cause the telephone to be a time waster.

- engaging in personal conversations during work hours
- failing to give the proper information to a co-worker, client, or customer
- failing to get the proper information from a caller; for example, name, number, and reason for call
- using the telephone when it would be more efficient to use e-mail or a fax

COMMUNICATION TIP

A short pencil is better than the longest memory. When in doubt, write things down.

The telephone can become an ineffective means of communication when it is not used properly.

Inadequate Planning

Many individuals never plan what needs to be done on a particular day. Lack of planning can cause both you and your supervisor problems. Consider this situation.

> Your supervisor gives you a report on Friday afternoon which must be completed by Monday afternoon. You understand that the job is high priority; however, the report is not lengthy and you do not analyze how long it will take you to produce it. On Monday morning you have numerous interruptions; you do not begin the report until Monday afternoon at 2 p.m. As you get into the report, you see that it is very involved; there is no way that you will be able to finish by 5 p.m. Your employer is unhappy and you are embarrassed and frustrated when you have to admit to your employer that the report is not completed.
>
> Your lack of planning resulted in an important report not being produced in a timely manner. Lack of planning can cause serious problems—even job loss.

Improper Handling of Visitors

As an office professional, your responsibility is to make visitors feel comfortable and welcome. That does not mean, however, that you must entertain the visitors while they are waiting to see your employer. Also, you should not engage in chitchat for long periods of time with co-workers. Certainly, if a co-worker comes by on a professional errand, it is okay to engage in the pleasantries such as, "Good morning, how is your day going?" but you should not spend ten to twenty minutes in idle chitchat.

Disorganization

Does your desk have a mountain of file folders, with their contents scattered everywhere? Are there half-finished projects, half-finished memorandums, and a stack of filing that is three weeks old? Disorganized individuals are a serious liability to their organization. They cannot be depended upon to provide information in a timely manner to others. They forget where the information is; they never meet deadlines because they have not written them down. They waste an enormous amount of their own time and other people's time in searching for files, phone numbers, reports, and other needed information.

When your desk is disorganized, it is difficult to get work done quickly and efficiently.

COMMUNICATION TIP

Stop reading junk mail.

Procrastination

Procrastination is defined as postponing or needlessly delaying a project or something that has to be done. Many of us are guilty of procrastination. We postpone a project because we are afraid that we will fail at it, because we are not interested in the work, and even because we are angry with the person who delegated it to us.

Of course, we do not want to admit any of these real reasons, so we make excuses such as the following:

- I have too many other projects.

- I do not have what I need to do the job.

- Before I can get started, I have to consult with my supervisor.

- There really is no rush to begin; it is not due for three weeks.

Procrastinators are late for meetings, put off handling projects, and do not return telephone calls. Procrastinators may be such relaxed, easygoing people that the procrastination does not bother them as much as others. They can still create stress for themselves with their last minute efforts, and the stress they put on other members of their work group can be significant.

Self Check C

What are your time wasters? Do you know? Take a few moments to consider them and write them down in the space provided here.

_____

_____

_____

_____

_____

TIME MANAGEMENT TECHNIQUES

You have considered the importance of time management, and you understand that time is a resource that must be used well. You have looked at some of the time wasters that we all face. Now attempt to understand how you might do a better job of managing yourself in relation to time. This area is one that all of us must work on constantly.

We never will become such effective time managers that we can forget about the constraints of time. If we pay attention to effective management techniques, however, we will find that not only do we seem to have more time to get our tasks done but that we also have reduced the stress in our lives considerably.

Set Goals

A **goal** is an objective, a purpose, or an end that is to be achieved. The idea of establishing goals makes many people feel uncomfortable. It has something to do with writing the goal down and then being expected to do it. It is like setting New Year's resolutions. How many of us set New Year's resolutions in good faith and then fail to reach any of them? If we even allow ourselves to think of these resolutions at a later date, we feel a vague sense of guilt about not having accomplished what we set out to do.

Goal setting can produce this same type of hesitancy and guilt. If we are to accomplish anything on our job and in our personal lives, setting goals is essential. An old Chinese proverb states, "If you do not know where you are going, any road will take you there." So it is. If we do not establish our goals, we become very undirected and may wind up someplace we did not intend to go.

Organizational Goals. Most organizations are involved in strategic and organizational planning. When these plans are written, there are definite goals to be accomplished and deadlines established in meeting these goals. Employees are usually brought into the planning process. In fact, companies often ask employees to write action plans that reflect what they will be accomplishing to meet the goals of the organization. Then, during evaluation, the employees are evaluated on how well they have met these goals.

Personal Goals. Personal goal setting is also important, and can take the form of deciding:

- on your career goals—what you want to be doing and where you want to be in five or ten years;

- when you want to purchase a house;

- when or if you want to start a family;

- where you want to live.

Goal Attributes. Effective goals must be achievable. They should stretch you so that you will have the opportunity for growth. They should be specific and measurable. These attributes, plus additional ones, are explained here.

- A goal should stretch you. A goal should motivate you to do more than you have been doing. It should motivate you to reach a higher level of accomplishment.

- A goal must be attainable. Just as your goals should stretch you, they also should not be unrealistically high. Goals should be achievable with hard work, appropriate skills, and dedication to the task.

- A goal must be specific and measurable. If your goal is too vague, you will not know when you have achieved it. For example, "to become a more effective communicator" is a goal that is too vague. How can you become a more effective communicator? You should determine the behaviors that will allow you to accomplish your goal. For example, your goal might be stated as, "I am going to become a more effective communicator by using paraphrasing, direct and simple language, and listening to others."

Then, your next step is to establish methods for measuring the accomplishment of your objective. In the communication situation, you might determine that you are going to measure the accomplishment in the following way: "In order to determine if I have accomplished my objective, I will ask three people within my workgroup to evaluate my communication skills."

- A goal must have a deadline. Deadlines allow us to track to see if the goal has been accomplished. In the communication example just given, you might set yourself this deadline: "Evaluation of my communication goal will occur by December 20, 1999" (within three months after it was set).

- A goal should be flexible. Sometimes conditions external to you impact your goals to the point that you cannot accomplish them. When this occurs, do not cling stubbornly to something that is no longer possible; but do not be too quick to mark off your goal. It may be that by working smarter you can offset the external factors. Also, you may be able to revise your goal or establish a different time frame for completion.

Analyze Your Time

Although you might feel that you know exactly how you spend your time, most of us in reality do not. It is a good idea to check periodically how you are spending time. You might be surprised at what is taking your time, and you might also discover some time wasters as you analyze your time.

Log Your Time. One way to determine how you spend your time is to chart on a time log the amount of time you spend in various daily activities. Certainly, you should not become a slave to the log. It is not important that you be accurate to the second or minute. It is important, however, that you are faithful to the process for a period of one or two weeks so you might have a realistic picture of how you are spending your time. Figure 14-1 shows a time log.

DAILY TIME LOG			
Name _____ Day _____ Date _____			
Time	Activity	Priority	Nature of Interruptions
		1 2 3	

Figure 14-1   Time log.

Analyze the Log. Your next step is to analyze your time log to discover ways in which you can improve the management of your time. Ask yourself these questions.

- What was the most productive period of the day? Why?

- What was the least productive period of the day? Why?

- Who or what accounted for the interruptions?

- Can the interruptions be minimized or eliminated?

- What activities needed more time?

- On what activities could I spend less time and still get the desired results?

Prepare an Action Plan. After you analyze your log, the next step is to do an action plan. The purpose of the plan is to set goals for yourself as to how you will increase your time management efficiency.

September						
Sunday	**Monday**	**Tuesday**	**Wednesday**	**Thursday**	**Friday**	**Saturday**
28	29	30	31	1	2	3
4	Labor Day 5	6	7 *Introductory phone call*	8 *Send brochure*	9	10
11	12 *Call to arrange presentation*	13	14	15	16	17
18	19 *10:00 a.m. Presentation*	20 *Follow-up Call*	21			24
25	26	27	28			1

My To-Do List

Task	Priority
Make phone call	A
Order brochures	B
Work on presentation	C

Figure 14-2   To-do list.

Use Good Techniques

Here is a sampling of techniques that will help you manage yourself in relation to your time. Obviously, there are numerous other effective time management techniques.

Set Priorities. Many times it will be impossible for you to do everything that you are asked to do in one day. Thus, you must be able to set priorities—to distinguish between the most important and least important jobs and determine the order in which they should be completed. If you are new to a job, you probably will have to have help from your supervisor to determine what tasks are the most important. Once you learn more about your position and your supervisor, you should be able to establish priorities on your own.

Prepare Daily To-Do Lists. Before you leave for the day, it is a good idea to prepare a to-do list for the next day. List all the tasks, activities, and projects that you need to accomplish and then review your list. Mark the most important items *A*; less important items *B*; those remaining *C*. Use your list, with priorities in place, to:

- arrange papers on your desk in priority order, with the *A*s in one pile, *B*s in another, and *C*s in another;

- mark telephone message slips with *A*, *B*, or *C*.

The next day as you complete the items on your to-do list, mark them off. This step gives you a sense of accomplishment in addition to calling your attention to what still needs to be accomplished. As you prepare your to-do list for the next day, use the present list. If there are items that you have not been able to accomplish, transfer these items to the to-do list for the next day. A sample to-do list is shown in Figure 14-2.

COMMUNICATION TIP

Keep your to-do list on your computer; updating and establishing priorities can be done quickly with a computerized to-do list.

Simplify Repetitive Tasks. If you find yourself keyboarding a form numerous times, simplify the process. Prepare a template on your computer. Do you find yourself looking up the same address or telephone number several times? Make yourself a list of frequently used addresses and telephone numbers. Store these on your computer. Simplifying a repetitive task takes time to organize initially, but in the long run the time savings can be significant.

Conquer Procrastination. Pick one area where procrastination plagues you and conquer it. For example, assume that you always put off filing. You find yourself having two and three weeks of filing stacked on your desk, and you are constantly having to rummage through the papers for something your employer needs. In your list of priorities, set aside twenty or thirty minutes each day (or whatever time you need) for filing; put it on your to-do list. Check it off when you have accomplished it.

The following include other ways in which you might conquer procrastination.

- Focus on one task at a time.

- Give yourself deadlines and meet them.

- Tackle the most difficult tasks first.

- Do not let perfectionism paralyze you; do not be afraid to make mistakes.

- Recognize that you have developed the habit of putting things off; then take steps to correct the habit; for example, create whatever visual reminders you need. You might make a sign for your desk reminding you not to procrastinate. Do not let yourself make exceptions by saying, "It is okay to procrastinate on this task." A lapse is like a skid in a car; it takes much more effort to recover than to maintain control from the outset.

Handle Paper Once. Do you ever find yourself rereading a piece of paper or shuffling it from the top of the stack to the bottom of the stack several times? Most of us do. In fact, many time management experts claim that handling paper over and over is the biggest paperwork time waster. The basic rule is to handle paper once. Read it, route it, file it, or answer it. Get if off your desk as quickly as possible.

Organize Your Work Area. When you are working on a project, clear your desk of materials that relate to other projects. Put these materials in a file folder, label the folder with the name of the project, and place the folder in your drawer.

Keep in and out trays on your desk, and label the trays so that it is clear which is for incoming material and which is for outgoing material. If space permits, you may wish to have a tray for material to be filed on your desk. Keep frequently used supplies such as pencils, pens, and paper clips in the center drawer of your desk. Divide your paper into letterhead, plain bond, memorandum, and other types of paper that you use.

COMMUNICATION TIP

Vary your repetitive tasks to ease the boredom. For example, file for twenty minutes, sort mail for ten minutes, and prepare mailing lists for fifteen minutes.

HUMAN RELATIONS

Your goal is to get control and then stay in control of your paperwork.

COMMUNICATION TIP

Spend a few moments at the end of each day getting your desk organized. You will feel much better about coming to work the next day if your desk is well organized.

Keeping your work area organized increases your productivity.

Reduce Interruptions. Interruptions can be frustrating time wasters. Controlling or minimizing interruptions is crucial to efficient time management. Here are some suggestions for reducing telephone and visitor interruptions.

Telephone

- Give and record correct information during telephone calls.

- When placing calls, identify yourself, your supervisor (if you are placing a call for that person), and what you need.

- If the person called is not in, find out when the person will return.

- When taking incoming calls, find out who is calling and the nature of the call.

- If you are taking a call for your supervisor who is not in, let the person know when your supervisor is expected.

- If you take a message, repeat the name, number, and message to the caller to confirm the accuracy.

- When you have several calls to make, group them and make the calls when the persons are likely to be in the office. Early morning is usually a good time to reach people.

- Keep your personal calls to a minimum. Let your friends know that they should not call you at the office.

- Use e-mail and faxes as alternatives to phone tag.

Visitors

- Set up appointments for visitors. Discourage people from dropping by unexpectedly to see you or your supervisor.

- Make visitors welcome, but do not make small talk for extended periods. Continue with your work.

- Discourage your co-workers from dropping by to socialize with you. You can socialize on breaks and at lunch. Make it clear that during working hours it is your responsibility to work.

Use Good Communication Techniques. If your supervisor asks you to do something, be sure that you understand exactly what you are to do. Paraphrase what you believe was said if you are not clear. Do not be afraid to ask questions. Transmit ideas in simple, clear terms. Define terms if necessary.

Listen carefully when someone is talking. When you are communicating with an individual face-to-face, use good eye contact. Be sensitive to the person's body language and to the words the person is saying. Keep your mind open to new ideas; refrain from passing judgment on what the speaker is saying.

TIME MANAGEMENT SYSTEMS

Many systems will help you to use your time well. These systems may be manual or electronic.

Manual Systems

One type of manual system is a calendar that allows you to record all appointments for the day, week, month, and year. If you use a manual calendar, keep all activities logged on the same calendar.

COMMUNICATION TIP

Learn to say "no" when it is appropriate. Learn to delegate to others or to ask for help if the task cannot be done in the time allotted.

Planning systems are also available. These systems include calendars; but they also include places to record prioritized daily tasks and appointments, monthly planning calendars for future years, sheets for recording goals, telephone and address directories, and delegation sheets.

Another type of manual system is a **tickler file.** This file is a chronological record of items to be completed. The system may be one that you design yourself or that you purchase. If you are setting up the system, a guide for the current month is placed in the front of the file followed by a separate guide for each day of the month. At the back of the file are guides for each month of the year. A tickler file is shown in Figure 14-3. To use this file, you write notes on index cards of tasks that need to be accomplished and file them behind the appropriate dates.

Figure 14-3   Tickler file.

Electronic Systems

One type of electronic system is an electronic calendar. These systems are used frequently in the office. Individual appointments and meetings are recorded on the calendar. Electronic calendars are usually networked within the office so executive calendars may be easily coordinated.

PIM software (which you learned about in Chapter 4) is still another type of electronic system which allows you to organize your work quickly and efficiently. Several companies produce this type of software which consists of user-friendly programs that feature calendaring, tracking to-do lists, address keeping, call logging, group scheduling, yearly planning, and notepads for storing text and graphics, to name a few. Software programs available include: Lotus Organizer, Day-Timer Organizer, and Sidekick for Windows.

YOUR POWER AND POTENTIAL

If you are to thrive in the business world of today, to master the multitude of changes that will be coming your way in the form of technology, and to be productive and happy in your work, you must be able to realize your full power and potential. When you are stressed to the point of burnout on your job and when you are constantly fighting too few hours in the day to accomplish what you must accomplish, you are not able to realize your full power and potential. By putting to use the techniques presented in this chapter you have a chance not only to succeed in your job but also to thrive in the world of change.

CHAPTER SUMMARY

This summary will help you remember the important points covered in this chapter.

- Stress is the body's response to a demand placed upon it. Chronic stress occurs when a distressful situation is prolonged with no rest or recuperation for the body. Chronic stress can cause physical and emotional problems.

- Factors in our society that contribute to stress are work overload, dual-career families, single-parent families, elderly family members, economic pressures, and distressing work conditions.

- Stress reducers include balancing work and play, knowing the difference between achievement and perfection, recognizing our limits, exercising, eating right, getting enough sleep, and managing ourselves in relation to our time.

- Time is a unique resource; it cannot be bought, sold, borrowed, rented, saved, or manufactured. It is the only resource that must be spent the minute it is received.

- Time wasters include ineffective communication, poor telephone usage, inadequate planning, improper handling of visitors, disorganization, and procrastination.

- Good time management techniques include setting goals, analyzing our time, setting priorities, preparing daily to-do lists, simplifying repetitive tasks, conquering procrastination, handling paper once, organizing our work areas, keeping in and out trays on our desks, reducing interruptions, and using good communication techniques.

- Time management systems such as calendaring, tickler files, and computer software can help us manage ourselves in relation to our time.

CHAPTER GLOSSARY

The following terms were introduced in this chapter. To help you review, definitions are given here.

- **Downsize** (p. 329)–Reduction of the number of employees within a business.

- **Rightsize** (p. 329)–Determining the most efficient and effective number of employees and organizational structure.

- **Virtual office** (p. 329)–An office created at any place and at any time through the use of technology.

- **Stress** (p. 329)–The body's response to a demand placed upon it.

- **Chronic stress** (p. 329)–Occurs when a distressful situation is prolonged with no rest or recuperation for the body; it can cause physical and emotional problems.

- **Burnout** (p. 329)–An employee consistently has low productivity and low motivation and has a general attitude of disinterest in the job.

- **Perfectionism** (p. 332)–The propensity for setting extremely high standards and being displeased with anything else.

- **Time management** (p. 335)–The way in which we manage ourselves and our tasks in relation to the time that we have.

- **Time** (p. 335)–A resource that cannot be bought, sold, borrowed, rented, saved, or manufactured. It is the only resource that must be spent the minute it is received.

- **Procrastination** (p. 337)–The act of postponing or needlessly delaying a project or something that has to be done.

- **Goal** (p. 337)–An objective, a purpose, or an end that is to be achieved.

- **Tickler file** (p. 342)–A chronological file by date order.

DISCUSSION ITEMS

These discussion items provide an opportunity for you to test your understanding of the chapter through discussion with your classmates and your instructor.

1. Is all stress unhealthy? Explain.
2. List and explain five causes of stress.
3. Explain what is meant by "knowing the difference between achievement and perfection."
4. How does exercise help reduce stress?
5. List and explain five time wasters.
6. How does goal setting relate to time management?

CASE STUDY

Claudia Shaeffer has worked in the Human Resources Division of Koronet International for five years. Claudia is in charge of employee benefits. She is an excellent employee—very competent, knowledgeable about human resources (holds an MBA with a specialty in management), loyal, dependable, and respected by her colleagues. Two years ago, a new director of human resources was hired. Claudia has tried to work with him, but the situation does not get better—it merely gets worse. He gives her no information. When he asks her to prepare a report, it is done always at the last minute; for example, he often gives her approximately two hours to do a report that should take at least a week to do well. He lies to her about policies and directions that are being set. She has

talked with him repeatedly about the issues. Claudia is not afraid to address the issues. When she talks to him, he listens but never responds. He has never complained about her work; she believes that he knows she does a good job. Claudia has considered leaving the job; however, she has two more years until she is vested in the retirement system. If she left now, she would lose all of her retirement benefits. Recently, Claudia began to have health problems. She went to her physician; he told her it was stress related. He also stated she needed to take at least three months off. Claudia did so. The three months have passed, and Claudia is ready to come back to work.

What suggestions would you make to Claudia to decrease the stress on her job?

OFFICE TASKS

OFFICE TASK 14-1 (Objectives 1, 2, and 3)
Analyze the two cases presented here, then respond to the items following the cases in a memorandum addressed to your instructor. A memorandum form is provided on the Student Data Template Disk, file OT14-1.

Two of your friends (Johanna and Juan) who work in offices in your building are having problems; they have both told you their situations which are given here.

Johanna's Situation

Johanna has worked for the company for three years. Recently, she was promoted to administrative assistant for the president of the company. The job is a demanding one. Her responsibilities include setting up meetings, making travel arrangements for the president and the board of trustees, arranging meals before the monthly board meetings, and responding to calls from the board of trustees about various items. In addition, she supervises two office assistants and takes minutes at the board meetings and the biweekly staff meetings called by the president, along with numerous other projects.

Johanna is attempting to employ a new office assistant, since one assistant has recently left for another position. This task is taking a long time. She is using a temporary employee until she can employ someone full time.

Johanna has four children, and she and her husband are in the process of getting a divorce. Her husband has fought her throughout the process. The situation at home is very difficult.

Johanna likes her job, but she is not being as effective as she knows that she can be.

1. Are there stressors in Johanna's work environment? If so, what are they?

2. What are the stressors in Johanna's home environment?

3. What might Johanna do to reduce some of the stress?

Juan's Situation

Juan has been working for Ingram Travel Agency for two years. The company is small, and there have been several personnel cutbacks since Juan began. Recently, there have been additional cutbacks. Now there are only two office assistants in the company (previously there were four). The other remaining office assistant has been with the company for only six months. Because Juan knows the operation well and has been with the company for two years, he has been asked to assume most of the responsibilities of the two assistants who have left.

Juan has always felt good about his abilities and skills. He is able to produce large amounts of work quickly. For the last two months, however, he has not been able to see the top of his desk. His supervisor has become irritable with him on several occasions when work was not completed on time. There never seems to be an end to the amount of work stacked on his desk; he cannot get caught up. Recently Juan has not been feeling well or sleeping well. He wakes up two and three times a night thinking about the office. He has resorted to taking sleeping pills to get some rest at night.

1. Identify the factors that have contributed to Juan's stress.

2. What steps can Juan take to minimize his stress?

3. To minimize future stress, how should Juan respond if he is faced with a similar situation?

OFFICE TASK 14-2 (Objectives 1, 2, 3, and 4)

Team with three of your classmates on this project. Read four recent articles on stress and time management. Write your findings in a memorandum to your instructor; list all references that you used. A memorandum form is provided on the Student Data Template Disk, file OT14-2.

OFFICE TASK 14-3 (Objective 3)

Identify the stressors that you have in your life at the present time. These stressors may be at home, at school, or in the office. Next, identify ways in which you can relieve these stressors. Practice implementing these stress controls for two weeks. Write a memorandum to your instructor explaining what stress controls you implemented and how successful these stress controls were in relieving your stress. A memorandum form is provided on the Student Data Template Disk, file OT14-3.

OFFICE TASK 14-4 (Objectives 4, 5, and 6)

On the Student Data Template Disk, file OT14-4 is a similated screen from your PIM software and an e-mail message from Ms. Marquette appears on OT14-4B. Considering both of these items, place your to-do list in priority order, adding the items which need to be added from Ms. Marquette's memo. Assign an *A* to the items requiring immediate attention, *B* to those items that should be dealt with this week, and *C* to those items that you should begin work on as soon as possible but have no immediate deadline. Print out your new prioritized to-do list and hand in to your instructor.

OFFICE TASK 14-5 (Objectives 5 and 6)

On the Student Data Template Disk, file OT14-5 is a time log form; print out five copies of the form. For the next five days, log the time you spend in various activities on the form. If you are employed, log the time you spend in activities at work. If you are not employed, log the way you use your personal time.

Now analyze the way you spent your time during the five days. On the Student Data Template

Disk, file OT14-5B are questions for you to answer to help you analyze your time. After you have analyzed the way you used your time, prepare an action plan using the form given on the Student Data Template Disk, file OT14-5C. Indicate what you will be doing to make more effective use of your time. Print out one copy of 14-5B and 14-5C and turn in to your instructor.

OFFICE TASK 14-6 (Objectives 5 and 6)
On the Student Data Template Disk, file OT14-6 is a time effectiveness questionnaire. Respond to the statements given. Then prepare an action plan, using the form provided on the Student Data Template Disk, file OT14-5B. Indicate what you will be doing to make more effective use of your time. Turn in the action plan to your instructor.

ENGLISH USAGE CHALLENGE DRILL

Correct the following sentences. Cite the grammar rule that is applicable to each sentence. Before you begin, refresh your memory of grammar rules by reviewing capitalization.

1. He gave three reasons for not being on time: (1) bad weather caused traffic slowdowns. (2) the time listed on his calendar was incorrect. (3) he had to stop for gasoline.

2. The reasons for the delay were: Bad weather, Poor scheduling, and Equipment failure.

3. "Of course," she added, "The project will take time."

4. I was introduced to senator George Aikens.

5. Mr. Monroe is President of the company.

ASSESSMENT OF CHAPTER OBJECTIVES

Now that you have completed the chapter and the office tasks, take a few moments to review the following learning objectives which you were given at the beginning of this chapter. Did you accomplish these objectives? If so, explain how in the space provided. If you were unable to accomplish these objectives, give your reason for not doing so. Your instructor may want to review your answers.

I accomplished these objectives:

1. Define the causes of stress. Yes _____ No _____
   Explain how you accomplished this objective.
   _____
   _____
   _____

2. Identify stress reducers. Yes _____ No _____
   Explain how you accomplished this objective.
   _____
   _____
   _____

3. Implement stress controls. Yes _____ No _____
   Explain how you accomplished this objective.
   _____
   _____
   _____

4. Determine the importance of utilizing time well.
   Yes _____ No _____
   Explain how you accomplished this objective.
   _____
   _____
   _____

5. Identify time wasters. Yes _____ No _____
   Explain how you accomplished this objective.
   _____
   _____
   _____

6. Establish effective time management techniques.
   Yes _____ No _____
   Explain how you accomplished this objective.
   _____
   _____
   _____

Provide reasons for failing to accomplish any of the objectives.
_____
_____
_____
_____

CHAPTER 15

LEADING OTHERS

LEARNING OBJECTIVES

1. **Determine what unique leadership needs exist in the twenty-first century.**
2. **Describe the characteristics of effective leaders.**
3. **Define the essential management responsibilities.**
4. **Analyze how leadership is earned.**

As you assume positions of greater responsibility in the office, you may have one or more persons reporting to you. Being an effective manager, one who is able to inspire people to produce at their maximum, demands that you understand and apply basic leadership and management theory. This chapter is designed to help you become effective in leadership and management roles.

Even if you do not become a manager or supervisor, this chapter will be helpful to you when you have the opportunity to assume leadership roles in diverse areas. For example, you may assume a leadership role in

- *leading a team within the office in solving some problem;*

- *determining a new document management system which will be used throughout the department;*

- *serving as an officer in a professional organization;*

- *leading in your personal life through working with your spouse and children to manage the home environment;*

- *leading through taking responsible roles in civic organizations and church functions.*

Whatever form it takes, most of us find ourselves in leadership roles or certainly having the opportunity to take leadership roles at numerous points throughout our lives. By studying this chapter, you will understand some of the important aspects of leadership.

LEADERSHIP IN THE TWENTY-FIRST CENTURY

Throughout this book you have learned that change (due to technology, the information explosion, and demographics, to name some of the factors) will be constant in the twenty-first century. In addition, you have learned that we must consider ourselves part of a global community. Even if we wanted to think of the United States in isolation, we cannot. Technology allows us to communicate on a worldwide basis, pulling together people of diverse backgrounds and cultures. Leadership in the twenty-first century demands two unique skills—skills that were not essential in the past but are imperative now. These skills are change mastery and an international perspective.

CHANGE MASTERY

The leader in the twenty-first century not only understands change but also embraces change; however, embracing change is not easy. Change can be scary and even threatening to many people. The successful leader sees change as challenging but filled with opportunity. This kind of leader expects the future to be filled with shifting variables and understands that disruptions are an inevitable part of the changing world. The twenty-first century leader

- considers long-term results over short-term results;
- stresses effectiveness over efficiency only;

- thinks strategically rather than operationally;

- is proactive to situations rather than reactive;

- is driven by plans rather than problems.

INTERNATIONAL PERSPECTIVE

The organization of the twenty-first century will draw resources—financial, human, and technical—from all over the world. To be effective, the leader must understand and be able to function in an **interdependent** world. This interdependent world is made possible by instantaneous communication through television, computers, fax, and the World Wide Web; efficient global transportation systems; and consumer tastes which are becoming more universal. Think for a moment about the food industry. McDonald's is worldwide; when visiting countries in Europe and Asia, Americans can rather easily satisfy their need for what has been considered an American staple in the past—the hamburger. Today, that American staple has become a food enjoyed worldwide. So, too, is food from other nations common in the diet of Americans. Sushi bars are now in local American grocery stores, in addition to restaurants specializing in Japanese food. Thai and Korean restaurants are easily found in most American cities; enchiladas, tacos, and tortillas are staples in most Americans' diets.

The effective organization of the next century cannot think and act independently. Organizations must cultivate global interdependence to lead into the twenty-first century. The marketing of products and services worldwide (as illustrated in the McDonald's example) also means that human, financial, and technical resources must be considered in a worldwide market. When Americans open business operations in China, for example, employees consist of Americans, Chinese, and people of other nationalities. In other words, the labor pool is a worldwide pool. This same concept is true as Japanese businesses, for example, open businesses in America. Consider the Toyota plants that operate in the United States. The personnel are international. Our interdependency will only continue to grow. What was once considered the far reaches of the world are now coming closer to all of us—almost as if they are right next door. The responsibility of leaders in this worldwide economy is truly awesome.

For continued growth, corporations such as Proctor & Gamble must have a global perspective. *Erik Von Fischer/Photonics Graphics.*

CHARACTERISTICS OF AN EFFECTIVE LEADER

What are the characteristics of an effective leader in this global world of change? Here are a few important ones for your consideration.

UNDERSTANDS SELF

If leaders are to be effective, they must understand (not just superficially but deeply) who they are. We are shaped by our background and experiences. Our families, our friends, the schools we have attended, and society in general have told us how we should behave and what we should value. If we are truly to understand ourselves, however, we must at some point in our lives decide for ourselves what is important. How can we really know who we are? These ideas will help you.

- Be willing to separate who you are from what the world thinks you should be. This statement does not mean that the teachings you have learned are not important. Of course, they are. At some point, however, you must decide what is important to you. For example, your mother or father may have wanted you to be a medical doctor. Not only are you not interested in the field, but you have no aptitude for the sciences. The quicker you understand and accept that you have the ability to decide what is best for you, the quicker you will be on your way to understanding and being your own self.

349

- Be willing to accept responsibility. Life is about accepting responsibility for your actions. Have you ever known someone who never made a mistake, never made an error, or never admitted to being wrong? Most of us have had some experience with this type of individual. Unfortunately, this type of person usually has very little understanding of self. Knowing self means that we recognize our strengths and our weaknesses. We know what we can and cannot do. We know that all human beings make mistakes, and we are willing to admit when we make one. To make an error is not unique or even unforgivable. To continue to make the same error and to not learn from our mistakes are unforgivable. Knowing ourselves means that we accept our humanness—we do make mistakes, but we do not attempt to pass this blame on to others.

- Be willing to reflect on past experience. Reflecting on experience means having a dialogue with yourself. What really happened? Why did it happen? How did it affect me? What can I learn from the experience? By reflecting on your experiences, you can learn and grow. If the experience was unpleasant, you analyze why. What went wrong? Why did it go wrong? You can then strive to never make the same mistake again.

- Understand that self-knowledge is a lifetime process. Just as the world changes, individuals change with new experiences and new knowledge. If we are going to understand ourselves, we must commit to continuing the process through life. We must continue to explore our own depths, to reflect on our experiences, and to seek challenges.

BUILDS A SHARED VISION

You learned in Chapter 6 that the ethical organization is visionary. The effective leader is able to build the shared vision of the organization with employees within the organization. Building a vision with employees means involving employees at all levels of the organization in the vision. It means that leaders help employees consider these possible questions.

- What products or services does the organization produce? What should it produce?

- What values does the organization have? What values should it have?

- What contributions should the organization make to the community?

- What reputation does the organization have? What reputation should it have?

- Who are the clients and customers of the organization?

- How do people work together within the organization?

- Do the values of the individuals within the organization match the values of the organization?

- What contributions do individuals within the organization make?

Effective leaders help employees to understand the organization's vision and how their individual goals and objectives can support the vision of the organization.

The effective leader works with employees to build a shared vision.

COMMUNICATION TIP

Put the company's vision on the back of all business cards; make attractive posters of the company's vision; place these posters at all entrances to the business.

IS SERVICE ORIENTED

Effective leaders consider service to others as primary. In other words, effective leaders are not concerned first with building a career for themselves but in understanding how they can serve the organization, the external community, and people within the organization. The effective leader is service oriented around principles, and has deep-seated values. For example, these values may be commitment to helping people grow, commitment to diversity, and commitment to helping the world to be a better place to live. When effective leaders live by a set of principles, they are said to have **legitimate power.**

To understand legitimate power, contrast this type of power with two other negative types of power which ineffective managers sometimes use. One type is referred to as **coercive power.** With coercive power, the manager creates fear in the follower that either something bad will happen or something good will be taken away if the manager is not "obeyed." Out of fear of losing a job, for example, the individual will acquiesce to the manager. The second type of negative power is referred to as **utility power.** With utility power, the relationship is based on a useful exchange of goods and services between the manager and the employees. For example, the employees have something the manager wants (talent, time, energy) and the manager has something the employees want (promotions, security, information). The employees operate from the belief that the manager will do something for them if they will do what the manager wants.

Legitimate power uses neither of these negative "if you do something for me, I will do something for you" approaches. The leader who has legitimate power is true to inner principles, and leads from this principle-centered approach. Employees can then respond because they believe in the "right" of what is being done. There is no blind faith or servitude on the part of the employee but thoughtful acceptance or open disagreement (with open discussion) concerning the goals of the organization and the individual. The leader and the employees move forward because of their faith, respect, and trust in each other.

EMPOWERS OTHERS

Power, according to the dictionary, means "the ability or official capacity to exercise control;

authority." Because the prefix "em" means "to put on to" or "to cover with," **empowering** means the passing on of authority or responsibility to others.

Leaders empower people when they

- provide the employees access to information that will help them do their job better;
- allow employees to take on more responsibility;
- allow employees a voice in decision making.

Empowered employees feel a sense of ownership and control over their jobs, responsibility for their work, and ability to get their jobs done. Empowered employees usually are happier individuals—they trust the organization, feel a part of it, and enjoy the rewards that the job provides.

The leader who empowers people has a core belief in people, and believes that people are basically good, honest, and well intentioned. The leader believes that people will do the right thing when they have the resources available to them to accomplish the task. This type of leader understands that leadership is doing the right thing—that leadership is operating from a central core of values even in the most difficult situations.

The effective leader empowers others by providing employees access to information. *Courtesy of International Business Machines, Inc.*

REWARDS RISK TAKING

The organization of the twenty-first century, with change as a constant, will face risks daily. To ignore the risks does not make them go away. The organization cannot take refuge in status quo, conformity to the norm, or security in the past. None of these stances make sense if the organization is to be successful. The organization must constantly be willing to see new answers to problems, to try new approaches, and to be flexible. If the organization is to be successful, it must have leaders who not only take risks themselves but also encourage others to take risks.

Here are some keys to successful risk taking.

- Trust your own abilities. Do not place limits on your ability to learn and improve. Just as a small child you did not doubt yourself because you could not read (knowing and looking forward to going to school so that you could learn to read), you should not doubt your ability to learn and try new things when you are 30, 50, or even 70 years young.

- Be open minded. Our assumptions can prevent us from seeing new possibilities. When analyzing situations that need solving, we need to discard our old assumptions. Where would we be today if Columbus and his courageous colleagues had believed the world was flat as did almost everyone in the world at that time? Where would we be today if Wilbur and Orville Wright had not believed that it was possible to build a "flying machine."

- Develop your intuitive powers. Subconsciously, we take note of any number of things that our conscious mind does not realize. However, these subconscious notations can be brought to the surface of our consciousness if we listen carefully to ourselves (our intuition).

- Overcome the fear of making mistakes. Certainly, when trying something new, you will make mistakes. What you need to consider when taking risks is the likelihood of success. You would not want to jump off a ten-story building thinking that maybe you would live through it. That would be a foolish and senseless risk. Listen to your intuition. Most people know intuitively when a risk makes sense and when it does not. Sam Walton in building Wal-Mart went through many failures and difficult times. Yet, his vision was so clear and his understanding of what would yield success so deep that the risks and even temporary failures were well worth it.

- Develop a support team. When you feel you have made a mistake, supportive colleagues can help you analyze your situation to determine what to do next. When your colleagues make mistakes, you can help them analyze the situation. Support teams can help each other in the bad times and cheer for each other in the good times.[1]

The task of the effective manager is to build an environment that supports risk taking. Employees need to know that they will not be "punished" for taking appropriate risks. They need to know that the organization will support their risk-taking ventures and reward their successes. They need to know that the leader encourages their risk taking, knowing that failures will occur sometimes. These failures, however, will never be catastrophic for the individual taking the risk.

MOVES THROUGH CHAOS

The effective leader learns from the surrounding chaos in this changing world and, in fact, is often shaped by that chaos. In this case, "shaping" means that the leader learns from both the good and bad experiences which happen during times of chaos. You have already learned that when you take risks, you often make mistakes. Mistakes are an inevitable outcome of continued risk taking. The effective leader takes these mistakes, learns from them, and builds on

---

[1]Kline, Peter and Bernard Saunders, *Ten Steps to a Learning Organization* (Virginia: Great Ocean Publishers, Inc., 1993), 98–103.

COMMUNICATION TIP

Develop a risk-taker award to be given to employees who take risks.

the lessons learned from the failure to help ensure success the next time. For example, numerous highly successful people have been fired, but they do not let the fact that they have been fired keep them from being successful in their next venture. They learn what they can from the firing, discard what is not meaningful, and continue to try to make a difference in the world. In other words, they are driven by their own inner strengths and messages.

Chaos is an inevitable part of being a leader in the twenty-first century. The successful leader accepts this inevitability, moves with it, and therefore practices the art of meeting individuals and situations where they are and moving with them to bring about the desired outcomes.

KNOWS HOW TO FOLLOW

The effective leader knows the importance of stepping back and being a follower when the situation demands it. This leader understands that leaders are followers at times and followers are leaders at times. A **bilateralness** (affecting two sides equally) exists, with the leader not only understanding the importance of following but having the trust in others to know that they, given the proper opportunities and training, can be leaders, too.

Self Check

Stop for a few minutes and consider the characteristics that you believe you already possess of an effective leader. List those characteristics here, stating why you believe you are effective in each area.

_____

_____

_____

_____

Now list the characteristics that you would like to begin to work on during the remainder of this course. List at least two characteristics, stating how you plan to develop them.

_____

_____

_____

_____

LEADERSHIP AND MANAGEMENT CONTRASTED

Leadership is defined as doing the right thing whereas **management** is defined as doing things right. The effective leader operates around a clearly defined set of values, with those values centering on what is right for an organization and for the people who exist in that organization. Effective leadership relies on the leader bringing the appropriate set of values to the work environment. There is no real way to assess the values of the leader in isolation; they are apparent as the leader moves an organization and the individuals within it to accomplish goals that benefit not only the organization but also the external community and the individuals within the organization. The importance of leadership can never be diminished, and the numerous books written on leadership attest to the fact that true leadership is to be valued and treated with the utmost respect.

By contrast, management can be considered a subset of leadership; for example, the functions of management include planning, organizing, recruiting, training, controlling, and evaluating. These activities are relatively concrete and can be quantified, measured, and assessed. If an organization is to do things right, these functions must be understood and carried out effectively.

EFFECTIVE LEADERSHIP AND MANAGEMENT: A BLEND

Management has been a body of study for years. Numerous books have been written; management courses are a standard part of business degrees; the term "manager" is used as a title in most organizations. The tasks of management are relatively clear and understood by most professionals. Although it is possible to make a case for a clear distinction between leadership and management, the most effective managers are also effective leaders. In considering this concept, you need to be aware of three individuals who have written extensively about effective organizations and effective people within organizations—W. Edwards Deming, Stephen R. Covey, and Peter Senge. These individuals' ideas are accepted and widely used in the corporate world today. They approach leadership and management as a totality, stressing that effective management is an integral part of effective leadership. In other words, one cannot exist without the other.

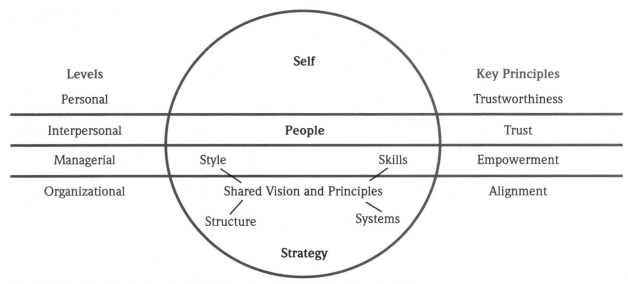

Levels		Key Principles
Personal	**Self**	Trustworthiness
Interpersonal	**People**	Trust
Managerial	Style Skills	Empowerment
Organizational	Shared Vision and Principles	Alignment
	Structure Systems	
	Strategy	

Figure 15-1   Principle-centered leadership has four levels and four key principles.

In Chapter 1, you learned about total quality management and Deming's fourteen principles. Total quality management is a philosophy that espouses the necessity of continuous improvement within the organization. This planning and improvement is guided by feedback from clients and customers—both internal and external. The key, according to Deming, is to listen to individuals who have a stake in the organization, whether they be clients, customers, or employees. One deadly disease of an organization is to lack constancy of purpose—to not have long-range plans for staying in business.

Stephen Covey in *Principle-Centered Leadership*[2] stresses that the key to a total quality organization is having total quality people within the organization. He describes the four levels to principle-centered leadership and four key principles. Figure 15-1 gives these levels and principles. Notice that the first level is personal. Covey contends that without personal and professional development one cannot be effective as a manager within an organization.

Peter Senge sets out his philosophy of leadership and management within an organization through his work *The Fifth Discipline*.[3] Senge contends that it is essential to build a learning organization through personal mastery, mental models, shared vision, and team learning. He also contends that building a learning organization is a continual process, stating that " . . . a corporation cannot be excellent in the sense of having arrived at a permanent excellence; it is always in the state of practicing the disciplines of learning, of becoming better or worse."[4]

MANAGEMENT RESPONSIBILITIES

If you are to be successful in a supervisory role, you need to understand how to effectively perform the basic management responsibilities including planning, organizing, recruiting and employing, training, motivating, delegating, and evaluating. These functions are presented here.

PLAN

Planning is one crucial function of management. Without proper planning, an organization and the individuals within it do not know where they are going. A major part of the planning process is setting goals and objectives. Although all organizations have goals and objectives, they may be loosely defined or not defined at all in writing. Defining them in writing and establishing measurable results involve a process recommended by Peter Drucker[5]

[2]Covey, Stephen R., *Principle-Centered Leadership* (New York: Summit Books, 1990).

[3]Senge, Peter, *The Fifth Discipline* (New York: Doubleday/Currency, 1990).

[4]*Ibid.*, 11.

[5]Drucker, Peter, *The Practice of Management* (New York: Harper and Row, Publishers, 1954).

over thirty years ago. In a seminal work entitled *The Practice of Management,* Drucker set forth the process that came to be known as **management by objectives (MBO).** Although it has taken on numerous forms and variations, it is still used extensively today.

The planning process in which goals and objectives are set is usually done for a one-year period, which is called **short-range planning,** and for a three- to five-year period, which is called **long-range planning.** Many times the overall goals of the company are set by top level administrators; that is, the board of directors, the president, and the executive vice-presidents. Once these goals have been determined, they are distributed to the managers and supervisors in the organization. Then the supervisors set objectives for their particular work unit and the managers for their particular division. The supervisors and managers are responsible for the contributions that their work units or divisions make to the departments above and below them.

Think for a moment about what your role in the planning process might be as an office professional supervising support staff. You may be included in helping to set the objectives of the department in which you work. The responsibility for setting departmental objectives rests with the managers of the department, but some organizations include their employees in this planning process. If you have management responsibilities, the possibility of your being included is greater.

Once you have participated in the setting of objectives for your department, you will have a greater understanding of the objectives and goals of the company. Even if you do not help set the objectives of your department, you will engage in planning the activities of your unit. That planning includes setting objectives. All employees in the unit need to understand what they are expected to produce. You should have a planning session at least once a year, and preferably every six months, to look at what your unit should be accomplishing for the year. During this planning session, you and the employees determine what should be accomplished, when it will be accomplished, the costs of accomplishing the objectives, and how the objectives will be measured. Assume, for example, that one of your objectives is to revise the document management system within your division. The objective might be written in this manner:

Revise the document management system from an alphabetic system to a subject system by April 15. After two months of use, the system will be evaluated by all users within the division; the evaluation will be written by the manager, in conjunction with two of the team members. The cost of the system is in personnel and supplies (with an approximate cost of $500 for supplies).

ORGANIZE

Once the planning has been done, the work must be organized. Organization involves bringing together all resources—people, time, money, and equipment—in the most effective way to accomplish the goals. The three factors that enter into how the work is organized are span of control, job analysis, and work periods.

Span of Control

Span of control refers to the number of employees who are directly supervised by one person. There is no formula that rigidly defines the span of control. The number is determined more by the philosophy of management. You learned in Chapter 1 that organizations are flatter today (fewer levels of hierarchy). A flattened organizational structure usually means that the span of control is greater than in the past. For example, rather than supervising three to five individuals, a manager may supervise as many as thirty people. Here are some questions that need to be asked when considering span of control.

- Is the organization a hierarchical one or is it committed to a flat organization?

- Is the manager highly skilled and experienced? (Can the manager assume the responsibilities of an expanded reporting structure? Does the manager have the skills to do so?)

- Are the workgroup members highly skilled and knowledgeable?

- Is the work that the group is performing similar in nature?

- Is the workgroup given a great degree of autonomy? (Is the workgroup allowed to make decisions without checking with the supervisor?)

Job Analysis

A second factor in the organization of work is job analysis. To perform a job analysis, a supervisor must determine the requirements of a job and the qualifications needed by personnel to get the job done. Once this information is determined, it is usually compiled into a job description such as the one in Figure 15-2. The job description includes skills, training, education necessary for the job, and a list of the job duties. Most companies have job descriptions for all employees. Such an approach is helpful not only in the hiring process but also in letting employees know what they are expected to do.

Work Periods

A third factor to consider in organizing work is the time in which the work is to be performed. In the past, the workweek has traditionally spanned from 8 or 9 a.m. to 5 p.m. However, there are numerous changes today. You learned in Chapter 1 about flextime, four-day weeks, job sharing, and the virtual office (with people working from various locations and at various times). These factors impact the way the supervisor organizes the work of a particular division.

RECRUIT AND EMPLOY

In recruiting office professionals, a company makes use of several sources—employment agencies, newspaper advertisements, Internet advertisements, recommendations from employees, college and university placement offices, and so forth. Companies usually establish procedures through their human resources departments which outline how a company will recruit employees. There are certain legal considerations; for example, when placing advertisements, care should be taken to ensure that the wording of the advertisement does not conflict with fair employment practice laws. Discrimination statutes prohibit advertisements that show

Job Description

Job Title: Administrative Assistant
Company: Koronet International
Department: Vice President of Community Relations
Reports to: Jacqueline Marquette

Skills and Training

The position of Administrative Assistant requires excellent organizational and human relations skills. The position requires the ability to screen and establish priorities on projects and to supervise office support staff. Excellent oral and written communication skills are necessary.

Basic skills include computer (word processing, spreadsheet, and graphics software), document management, grammar and composition, and accurate keyboarding at 80 wpm.

Education and Experience

Four years of office experience; an associate degree in business.

Duties

1. Composing letters, memorandums, and reports.

2. Keying correspondence and reports.

3. Developing spreadsheets.

4. Maintaining a document management system.

5. Planning meetings and conferences.

6. Handling requests from the external community.

7. Supervising office support staff.

Figure 15-2

preferences in terms of race, religion, gender, age, or physical disabilities. An employer cannot advertise for a particular age group. Thus, expressions such as "young person" or "retired person" cannot be used in advertisements. If you are recruiting employees, check with the appropriate individuals within your company to make sure you are observing the company rules and any legal guidelines.

Once applicants are recruited, use the following three major tools for screening and selection.

- written application
- personal interview
- testing procedures

The manager or a team of people may review the applications. When reviewing the applications, you should be clear as to the skills, education, and experience that you desire. These questions will help keep you and the team on track.

- What type of person are we seeking?
- What qualifications does that person need to have?
- What education and experience does the person need?

With your criteria in mind, screen the applications and select the most qualified individuals to interview.

You may choose to interview individually, use a team, or a combination of the two. Before the interviewing process begins, write a list of questions that will be asked of each candidate. Such a list keeps you and the team on target as you begin the interviewing process and helps you treat all interviewees with fairness and consistency. It also helps remind you about questions you cannot legally ask. The following questions are unlawful to ask during the interview.

- Are you married? Single? Divorced? Separated?
- What is the date of your birth?
- Is your spouse a United States citizen?
- Where were you born?
- To what clubs do you belong?
- What are the ages of your children?
- What church do you attend?

It is imperative that you keep up with the latest laws concerning discrimination and interviewing procedures. You can inadvertently place your company in jeopardy of a discrimination suit if you are not knowledgeable of the laws.

Set aside enough time for a thorough interview. You will probably need to spend an hour or more with each applicant. Do not consider this time wasted. Hiring the right person for a job is one of the most important things you will do as a manager.

The third screening tool is the test. Here, too, legal considerations are important. The use of tests in selecting office professionals is not prohibited, but testing practices that have a discriminatory effect are prohibited. Keep in mind that the test must measure the person's qualifications for the job and not the person as an individual. If you are employing an office professional, for example, and a requirement of the job is that the person be able to key at a certain rate with a certain degree of accuracy, you can give the person a keyboarding test to discover the necessary skills. You can also give an office professional grammar and spelling tests because the individual will be required to produce documents that are free of grammatical and spelling errors. You cannot ask a person to take a math proficiency test unless the use of math is necessary in performing the job.

TRAINING

Training for which the manager is responsible is twofold—individual training and team training. Both types are presented here.

Many companies conduct training sessions to better educate their employees. *Hewlett Packard.*

357

Individual Training

Once a person is employed, the next step is to assist that person in developing the knowledge to be successful on the job. Certainly, the individual comes in with a set of skills; however, remember that the person probably knows little or nothing about how your company works. To be successful, that person must learn quickly about proper company procedure. As a manager, you have an obligation in this area.

In addition to entry-level training, the rapid changes in technology make it necessary to provide job up-date training for office professionals. The company, for example, may purchase a new software program. The employee will need training to become proficient on this software.

Still another type of training for which a supervisor may be responsible is preparation for promotion. Company programs for promoting qualified office workers improve employee morale. Supervisors should be constantly alert for employees who show promotion capabilities and use every opportunity to encourage and develop these employees. Additional training may be available through company-sponsored seminars, through tuition-reimbursed courses at local colleges, or through job internship or rotation plans in which the employee spends a period of time learning various jobs.

Team Training

The use of extensive teams within the office demands that the manager be involved in training teams. Generally, teams cannot function at their highest degree of productivity without training as to how to accomplish tasks together and interpersonal skill development. Here are some skills that are generally necessary for all team members as they work together.

- listening—summarizing, checking for understanding, and giving and receiving feedback

- communication—communicating with other team members, clients and customers, and the team leader

- conflict resolution—identifying and resolving conflicts within the team or with individuals outside the team

- influencing others—gaining commitment as a team and as individuals

- team job skills—cross-training and coaching

- developing solutions—creatively generating and sorting alternative solutions to issues

- ensuring ongoing quality—determining how results will be continually measured

- technical capability—the technical expertise needed to get the task done

In addition, as a manager working with teams, heed the following caveats to be successful.

- Do not **micromanage** (tell the team every step to take).

- Empower the team; give them the information needed to get the job done.

- Trust the team; once they have the information, trust them to produce the best possible solutions to problems.

- Take a strong stand with the team when needed; if the team is not accomplishing the task or is getting bogged down in personality issues, let them know that such behaviors are not acceptable.

- Check on the team's development. Are they communicating with and trusting each other? Do they know the purpose of the team? Do they understand their individual roles? Is each member involved in the process and product?

MOTIVATE

Motivation comes from the Latin word meaning "to move." The two types are **extrinsic motivation** (relying on factors such as salary increases or promotions) or **intrinsic motivation** (coming from within the person—something gets done because it is the right thing, fits the individual's values, and

---

COMMUNICATION TIP

Select an employee of the month; honor that person with a gift certificate and hang the employee's picture in a prominent place for the month.

so forth). Figure 15-3 lists both intrinsic and extrinsic motivational techniques which will help motivate others.

Motivation Techniques

1. Set objectives. Help the employees you supervise establish challenging, measurable objectives. Then, help them commit themselves to achieving the objectives. This approach requires follow-through and planning on the part of the supervisor. You must not only know the objectives, but you must also follow up to see that the employee has achieved these objectives.

2. Give recognition. As a supervisor, you need to train yourself to become sensitive to the accomplishments of others. You can give recognition in a number of ways—verbal praise for a job well done, a thank-you letter written to the employee, recognition in the company newsletter, and so forth.

3. Develop a team. Individuals need to be an accepted member of a group. As a supervisor you can capitalize on this need by building a team of people who work together well. Productivity can be increased when each person in the group contributes to the overall effectiveness of the team.

4. Pay for the job. As a supervisor, know what your employees do and then pay for the job. Reward the employees who consistently give you outstanding performance with good salary increases.

5. Delegate work. Employees enjoy doing meaningful and challenging work. Provide them this opportunity by delegating significant projects to them.

Figure 15-3

DELEGATE

Delegation means assigning tasks to others and empowering others by giving them the appropriate information to get a job done. Delegation can be difficult for a manager, particularly one who has a need to control all parts of the job; however, one widely accepted definition of management is "getting work done through others." No manager can possibly do it all. Delegation is a necessity. Obviously, delegation means that employees are given the proper information and training before being given a task. They should then be trusted to perform.

EVALUATE

Performance evaluation occurs regardless of a formal evaluation program. It is a consequence of the way jobs are designed and organizations are structured. Supervisors are constantly observing the way the people reporting to them are performing. Most companies have formal evaluation periods in which personnel are evaluated every six months or every year. These evaluations may be individual evaluations, team evaluations, and workgroup evaluations.

Individual Evaluation

Individual evaluations are generally essential even if team evaluations occur. Most companies have forms and a process developed for evaluation which come from the human resources departments. This particular department may use a team within the company to develop the evaluation system. Once it is developed, it should be consistently followed throughout the organization. Usually the process involves the individual doing a self-evaluation and the supervisor preparing an evaluation. In the evaluation conference, both evaluations are discussed and a final evaluation document is prepared. The evaluation conference should be open. If the employee gives the supervisor new information that applies to the evaluation, the supervisor should accept that information and reflect it on the evaluation form. Read Figure 15-4 carefully; the techniques here will help you understand how to effectively evaluate an employee.

Team Evaluation

Some companies use team evaluations; that is, employees who work together as a team are asked to evaluate each other. These team evaluations may be given to the supervisors of the people involved in the team or discussed among the team members only. If the team members discuss the evaluation, the team leader needs to take a strong position in the process to ensure that the team evaluation session does not become a "fault-finding" or "blaming others" situation. Guidelines should be given to the team before the evaluation is done. The team leader should stress that the evaluation should concentrate on whether the team was able to

Evaluation Techniques

1. Evaluate performance on a day-to-day basis. Employees should always know how they are doing. If a report or letter is not written or formatted as it should be, let the person know immediately. Also, praise a job well done. Give employees immediate feedback as to their performance. Do not save all criticism or all praise for a yearly evaluation session.

2. Allow adequate time for the evaluation. The performance evaluation is important for both you and the employee. Set aside enough time on your calendar to do it well. You need to spend an hour or two with each employee. Also, be sure that the place is appropriate. If you are using your office, ask that you not be interrupted. It is best to close the door so that visitors will not drop in.

3. Give credit where credit is due. Be certain that you praise the employee for work well done. Too many managers consider an evaluation period a time for criticism only. It is not. It is a time to look at the total work of the employee. In what areas is the employee performing in an exemplary manner? An average manner? Below expectations?

4. Be fair. Analyze the employee's work based on established criteria of performance, not on how well you like or dislike the employee. Stay away from personality traits. Stress job performance. In discussing errors, suggest ways that the work could have been performed satisfactorily. Give the employee an opportunity to suggest possible alternatives. Word your comments as positively as possible. For example, do not say, "Your performance is a problem." Instead say, "You are doing well in these areas (then identify the areas), and improvement is needed in these areas."

5. Listen to what the employee is saying. Too often we listen to others with only half an ear. The employee often comes to an evaluation session with a certain amount of anxiety and perhaps even hostility. Let the person talk. By talking, the person can usually release much of the anxiety and thus be more receptive to constructive criticism.

6. Avoid personal areas. Sometimes a supervisor, with the best of intentions, will become too involved in the employee's personal life. Do not try to counsel an employee about problems that should be handled only by a qualified professional.

7. Establish attainable objectives for improvement. Help the employee set realistic objectives for improvement. It is a good idea to ask the employee to put these objectives in writing. A plan of action for improvement may be developed, with dates set for the accomplishment of each objective. Remember, this plan of action is a growth plan for improvement; praise the employee for improvement.

Figure 15-4

successfully complete the task and contributions made by individual members to the task.

Workgroup Evaluation

You learned earlier that workgroups set objectives in relation to the overall goals established by the company. These objectives must be measurable; the workgroup must know whether they accomplished their objectives. The manager and the workgroup might also evaluate what needs to be improved during the next six months or year by using a total quality approach. In using this approach, here are some questions which might be asked.

- What needs to be improved? Is it customer or client service? Is it internal service?

- Where does the workgroup want to be? Once the area of improvement has been identified, realistic targets must be set?

- What actions should we take to improve in the area(s) identified?

- Who does what, when? This stage is when the action plan is developed. The action plan will include specific tasks to be achieved, and state who is responsible, the problems to be overcome, and what is needed to achieve a solution. The tasks to be achieved are integrated into the regular planning process through established objectives.

- How do we know if the action is working? Once the action plan is implemented, it is monitored to determine if the desired results are achieved.

- How can we ensure that the problem will not reoccur? Once results are achieved, procedures, training, and other necessary measures are taken to ensure that the problem does not reoccur.

- What have we learned? The improvement process, problem solving, and teamwork are analyzed. Areas where difficulties occurred are reviewed so that improved performance is ensured for the future.

THE RIGHT TO LEAD

You have learned in this chapter that the effective leader has certain characteristics and is willing to consistently follow personal values to help the organization and people within the organization to learn and grow. You have learned that a number of management responsibilities are necessary for an organization to function efficiently. You have learned that there is a definite link between good leaders and good managers. Although management tasks are more concrete, each manager (to be the most effective) must have leadership characteristics—those characteristics that ensure that the organization is focused on doing what is right.

Needless to say, not all individuals have the characteristics mentioned in this chapter and not all individuals are interested in developing these traits. The process of learning how to lead is a continual one. No one person is born with the right to lead. Leadership is earned by those individuals who sincerely demonstrate in their daily lives the commitment to the skills defined here. Only then is leadership earned.

CHAPTER SUMMARY

This summary will help you remember the important points covered in this chapter.

- Leadership in the twenty-first century requires two unique skills—change mastery and an international perspective.

- An effective leader has the following characteristics.

  a. understands self

  b. builds a shared vision

  c. is service oriented

  d. empowers others

  e. rewards risk taking

  f. moves through chaos

  g. knows how to follow

- Leadership can be defined as doing the right thing, whereas management is defined as doing things right.

- Although management responsibilities are more concrete and can be quantified, measured, and assessed, truly effective management and effective leadership are a blend. The effective manager is also an effective leader.

- Management responsibilities include:

  a. planning

  b. organizing

  c. recruiting and employing

  d. training

  e. motivating

  f. delegating

  g. evaluating

- The process of learning how to lead is continual. No one person is born with the right to lead. Leadership is earned by those individuals who sincerely demonstrate in their daily lives the commitment to develop the needed leadership characteristics.

CHAPTER GLOSSARY

The following terms were introduced in this chapter. To help you review, definitions are given here.

- **Interdependent** (p. 349)–A state where individuals within the world are mutually dependent on each other for various resources; for example, human, financial, and technical resources.

- **Legitimate power** (p. 351)–Given to leaders who live by a set of principles.

- **Coercive power** (p. 351)–Power in which the manager creates fear in the follower that either something bad will happen or something good will be taken away if the manager is not "obeyed."

- **Utility power** (p. 351)–A relationship between the manager and employees based on a useful exchange of goods and services between the two.

Each operates from the belief that the other will do what is required if both provide the necessary goods or services to each other.

- **Power** (p. 351)–the ability or official capacity to exercise control; authority.

- **Empower** (p. 351)–The passing on of authority or responsibility to others.

- **Bilateralness** (p. 353)–Affecting two sides equally.

- **Leadership** (p. 353)–Doing the right thing.

- **Management** (p. 353)–Doing things right.

- **Management by objectives (MBO)** (p. 355)–The process of establishing written objectives that can be measured and evaluated.

- **Short-range planning** (p. 355)–Planning for a one-year period.

- **Long-range planning** (p. 355)–Planning for a three- to five-year period.

- **Span of control** (p. 355)–The number of employees who are directly supervised by one person.

- **Micromanage** (p. 358)–Telling individuals within an organization each step to take when they are working on a project.

- **Motivation** (p. 358)–To move.

- **Extrinsic motivation** (p. 358)–Relying on external factors to move someone or something.

- **Intrinsic motivation** (p. 358)–Coming from within the individual and satisfying an internal need; for example, feeling good about an accomplishment.

DISCUSSION ITEMS

These discussion items provide an opportunity for you to test your understanding of the chapter through discussion with your classmates and your instructor.

1. Explain the two unique leadership needs that exist in the twenty-first century.

2. List the characteristics of an effective leader.

3. Explain the difference between legitimate power, coercive power, and utility power.

4. Explain the difference between leadership and management. What is meant by the statement: There cannot be effective management without effective leadership?

5. Define the essential functions of management.

6. What is meant by MBO? Explain how it is used within an organization.

CASE STUDY

Ms. Marquette appointed a team of people, with you as the team leader, to consider the objectives your workgroup needs to accomplish for the next year. She gave you the organizational goals which were recently set by the board of directors and the president of the company. You met with your workgroup for the first time last week. You thought the meeting went well. There was an open discussion of the strengths and weaknesses of the workgroup and what needs to be done to improve service to customers. Although no decisions were reached, the group seemed to be heading in several directions that are appropriate for the workgroup.

This morning one team member came by your office for a "chat." He was upset because he thought a statement made about the weakness of the workgroup was directed at him. He informed you that he expected you to not let the discussion head in that direction in the future. He also stated

that he was doing an excellent job, and he did not need to improve. He said at the next meeting that he was going to talk about several issues that he has with certain other members of the workgroup. You tried to tell him that you did not feel the group was criticizing him at all. The group was merely talking about where the workgroup could improve in service to customers. He refused to listen to you.

This man is very controlling. He always believes he is right, and he has openly stated on several occasions that he does not make mistakes. He never wants to change anything, always contending that "status quo" is perfect.

You want to develop a plan that is meaningful for your workgroup. You do not feel that this person should be allowed to cause problems within the group; however, you do not know how to handle the situation. What should you do? Should you seek help from Ms. Marquette? The man does report to her. Should you try to talk with him again?

OFFICE TASKS

OFFICE TASK 15-1 (Objectives 1, 2, 3, and 4)

Work as a team with four of your classmates on this assignment. Interview two top level executives (presidents or vice presidents, if possible). Ask the executives the following questions.

- How will leadership be different in the twenty-first century than it was in the twentieth century?

- What do you consider the characteristics of an effective leader?

- How did you develop your leadership skills?

- Is there a definable difference between leadership and management? If so, what is it?

- How is the planning process conducted in your organization?

- Do you provide training opportunities for employees? If so, what are they?

- What process do you use to evaluate employees?

Summarize your findings and report them orally to the class.

OFFICE TASK 15-2 (Objective 3)

A recent study by Human Resources has shown that the absentee rate for Koronet has gone up for the second year in a row. The absentee rate for 1994–1998 is shown on the Student Data Template Disk, file OT15-2. Using the data, create a bar graph to illustrate the rising absentee rate; project the same percentage of increase this year out for the next two years. Compose a memorandum to Ms. Marquette, providing recommendations for reducing the absentee rate based on information you have learned in this chapter. Include the bar graph as an attachment to the memorandum. A memo form is provided on the Student Data Template Disk, file OT15-2B. Turn in the memorandum and bar graph to the instructor.

ENGLISH USAGE CHALLENGE DRILL

Correct the following sentences. Cite the grammar rule that is applicable to each sentence. Before you begin, refresh your memory of grammar rules by reviewing possessives.

1. Jane Withers's coat was lost.
2. I will be going to the doctors tomorrow.
3. Mavis' pet lizard likes to eat flies.
4. The childrens talking bothered me.
5. The CEOs office was extremely large.

ASSESSMENT OF CHAPTER OBJECTIVES

Now that you have completed the chapter and the office tasks, take a few moments to review the following learning objectives which you were given at the beginning of this chapter. Did you accomplish these objectives? If so, explain how in the space provided. If you were unable to accomplish these objectives, give your reason for not doing so. Your instructor may want to review your answers.

I accomplished these objectives:

1. Determine what unique leadership needs exist in the twenty-first century. Yes ____ No ____ Explain how you accomplished this objective.

_____

_____

_____

2. Describe the characteristics of effective leaders.
Yes _____ No _____
Explain how you accomplished this objective.

_____

_____

_____

3. Define the essential management responsibilities. Yes _____ No _____
Explain how you accomplished this objective.

_____

_____

_____

4. Analyze how leadership is earned.
Yes _____ No _____
Explain how you accomplished this objective.

_____

_____

_____

Provide reasons for failing to accomplish any of the objectives.

_____

_____

_____

_____

_____

_____

_____

_____

_____

_____

FINLEY A. LANIER, JR.'S CASE SOLUTION

Here is how I handled the situation. First, I ascertained who was to receive the packet by checking the mailing lists of persons in the field. These included over 250 store managers, 204 sales reps, 21 sales managers, 4 directors of marketing in four districts, inside "hotline" personnel, and international and domestic personnel. I prepared labels for each and the proper stickers for each envelope.

Second, I completed a set of what was to be shipped in each packet and gave the completed packet, plus mailing labels and stickers, to the mailroom supervisor with instructions as to where the materials for the packets were located. All of this information had to be shrink-wrapped and labeled. I gave the supervisor enough information to locate the material, get it into the mailroom, and complete the shrink-wrapping procedure.

Third, I sent the master list of items to the duplication department instructing the supervisor of the number of copies of each item and where to send them when this process was completed.

Fourth, I was in constant communication with the duplicating center and shipping department to make sure that all systems were go and whatever was needed to complete the job was on hand.

The job was completed and out the door as scheduled. However, without excellent communication and teamwork the problem could not have been solved in such a short time. I determined who needed to be involved in the job, got their support, and gave them good instructions on what needed to be done.

The skills that were crucial to getting the job accomplished included organizational skills, a knowledge of the company, and communication and teamwork skills.

REFERENCE GUIDE

This guide provides an easy-to-use reference to English rules and basic formats for letters and reports that you use daily in written and oral communication. To help you review the basics, it is a good idea to read through the guide at the beginning of the course and to also review it as questions arise when you are preparing materials for this course. The parts of the guide are

- Abbreviations
- Capitalization
- Letters
  - Letter and Punctuation
  - Styles
  - Envelope Addressing
  - Placement of Letter Parts
- Nonsexist Language
- Numbers
- Often Misused Words and Phrases
- Parallel Construction
- Plurals and Possessives
- Pronouns
- Punctuation
- Proofreaders' Marks
- Report Format
- Spelling Rules
- Subject and Verb Agreement
- Word Division

ABBREVIATIONS

1. Academic degrees are generally abbreviated; periods are generally not used with the abbreviation.

   PhD
   MA
   BBA

2. Many companies and professional organizations are known by abbreviated names. These abbreviated names are typed in capital letters with no periods and no spaces between the letters.

   IBM International Business Machines
   YMCA Young Men's Christian Association

3. Certain expressions are abbreviated.

   e.g. exempli gratia (for example)
   etc. et cetera (and so forth)
   i.e. id est (that is)

4. Names of countries should be abbreviated only in tabulations or enumerations and should be written in capital letters; periods may be used in these abbreviations.

   U.S.A. or USA

5. Abbreviations for government agencies are usually written in capital letters with no periods and no spaces between the letters.

   FTC Federal Trade Commission
   CIA Central Intelligence Agency

6. The personal titles *Mr., Mrs., Ms., Messrs.,* and *Dr.* are abbreviated when written before a name.

   Mrs. Ellen Herrera   Messrs. Fleming and Brown

7. Other personal titles such as *Rev., Hon., Prof., Gen., Col., Capt.,* and *Lieut.* may be abbreviated when they precede a surname and a given name. When only the surname is used, these titles should be spelled out.

   Prof. Mark Huddleston
   Professor Huddleston

8. The titles *Reverend* and *Honorable* are spelled out if preceded by *the.*

   The Honorable Marjorie Popham

9. Use only one period if an abbreviation containing a period falls at the end of a sentence. In sentences ending with a question mark or an exclamation mark, place the punctuation mark directly after the period.

   The play began at 8:15 p.m.
   Does the class start at 9:30 a.m.?

10. Avoid abbreviating the following categories of words unless these words appear in tabulations or enumerations.

- names of territories and possessions of the United States, countries, states, and cities
- names of months
- days of the week
- given names, such as *Wm.* for *William*
- words such as *avenue, boulevard, court, street, drive, road, building*
- parts of company names such as *Bros., Co., Corp.* unless the words are abbreviated in the official company name
- compass directions when they are part of an address; use *North, South, East, West. NW, NE, SE,* and *SW* may be abbreviated after a street name, however.
- The word *number* unless it is followed by a numeral.

CAPITALIZATION

1. The first word of every sentence should be capitalized.

2. The first word of a complete direct quotation should be capitalized.

3. The first word of a salutation and all nouns used in the salutation should be capitalized.

4. The first word in a complimentary close should be capitalized.

5. Capitalize the first word after a colon only when the colon introduces a complete passage or sentence having independent meaning.

   In conclusion I wish to say: "The survey shows that. . . ."

   If the material following a colon is dependent on the preceding clause, the first word after the colon is not capitalized.

   I present the following three reasons for changing: the volume of business does not justify the expense; we are short of people; the product is decreasing in popularity.

6. Capitalize the names of associations, buildings, churches, hotels, streets, organizations, and clubs.

   The Business Club, Merchandise Mart, Central Christian Church, Peabody Hotel, Seventh Avenue, Administrative Management Society, Chicago Chamber of Commerce

7. All proper names should be capitalized.

   Great Britain, John G. Hammitt, Mexico

8. Capitalize names that are derived from proper names.

   American, Chinese

   Do not, however, capitalize words that are derived from proper nouns and that have developed a special meaning.

   pasteurized milk, china dishes, morocco leather

9. Capitalize special names for regions and localities.

   North Central States, the Far East, the East Side, the Hoosier State

   Do not, however, capitalize adjectives derived from such names or localities that are used as directional parts of states and countries.

   far eastern lands, the southern United States, southern Illinois

10. Capitalize names of government boards, agencies, bureaus, departments, and commissions.

    Civil Service Commission, Social Security Board, Bureau of Navigation

11. Capitalize names of the deity, the Bible, holy days, and religious denominations.

    God, Easter, Yom Kippur, Genesis, Church of Christ

12. Capitalize the names of holidays.

    Memorial Day, Labor Day

13. Capitalize words used before numbers and numerals, with the exception of the common word, such as *page, line,* and *verse.*

    The reservation is Lower 6, Car 27.
    He found the material in Part 3, Chapter X.

14. Any title that signifies rank, honor, and respect, and that immediately precedes an individual's name should be capitalized. Do not capitalize a title that follows a name.

    She asked President Harry G. Sanders to preside.
    He was attended by Dr. Howard Richards.
    Dr. Fulton is president of the company.

15. Academic degrees should be capitalized when they precede or follow an individual's name.

    Mrs. Constance R. Collins, PhD, was invited to direct the program.
    Fred R. Bowling, Master of Arts

16. Capitalize titles of high-ranking government officers when the title is used in place of the proper name in referring to a specific person.

    Our Senator invited us to visit him in Washington. The President will return to Washington soon.

17. Capitalize military and naval titles signifying rank.

    Captain Meyers, Lieutenant White, Lieutenant Commander Murphy

LETTERS

This section provides a review of letter styles, punctuation styles, envelope addressing, and placement of letter parts.

LETTER AND PUNCTUATION STYLES

Letters may be keyed in a block or modified block style, with blocked or indented paragraphs. Figure 1 shows a block style with blocked paragraphs. (When using a block letter style, the paragraphs must be blocked.) Notice in the block letter style, every line begins at the left margin. Figure 2 shows a modified block style, with indented paragraphs. (When using a modified block style, the paragraphs may be blocked or indented.) In the modified block style, the date line and the closing lines begin at center point or end flush with the right margin. Open punctuation has no punctuation after the salutation and no punctuation after the complimentary close. When using mixed punctuation, there is a colon after the salutation and a comma after the complimentary close. Notice the open punctuation style in Figure 1 and the mixed punctuation style in Figure 2.

ENVELOPE ADDRESSING

Optical character readers (OCRs) used in the U.S. Post Office are programmed to scan a specific area, so the address must be placed appropriately. With a No. 10 envelope (the standard size used in offices), the address is placed 2½" from the top of the envelope and 4" from the left edge. The address is keyed in all caps with no punctuation. Two-letter state abbreviations should be used, along with the 9-digit ZIP code.

Notations to the post office such as REGISTERED should be keyed below the stamp at least three lines above the address in all caps.

Notations such as HOLD FOR ARRIVAL, CONFIDENTIAL, and PLEASE FORWARD should be keyed a triple space below the return address and three spaces from the left edge of the envelope. Figure 3 shows the placement of the address on the envelope.

PLACEMENT OF LETTER PARTS

Date line—Key a double space below the last line of the letterhead.

Inside address—Key three to nine lines below the date, depending on the letter's length.

Attention line—Key a double space below the address and a double space above the salutation.

Salutation—Key a double space below the address or a double space below the attention line.

Subject or reference line—Key a double space below the salutation.

Body—Key a double space below the salutation or a double space below the subject line.

Second page heading—Key approximately 1" from the top. Key the addressee's name, the page number, and the date in a three-line block at the left margin. Or, use a one-line arrangement and key the addressee's name at the left margin, center the page number, and position the date to end at the right margin.

Complimentary close—Key a double space below the last line of the body.

Name and title of writer—Key a quadruple space below the complimentary close or the company name, if used.

Reference initials—Key a double space below the name and title.

Enclosure—Key a double space below the reference initials.

Postscript—Key a double space below the reference initials or the last keyed line.

Copy notation—Key a double space below the reference initials or the last keyed line. If a copy notation and a postscript are both used, the postscript is a double space below the copy notation.

NONSEXIST LANGUAGE

Inclusive usage in language (incorporating both sexes) is extremely important in writing. Exclusive language (words which by their form or meaning discriminate on the basis of gender) should be avoided. Examples of exclusive language include

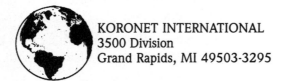

KORONET INTERNATIONAL
3500 Division
Grand Rapids, MI 49503-3295

December 21, 1999

Tricounty Building Corporation
Attention Mr. Harold Chad
2395 36th Street
Ada, MI 48301

Ladies and Gentlemen

Thank you for your order for three executive chairs and three
desks. The order will be shipped to you on January 5, 2000.
I understand that you are interested in one of our designers
working with you on furniture for a new building which you
anticipate completing in October. As manager of the department,
I will be calling your office in the next week to schedule an
appointment with you.

We at Koronet are pleased that you are using our furniture, and
I look forward to working with you on furniture designs for the
new building.

Sincerely

J. Allen McGregory
Manager, Interior Design
lc

Figure 1   Block letter style, open punctuation.

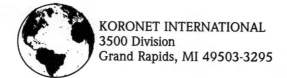

KORONET INTERNATIONAL
3500 Division
Grand Rapids, MI 49503-3295

December 21, 1999

Mrs. Helena Andrews
Fetzer Foundation
2356 Old Kent Road
Kalamazoo, MI 49003

Dear Mrs. Andrews:

    Koronet is sponsoring a community seminar on management
techniques for non-profit organizations. I understand that
Fetzer has an interest in non-profits. Would you be interested
in talking about co-sponsoring this seminar with Koronet? I
know that your expertise would add greatly to the quality of
the seminar.

    I will be calling you within the next week to talk about
this possibility.

                    Sincerely,

                    Jacqueline Marquette

                    Jacqueline Marquette
                    Vice President of Community Relations

lc

Figure 2   Modified block letter style, mixed punctuation.

```
┌─────────────────────────────────────────────────────────────────┐
│                                                                   │
│  CONFIDENTIAL                                       REGISTERED     │
│                                                                   │
│                                                                   │
│                  TRICOUNTY BUILDING CORPORATION                   │
│                  ATTENTION MR HAROLD CHAD                         │
│                  2395 36TH STREET                                │
│                  ADA, MI 48301                                   │
│                                                                   │
│                                                                   │
└─────────────────────────────────────────────────────────────────┘
```

Figure 3   Placement of address on envelope.

words such as *craftsman, weatherman, fireman, policeman,* and so forth. Other examples of exclusive language include such statements as:

The teacher asked everyone to state his name.
The executive answered his phone.

In writing and speaking, gender bias statements should be eliminated. For example, *weatherman* becomes *weatherperson, policeman* becomes *police officer.*

The teacher asked everyone to give his or her name.
The executive answered the phone.

NUMBERS

1. Spell out numbers one through ten; use figures for numbers above ten.

   We ordered *ten* coats and *four* dresses.
   About 60 letters were keyed.

2. If there are numbers above and below ten in correspondence, be consistent—either spell out all numbers or place all numbers in figures. If most of the numbers are below ten, put them in words. If most are above ten, express them in all figures.

   Please order 12 memo pads, 2 reams of paper, and 11 boxes of envelopes.

3. Numbers in the millions or higher may be expressed in the following manner to aid comprehension.

   3 *billion* (rather than 3,000,000,000)

4. Always spell out a number that begins a sentence.

   Five hundred books were ordered.

5. If the numbers are large, rearrange the wording of the sentence so that the number is not the first word of the sentence.

   We had a good year in 1999.
   Not: Nineteen hundred and ninety-nine was a good year.

6. Spell out indefinite numbers and amounts.

   A *few hundred* voters

7. Spell out all ordinals (first, second, third, etc.) that can be expressed in words.

   The store's *twenty-fifth* anniversary was held this week.

8. When adjacent numbers are written in words or written in figures, use a comma to separate them.

   On car 33, 450 cartons are being shipped.

9. House or building numbers are written in figures. However, when the number *one* appears by itself, it is spelled out. Numbers one through ten in street names are spelled out. Numbers above ten are written in figures. When figures are used for both the house number and the street name, use a hyphen that is preceded and followed by a space.

   101 Building
   One Main Place
   21301 Fifth Avenue
   122 - 33d Street

10. Ages are usually spelled out except when the age is stated exactly in years, months, and days.

When ages are presented in tabular form, they are written in figures.

She is eighteen years old.
He is 2 years, 10 months, and 18 days old.

Name	Age
Jones, Edward	19
King, Ruth	21

11. Use figures to express dates written in normal month-day-year order. Do not use *th, nd,* or *rd* following the date.

    May 8, 1999
    Not: May 8th, 1999

12. Fractions should be spelled out unless they are part of mixed numbers. Use a hyphen to separate the numerator and denominator of fractions written in words when the fraction is used as an adjective.

    three-fourths inch
    5⅝

13. In legal documents, numbers may be written in both words and figures.

    One Hundred Thirty-Four and 30/100 Dollars ($134.30)

14. Amounts of money are usually expressed in figures. Indefinite money amounts are written in words.

    $100
    $3.27
    several hundred dollars

15. Express percentages in figures; spell out the word *percent.*

    10 percent

16. To form the plural of figures, add *s.*

    Technological advances will increase in the 1980s.

17. In times of day, use figures with a.m. and p.m.; spell out numbers with the word *o'clock.* In formal usage, all times are spelled out.

    9 a.m.
    10 p.m.
    eight o'clock in the evening

OFTEN MISUSED WORDS AND PHRASES

1. **A or an before the letter h**

   A is used before all consonant sounds, including *h* when sounded.

   An is used before all vowel sounds, except long *u* and before words beginning with a silent *h.*

   a historic event, **an** honor, **a** hotel

2. **A while, awhile**

   A while is a noun meaning a short time.
   We plan to go home in **a while.**

   Awhile is an adverb meaning a short time.
   She wrote the poem **awhile** ago.

3. **About, at**

   Use either **about** or **at**—not both.
   He will leave **about** noon.
   He will leave **at** noon.

4. **Accept, except**

   Accept means to receive; it is always a verb.
   I **accept** the gift.

   Except as a preposition means with the exception of.
   Everyone left **except** him.

   Except as a verb means to exclude.
   When the sentence was **excepted,** the committee approved the report.

5. **Addition, edition**

   Addition is the process of adding.
   They plan to add an **addition** to the building.

   Edition is a particular **version** of printed material.
   This is the fourth **edition** of the book.

6. **Advice, advise**

   Advice is a noun meaning a recommendation.
   She did not follow my **advice.**

   Advise is a verb meaning to counsel.
   The counselor will **advise** you.

7. **All, all of**

   Use **all;** *of* is redundant. If a pronoun follows all, reword the sentence.
   Check **all** the items.
   They are **all** going.

8. **All right, alright**

   All right is the only correct usage. Alright is incorrect.

9. **Among, between**

   Among is used when referring to three or more persons or things.
   The inheritance was divided **among** the four relatives.

   Between is used when referring to two persons or things.
   The choice is **between** you and me.

10. **Appraise, apprise**

Appraise means to set a value on; **apprise** means to inform.

The house was **appraised** at $200,000.
I was **apprised** of the situation by Jack.

11. **Bad, badly**

Bad is an adjective and should be used after verbs of sense; **badly** is an adverb.

He feels **bad** about losing. She looks **bad**.
The football team played **badly** tonight.

12. **Biannual, biennial**

Biannual means occurring twice a year.

The **biannual** meeting will be held next month.

Biennial means occurring once every two years.

The **biennial** evaluation will be done in May.

13. **Bimonthly, semimonthly**

Bimonthly means every two months; **semimonthly** means twice a month.

The report will be run on a **bimonthly** basis.
I receive my paycheck **semimonthly**.

14. **Can, may**

Can means to be able to; **may** means to have permission.

The diskette **can** be copied.
He **may** leave when the report is finished.

15. **Capital, capitol**

Capital is used unless you are referring to the building that houses a **government**.

Austin is the **capital** of Texas.
We toured the United States **Capitol** in Washington.

16. **Cite, sight, site**

Cite means to quote; **sight** means vision; **site** means location.

She **cited** the correct reference.
That is a pleasant **sight**.
They **sighted** a whale.
The **site** for the new building will be determined soon.

17. **Complement, compliment**

Complement means to complete, fill, or make perfect; **compliment** means to praise.

His thorough report **complemented** the presentation.
I **complimented** Jane on her new dress.

18. **Council, counsel**

Council is a noun meaning a governing body.
The **council** meets today.

Counsel as a noun means advice; it also means a lawyer.

Counsel as a verb means to advise.
Dr. Baker's **counsel** helped Chris overcome her fears.
Counsel was consulted on the case.
He is there to **counsel** you.

19. **Desert, desert, dessert**

Desert may mean a barren or arid region with low rainfall.

We traveled through the **desert** of Arizona.

Desert may mean to abandon.
He **deserted** his family.

Dessert is a sweet usually served at the end of a meal.
We had ice cream for **dessert**.

20. **Farther, further**

Farther refers to distance; **further** refers to a greater degree or extent.
The store is a mile **farther** down the road.
We will discuss the matter **further** on Saturday.

21. **Good, well**

Both **good** and **well** are adjectives. **Well** is used to mean in fine health; **good** is used to mean pleasant or attractive.
I feel **well**.
She feels **good** about her job.

22. **Got, gotten**

Go is preferred to **gotten** as the past participle of get. It is colloquial when used for must or ought.
I've **got** to get up at 6:00 a.m.
Improved: I must get up at 6:00 a.m.

23. **In, into**

Into is a preposition suggesting motion. **In** is a preposition implying place in which.
She went **into** the room (she was on her way and not yet in the room).
She is sitting **in** the room (she is already in the room).

24. **Its, it's**

Its is the possessive form of it.
The family had **its** reunion yesterday.

It's is the contraction of it is.
It's probably going to rain.

25. **Percent, per cent, percentage**

Percent is the correct usage; not **per cent**.

Percentage is also one word and should not be used with numbers.

26. **Principal, principle**

    Principal as an adjective means main; as a noun it means the main person or a capital sum.

    The **principal** actor was outstanding.
    The **principals** in the case are present.

    Principle is a noun meaning a rule, guide, truth; it never refers directly to a person.

    She held steadfast to her **principles**.

27. **Respectfully, respectively**

    Respectfully means in a courteous manner; **respectively** refers to being considered singly in a particular order.

    She **respectfully** asked for her grade report.
    The first, second, and third awards will go to Richard, Sarah, and Christine, **respectively**.

28. **Stationary, stationery**

    Stationary means stable or fixed; **stationery** is writing paper.

    The ladder seems **stationary**.
    Order three boxes of **stationery**.

29. **That, which, who**

    Who is used to refer to persons; **which** refers to animals and inanimate objects; **that** is used to refer to animals, inanimate objects, or a classification of persons.

    Patricia is a woman **who** understands what she is doing.
    Which books do you mean?
    The animal **that** I saw yesterday belonged to Harold.

30. **Who, whom**

    Who is used as the subject of a verb; **whom** is used as an object of a verb or preposition.

    Send it to the people **who** asked for it.
    Whom shall I ask first?
    It does not matter **who** did what to **whom**.

PARALLEL CONSTRUCTION

Parts of a sentence that are parallel in meaning should be parallel in structure. Writers should balance a word with a word, a phrase with a phrase, a clause with a clause, and a sentence with a sentence.

For example:

NO   The parents tried pleading, threats, and shouting.

YES   The parents tried pleading, threatening, and shouting.

NO   In undeveloped countries, don't drink the water; in developed countries, the air is dangerous to your health.

YES   In undeveloped countries, don't drink the water; in developed countries, don't breathe the air.

PLURALS AND POSSESSIVES

1. When a compound word contains a noun and is hyphenated or made up of two or more words, the principal word takes an *s* to form the plural. If there is no principal word, add an *s* to the end of the compound word.

   Commanders in chief   runners-up
   mothers-in-law   forget-me-nots
   passersby

2. The plural of letters is formed by adding *s* or *'s*. The apostrophe is unnecessary except when confusion might result.

   CPAs
   dotting the I's

3. Singular nouns form the possessive by adding *'s*. If a singular noun has two or more syllables and if the last syllable is not accented and is preceded by a sibilant sound (*s, x, z*), add only the apostrophe for ease of pronunciation.

   the person's computer   Mrs. Jones's office
   the department's rules   Ulysses' voyage

4. Plural nouns form the possessive by adding an apostrophe if the plural ends in *s* or by adding *'s* when the plural does not end in *s*.

   the boy's grades
   ladies' wear
   the children's bicycle

5. When a verb form ending in *ing* is used as a noun (gerund), a noun or pronoun before it takes the possessive form.

   Mr. Ware's talking was not anticipated.
   Their shouting disturbed me.

6. To form the possessive of a compound word, add the possessive ending to the last syllable.

   Her mother-in-law's gift arrived.
   The commander-in-chief's address was well received.

7. Joint possession is indicated by adding the possessive end to the last noun.

   We are near Jan and Mike's store.
   Drs. Edison and Martin's article was published this week.

8. In idiomatic construction, possessive form is often used.

   a day's work   two weeks' vacation

9. The possessive form is used in cases when the noun modified is not expressed.

   Take it to the plumber's. (shop)

10. The possessive form of personal pronouns is written without an apostrophe.

This book is hers.
She will deliver yours tomorrow.

PRONOUNS

1. A pronoun agrees with its antecedent (the word for which the pronoun stands) in number, gender, and person.

Roger wants to know if *his* book is at your house.

2. A plural pronoun is used when the antecedent consists of two nouns joined by *and.*

Mary and *Tomie* are bringing their stereo.

3. A singular pronoun is used when the antecedent consists of two singular nouns joined by *or* or *nor.* A plural pronoun is used when the antecedent consists of two plural nouns joined by *or* or *nor.*

Neither *Elizabeth* nor *Johann* wants to do *her* part.
Either the *men* or the *women* will do *their* share.

4. Do not confuse certain possessive pronouns with contractions that sound alike.

its (possessive)	it's (it is)
their (possessive)	they're (they are)
theirs (possessive)	there's (there is)
your (possessive)	you're (you are)
whose (possessive)	who's (who is)

As a test for the use of a possessive pronoun or a contraction, try to substitute *it is, they are, it has, there has, there is,* or *you are.* Use the corresponding possessive form if the substitution does not make sense.

Your wording is correct.
You're wording that sentence incorrectly.
Whose book is it?
Who's the owner of this typewriter?

5. Use *who* and *that* when referring to persons.

He is the boy *who* does well in keyboarding.
She is the type of *person that we* like to employ.

6. Use which and that when referring to places, objects, and animals.

The card *that I* sent you was mailed last week.
The fox, *which* is very sly, caught the skunk.

7. A pronoun in the objective case functions as a direct object, indirect object, or the object of a preposition. Objective pronouns include *me, you, him, her, it, us, them, whom, whomever.*

The movie was an emotional experience for *her* and *me.* (The pronouns "her" and "me" are in the objective case, because they function as the object of a preposition in this sentence.)

8. A linking verb connects a subject to a word that renames it. Linking verbs indicate a state of being—*am, is, are, was, were,* etc.—relate to the senses, or indicate a condition. A pronoun coming after any linking verb renames the subject so it must be in the subjective case. Subjective pronouns include *I, you, she, he, it, we, they, who, whoever.*

It is *I* who will attend the play.

9. The pronouns *who* and *whoever* are in the subjective case and are used as the subject of a sentence or clause.

Whoever is in charge will be required to stay late.

10. At the beginning of questions, use *who* if the question is about the subject and *whom* if the question is about the object.

Who is going to the party?
Whom can we expect to give the welcoming address?

11. Reflexive pronouns reflect back to the antecedent. Reflexive pronouns include *myself, herself, himself, themselves,* and other *self* or *selves* words.

I intend to do the painting by *myself.*

PUNCTUATION

Correct punctuation is based on certain accepted rules and principles rather than on the whims of the writer. Punctuation is also important if the reader is to correctly interpret the writer's thoughts. The summary of rules given in this reference guide will be helpful in using correct punctuation.

THE PERIOD

The period indicates a full stop and is used

1. At the end of a complete declarative or imperative sentence.

2. After abbreviations and after a single or double initial that represents a word.

acct.	etc.
U. S.	viz.
N. E.	i.e.

However, some abbreviations that are made up of several initial letters do not require periods.

FDIC (Federal Deposit Insurance Corporation)
FEPC (Fair Employment Practices Committee)
AAA (American Automobile Association)
YWCA (Young Women's Christian Association)

PROOFREADERS' MARKS

Symbol	Meaning	Marked Copy	Corrected Copy
Cap or ≡	Capitalize	dallas, texas	Dallas, Texas
∧	Insert	two people *or three*	two or three people
ℛ	Delete	the man and woman	the man
⊏	Move to left	human relations	human relations
#	Add space	follow these	follow these
lc	Lowercase letter	in the Fall of 1999	in the fall of 1999
◠	Close up space	sum mer	summer
tr or ∾	Transpose	When is it	When it is
⊐	Move to right	skills for	skills for
		living	living
∨	Insert apostrophe	Macs book	Mac's book
∨∨	Insert quotation marks	She said, No.	She said, "No."
⊔	Move down	n falle	fallen
⊓	Move up	straigh t	straight
¶	Paragraph	¶ The first and third page	The first and third page
No new ¶	No new paragraph	No new ¶ The first and third page	The first and third page
sp	Spell out	Dr.	Doctor
stet or · · · · ·	Let it stand; ignore correction	most efficient worker	most efficient worker
_____	Underline or italics	Business World	*Business World*
⊙	Insert period	the last word	the last word.

3. Between dollars and cents. A period and cipher are not required when an amount in even dollars is expressed in figures.

$42.65 $1.47 $25

4. To indicate a decimal.

3.5 bushels   12.65 percent   6.25 feet

THE COMMA

Use the comma:

1. To separate coordinate clauses that are connected by conjunctions, such as *and, but, or, for, neither, nor,* unless the clauses are short and closely connected.

We have a supply on hand, *but* I think we should order an additional quantity.
She had to work late, *for* the auditors were examining the books.

2. To set off a subordinate clause that precedes the main clause.

Assuming that there will be no changes, I suggest that you proceed with your instructions.

3. After an introductory phrase containing a verb form.

To finish his work, he remained at the office after hours.
After planning the program, she proceeded to put it into effect.

If an introductory phrase does not contain a verb, it usually is not followed by a comma.

After much deliberation, the plan was revoked.
Because of the vacation period we have been extremely busy.

4. To set off a nonrestrictive clause.

Our group, which had never lost a debate, won the grand prize.

5. To set off a nonrestrictive phrase.

The beacon, rising proudly toward the sky, guided the pilots safely home.

6. To separate from the rest of the sentence a word or a group of words that breaks the continuity of a sentence.

The secretary, even though his work was completed, was always willing to help others.

7. To separate parenthetical expressions from the rest of the sentence.

We have, as you know, two persons who can handle the reorganization.

8. To set off names used in direct address or to set off explanatory phrases or clauses.

I think you, Mr. Bennett, will agree with the statement. Ms. Linda Tom, our vice president, will be in your city soon.

9. To separate from the rest of the sentence expressions that, without punctuation, might be interpreted incorrectly.

Misleading: Ever since we have filed our reports monthly.
Better: Ever since, we have filed our reports monthly.

10. To separate words or groups of words when they are used in a series of three or more.

Most executives agree that dependability, trustworthiness, ambition, and judgment are required of their office workers.
Again I emphasize that factory organization, correlation of sales and production, and a good office organization are all necessary for maximum results.

11. To set off introductory words.

For example, the musical was not as lyrical as the last musical I saw.
Thus, both the man and the boy felt a degree of discrimination.

12. To separate coordinate adjectives. Coordinate adjectives are two or more adjectives that equally modify a noun.

The large, insensitive audience laughed loudly at the mistake.

13. To set off short quotations from the rest of the sentence.

He said, "I shall be there."
"The committees have agreed," he said, "to work together on the project."

14. To separate the name of a city from the name of a state.

Our southern branch is located in Atlanta, Georgia.

15. To separate abbreviations of titles from the name.

William R. Warner, Jr.
Ramona Sanchez, Ph.D.

16. To set off conjunctive adverbs such as *however* and *therefore.*

I, however, do not agree with the statement.
According to the rule, therefore, we must not penalize the student for this infraction.

17. To separate the date from the year. Within a sentence, use a comma on both sides of the year in a full date.

The anniversary party was planned for June 18, 2000.
He plans to attend the management seminar schedule for April 15, 1998, at the Hilton Hotel.

18. Do not use a comma in numbers in an address even when there are four are more digits.

The house number was 3100 Edmonds Drive.

19. Do not use a comma in a date that contains the month with only a day or the month with only a year.

The accident occurred on June 10.
The major event for June 1998 was the ethics seminar.

THE SEMICOLON

The semicolon should be used in the following instances:

1. Between independent groups of clauses that are long or that contain parts that are separated by commas.

He was outstanding in his knowledge of typing, shorthand, spelling, and related subjects; but he was lacking in many desirable personal qualities.

2. Between compound sentences when the conjunction is omitted.

Many executives would rather dictate to a machine than to a secretary; the machine won't talk back.

3. To precede expressions such as *namely* or *viz., for example* or *e.g., that is* or *i.e.,* when used to introduce a clause.

We selected the machine for two reasons; namely, because it is as reasonable in price as any other and because it does better work than others.
There are several reasons for changing the routine of handling mail; i.e., to reduce postage, to conserve time, and to place responsibility.

4. In a series of well-defined units when special emphasis is desired.

Emphatic: The prudent secretary considers the future; he or she makes sure that all the requirements are obtained, and he or she uses his or her talents to successfully attain the desired goal.

Less emphatic: The prudent secretary considers the future, makes sure that all the requirements are obtained, and uses his or her talents to successfully attain the desired goal.

5. Before a coordinating conjunction joining independent clauses containing commas.

When the task is difficult, the time spent is usually great; and the rewards can be equally great.

THE COLON

The colon is recommended in the following instances:

1. After the salutation in a business letter except when open punctuation is used.

Ladies and Gentlemen:
Dear Ms. Carroll:

2. Following introductory expressions, such as *the following, thus, as follows,* and other expressions that precede enumerations.

Please send the following by parcel post:
Officers were elected as follows: president, _____; vice president, _____; secretary treasurer, _____ .

3. To separate hours and minutes when indicating time.

2:10 p.m.   4:45 p.m.   12:15 a.m.

4. To introduce a long quotation.

The agreement read: "We the undersigned hereby agree . . ."

5. To separate two independent groups having no connecting words between them and in which the second group explains or expands the statement in the first group.

We selected the machine for one reason: in competitive tests it surpassed all other machines.

THE QUESTION MARK

The question mark should be used in the following instances:

1. After each direct question.

When do you expect to arrive in Philadelphia?
An exception to the foregoing rule is a sentence that is phrased in the form of a question, merely as a matter of courtesy, when it is actually a request.
Will you please send us an up-to-date statement of our account.

2. After each question in a series of questions within one sentence.

What is your opinion of the IBM word processor? the Xerox? the CPT?

EXCLAMATION POINT

The exclamation point is ordinarily used after words or groups of words that express command, strong feeling, emotion, or an exclamation.

Don't waste office supplies!
It can't be done!
Stop!

THE DASH

The dash is used in the following instances:

1. To indicate an omission of letters or figures.

Dear Mr.—
Date the letter July 16, 19—.

2. Sometimes in letters, especially sales letters, to cause a definite stop in reading the letter. Usually the dash is used in such cases for increased emphasis. One must be careful, however, not to overdo the use of the dash.

This book is not a revision of an old book—it is a brand new book.

3. To separate parenthetical expressions when unusual emphasis is desired on the parenthetical expression.

These sales arguments—and every one of them is important—should result in getting the order.

THE APOSTROPHE

The apostrophe should be used:

1. To indicate possession.

The boy's coat; the ladies' dresses; the girl's book.

   a. To the possessive singular, add *'s* to the noun.

man's work
bird's wing
hostess's plans

   An exception to this rule is made when the word following the possessive begins with an *s* sound.

for goodness' sake
for conscience' sakes

   b. To form the possessive of a plural noun ending in an *s* or *z* sound, add only the apostrophe (') to the plural noun.

workers' rights
hostesses' duties

   c. If the plural noun does not end in *s* or *z* sounds, add t*'s* to the plural noun.

women's clothes
alumni's donations

   d. Proper names that end in an *s* sound form the possessive singular by adding *'s.*

Williams's house
Fox's automobile

   e. Proper names ending in *s* form the possessive plural by adding the apostrophe only.

The Walters' property faces the Jones' swimming pool.

2. To indicate the omission of a letter or letters in a contraction.

it's (it is), you're (you are), we'll (we shall)

3. To indicate the plurals of letters, figures, words, and abbreviations.

Don't forget to dot your i's and cross your t's.
I can add easily by 2's and 4's, but I have difficulty with 6's and 8's.
More direct letters can be written by using shorter sentences and by omitting and's and but's.
Two of the speakers were PhD's.

QUOTATION MARKS

Certain basic rules should be followed in using quotation marks. These rules are as follows:

1. When a quotation mark is used with a comma or a period, the comma or period should be placed inside the quotation mark.

She said, "I plan to complete my program in college before seeking a position."

2. When a quotation mark is used with a semicolon or a colon, the semicolon or colon should be placed outside the quotation mark.

The treasurer said, "I plan to go by train"; others in the group stated that they would go by plane.

3. When more than one paragraph of quoted material is used, quotation marks should appear at the beginning of each paragraph and at the end of the last paragraph.

Quotation marks are used in the following instances:

   a. Before and after direct quotations.

The author states, "Too frequent use of certain words weakens the appeal."

   b. To indicate a quotation within a quotation, use single quotation marks.

The author states, "Too frequent use of 'very' and 'most' weakens the appeal."

   c. To indicate the title of a published article.

Have you read the article, "Automation in the Office"?
He asked, "Have you read 'Automation in the Office'?"

OMISSION MARKS OR ELLIPSES

Ellipses marks (. . . or ***) are frequently used to denote the omission of letters or words in quoted material. If the material omitted ends in a period, four omission marks are used (. . . .). If the material omitted is elsewhere in the quoted material, three omission marks are used (. . .).

> He quoted the proverb, "A soft answer turneth away wrath: but. . . ."
>
> She quoted Plato, "Nothing is more unworthy of a wise man . . . than to have allowed more time for trifling and useless things than they deserved."

PARENTHESES

Although parentheses are frequently used as a catch-all in writing, they are correctly used in the following instances:

1. When amounts expressed in words are followed by figures.

   > He agreed to pay twenty-five dollars ($25) as soon as possible.

2. Around words that are used as parenthetical expressions.

   > Our letter costs (excluding paper and postage) are much too high for this type of business.

3. To indicate technical references.

   > Sodium chloride (NaCl) is the chemical name for common table salt.

4. When enumerations are included in narrative form.

   > The reasons for his resignation were three: (1) advanced age, (2) failing health, and (3) a desire to travel.

REPORT FORMAT

In keying reports, follow these guidelines.

TITLE PAGE

Include the title of the report and name and title of the person writing the report, plus the date of the report. Center all items on the page, with the title of the report in all caps, approximately one-third from the top of the page. Leave approximately 2 to 2½" and key the name and title of the person writing the report. Leave approximately 2 to 2½ additional inches and key the date.

TABLE OF CONTENTS

Center *Table of Contents* approximately 2" from the top of the page. Key main headings and sub-headings in order, using leaders (periods every other space) to the page number. Use a combination of double and single spacing. Center the page number 1" from the bottom of the page using lowercase Roman numerals.

BODY OF THE REPORT

Center the title of the report 1½ to 2" from the top of the page. Set the left margin for 1½" if left-bound, 1" if unbound; use 1" top and bottom margins. Number the first page of the body 1" from the bottom at the center or do not number at all. Number all other pages of the report using Arabic numbers keyed 1" from the top of the page at the right margin or centered 1" from the bottom. The report may be double or single spaced.

TABLES, CHARTS, AND GRAPHS

Number the tables, charts, and graphs consecutively throughout the report. Identify all tables, charts, and graphs with the word *Figure* followed by the number. Give each graphic a title.

FOOTNOTES/ENDNOTES

Follow an acceptable style of footnote or endnote (APA, MILA, or traditional style).

BIBLIOGRAPHY

Follow an acceptable bibliography style consistent with the footnote or endnote style. Provide separate sections for books, articles, and government publications. Center the word *Bibliography* 1½ to 2" from the top of the page. Use the same margins as in the report.

SPELLING RULES

1. Put *i* before *e* except after *c* or when sounded like *a* as in neighbor or weigh.

   Exceptions: either, neither, seize, weird, leisure, financier, conscience.

2. When a one-syllable word ends in a single consonant and when that final consonant is preceded by a single vowel, double the final consonant before a suffix that begins with a vowel or the suffix *y*.

run	running
drop	dropped
bag	baggage
skin	skinny

3. When a word of more than one syllable ends in a single consonant, when that final consonant is preceded by a single vowel, and when the word is accented on the last syllable, double the final consonant before a suffix that begins with a vowel.

begin	beginning
concur	concurrent

When the accent does not fall on the last syllable, do not double the final consonant before a suffix that begins with a vowel.

travel	traveler
differ	differing

4. When the final consonant in a word of one or more syllables is preceded by another consonant or by two vowels, do not double the final consonant before any suffix.

look	looked
deceit	deceitful
act	acting
warm	warmly

5. Words ending in silent *e* generally drop the *e* before a suffix that begins with a vowel.

guide	guidance
use	usable

6. Words ending in silent *e* generally retain the *e* before a suffix that begins with a consonant unless another vowel precedes the final *e.*

hate	hateful
due	duly
excite	excitement
argue	argument

7. Words ending in *ie* drop the *e* and change the *i* to *y* before adding *ing.*

lie	lying
die	dying

8. Words ending in *ce* or *ge* generally retain the final *e* before the suffixes *able* and *ous* but drop the final *e* before the suffixes *ible* and *ing.*

manage	manageable
force	forcible

9. When a word ends in *c,* insert a *k* before adding a suffix beginning with *e, i,* or *y.*

picnic	picnicking

10. Words ending in *y* preceded by a consonant generally change the *y* to *i* before any suffix except one beginning with *i.*

modify	modifying	modifier
lonely	lonelier	

11. Words ending in *o* preceded by a vowel form the plural by adding *s.* Words ending in *o* preceded by a consonant generally form the plural by adding *es.*

folio	folios
potato	potatoes

12. Words ending in *y* preceded by a vowel form the plural by adding *s;* words ending in *y* preceded by a consonant change the *y* to *i* and add *es* to form the plural.

attorney	attorneys
lady	ladies

SUBJECT AND VERB AGREEMENT

This section presents a review of some of the basic rules concerning subject-verb agreement.

1. When the subject consists of two singular nouns and/or pronouns connected by *or, either . . . or, neither . . . nor,* or *not only . . . but also,* a singular verb is required.

   Jane or *Bob has* the letter.
   Either *Ruth* or *Marge plans* to attend.
   Not only a *book* but also *paper is* needed.

2. When the subject consists of two plural nouns and/or pronouns connected by *or, either . . . or, neither . . . nor,* or *not only . . . but also,* a plural verb is required.

   Neither the *secretaries* nor the *typists have* access to that information.

3. When the subject is made up of both singular and plural nouns and/or pronouns connected by *or, either . . . or, neither . . . nor,* or *not only . . . but also,* the verb agrees with the last noun or pronoun mentioned before the verb.

   Either *Ms. Rogers* or the *assistants have* access to that information.
   Neither the *men* nor *Jo is* working.

4. Disregard intervening phrases and clauses when establishing agreement between subject and verb. *One of* is considered singular.

   One of the men *wants* to go to the convention.

5. The words *each, every, either, neither, one,* and *another* are singular. When they are used as subjects or as adjectives modifying subjects, a singular verb is required.

   Each person *is* deserving of the award.
   Neither boy *rides* the bicycle well.

6. The following pronouns are always singular and require a singular verb:

anybody	everybody	nobody	somebody
anyone	everyone	nothing	something
anything	everything	no one	someone

   Everyone plans to attend the meeting.
   Anyone is welcome at the concert.

7. *Both, few, many, others,* and *several* are always plural. When they are used as subjects or adjectives modifying subjects, a plural verb is required.

   Several members *were* asked to make presentations.
   Both women *are* going to apply.

8. *All, none, any, some, more,* and *most* may be singular or plural, depending on the noun to which they refer.

   Some of the supplies *are* missing.
   Some of that paper *is* needed.

9. A collective noun is a word that is singular in form but represents a group of persons or things. For example, the following words are collective nouns: *committee, company, department, public, class, board.* These rules determine the form of the verb to be used with a collective noun.

   a. When the members of a group are thought of as one unit, the verb should be singular.

      The *committee has* voted unanimously to begin the study.

   b. When members of the group are thought of as separate units, the verb should be plural.

      The *board are* not in agreement on the decision that should be made.

10. *The number* has a singular meaning and requires a singular verb; *a number* has a plural meaning and requires a plural verb.

    A number of people *are* planning to attend.
    The number of requests *is* surprising.

11. Geographic locations are considered as singular and used with a singular verb when referring to one location. When reference is made to separate islands with a geographic location, the plural form is used with a plural verb.

    The Hawaiian Islands has been their vacation spot for years.
    The Caribbean Islands have distinct cultures.

WORD DIVISION

1. Divide words between syllables.

   moun-tain

2. Do not divide words of five or fewer letters (preferably six or fewer).

   apple
   among
   finger

3. Do not divide one-syllable words.

   helped
   eighth

4. If a one-letter syllable falls within a word, divide the word after the one-letter syllable.

   regu-late
   sepa-rate

5. If two one-letter syllables occur together within a word, divide between the one-letter syllables.

   continu-ation
   radi-ator

6. Divide between double consonants that appear within a word. Also, when the final consonant of a base word is doubled to add a suffix, divide between the double consonants.

   neces-sary
   commit-ted

7. When a base word ends in a double consonant, divide between the base word and the suffix.

   tell-ing
   careless-ness

8. Divide hyphenated compound words at existing hyphens only.

two-thirds
self-control

9. Avoid dividing a date, personal name, or address. If it is absolutely necessary, maximize readability by doing the following:
   a. Divide a date between the day and the year.
   b. Divide a personal name between the first name and surname.
   c. Divide an address between the city and state.

10. Avoid dividing figures, abbreviations, and symbols.

$20,000
YMCA
#109

11. Do not divide contractions.

he'll
wouldn't

12. Divide no more than three or four words on a typewritten page.

13. Avoid dividing words at the end of the first and last lines of a paragraph.

14. Do not divide the last word on a page.

15. The first part of a divided word must contain at least two letters; the latter part must contain at least three.

around (not a-round)
lately (not late-ly)

INDEX

nonverbal, 115–19
  body language, 118
  space, 119
  time, 119
  voice quality, 119
  process of, 115–16
  resolutions, 122–24
  sexual harassment, 121
  techniques, 122
  verbal, 115–19
Communications software, 92
  defined, 101
Community, commitment to,
    by organization, 132
Compact disk read-only memory.
    See CD-ROM
Company mission statement, sample, 134
Company-owned planes, 245
Company walk-ins, 29
  for job information, 29
Compressed workweek, 11
  defined, 21
Computer-aided retrieval
  defined, 322
  document management, 298
Computer back-up of data, 97
Computer care, 97
Computer classifications, 52–54
  mainframes, 52
  microcomputers, 53–54
  minicomputers, 52
  supercomputers, 52
  supermicros, 53–54
  superminis, 52
Computer conferencing, 224
  defined, 240
Computer hardware, 51–80
Computer history, 51–52
Computer input microfilm, 297
  defined, 322
Computer keyboards, 54
Computer networks, 62–64
Computer output microfilm, 297
  defined, 322
Computer security procedures, 97–98
Computer viruses, 98–99
  defined, 101
  transmission pattern of, 99
Conference on Fair Use, 69
Conferences, duties involved, 237–38
Confidentiality
  defined, 21
  importance of, 15, 135
Conflict resolution, 122, 124
Continuous quality improvement, 9
  defined, 21
Control unit, computer, 58
Cooperativeness, of employee,
    importance of, 136
Copier-printers, 65

Copiers, 64–69
  categories of, 64–66
  color, 65
  features, 66
  high-volume, 65
  low-volume, 65
  maintenance, 67
  mid-volume, 65
  personal, 65
  quality, 66
  selection of, 69
Copyright law, use of copier and, 68–69
Cordless telephones, 156
Corporate culture, 133–34
Corporate directories, 189
Correspondence
  coherence of, 179–81
  courteousness in, 177
  effective, 175–81
  international, 191
  negative words, 178
  objective of, 181–82
  paragraphs, 179–81
  parallel structures, 181
  planning, 181–82
  positive words, 178
  promptness, 178
  proofreading tips, 177
  readability level, 181
  tone, 178
  topic sentence, of paragraph, 179
  written, 173
Covey, Stephen, contribution of, 133
CPS. *See* Certified professional secretary
CQI. *See* Continuous quality improvement
Creativity, in presentations, 204–6
  defined, 21, 204, 213
Critical thinking
  defined, 21
  derivation of term, 14
  skills in, 14
Criticism, employee acceptance of,
    134–35
Crystal display, on telephone, 157
Cultural differences, 112–14
Culture
  of corporation, 133–34
  defined, 21
Cursor control keypad, for computer, 54
  defined, 74
Customers, employee respect for, 136

Database management, 90, 295
  defined, 321
Decision-making, effectiveness in, 26
Defragmenter, disk, 97

Deming, W. Edwards, contribution of,
    9, 10
Deming's Management Principles, 10
Density of disk, 58
Dependability, of employee, 135
  importance of, 15
Desktop publishing
  process of, 91
  software, 91
Dialing, of telephone, 157
Discrimination, 119–21
  actions against, 124
  defined
  laws governing, 120
Disks, 58
  defragmenter, 97
  defined, 101
Diversity
  commitment to, by organization, 132
  of labor force, 6
Document management, 294–325
  confidentiality, 299
  defined, 294, 321
  designing files, 298
  disposing of materials, 299
  electronic image storage, 317–20
  equipment, manual, 314–17
  indexing, 299–306
  maintaining files, 298
  manual systems, 298, 310–14
    supplies for, 314–17
  responsibilities, 298–99
  software, 319–20
  storage, 298–99, 306–10
  systems for, 295–98
  trends in, 320
Document shredding, 287
Domestic travel, arrangements for, 244–47
DOS, 82–83
  defined, 100
Downsizing, of organization, 7–9
  stress and, 329
Drawing programs, 87
Dual career families, stress and, 330

e-mail, 62, 173–74, 278
  defined, 76
Eating habits, stress and, 334
Eckert, John, development of computer, 52
Economic pressures, stress and, 330
Economy, global, 7
Edited document, sample, 105–6
Education, resume listing of, 32
Elderly family members, stress and, 330
Electrical Numerical Integrator and
    Calculator. *See* ENIAC

Electronic blackboard, 223
  defined, 240
Electronic document management
      systems. *See* Document
      management
Electronic mail. *See* e-mail
Electronic meetings, 223–25
Emergencies, in employment, 142
Employee ethics, 134–38
Employees, commitment to, by
      organization, 133
Employment agencies, 28
Employment application, 34, 36
  defined, 47
  sample, 36–37
Employment interview, 40
  follow up, 41
  questions commonly asked, 39
Endnotes, of report, 190
English usage, expertise in, 13
ENIAC, development of computer, 52
Environment of office, 5–24
Environmental responsibility of
      organization, 131, 133
Erasable disk, 59
  defined, 75
Ethical issues, in work environment,
      130–44
Evaluation, of performance, 44
EWI. *See* Executive Women International
Executive Women International, 18
Exercise, stress and, 333
Exit interview, 45
  defined, 47
Expectations, of supervisor, regarding
      office callers, 197
Express mail, 272
  rate chart for, 273
Extemporaneous presentation, 207
External storage devices, computer,
      58–59
Extracurricular activities, resume listing,
      32
Extrinsic motivation, 358
  defined, 363
Eye contact, in communication, 118
Eyestrain, employment and, 141

F

Facsimile. *See* Fax
Fatigue, employment and, 141
Fax
  broadcasting, 70, 76
  color, 70
  defined, 76
  features of, 70
  portable, 70

process of, 70–71, 279
  selection of, 70–71
Fax-on-demand, 70
  defined, 76
Federal Copyright Law P.L. 94–553, 68
FEDEX, 277
Fiber optics, development of, 153
The Fifth Discipline, 133
File folders, for manual storage, 314–15
First-class accommodations, 245
  defined, 262
First-class mail, 272
Flattened organization, 7–9
  chief executive officer, in
      organizational structure, 8
  organizational structures, 8–9
  quality focus, 9–10
  temporary employees, 8
  vs. traditional hierarchical structure, 8
Flextime, 11
  defined, 21
Flight classifications, 245
Floppy disk, 58
  defined, 75
Floppy drives, 53
Follow-up letter, after interview, 41
  defined, 47
Footnotes, of report, 190
Foreign-born population, in United States,
      111–12
Format, of resume, 34
Fortune, 16
Fourth-class mail, 273
  rate chart for, 274
FrameMaker desktop publishing software
      program, 91
France, cultural differences with, 113
Free addresses, usage of term, 138
From Nine to Five, 16
Fry, William, contribution of, 329–31
Function keypad, 54
  defined, 74
Functional resume
  defined, 47
  sample, 33

G

Gates, Bill, contribution of, 71
Gender differences, 6–7
Gender discrimination, 121
Gigabytes, 57
Global economy, 7
Global Market Surveys, 189
Global Network Navigator, 255
Goals, setting, 337
Graphical user interface, 56
  defined, 75

Graphics, 87–89
  color, 89
Greeting of visitors, 198
Ground transportation, arrangements for,
      246
Growth, professional, importance of,
      16–18

H

Handheld scanners, 55
Handshakes as greeting, universality of,
      114
Hard disk, 59
  defined, 75
Hard drives, 53
  defined, 74
Hardware, 54
  computer, 51–80
Health issues, in employment, 139–42
Health precautions, international travel,
      249
Hierarchical organizational structure, 8
High density disk, 58
Hollerith, Herman, development of
      computer, 51
Home Computing, 10
Honesty
  of employee, 136–37
  of organization, 132
Honors, in resume listing, 32
Hoteling, usage of term, 138
Human relations skills, 13–14

I

Icons, use of, 82
Identified ringing feature, on telephone,
      157
Illustrations, list of, of report, 190
Image, professional, importance of, 16
Impact printers, 60
Impromptu presentation, 207
*Industry and Development: Global
      Report,* 189
Information, on jobs, sources of, 27–29
Information Age, entering into, 5
Information management, 90–91.
      See also Document management
Initiative
  defined, 21
  importance of, 15
Input devices, 54–56
Insured mail, 274
Integrated software, 86
  defined, 101